A MOMENT OF EQUALITY FOR LATIN AMERICA?

T0361967

A Moment of Equality for Latin America?
Challenges for Redistribution

Edited by

BARBARA FRITZ
Freie Universität Berlin, Germany

LENA LAVINAS
Federal University of Rio de Janeiro, Brazil

Routledge
Taylor & Francis Group

LONDON AND NEW YORK

First published 2015 by Ashgate Publishing

2 Park Square, Milton Park, Abingdon, Oxfordshire OX14 4RN
52 Vanderbilt Avenue, New York, NY 10017

Routledge is an imprint of the Taylor & Francis Group, an informa business

First issued in paperback 2020

British Library Cataloguing in Publication Data
A catalogue record for this book is available from the British Library

The Library of Congress has cataloged the printed edition as follows:
Fritz, Barbara, 1964–
  A moment of equality for Latin America? : challenges for redistribution / by Barbara Fritz and Lena Lavinas.
    pages cm. – (Entangled inequalities : exploring global asymmetries)
  Includes bibliographical references and index.
  ISBN 978-1-4724-4672-5 (hardback : alk. paper)
  1. Income distribution–Latin America. 2. Equality–Latin America. 3. Latin America–Social policy–21st century. I. Lavinas, Lena. II. Title.
  HC130.I5F75 2015
  339.2098–dc23

                                                                2015011056

ISBN 978-1-4724-4672-5 (hbk)
ISBN 978-0-367-59801-3 (pbk)

Contents

List of Figures

List of Tables

Notes on Contributors

Bielschowsky, Ricardo worked at UN-CEPAL for 20 years, recently as the director of its Brazilian bureau. He is now an Associate Professor at the Federal University of Rio de Janeiro (UFRJ), having published over 60 books and papers on development and economic thought in Brazil and in Latin America.

Braig, Marianne is a Professor of Political Science at the Freie Universität Berlin, in the Institute for Latin American Studies—LAI. Her current research projects and publications deal with the topics of "Political cultures and statehood" and "Entangled inequalities between regions (especially Latin America, Europe and China)."

Costa, Sérgio is a Professor of Sociology at the Freie Universität Berlin as well as one of the spokespersons of desiguALdades.net, the Research Network on Interdependent Inequalities in Latin America. Trained in Economics and Sociology in Brazil and Germany, he obtained his B.A. and M.A. at the Federal University of Minas Gerais (UFMG), and his Ph.D and "Habilitation" from the Freie Universität Berlin.

Fagnani, Eduardo is a Professor at UNICAMP's Institute of Economy, researcher at the Center for Union and Labor Studies (CESIT) and coordinator of the Plataforma Política Social—Agenda para o Desenvolvimento www.plataformapoliticasocial.com.

Fritz, Barbara is Professor for Economics at the Institute for Latin American Studies and the Department of Economics of the Freie Universität Berlin. Her fields of expertise are development economics and international macroeconomics, money, and finance, with a special focus on Latin America.

Gentil, Denise holds a Ph.D. in Economics from the Institute of Economics (I.E.) at the Federal University of Rio de Janeiro (UFRJ), where she is currently an Associate Professor.

Haldenwang, Christian von is a Senior Researcher at the German Development Institute/Deutsches Institut für Entwicklungspolitik (DIE). He holds a Ph.D. in Political Science and an M.A. in Political Science and Philosophy.

Hermann, Jennifer holds a Ph.D. in Economics from the Institute of Economics (I.E.) at the Universidade Federal University of Rio de Janeiro (UFRJ). She is currently an Associate Professor at the same Institute, and has co-authored the book *Economia Brasileira Contemporânea: 1945/2004* (Campus, 2005 and 2011).

Jiménez, Juan Pablo is an Economic Affairs Officer at the Economic Commission for Latin America and the Caribbean (CEPAL) and a Visiting Fellow at the International Centre for Economic Development (ICER) and the Research Network on Interdependent Inequalities (DesiguALdades.net).

Lavinas, Lena is an Associate Professor at the Institute of Economics at the Federal University of Rio de Janeiro (UFRJ) and Senior Researcher (Level 1) at the Brazilian National Research Council (CNPQ). She is a Research Fellow at desigualdes.net (Freie Universitat). Most of her research focuses on social policies.

Lo Vuolo, Rubén is an Economist and Academic Director of the Interdisciplinary Center for the Studies of Public Policy (Ciepp) in Buenos Aires, Argentina, and teaches graduate courses at various universities in Argentina.

López Azcúnaga, Isabel is a PhD Candidate and has a Master's in International Economy and Development from the Universidad Complutense de Madrid. She works as a consultant for CEPAL.

Pérez Sáinz, Juan Pablo holds a Doctorate in Economics from Vrije Universiteit, Brussels, Belgium. He is currently a researcher at Facultad Latinoamericana de Ciencias Sociales (FLACSO), Costa Rica.

Puhle, Hans-Jürgen is Professor Emeritus of Political Science at the Institute of Political Science, Goethe Universität, Frankfurt am Main, Germany. He has published over 30 books and over 150 academic articles in various fields such as social history, comparative politics, and political theory.

Saboia, João is a Professor at the Institute of Economics (I.E.) at the Federal University of Rio de Janeiro (UFRJ). He received the 2007 Jabuti Award for co-editing the best book of the year in Economics and Business Administration, entitled *Celso Furtado e o Século XXI*.

Simões, André holds a Ph.D. in Economics from the Institute of Economics (I.E.) at the Federal University of Rio de Janeiro (UFRJ) and currently works in the Department of Population and Social Indicators at the Brazilian Institute of Geography and Statistics (IBGE).

Therborn, Göran is Professor Emeritus of Sociology at the University of Cambridge, UK and an Affiliated Professor of Sociology at Linnaeus University, Sweden. His works have been published in 24 languages. His latest books are *The Killing Fields of Inequality* (Cambidrige, Polity 2013) and *El Mundo. Una guía para principantes* (México, Océano 2012). He is a civic intellectual, with a lifetime commitment to universal freedom and equality.

Valdés, Maria Fernanda is an Associate Researcher at the international research network desiguALdades.net at Freie Universität Berlin, where she has been researching inequality and tax policy in Latin America.

Acknowledgements

This volume would not have seen the light of the day without the support of many people and institutions.

Firstly, the research network on interdependent inequalities in Latin America, desiguALdades.net (www.desigualdades.net), provided far more than generous financial support. Coordinated mainly by the Institute for Latin American Studies of the Freie Universität Berlin and the Ibero-American Institute of the Prussian Cultural Heritage Foundation in Berlin, and funded by the German Federal Ministry of Education and Research (BMBF), this interdisciplinary, international, and multi-institutional research network created not merely a virtual platform, but a real stage for reflection and knowledge creation, over four years with researchers from many places and institutions and a huge variety of approaches to the issue of the entangled inequalities of Latin America. A vast collection of working papers synthesizes an intellectual and academic trajectory which is plural and overspills conventional disciplinary borders.

As a truly international endeavor, this book also has considerable Brazilian participation, in both intellectual and financial terms. A series of outstanding institutions from academia and beyond helped bring about an international conference in Rio de Janeiro with a large number of participants. This seminar was supported and funded by the Institute of Economics at the UFRJ (I.E./UFRJ), the International Celso Furtado Center for Development Policies, the Institute of Economics at UNICAMP (I.E./UNICAMP), and the National Bank of Economic and Social Development (BNDES). In parallel, the Celso Furtado Center is also publishing the Portuguese version of this edited volume.

But there was still a long way to go before a book could emerge out of part of the conference contributions, plus a few papers from other sources. Our special thanks go here to Rubén Lo Vuolo and Göran Therborn, who served on the editorial council and had a fundamental role in improving the articles with insightful comments and helping the authors to review their contributions, in some cases more than twice.

No less important in this enterprise was the backstage support we received from a highly transnational team. Our thanks go to Denise Uderman, our superb Rio-based coordinator for both the workshop and the book, to Flora Thomson-DeVeaux for perfect and timely translation and editing support, to Anna Wickes-Neira for dealing with all financial issues, to Tom Norton for copy-editing and indexing, and to Neil Jordan from Ashgate for his continuous support.

Last but not least, we are truly grateful to Sérgio Costa, who offered us the honor of putting together the inaugural volume in the book series entitled "Entangled Inequalities: Exploring Global Asymmetries," and who, alongside Marianne Braig and Barbara Göbel, acted as the spiritus rector of the whole endeavor.

SPONSORED BY THE

Federal Ministry
of Education
and Research

desiguALdades.net
Research Network on Interdependent
Inequalities in Latin America

Foreword

Marianne Braig

The growing social gap between the rich and the poor has once again become an important social *problématique* and is attracting increased attention in social science research. The research network *desiguALdades.net* forms part of an ongoing revitalization of the study of inequalities from both national and global perspectives, bringing together experts on social inequalities and experts on Latin America. The objective of *desiguALdades.net* is to make a contribution to research on social inequalities in Latin America.

The intersections of different types of social inequalities and the global interdependencies of local constellations of social inequalities beyond the nation-state are at the focus of these analyses. While considering the particularities of Latin American inequalities, it is important to include other dimensions in the debate over the creation and reproduction of social inequalities. With special focus on the multidimensionality and interdependencies of social inequalities, scholars address the roots and dynamics of persistent inequalities in the region. Through empirical research on Latin America, the network seeks to contribute to a more diverse understanding of social inequalities, taking in multidimensional and transregional interdependencies.

Latin America is critical for understanding social inequalities for two seemingly contradictory reasons. It is the only region that has seen a reduction in inequalities in selected countries over the past 20 years. Recent reductions in inequality notwithstanding, however, Latin America remains one of the most unequal regions in the world.

In the discussion over the question of how to reduce inequalities, there is a widely shared consensus as to the positive effects that state action can have in making societies more equal. Hence, Latin American states are held to be the most powerful and important actors in reducing inequalities and related patterns of socioeconomic and political exclusion in the region. Such an approach, however, tends to underestimate two central aspects. The first is the question of politics, understood as struggles over the definition and implementation of state policies at a specific historical moment, in the making of inequalities in Latin America. The second has to do with the institutional legacies responsible for the reproduction of inequalities over time.

Against this background, this publication is bringing politics, and economic politics in particular, back onto the stage of research on social inequalities and attempts to explore the limits to distribution and redistribution over the last two decades.

Intensive cooperation between Brazilian and German research and funding institutions made it possible to bring together experts from Europe and Latin America in the international seminar on "Challenges and Limits of Redistributive Policies in Latin America," and to publish the results of their debates and exchanges.

PART I
Opening the Question

Chapter 1
Redistribution and Persistent Challenges: An Introduction

Lena Lavinas and Barbara Fritz

The Latin American continent has seen an unprecedented drop in income inequality amidst a vigorous return to economic growth, with indicators at levels not seen for quite some time (4.1% p.a. on average for the region as a whole from 2004–2013, as opposed to 2.7% p.a. for the period 1984–2003, according to IMF, 2014). This recent growth with equity has been cast as a paradox (Boyer, 2014), as it goes against the grain of tendencies observed in other regions around the world at the turn of this century, as well as the trajectory of this region over the 20th century. In Göran Therborn's words, in the chapter that lends the book its title, Latin America is experiencing a "moment of equality." Is this unexpected inversion simply a parenthesis in the development of Latin America, or a historical breakthrough in a region marked by extraordinary levels of inequality? To what extent does this virtuous coincidence reflect structural changes capable of ushering in a new era in development, free of the impasses that for decades hindered the expansionary potential of such a rich, diverse, and plural region?

Many studies have attempted to explain this phenomenon. A convergence in the literature indicates that this state of affairs is not simply the result of significant economic growth over the period, but also of key political interventions. What policies were these? What did they stipulate, and how sustainable will they prove in the effort to maintain a continuous reduction of inequality indices in Latin America in the middle and long term? On these points, the critical consensus splits in many directions.

Most scholars who have examined the novelty of this "moment of equality" in Latin America recognize that it has become the stage for new experiments in the field of public policy, with clear effects in terms of reduced social and economic disparities. Authors such as Lustig and López Calva (2010) have seen, beyond the substantial economic growth of the 2000s, a notable increase in the education levels of the less fortunate classes, and the subsequent reduction in skill premium as the principal factor driving income disparities down—an explanation also adopted by Tsounta and Osueke (2014). The latter add other explanatory factors, such as the considerable rise in direct investments and high levels of tax collection. Cornia, in a recent compilation focusing on the subject, has even detected the gradual emergence of a new model, dubbed "open-economy growth with equity" (Cornia, 2014: p. 4). Working off a series of country studies for the years 2002–2010, he indicates a broad array of factors and economic, fiscal, and social policies that were fundamental to the exceptional fall in inequality, against the tide of global trends. Cornia concludes that this phenomenon, irrespective of the political orientation or economic structure prevalent in the countries in the region, is also the result of an improvement in external conditions, changes in the dependency ratio and activity rates, and the adoption of fiscal and employment policies.

This book takes a different tack. Instead of segregating its analysis by policy fields or by interpreting the measurable effects of specific interventions in a number of areas, so as to evaluate the contribution of each to the recent fall in inequality in Latin America, it brings together specialists from the fields of social, macroeconomic, and fiscal studies to discuss the interdependences that may restrict—or, rather, boost—the dynamics of inequality reproduction.

The jumping-off point is reference to a broad concept of inequalities as multidimensional and interdependent, as well as transnational. This was developed through the international research network *desiguALdades* (www.desigualdades.net; see Braig et al., 2013), in collaboration with a wide-ranging and multidisciplinary array of academics working on the topic. Both the network and the conceptual field structuring the collection are especially influenced by dialogue with structuralist and neostructuralist thought. These currents of economic thinking are both relevant and crucial in reflections currently taking shape across the region around the advances and stumbles that have marked the return to a new trajectory of development with greater social inclusion, at the turn of this century.

As the reading of many of the chapters in this collection will reveal, the Prebischian and Furtadian analytical framework[1] for interpreting the causes of Latin America's underdevelopment and its peripheral place on the international stage retains great freshness and pertinence in approaching the challenges that lie ahead. Other referential frameworks brought into the debate on growth and redistribution are the return to a Keynesian approach regarding the centrality of social spending, on one hand, and the relevance of fiscal policy in the construction of a fairer and more sustained redistributive pattern, on the other. Speaking from various schools of thought, these chapters ask whether the return to economic growth with a more egalitarian income distribution has managed to overcome the profound social and productive heterogeneity of the region; the weakness of its institutions; the bottlenecks to innovation and continued technological progress, inhibiting productivity gains; its low investment capacity; its recurrent external vulnerability; the stumbling-blocks of the process of late industrialization; and prevailing resilience to structural changes that might sustainably promote the deconcentration of wealth, thus broadening opportunities. These issues, which have dominated the regional agenda since the 1950s, have taken on new vigor in the context of the regulatory scheme introduced by so-called "neoliberal" reforms in the reestablishment of market mechanisms, particularly so in recent decades. During this period, most countries in the region sought, albeit in quite different ways, to forge instruments and policies that might help them overcome two decades of stagnation and crises, rising poverty and inequality, loss of competitiveness, and the absence of leadership on the international political stage.

While the issues that marked seminal structuralist thought remain atop the regional agenda, others have become equally relevant and urgent. The recognition of the persistence of marked ethnic/racial and gender inequalities, and the place of nature and the preservation of the extraordinary biodiversity of the region, are just two of the countless points that spell out the complexity of the formulation of alternatives that may support sustained and inclusive development in Latin America. At the turn of the 1990s, Fajnzylber (1990) had

---

1   Raúl Prebisch and Celso Furtado were the two greatest masterminds of Latin American structuralist thought in the seminal postwar period, when they constructed a new chapter in the analysis of economic development. They formulated concepts and interpretations around the underdevelopment of the region and laid the foundations for an historical-structuralist analysis of the motives of Latin America's relative backwardness and its integration into the global economy.

warned that it would be impossible to move forward without linking growth and equity in development strategies. Indeed, it was precisely amidst a new phase of economic growth with falling inequality, then, that new redistributive conflicts and the struggle for human rights dovetailed, revealing an intricate web of interdependent and entangled asymmetries.

This book proffers a dense debate around the advances, limits, and, above all, the quality of this "moment of equality," underscoring the interdependence of macroeconomic, fiscal, and social policies. By focusing on the challenges and limits of redistributive policies in Latin America, this edited volume seeks to synthesize and update the discussion on the topic. To what extent does inequality reduction reflect changes in both public funding and public spending? How much is it backed by the provision of public goods? What sorts of coordination and convergence between macroeconomic and social policy have come forth over the course of this recovery? How to face the challenge of increasing productivity? Our preliminary analysis of these changes reveals a highly complex state of affairs. The 21st century has brought new energy and hope, but has likely not undone the multiple restrictions that characterized the "problematic expansion"[2] (Bielschowsky, 2000) of Latin America.

Although practically all countries in Latin America have seen economic growth with improved redistribution, there are significant differences between their trajectories. This book highlights those singularities even as it formulates a diagnosis for the region as a whole. Without excluding original processes, such as those seen in certain Andean countries with policies of high redistributive impact, this work privileges an interpretation of Brazil's trajectory. Beyond its weight in the GDP of Latin America and the Caribbean (39.7% in 2013, according to the World DataBank), Brazil has emerged as a paradigm over the last decade, given the success of its genuine mix of (relatively conservative) economic policies and (active) social policies.

The phenomenon of the reduction of social and economic inequalities is still recent, and will thus call for redoubled efforts in forging a more conclusive and definitive evaluation of both the trajectory sought and the conquests consolidated. The chapters in this volume present critical arguments, as opposed to readings whose paeans to progress achieved may speak more to the novelty of the strategy at hand than a rigorous evaluation of its ultimate result. It would be impossible to ignore that there have been significant and remarkable results. Nor can we turn a blind eye to the persistence of a legacy of hurdles and brick walls facing full citizenship, which promises to drive structural transformations in both the productive sphere and the institutions that guide values and norms.

Latin America's fall in inequality over recent years evidences, above all, a successful process of recuperation, essentially wiping out the severely deleterious effects of two decades of neoliberal experimentation on the continent. A key point in this respect is the significant upward trend in Gini indices in the majority of Latin American states, as seen amidst adjustment policies and unbridled economic opening. Likewise, the numbers of the poor rose notably, going from 136 million to 225 million from 1980 to 2002 (CEPAL, 2011) in the wake of the costs of stabilization policies and an ideology resistant to public social protection systems. Spending cuts and the privatization of public provision of services contributed to exacerbating the negative externalities of what had been cast as a lifeline for Latin America.

---

2 For Bielschowsky (2000: p. 32), problematic expansion denotes phases of growth in Latin America marked by a persistent discrepancy between industrial and productive modernization, on one hand, and the transformation of economic and institutional structures, on the other, in the effort to overcome the reproduction of underdevelopment.

Thus, the century now beginning offers the reassurance of a trend reversal. The profoundly unjust, determinant starting-point of a dependent, peripheral capitalism has been left behind, even as elites' consumption predominated, fueling a development model that never went beyond its premises.

Given this context, the question is whether, beyond recovering from the losses that undercut and delayed social change and frustrated hopes for greater equality and well-being, which forged resistance to the authoritarianism of both dictatorial regimes and the market on the continent, there might lie such a "moment of equality," and whether it can spur on an even greater leap, with even more remarkable structural repercussions, able to ensure a sustainable, substantive socioeconomic trajectory that might finally break with the region's underdeveloped roots.

Counterpoints

This volume opens with a chapter from Göran Therborn, wielding a global lens in order to contextualize and emphasize the singularity of the current "moment of equality" in Latin America, described as "virtually the only ray of light" in the "contemporary darkness of accelerating economic inequality." He compares Latin America's trajectory to other historical periods that brought the reduction of multiple inequalities, especially during the postwar period (1945–1975/80), which brought favorable changes in many regions across the world, such as North America, almost all of Europe, Northeast Asia, and Oceania, Australia and New Zealand. Despite the temporal difference, he identifies commonalities between the Latin America of the turn of this century and the *trente glorieuses* that transformed Western democracies. But Therborn also emphasizes profound differences between historical moments marked by processes of social equalization, geopolitical context among them. From this comparative perspective, he evaluates the Latin American moment as being one of respectable proportions, especially considering processes of "existential equalization," as a wealth of ethnic, racial, and gender issues have bloomed on the political and institutional scene. Nevertheless, the author makes it plain that despite a clear tendency towards decline, hemispheric inequality still persists "at Andean levels," far above figures seen in other regions; and he points out present and worrisome risks, such as the ongoing deindustrialization of the region or the favorable context of the commodities boom, making this moment of equality both unprecedented and demonstrably fragile. Although their political bases and their power when dealing with regional executives remain intact, pro-equity Latin American governments cannot camouflage their limits or vulnerabilities.

Like Therborn, Sáinz, in examining these recent trends, sees a factor in the "expansion of basic citizenship," especially so in those countries that saw Bolivarian revolutions (Venezuela, Bolivia, and Ecuador). In his opinion, while the distributive sphere was not enough to revert inequalities in the countries studied, the break with a highly exclusive pattern came through redistribution. The author affirms that, beyond conditional cash transfer programs and increased social security coverage, the increase in social spending by an unprecedented magnitude wrought profound transformations in the three countries in question. Two aspects contributed to realize the potential of voluntary redistributive mechanisms in a "postneoliberal" context. On one hand, broad-based political coalitions, supported by popular and historically marginalized subaltern sectors, legitimized a new, heretofore unseen redistributive pattern. This pattern is rooted in the recognition of the rights of citizenship, which Sáinz sees as difficult to posteriorly contest or annul, as the process has empowered once-"invisibilized" social groups. Though these economies continue to focus on the extraction and exportation of primary goods, reinforcing their dependence on the commodity cycle, the author believes that the so-called progressive neo-extractivist model made it possible to reserve funds and shift revenues in order to finance social citizenship. While the future may present a heavy bill in economic, environmental and social terms, for Sáinz, Venezuela, Ecuador, and Bolivia managed to break away from a historical trend of profound socioeconomic asymmetries.

This interpretation is not echoed, however, by other authors in this volume, especially, but not exclusively, in examining the case of Brazil. For some, the quality and structure of social spending seem to have significantly restricted their effectiveness in fighting inequalities. This is the point of view put forth most emphatically by Lo Vuolo, Lavinas, and Simões, Jiménez and Azcúnaga, and Hermann and Gentil, as they emphasize the persistence in the region of low complementarity between macroeconomic and social policy.

Taking a balance of the 20th century, Lo Vuolo runs down the structural factors that have been gnawing away at the pillars of a more egalitarian development in Latin America and explain the limits on redistribution. After identifying three distinct models for coordinating economic and social policy (the ISI regime, from the '50s to the '70s; the neoliberal solutions of the '90s; and, finally, the recent phase of growth with inclusion), the author affirms that "the distributional issue is again a dependent variable of a sound macroeconomic policy and growth." This argument rests on the fact that trends in the shrinkage or expansion of social spending converge with economic and political cycles. The frequency of crises, a structural element in Latin America—given the permanence of high economic instability—makes social policies essentially secondary. They remain the adjustment factor, and this stands as one indication that structural change has not yet occurred. Another problem is considerable heterogeneity, unchallenged and reinforced by the structure of social policies that do not promote universality and greater social cohesion. Contrary to Sáinz's analysis, Lo Vuolo sees the persistence of structural heterogeneity and income and job insecurity as revealing "failures in the arena of the primary distribution [that] are not counterbalanced by progressive redistribution in the fiscal arena," a problem mainly stemming from the design of social policies,

Hermann and Gentil, taking Keynesian thought and the multiplier effects of social spending as their jumping-off point, underscore that, in the case of Brazil, public transfers (both contributive and noncontributive) played a key role in reducing income inequality and spurring economic growth, especially given their multiplier effect on GDP. They also recognize that these transfers contributed to an increase in tax revenue, given their strong impact on consumption. However, they conclude that the continued constriction of the offering of public goods and services, on one hand, and monetary policy (high interest rates and the appreciation of the exchange rate), on the other, have impeded virtuous complementarity between macroeconomic policy and redistribution.

Bielschowsky and Saboia also view the combination of high interest rates and appreciated exchange rates as conspiring against an enduring increase in manufacturing investments, hence limiting the chances of successfully promoting structural changes able to forge a new model of economic development, one based on growth with equity. This is also the central note in Lo Vuolo's argument, as he affirms that "social policies are not countercyclical because they are subordinated to the economic macroeconomic context" currently prevailing in Latin America.

Lavinas and Simões could not agree more, as they see the subordination of social policy to macroeconomic policy coming to the fore precisely in the structure of public spending, which is consistently focused more on the correction of market failures than the equalization of opportunities and the promotion of a more egalitarian society. They believe that the model of mass consumption that has emerged from this phase of growth, driven in large part by household consumption, has shown itself disconnected from the issue of productivity. This on its own compromises the possibility of a constant and sustainable decline in inequality in Latin America over the middle and long term. The authors argue that the strategy adopted by many countries in the region, of using social policy to foment market incorporation, made it possible to bypass, rather than face down, structural bottlenecks such as low work productivity and low competitiveness, which currently hamper the international integration of Latin America's economies and the emergence of stable, socially more just development at the domestic level. This second-best strategy, however, is no guarantee of a successful trajectory in overcoming profound structural heterogeneity and underdevelopment, which remain as the continent's hallmark, and a crucial source of the reproduction of inequalities.

Although he posits that mass consumption was itself a key factor in reducing inequalities, especially by virtue of having brought about a considerable expansion in formal employment, Bielschowsky recognizes that weak ties between investment and productivity gains have hindered the expansion of innovation-driven production chains. Hence, economic development itself may be aborted, since the region's always-latent external vulnerability may, during a downward spiral in commodity prices, lead to a new cycle of instability and refuel inequalities.

Saboia, meanwhile, turning to the Brazilian case, calls our attention to the element that led to a notable, timely synergy between social and economic policy, and which came about in the distributive sphere, despite lackluster productivity gains: the rise in the minimum wage. The author examines the extremely positive effects of the policy of elevating the minimum wage in real terms, adopted broadly across Latin America (except in Mexico) during a time of renewed economic growth. In privileging this mechanism as a vector for the greater incorporation of the working classes into the consumer market, many Latin American governments, Brazil's in particular, managed to reduce income disparities and poverty.

A clear consensus has emerged around the importance of the minimum wage, having been a strong institution in Latin America since the 1940s. The authors of this volume, while emphasizing insufficient coordination between macroeconomic and social policy, still recognize that the real increase in the minimum wage led to a reduction of income inequality, through redistributive effects brought about on the job market. Moreover, the existence of a minimum wage certainly served to promote the formalization of labor in the region.

Costa, in indicating various mechanisms for the reproduction of ongoing social inequalities, points to the fight against discrimination as the main pillar of public policies on racial and gender equality in Brazil, in keeping with larger patterns across Latin America. In his opinion, the incorporation of gender and race into state policies is a positive point. Nevertheless, the author concludes that relevant dimensions in the dynamic of reproduction of inequalities, such as the factor of exploitation, hoarding of opportunities, or hierarchization, to name just three, remain absent from or marginal to the design of interventions aimed at the reduction of asymmetries between groups organized by color (whites and blacks) or sex (women and men). This is to say that the formulation and structuring of public policies aimed at gender and racial equality betray a limited scope, as they have still not managed to appropriately translate the challenges of multidimensionality and intersectionality into the realm of concepts and actions. In this sense, he indicates lacunas that persist in the effective operationalization of entangled inequalities. In short, for Costa, public policies do matter and have to be reinforced, but their scope must be widened to simultaneously address distinct dimensions of inequality—only then can they be more effective in tackling gender, class and race asymmetries in the long run.

Fagnani's line of argument reinforces the understanding that in order for redistribution to be effective, the fragmentation, segmentation, and targeting of social policy must be overcome. In his chapter, the author vehemently criticizes the policies of minimum social standards that have been gaining traction as a strategy for overcoming inequality within a new institutional framework, that of the social protection floor. In his opinion, the reduction of entangled inequalities would lead to a breakthrough on underdevelopment. There is no possible path, in this sense, beyond the universalization of social policies and formal, real, solidarity. But the trajectory we have seen is the strengthening of residual policies. This is the dispute at hand. Some would have it that we have seen the success of minimal-state policy. In the Brazilian case, the author emphasizes that, in addition to changes in the job market—more employment and real gains in the minimum wage—it was the existence of Social Security as a strong institution that truly impeded backsliding and brought out positive effects in the sense of greater redistribution, particularly in terms of welfare and assistance.

In line with Lo Vuolo, Jiménez and Azcúnaga, and Valdés, point to the heart of the problem in emphasizing that this redistribution has come about without the indispensable contribution that is tax policy. Yes, there was an increase in fiscal space, as Jiménez and Azcúnaga rightly indicate, since fiscal revenues increased in the wake of the commodities boom, which led to nearly a decade of economic growth, and improvements in revenue-collecting efficiency (a high point of tax reforms, where they did come about on the continent). However, they emphasize, the tax burden remains low, on average, vis-a-vis the level of regional GDPs, thanks to a narrow base. Moreover, the structure of taxation remains regressive, with a focus on consumption and payroll, rather than income and wealth, and volatile, as it is highly dependent on the commodities cycle. Recent tax reforms did not substantially increase the progressivity of taxes (with Peru as a possible exception, in Valdés' eyes), nor did they break with their passive posture, which has inhibited a process of profound and systematic deconcentration of income. More damningly, they have compromised the State's ability to ensure the public provision of goods and services that might equalize opportunities and access, thus strengthening the market and the reproduction of inequalities.

After examining three tax variables relevant in determining equity (level of the tax burden, progressivity of the structure, and the behavior of tax collection vis-a-vis economic cycles) in five countries, Valdés concludes that the systems of taxation analyzed lack a relatively uniform pattern at the regional level, and even within a single country over a period of time. They may be procyclical in adverse periods or altogether anticyclical. Thus, their pro-equity potential remains compromised and timid. The author thus concludes that tax policy has not been used as an active redistribution policy tool. The strong interdependency between fiscal policy and inequality has been neglected by most Latin American countries as of late, which has served to hinder taxation's potential to reduce inequalities.

Haldenwang's text focuses on the topic of the vulnerability of fiscal revenues in terms of external shocks, examining a wide variety of developing countries in addition to Latin America. His econometric results indicate that, while the volatility of tax revenue reveals structural weaknesses in Latin America, the area has seen improvements in its macroeconomic and financial administration, as well as greater resilience to shocks in several countries across the region during the recent phase of growth. This being said, the author underscores that Latin American countries of average income, with manufacturing strongly represented in their exports, are demonstrably sensitive to global changes in terms of their tax revenue. This should be seen as a likely sign that not only technological content, but also a tax regime related to certain structural patterns of production, may be problematic. Finally, his results seem to demonstrate the existence of a "democracy rent," in the sense that low-income countries under democratic regimes seem to be less vulnerable to external shocks, this apparently a consequence of democratic systems' greater ability to avoid or compensate for revenue losses through public policy and political negotiations, maneuvering in terms of both revenue and spending.

A clear convergence, then, has emerged amongst various authors in this volume—Lo Vuolo, Lavinas and Simões, Costa, Hermann and Gentil, Sáinz, Jiménez and Azcúnaga, and Valdés—for whom the reduction of inequalities, while a hallmark of the first decade of the 21st century, has fallen short of what might have been possible. Two main motives appear, in this sense: the reduced scope of current policies—whether spending or tax policies, currently under reform—and weak institutional complementarity between social and macroeconomic policy, with the former subordinated to the latter, perennially serving as an adjustment factor.

One might also affirm that most of the authors here recognize that residual social policies have not guaranteed, nor will they guarantee greater redistribution in the sense of a continuous and robust fall in inequality in the region, which remains at excessively high levels regardless of one's point of comparison. This, after all, was precisely the structure of the social policies that marked this "moment of equality," which allows us to suppose that, if the spending structure that currently prevails in Latin America (targeted and conditional cash transfers in particular) is maintained, the chances of such effects spreading or at least holding up seem remote.

Pending Questions

Can we speak of a new model of development, present and active in Latin America at the turn of this century? There is no consensus as to the answer. For Therborn, given the vast diversity of Latin America's economies, it would be too simplistic to speak of a "regional pattern of growth." If there were a virtuous model at work, it might have led to a crowding-in effect; but this was not seen. This is a critical and still-pending element, as emphasized by Bielschowsky, Saboia, and Hermann and Gentil, especially so in the Brazilian case, but applicable to the region. This is yet another dimension of the weaknesses of coordination, in keeping with warnings from Lavinas and Simões, Lo Vuolo, Fagnani, and Costa—and the weakness at hand reveals precisely that social and economic action are not coordinated in an integrated, reflective, and cumulative fashion.

Among the countless institutional frailties that characterize Latin American development, and which are featured in this book, a positive institutional differential lies precisely in the existence, in most countries across the region, of an official minimum wage. The political decision to raise the minimum wage was the strongest institutional factor in reducing inequalities and boosting redistribution. Latin American democratic governments at the turn of this century were able to rightly prize an instrument inherited from the golden age of development and import substitution, lending it a place of pride in the consolidation of domestic mass consumer markets. This was the case with the minimum wage.

At the end of this period of renewed growth, however, it has become evident that the context did not favor the construction of new institutions, which would have proved indispensable to a change in the redistributive framework. For example, although fiscal policy increased its space as a factor in macroeconomic stabilization and made its collection more efficient, it was unable to redefine its structure so as promote progressivity in income redistribution.

Examining the pro-distribution reforms through the lens of political economy, it appears preferable, and more feasible, to overhaul existing institutions and give them greater importance. This was carried out, to a great extent, in Latin America. That said, the task of consolidating a moment of equality and overcoming underdevelopment calls for innovative institutional arrangements. These, in turn, as Göran Therborn indicates in the opening chapter, require political coalitions and an appropriate global context, allowing for redistribution to draw on the wealth of the economic elites, instead of preserving and multiplying it.

Latin America was undoubtedly host to the emergence of a new institutional framework in terms of rights, as indicated by the adoption of minimum social values in the fight against extreme poverty across the continent. As Therborn, Costa, and Sáinz rightly indicate, constitutional reforms and the creation of mechanisms for political intervention lent visibility and recognition to issues of ethnicity, race, gender, and the environment, both at the executive level and in the public sphere. These identity-related processes, dubbed "existential inequalities" by Therborn, are, in all their growing radicalism, an expression of the great vitality of Latin American societies over the period of democratic consolidation. Nevertheless, the great divide that still characterizes the continent is expressed, even beyond these cleavages, in the persistent deficits in the provision of public goods and services, as well as in the profoundly unequal access to them.

While the tempo of the construction of a new citizenship may differ from country to country, the universalization of rights remains unfinished and fragmented across the region. Conditional cash transfer programs—the most widely used tool in fighting poverty—have not even become a constitutionally guaranteed right. Rather, they depend on discretionary initiatives that have gained strength and legitimacy alongside social protection systems that are patently segregated and compartmentalized.

In the realm of macroeconomic policy, there was a clear attempt to give greater space to social policy, but with weak or deficient coordination. Graver still is the fact that such coordination was unable to slow down or revert the process of recommodification, which has emerged with new strength in South America. The region was able to reinsert itself into the global economy under very favorable conditions, given a remarkable high in commodity prices, but this was not enough to promote a virtuous trajectory of sustainable industrial development anchored in incremental, dynamic technological innovation.

It is still early for a definitive evaluation. However, the question remains as to whether the institutional framework developed at the height of this period of vigorous economic recovery will be able to sustain its genuinely positive results, and whether it can be honed in order to further pursue the reduction of economic and social inequalities. The challenge is thus to avoid backtracking, should the global economic context bring a steep slide in commodity prices—and, at the same time, to guarantee substantive advances that may finally ensure redistribution and structural change.

This is the warning that Pühle leaves us in his final comment: the agenda of the future calls for us to tackle structural reforms, the shaping of which demands creativity and originality in the search for functional equivalents that may support development and social justice in the long run.

Bibliography

Bielschowsky, R. (org.) (2000). *Cinquenta anos de pensamento na CEPAL.* Rio de Janeiro, Record.

Boyer, R. (2014). Is More Equality Possible in Latin America? A Challenge in a World of Contrasted but Interdependent Inequality Regimes. Desigualdades.net Working Paper No. 67; http://www.desigualdades.net/Resources/Working_Paper/67-WP-Boyer-Online.pdf?1393594018

Braig, M. et al. (2013). 'Soziale Ungleichheiten und globale Interdependenzen in Lateinamerika: eine Zwischenbilanz.' *desiguALdades.net Working Paper No. 4,* Berlin, Freie Universität.

CEPAL (2013). *Panorama Social de América Latina.* Santiago de Chile, CEPAL.

CEPAL (2011). *Panorama Social de América Latina.* Santiago de Chile, CEPAL.

Cornia, G.A. (2014). 'Recent Distributive Changes in Latin America: An Overview,' in Cornia, G.A. (ed.) (2014). *Falling Inequality in Latin America.* Oxford, Oxford University Press.

Fajnzylber, F. (1990). *Industrialization in Latin America: From the "Black Box" to the "Empty Box."* Santiago de Chile, CEPAL.

IMF (2014). *Fiscal Policy and Income Inequality.* Washington, DC, IMF, www.imf.org/external/np/pp/eng/2014/012314.pdf

IMF (2014). *Global Economic Outlook,* Washington, DC, IMF.

Lustig, N. and López-Calva, L.F. (eds.) (2010). *Declining Inequality in Latin America: A Decade of Progress?* Washington, DC, Brookings Institution Press, and New York, United Nations Development Programme (UNDP).

Tsounta, E. and Osueke, A.I. (2014). *What is Behind Latin America's Declining Income Inequality?* Washington, DC, IMF, https://www.imf.org/external/pubs/ft/wp/2014/wp14124.pdf

Chapter 2
Moments of Equality: Today's Latin America in a Global Historical Context

Göran Therborn

Latin American Inequality in a World Context

Latin American income inequality is notorious, and ancient. The European explorer Alexander von Humboldt (1822/1966) was shocked by it two centuries ago especially in New Spain, today's Mexico. Some African countries, like South Africa, now lead the world into the abyss of inequality, but no region of continental proportions, only sub-continental countries like China and India, can rival Latin American income inequality. The USA and Russia are not quite on par (Therborn, 2013: Table 10, with references). However, income distribution is not the whole story of inequality. The UNDP Human Development Reports have come to widen our horizons.

The figures shown in Table 2.1 should be seen as estimates rather than firm truths, and the South Asian income figure is most probably wrong, referring, as regional household surveys here usually do, to consumption, which is less unequally distributed, rather than to income. However, the world location of Latin America does not invite dispute. More quality of human life is lost in Latin America due to income inequality than in any other part of the world. But vital and educational inequality is lower than the world average. In terms of overall inequality of human development, Latin America is only slightly above world average, or plain average within the margins of error. Overall, Latin American inequality is the same as in the Arab states, but in the latter driven by educational inequality rather than income.

There is not yet any neat index of existential inequality—the unequal allocation of autonomy, recognition and respect to humans as persons—and the UNDP index of gender inequality—with its variables of maternal mortality, adolescent fertility, and gendering of parliamentary seats, secondary or higher education, and labor force participation—captures at most only one aspect of existential inequality with a weighting hardly above questioning. Nevertheless, the UNDP index says that Latin Americans are slightly below the world average of gender inequality, and better off than Arabs, South Asians, and Sub-Saharan Africans, but worse than post-Communist Eurasians, and far more unequal than "the very highly developed" (UNDP, 2013: p. 159).

Racial and ethnic diversity in Latin America also makes existential inequality a very salient issue. Along the mountainous backbone of the region, from Mexico to southern Chile, there are sizeable indigenous populations, majoritarian in Bolivia. In the Caribbean and along the plantation coasts of South America, from Venezuela and Colombia down to Rio de Janeiro, there are substantial populations of "*afrodescendentes*," as they are now officially called. Latin America never institutionalized White racism as in the United States, and its history is full of Mestizo and full-blood Indian leaders of different kinds, the 19th century Mexican Liberal Benito Juárez being the most impressive by current political

Table 2.1   Regional loss of human development index value due to inequality in 2012 (percentage loss)

Countries Group	Life expectancy	Education	Income	Overall Loss
Very high development	5.2	6.8	19.8	10.8
Arab States	16.7	39.8	17.5	25.4
East Asia & Pacific (China et al.)	14.2	21.9	27.2	21.3
[Eastern] Europe & Central Asia	11.7	10.5	16.3	12.9
Latin America & Caribbean	13.4	23.0	38.5	25.7
South Asia (India et al.)	27.0	42.0	15.9	29.1
Sub-Saharan Africa	39.0	35.3	30.4	35.0
World	19.0	27.0	23.5	23.3

Source: UNDP, Human Development Report 2013, p. 155.

standards. However, White racism is a very important Latin American legacy, down to this day. Brazil was, after all, the last country of the Hemisphere to abolish slavery, in 1888. The US civil rights struggles and advances of the 1960s had no equivalent in Brazil or in the other plantation countries of Latin America, hardly even an echo. The radical Bolivian revolution of 1952 saw itself and its tasks overwhelmingly in class terms, and Bolivia got its first Indian President only in 2006.

The Latin American Hour

Recent Latin American developments take on a global significance in a context of historical moments of change. In 2010, the UN Economic Commission for Latin America, CEPAL, heralded the arrival of "The Hour of Equality" (CEPAL, 2010). At a time when intra-national economic inequality was accelerating in North America and in most of Europe and of Asia, it was going down in Latin America, in 16 out of 18 countries with available data between 2000–2012 (CEPAL, 2013b: Table 1.6.4). (Costa Rica, once a modestly egalitarian country by generous Latin American standards but under neoliberal rule [possibly changing by the April 2014 Presidential election of a critic of it], being the only exception, together with Guatemala.)

When the most advantaged ten and one percent are increasing their share of national income in most rich countries, from USA to Australia via Sweden (OECD, 2011), the share of the top ten percent is going down in sixteen of eighteen reporting Latin American countries, including all the larger ones (Costa Rica and Guatemala being the exceptions, CEPAL, 2013: Table 1.6.3b). While a right-wing US economist is gleefully telling his compatriots that "average is over" (Cowen, 2013), the ratio of upper middle class to middle class income, the 95th to 50th percentile ratio, declined in seventeen of eighteen countries south of the border, Honduras being the sole exception (CEDLAS and World Bank, 2014, accessed 23.3.2014; the period is mostly 2000 to 2012).

In other words, current Latin American experience corroborates the idea that inequality is not a fate, nor equality a destiny. While capitalism harbors an inherent systemic tendency to ever increasing inequality, as Marx predicted and as Thomas Piketty (2013) has recently restated on an updated footing, contingent political economy keeps paths to equalization open.

Resource equalization in Latin America, of power (through democratization), of education, and of formal employment as well as of income, is accompanied by major strides towards existential equalization. The Brazilian Constitution of 1988 included a raft of far-reaching (and difficult to realize) social rights, the Bolivian of 2009 turned the colonially rooted Creole state into an officially "Plurinational" one, and new constitutions of Venezuela and Ecuador have added a new awareness of ethnic existential issues. Same-sex marriage was institutionalized in Mexico City (historically a vanguard of family legislation in Mexico) and in Argentina. A significant Black movement has finally developed in Brazil, and racial educational quotas are contributing to amending centuries of discrimination. Indigenous movements have harder battles (outside Bolivia) to fight, but have become recognized political players from Mexico to Chile.

Previous World Moments of Equality

Moments of equality have been rare in the history of industrial capitalism, almost as rare as revolutions, which have provided the most dramatic examples of the former. The French Revolution, at the dawn of contemporary capitalism, was the first, with effects, though fading, that outlasted the counter-revolutionary Restoration (Morrison, 2000: 235 ff.). In the 20th century the communist revolutions were major equalizers, and so were the two World Wars. The Depression stopped soaring inequality in the United States, but neither in the major states of Europe nor in Japan (Piketty, 2013; Atkinson and Piketty, 2010.)

However, the history of capitalist development has seen one prolonged period of peace when inegalitarian tendencies were kept at bay and equality was extended, in a variety of directions, not just income distribution. This was the period from 1945 to about 1975/1980. It was launched by the outcome of World War II, but it organized its own expanded reproduction of relative equality.

It was not global, but it was intercontinental in scope, comprising North America, most of Europe, east and west—fascistic regimes in Greece, Portugal, and Spain being the marginal exceptions[1]—Northeast Asia, and the Oceania of Australia and New Zealand. Latin America was not part of the confluence. Ironically, the most significant qualification of this exclusion was Peronist Argentina (Atkinson, Piketty and Saez, 2010: Table 13A.16), a country which had refused even token participation in the war as a US ally.

If there is any historical parallel to the current Latin American moment, it is this 1945–80 period, all of whose participants are now reciprocating the Latin American absence then. Even though some current Latin American governments are claiming to pursue a "socialism

---

1   They had their moment later, in 1985–2007, after democratization and joining the EU, inspired by the "European social model." On the Iberian case, see further Huber and Stephens (2012: p. 221ff., p. 251).

of the 21st century," for reasons of comparative simplicity, we had better leave out the Communist socialisms of the 20th, emerging from revolutions, and concentrate on the previous capitalist experience of equalization, in North America, Japan and the rest of capitalist Northeast Asia, and, above all, Western Europe.

Commonalities of Peacetime Equalization

There are two major parametric commonalities between Latin America of the first decade(s?) of the 21st century and the Intercontinental of 1945–1975/80. Most important is probably the political. Both are times in which the most aggressive anti-egalitarian ideologies and political forces are strongly discredited, Fascism or military dictatorship, and rightwing Liberalism.

The end of WWII meant a smashing of European Fascism and of Japanese militarism. Their survivors were in no position to defend a political agenda. In Latin America, only the Argentine junta was militarily defeated, but by 1990, the once-powerful militaries of the Southern Cone, and soon also those of Central America, were seen as barbarian monsters out of a nightmare. However, their mostly gradual phasing out, in a slowly lightening dawn, did not issue into a clear-cut turn to the left, like in the UK, where the electorate of July 1945 unceremoniously booted the Conservative war hero Winston Churchill out of office.

In Europe, and in North America, rightwing Liberalism was utterly discredited by the misery of the Depression of the 1930s, seen as very hard evidence that unregulated market liberalism has nothing positive to offer ordinary people. Friedrich von Hayek was then generally regarded as somewhat of a mad hermit in the desert, although his diatribe against a social-democratic welfare state, *The Road to Serfdom*, sold well, while failing to convince anybody outside a dwindling band of far-right marketeers.

Post-military Latin America was in a different political time. Militant, rightwing neoliberalism was in ascendancy, attuned to post-industrial financial capitalism and backed up by Anglo-Saxon firepower as well as intellectual power, the Washington Consensus—of the IMF, the World Bank, and the US Treasury—and by US academic departments of economics, headed by Chicago, the *consiglieri* of the Pinochet dictatorship. The only military junta with a clear economic program was the Chilean, and after its harsh economic punishments of the 1970s and its early 1980s crisis, this was experienced as an economics of boom. Aided by the negotiated return to democracy, Chilean neoliberalism survived its military Godfather. In Argentina and Bolivia, as well as in Mexico, via electoral fraud, neoliberalism was let out to go wild. In Brazil, after the disgrace of Collor, it was finally reined in by Cardoso, who nevertheless abstained from any significant social democratic approach to the abysmal inequalities of the country.

It took a good decade after the era of military dictatorships for rightwing liberalism to get utterly socially discredited in Argentina, Bolivia, Ecuador, Venezuela—all experiencing horrendous socio-economic crashes, of which the Argentine of 2001 had the widest reverberations—or at least have its hegemony eroded, as in Brazil, Chile, Mexico, Peru, Uruguay, and other countries.

But in the first decade of this century, there was a political-ideological commonality between Latin America and, on the other hand, post-World War II North America, Western Europe and capitalist Northeast Asia. Anti-egalitarian ideologies and politics were pushed to the margins, liberal as well as authoritarian ones.

A second commonality is economic growth. For the rich Tricontinental, 1945–75 was a period of unprecedented and unsurpassed rates of economic growth. Equalization was made much easier by accelerating positive-sum economic games. Economic growth in Latin America in the 2000s has not been unrivalled. But it has been substantial—4 percent annual average for the region for 2005–12, including a decline of 1.5% in 2009—and experienced against the background of the largely lost decades of the 1970s-1990s (CEPAL, 2013a: Table 2.1.1.).

Furthermore, there is a commonality of political process. Neither equalization was the product of one single political project or force. In Western Europe, both Christian and Social Democracy were major proponents. In France there were also Gaullists and progressive Republicans; in the UK there were "One Nation" Conservatives. US Republicans, from Eisenhower—who sent paratroopers against racist mobs in Little Rock—to Nixon, who expanded social services and economic regulations, were then not inimical to equality. In Northeast Asia, equalization had an ever wider range of crucial bedfellows, not only stalwart business conservatives in Japan, but also the Guomindang cadres of Taiwan and the Park Chung-Hee military dictatorship of South Korea, both concerned with boosting national cohesion.

Also in recent Latin America, equalization, though perhaps most radical in the most radical countries, such as Venezuela, Bolivia, and Argentina, has also been very significant in Peru, without any sustained left, and significant in Conservative Colombia, in Chile of the cautious *Concertación*, and in post-Salinas rightwing Mexico, while broad and well-organized centre-left coalitions have made substantial gradual changes in Brazil and Uruguay. We shall return to the results below.

This political polyvalence of equalization is noteworthy. The process has to be politically started, although the rich may lose part of their wealth in wars and depressions, but politics remains forever a complex art, irreducible to ideological programs. And it is always de facto shaped by economic constraints and opportunities.

Policy-wise, there are also some important similarities, as one might expect. Most important is the rise of a welfare state. By 1970, all democratic Western European states had become welfare states, in the specific meaning of devoting most of their expenditure to the welfare of their populations (i.e., social insurance and assistance, heath and other care, education). In the United States, this happened somewhat later, after the end of the Vietnam War (OECD data, see Therborn, 1984). The typical Latin America state (defined as population-weighted state average) became a welfare state around 2000. By the mid-nineties, Latin American social spending amounted to 46% of total public spending, but by the mid-2000s, 59% of public expenditure were for social purposes (CEPAL, 2012a: p. 158).

Social expenditure tends to be higher in more resourceful countries. Within Latin America, Mexico[2], Peru, and Colombia spend significantly less on social causes than one might expect from their GDP per capita, but also Venezuela, Ecuador, Nicaragua, and Bolivia are slightly below the expected regression line. Cuba, on the other hand, is far above, and well above are also Argentina, Uruguay, and Brazil. Somewhat higher are Costa Rica and Chile (CEPAL, 2012a: p. 161).

---

2 Mexican social spending is somewhat underreported, though, as that of sub-national governments is not included (CEPAL, 2013b: p. 193), but the country is quite substantially under-spending the Latin American average (CEPAL, 2013b: p. 194).

If we take a somewhat narrower definition of social expenditure, excluding education and concentrating on social security and welfare plus health, the most common definition for intercontinental, comparisons, Latin American social spending in 2009–10 comprised 12.3% of GDP 2009–10, up from 7.0 in 1991–92 (CEPAL, 2012a: Table 1A.1.).

The level reached in Latin America by 2010 is about the same as that of Western Europe in 1960, with its 11 (Germany, Sweden, UK) to 13 (France) percent range (Flora, 1983: p. 456). The change rate is rather similar to the West European of the 1950s, which was not a decade of major social advance in most of that region. The big quantitative expansion there came after 1960 (or rather 1965), almost doubling, up to 21–22% of GDP in West Germany, France, and Italy by 1974, but with more dispersion, between 14.5% in the UK and 24.4% in Sweden (Flora, 1983: p. 456). If Latin American countries want to develop their welfare states, the big jump lies ahead.

Differences

However, there are differences between the two historical moments, differences all indicating more constraints and larger difficulties for 21st century Latin America than to the North Atlantic and the Northeast Asian areas of the third quarter of the previous century.

Most obvious is the different geopolitical context. Post-WWII equalization was much driven by fear of and competition with Communism. This was strongest in Northeast Asia, inspiring extensive land reforms and adding to nationalist concerns with social cohesion. But it was important also in Western Europe, the epochal West German 1957 invention of the *dynamisierte Rente*, tying pension rights to the development of current wages, for instance, was part of a Christian Democratic project of rearmament. And it does not seem likely that a conservative US President would have sent federal troops to protect a handful de-segregated Black school children against Southern White mobs without the Cold War competition with the Soviet Union. Now, Communism as well as the USSR are gone as a social force, and whatever international attraction China may hold, it is no longer egalitarianism.

Not only political, but also economic history has increased the challenges facing Latin American egalitarians. Recent globalization has made capitalist development more dependent on international capital markets and much less on national integration and cooperation. The train of industry has now passed by Latin America, where de-industrialization has already begun. While manufacturing employment is still growing in numbers in several countries, its relative share, never predominant, is declining (CEPAL, 2012b: Table 1.) Current economic growth is above all a commodities boom, from soybeans to metals and oil. Large-scale, successful industrialization, as in the Northern Tricontinental after World War II, created widespread employment in jobs with a similar, relatively high productivity and corresponding pay. Developed industrial labour markets—after the vicious original accumulation studied by Marx—tend to sustain a certain amount of good wages egalitarianism. Huber and Stephens (2012: p. 145) found deindustrialization a major cause of rising Latin American inequality in the 1990s.

Commodity booms, on the other hand, produce rent economies with uncertain labor market effects. The land rent may be used for public social largesse and the boom utilized for raising minimum wages, as is currently the case in most of Latin America, but it may also be appropriated by a few, who then dole out portions of it in clientelistic patronage.

The social base of rent economies is always potentially oligarchic, and their revenues tend to be volatile.

The other visible post-industrial alternative capitalism, directed by financial capital, has strong tendencies towards a dualistic economy-cum-society of a luxurious "creative" class of financiers, their business supports, and entertainers, and a low-paid servant class, of cleaners, maids, nannies, teachers, gardeners, janitors, waiters, retail salespeople, and security guards. The US and the UK are showing the way. Latin American egalitarians will have to devise a new kind of a post-industrial economy and society.

Furthermore, the political props of today's Latin American equalization look more fragile than those of its predecessors, particularly in Western Europe and Northeast Asia. In the latter there was a solid development pact between, on one hand, a protected farming bloc, basking in its new-won gains of land reform, and, on the other, an outward-looking urban elite bent on export industrialization. Firm political structures kept up the pact, all dominating their national political stage, the Liberal-Democratic party of Japan, the Guomindang of Taiwan, and the iron-fist military dictatorship of General Park Chung-Hee in Korea, bolstered by large nationalist civilian associations.

In Continental Western Europe there was first of all Christian Democracy, well-organized mass membership parties, all with a substantial and influential trade union wing as well as deep religious connections in still largely non-secularized societies. To their left these Christian Democrats had big working class mass parties, Communist in France and Italy, Social Democratic in the rest. The most radical and consistent successful egalitarianism reigned in Scandinavia secularly weaned from Christian Democracy, through huge hegemonic Social Democratic parties, supported by the strongest trade union movement of the world. Britain, to say nothing of the United States, largely or wholly lacked these institutional props. Economic equalization never got very far there, and the neoliberal counter-offensive came earlier and more violently than in Western Europe or Northeast Asia.

Seen against this Eurasian background, current pro-equality Latin American governments look rather fragile, vulnerable or delimited. Venezuela's "Bolivarian Revolution" developed as a classic case of regional populism, by a charismatic leader and his followers—after the existing political system had gone completely bankrupt, without much of collective self-organization and institutionalization. It survived the death of Hugo Chávez just by a whisker, and is currently facing an implacable rightwing militant opposition under conditions of an at least partly self-inflicted—by corruption and mismanagement—economic crisis. There seems to be organized structuration behind Evo Morales' regime in Bolivia, but the country remains riven by an extremely fractious protest culture, much wider than the rightwing opposition, which is largely geographically confined.

The Ecuadorian government is perhaps most (intellectually) competently staffed among the three most radical regimes, all striving for a "Socialism of the 21st century," but, on the hand, its support, like that of the others honestly earned in democratic elections, is the least organized, in a country notorious for its volatile politics and weak institutions and organizations. Argentine Peronism contains everything, and its opposites, and the demise of its progressive Kirchner wing is on the horizon. What will happen then is an open question.

In the key country of Brazil, there is a government party with some resemblance to European Social Democracy, the Workers' Party (PT). But the PT is far from being a majoritarian party and depends on the personal charisma of Lula and on horse-trading alliance politics. Organized labour has not had much influence on the Lula and Dilma governments (Cf. Flores-Macías, 2012: p. 144 ff.). There is more structure to the "New

Majority" of Michelle Bachelet in Chile, now stretching from Christian Democracy to the Communist Party, and to the "Broad Front" of Uruguay, currently governing for a second presidential term, and with which labour has been able to march forward. Both coalitions are moving very cautiously, well aware of the narrow confines of inherited economic liberalism.

This brief schematic overview does not warrant any conclusion about the political future of equality in Latin America. It does show, though, that Latin American egalitarians face daunting tasks, with brittle or uncertain political resources, and without any support or spurring competition from the outside.

Historical Significance

The achievements of the Latin American Moment of Equality will be analyzed in the later chapters. Here, an attempt, obviously tentative and provisional rather than conclusive, shall be made to indicate its historical significance, to the history of Latin America and to the world.

One contribution of global importance has already been pointed out above. Even in the current wave of globalization, economic inequality is not governed by universal economic laws, such as of finance and technology, but is decisively shaped by national and regional political economies. US inequality is not necessarily going to be the destiny of us all.

We noted above that vital inequality in Latin America, as measured by life expectancy at birth, is below world average though well above the UNDP world of "very high human development." With respect to this, vital, dimension of inequality, like the others, the region harbours big inter-country differences. Least inequality of mortality and the highest average life expectancy we find in Cuba, second in the Americas, after Canada, with Chile coming third, having the same inequality of mortality as USA but slightly higher life expectancy. By far the worst situation festers in Bolivia, with a vital inequality almost as high as India's. Brazil is in the middle of the regional range, together with Colombia, Ecuador, Peru, and Venezuela, and Argentina, Mexico, and Uruguay in what might be named the upper middle group (UNDP, 2013: Tables 1 and 3). For the two decades, 1991–2010, there was a substantial reduction of spatial vital inequality across municipalities in Brazil (http://www.atlasbrasil.org.br/2013/ Access date: April 2, 2014), The distance between the national poles of social space, of two places in the Northeast and two in the South is currently twelve years of life expectancy at birth, which now is not very striking in the harsh international light, being equal to the distance of life-length between the Scottish metropolis of Glasgow and the London borough of Chelsea and Kensington. (http://www.pnud.org.br/IDH/Atlas2013.aspx?indiceAccordion=1&li=li_Atlas2013 Access date: April 2, 2014). The Brazilian spatial equalization has no contemporary equivalent in, for example, the UK, or Sweden, where the current municipal gap of life expectancy is 8.6 years is still somewhat lower. The general issue of vital inequality does not seem to have been firmly established on the Latin American political agenda yet. It is noteworthy, though, that Brazil, Ecuador, and Venezuela have embarked on extensive public health programmes directed to the most disadvantaged population. In both Brazil and Venezuela tackling the inequality of health involves large organized imports of Cuban doctors, who in Venezuela have also trained domestic 17,000 doctors[3].

---

3   Cristina Laurell, Mexican specialist on public health and occasional consultant to the Venezuelan government, oral communication, August 2014.

The egalitarians of the Northern Tricontinental were probably even less aware of vital inequalities than their Latin American successors, in particular since the infectious epidemic diseases were getting under control in the North. Nor were they much concerned with existential issues, even when they could hardly be denied. Blatant institutionalized racism continued in the United States after the war, and in continental Western Europe south of Scandinavia, marriage legislation was still proclaiming male superiority. Only in occupied Japan was gender equality introduced into family law—though not in practice (see further Therborn, 2004: Ch. 2).

In the 1970s the carapace of patriarchy was finally breaking in Western Europe, and now Latin America was placed at the centre of global gender politics. The immensely successful and influential UN Conference on Women took place in Mexico City in 1974. Gender emancipation became an integral part of the democratization process of the 1980s. One summary way of assessing how far it has gone may be to look at the UNDP "Gender-related development index," later changed into a "Gender inequality index." In 2001, Latin America was well behind Latin Europe, according to the former index. On the UNDP list, the least gender-unequal American countries ranked in the world as 34 (Argentina), 39, 41, and 43 (Uruguay, Costa Rica, Chile, respectively). Mexico had a national rank of 52, Brazil one of 58, and Venezuela 60. Portugal, the end light of Western Europe, ranked 23 (UNDP, 2003: Table 22).

By 2012, and according to a different manner of indexing[4], Latin America has certainly not climbed. While Spain is ranked 15 and Portugal 18, Cuba as the best Latin American country has rank 63, Chile 66, Argentina 71, Mexico 72, Brazil 85, and Venezuela 93 (UNDP, 2013: Table 4). Since the indices are so different, any fall backwards cannot be concluded, only that Latin America remains well behind Latin Europe. But there has been equalization; in 2001 the female labour force participation rate was in Mexico 48% of the male and in Brazil 52%, while in 2011 it was 55 and 74 percent, respectively In Portugal it increased from 72 to 83, and in Spain from 57 to 77 (UNDP, 2003: Table 25; UNDP, 2012: Table 4). On the other hand, gendered wage equalization, though predominant, has not been universal, apparently regressing in Argentina and Peru in 2000s while advancing rapidly in, for example, Mexico, from a lower level (CEPAL, 2009: Table 1.7.1).

Racial/ethnic aspects of existential inequality are a big issue in the Latin American moment of equality. In the process of post-military democratization, the indigenous peoples "erupted onto the agenda of democracy and development," as the UN Economic Commission put it (CEPAL, 2006: p. 145). This should be seen against the background of the UN International Decade for the Indigenous Peoples of the World, 1994–2004, and the 2007 Declaration of the Rights of Indigenous Peoples by the UN General Assembly (cf. Kempf, 2007). Indigenous movements and organizations have come to power in Bolivia, become important political forces in the other Andean countries, and non-negligible ones in almost the entire region, although in Brazil they are confined to the Amazonas. This mobilization and its recognition are in themselves moves against existential inequality. But for the indigenous peoples, existential equality is not just a matter of civil rights, but also a recognition of specific historical land rights, often of a sacred nature, against mining and

---

4   The first index included life expectancy at birth, adult literacy, overall school enrolment, and estimated earned income. The second maternal mortality rates, adolescent fertility rates, seats in parliament, proportion with at least secondary education, and labour force participation rates. It is hardly self-evident that the change is an improvement.

forestry companies or highway constructions. All of this has become very controversial, even in Bolivia and Ecuador, and in Guatemala the White Right is still ruling.

Under the hierarchization of racial/ethnic inequality in Latin America, by degrees of colour and looks, discrimination may have been less violent and humiliating than the dichotomous exclusion practiced in the United States. But limited and late educational and other national developments have come to mean severe socioeconomic disadvantages for Latin American ethnic minorities. On the eve of the current wave of equalization (1998–2002), it has been estimated that if Indians and Afro-descendants had the same schooling as people of European descent, poverty among the former would decrease from 58% to 39 in Bolivia, from 82% to 39 in Ecuador (in 1998), and from 72% to 51 in Mexico. In this calculation, schooling was less significant to Brazilian poverty (UNDP, 2010: p. 36).

Blacks in Brazil had only half the income of Whites (53%) in 2005. That was progress, from 1995, 48% (Soares et al., 2007: pp. 408–9), but below the US ratio of 62% in 2010 and 58% in 1980 (Noah, 2012: p. 44–5). The racial life expectancy gap gives a different picture. In 1990, even after a strong increase in the 1980s, the Brazilian White-Black gap was about six years (Faerstein, 2008), to seven in the US. By 2010, the gap in Brazil is only one year, while remaining at 4.5 in the US. Among Brazilian women, mixed race was a ticket to an extra year of life over (Chiavegatto Filho et al., 2014; Center for Disease Control and Prevention, 2011) In Brazil, racial equality is moving to centre stage, so far much more peacefully than in the United States. But its potential implications are far larger; at the 2010 census a majority of Brazilians, 50.9%, identified themselves as *Afro-descendentes* (CEPAL-CELADE, www.ecclac.cl/celade). Its political implications remain to be worked out. For instance, the predominantly Black and Brown city of Salvador has to this day never had a mayor of African descent, something with has been standard practice in Washington, D.C. since 1974.

The 2000s have seen a major reduction of poverty in Latin America from 44% of the population (according to the CEPAL definition, an absolute measure) in 2002 to 28% in 2012 (CEPAL, 2013a: Table 1.6.1). Most of it was achieved before the Northern financial crisis broke out. In 2009, the poverty rate stood at 33 (CEPAL, 2012: p. 53). Reduction occurred in all countries, but was most rapid in Ecuador, from 62 to 32%, Bolivia (from 64 to 36%), Venezuela, from 44 to 24%, Peru, from 55 to 37%, and Argentina, from 26 to 4% (urban areas only). Among the biggest countries, poverty diminished from 38 to 19% Brazil for 2001–12, but in Mexico positive change was concentrated in the 1998–2002 period, and between 2002 and 2012 indigence actually increased, from 12.6 to 14.2% of the population (CEPAL, 2013b: p. 87). Indigence and absolute poverty are highest in Honduras, Nicaragua, and Guatemala, befalling two thirds of all Hondurans and a majority of all Guatemalans and Nicaraguans (CEPAL, 2013a: Table 1.6.1). Poverty and indigence are still strongly skewed by race/ethnicity, though. In 2011, 29% of indigents and 15% of non-indigent poor belonged to ethnic minorities, while only 6% of people with incomes above 1.5 times the poverty line did (CEPAL, 2012a: p. 60).

Even after a decade of equalization, Latin America remains a region of high income inequality. Only one country, Uruguay, had a Gini coefficient of inequality below 40 (or 0.40) by 2012 (CEPAL, 2013b: Table 1A.3.). Even that is more unequal than any country of Western Europe, including the UK, and then Japan, South Korea, and Taiwan (Therborn, 2013: pp. 11–5). Nevertheless, equalization has been significant. In several countries the current level of inequality is no doubt unprecedented, but in Argentina it is above the level of 1953, towards the end of classical Peronism. The Brazilian Presidencies of Lula and Dilma have finally taken their country back to the level of inequality in 1960, before the anti-egalitarian spree of the military dictatorship, with a Gini coefficient around 50. Mexican income inequality does seem to be lower now than in 1950–63—then 50–55 instead of currently about 45—but the Mexican 95/50 ratio (of upper middle to middle class), 4.5 in 2012, is rather above to the ratio of 1989, 4.4, at the beginning of the neoliberal plunge in Mexico. (CEDLAS, 2014: Inequality tables; historical data from Weisshof, 1976: Table 2; and Fishlow, 1976: Tables 1–2).

Table 2.2   Income inequality reduction in Latin America, 2002–2012 (points of the Gini Coefficient)

Strong Reduction	Bolivia	− 14 (2011)
Substantial Reduction	Argentina	-10
	Nicaragua	-10 (2001–9)
	Venezuela	-10
	Ecuador	-9
	El Salvador	-9 (2001–12)
	Peru	-8
	Uruguay	-8 (urban data only)
	Brazil	-7 (2001–12)
Small Reduction	Chile	-4 (2003–11)
	Panama	-4
	Colombia	-3
	Dominican Republic	-2
	Mexico	-2
	Honduras	-2 (2002–10)
	Paraguay	-1 (2001–11)
Outliers of Increased Inequality	Guatemala	+4 (2002–6)
	Costa Rica	(+2) (uncertain comparability)

Source: CEPAL, 2013b: Table 1.A.3.

To explain this pattern, whose figures should all be read with a margin of error, is beyond the task of this contextualizing chapter. It does seem to point to two different forces, though. One is clearly political: radical Bolivia is on top, followed by the other left-leaning countries, and eight of the nine low-end states are all under conservative/neoliberal governments. Anti-racist inclusion and empowerment policies, minimum wage rises, pro-labour policies, and large-scale targeted progressive public transfers have been deployed by leftwing governments.

Secondly, the strong showing of Peru and Salvador, whose first decade of the new Millennium has included left-of-centre Presidents but with neither strong egalitarian ambitions nor power base, and, perhaps even more, the fact that inequality has decreased even in most countries with articulate conservative regimes, like Panama, Colombia, and Mexico, indicate something else at work as well. At least for the sake of raising the issue, without here being able to resolve it, we may refer to this second explanatory force of the

Latin American moment of equality as the regional 2000s pattern of economic growth and of social development. The decline of the income appropriation by the richest ten percent in almost all countries hardly owes anything to public redistributive measures in countries like Peru and Salvador and unlikely much more in Brazil or Mexico or Chile. Generally speaking, Latin American fiscal systems remain much less progressive and redistributive than those of the OECD countries, even after their neoliberal wave (Cf. OECD, 2014).

Now, given the diversity of the Latin American economies, it may be too simplistic to talk about "the" regional pattern of growth. However, three features seem to be common. Since the mid-1990s, Latin America has had a strong educational development, in part no doubt driven by progressive politics, but also indicating wider social change, and a democratic dividend after the dictatorships, very clearly visible in the case of Brazil (*O Globo* 13.10.2013: p. 3*)*. The strongest equalization of education has been registered in El Salvador, followed by Mexico and Brazil (Cornia and Martorano, 2010: Figure 5). Econometric studies have also found that income returns to educational credentials have generally declined in Latin America in the first decade of the 2000s (Barros, 2010; Cornia and Martorano, 2010; Gasparini and Lustig, 2011; Lustig et al., 2012). A massive expansion of education was, of course, a major feature of the Northern moment of equality, from the late 1940s to the 1970s.

Secondly, in contrast to the US, the UK, and Sweden, three countries of accelerating inequality, though at significantly different speeds, finance does not seem to have grown in importance in Latin America, perhaps a lesson from previous crises. The rapid growth of the real economy may also have put finance out of the driving seat. However, distributional data on finance and capital income in Latin America are scarce.

Thirdly, the hemispheric commodity boom, the engine of growth, does not put any extra premium on education credentials, although it often generates oligarchic rent appropriation. Here again, recent democratization, being carried by societal mass movements, has probably played a positive role.

But national differentials other than public policies of redistribution must also have been at work. In Central America, for instance, migrants' remittances are likely to have had a different channeling in El Salvador than in Guatemala and Honduras.

How does recent Latin American income equalization fare in comparison with the Northern experience? Between 1947 and 1980, the Swedish Gini coefficient (of disposable income, after tax and transfers) went down by around ten points, from 30 to 20 (Björklund and Jäntti, 2011: pp. 35, 38), about the same as in Nicaragua and Venezuela, but spread out over three decades instead of one or less. Now, historical Gini coefficients are rare, but some comparable data on shares by income deciles are available.

The current Latin American moment stands up quite well in a historical comparison with the Northern experience, and Bolivia stands out as a beacon. It has turned recent US experience upside down; in Bolivia all the deciles except the top one increased their share of the national income. The absolute numbers should be consumed with a fair amount of salt though. Historical income distribution data have a shaky comparability.

In the UK, the after-tax income share of the top ten percent declined by four percentage points between 1949 and 1974, to 24.8% of the total (Hills, 2004: p. 27), a level still far off in Latin America. Only in Uruguay (28%) did the richest tenth claim less than thirty percent of the nation's income, in Venezuela plain thirty, in Mexico just under forty, while in Chile and Brazil well above (CEPAL, 2013a: Table 1.6.3).

Table 2.3   **Moments of equality compared, Northern Countries 1950–70, Latin American 2000–2012: Change of the appropriation of national income by the most prosperous ten percent (share reduction in percentage points)**

France	6.9
West Germany	2.3
Sweden	4.8
UK	5.7
Japan	1.9a
USA	0.5b
Argentina	6.4c
Bolivia	16.0
Brazil	6.6
Chile	4.0
Ecuador	9.8
Mexico	3.8
Nicaragua	9.8
Venezuela	5.0

Notes: a. 1960–1970; b. 1950–60: 1.9; c. Urban areas only.
Sources: Europe, Japan, USA: Kaelble, 2007: p. 213.

Conclusion: Of Limited Conclusiveness

The first decade of the 21st century has been a bright moment of equality in Latin American history. In a historical global light, the Latin America achievement in the 2000s is of quite respectable proportions, and comparable to that of the European "Trente Glorieuses" after World War II. In the contemporary darkness of accelerating economic inequality, Latin America has provided virtually the only ray of light. Almost alone in the world, it has demonstrated the continued possibility of equalization.

Most strides have been made with respect to existential equalization, of indigenous peoples, of women, and of Afro-descendants, above all. Some vital equalization seems to have taken place, but it remains far from clear just how much and how general it has been. Economic inequality has gone down in Latin America, while rising in most of the rest of the world.

But hemispheric inequality is still operating at Andean levels, well above that of any European country, even capitalist Russia. The current hyping of a "rising middle class" is obscuring the region's persistent inequalities. The 95/50 income ratio between the beginning of the upper class (the 95th percentile) and the middle class median earner, currently 4.6 in Brazil and 4.5 in Mexico, is still higher than it was in the German Reich of 1913 (at 3.8 times the median) (Flora 1987: 652). And what kind of "middle class society" is Brazil, when a "typical" "traditional middle class" income is more than ten times that of minimum wage-earners? (Singer 2014: 29)

Will equalization efforts keep their momentum? This is the point where a conclusion drifts into inconclusiveness. The European post-World War II experience was not a general, straight line advance. It contained large international variation and a hilly path over time, with several ups and downs and with valleys of unchanging walking. It seems reasonable to expect some similar complexity in Latin America of the 21st century.

The hemispheric moment of equality is still on currently. New egalitarian protest movements, for instance in Brazil and Chile, have added to its thrust, while shaking the left-of centre governments in office. Anyway, the easy part of a profound equalization process is about to end, the reduction of extreme poverty, riding on a wave of popular anger over the crashes of neoliberalism, and sustained by soaring Chinese raw materials demand. The privileges of the upper class are still intact, the political contexts are getting more complicated, and the China-driven boom of commodity prices is embedded in uncertainty.

Already in 2012 there were indications of a stalling of the economic equalization process, in both the biggest countries, Brazil and Mexico, as well as in two of the three radical states, Ecuador and Venezuela (CEPAL 2013b: Tables 1A.1–3). Since then, the economic as well as the political crisis of Venezuela has deepened, and Argentina is pushed to debt default, implying serious economic problems, by hostile US actors, the vulture funds and the US judiciary.

On the other hand, so far, not a single one of the egalitarian governments and movements which have created the Latin American moment of equality has been defeated. But they are all fully functioning elective democracies, and the best definition of a democratic election is that its outcome is uncertain. The only warranted conclusion at the time of writing, is that the Latin American moment of equality is not concluded.

Bibliography

Atkinson, A. and Piketty, T. (eds). (2010). *Top Incomes.* Oxford, Oxford University Press.

Atkinson, A., Piketty, T. and Saez, E. (2010). 'Top incomes in the long run of history,' in Atkinson, A. and Piketty, T. (eds). (2010). *Top Incomes.* Oxford, Oxford University Press.

Barros, R. et al. (2010). 'Markets, the state and the dynamics of inequality: Brazil's case study,' in López Calva, L.F. and Lustig, N. (eds). (2010). *Declining Inequality in Latin America: A Decade of Progress?* Washington D.C., Brookings Institution.

Björklund, A. and Jäntti, M. (2011). *Inkomstfördelningen i Sverige.* Stockholm, SNS.

CEDLAS and The World Bank (2014). *Socio-Economic Database for Latin America and the Caribbean.* La Plata, CEDLAS. Available at http://sedlac.econo.unlp.edu.ar/eng/ (Accessed 25–27 March 2014).

Center for Disease Control and Prevention 2011. *National Vital Statistics Reports 60:3.* http:// www.cdc.gov/nchs/products/nvsr.htm

CEPAL 2006. *Panorama Social de América Latina.* Santiago de Chile, CEPAL

CEPAL 2009. *Panorama Social de América Latina.* Santiago de Chile, CEPAL

CEPAL (2010). *La Hora de Igualdad.* Santiago de Chile, CEPAL.

CEPAL (2012a). *Panorama Social 2012.* Santiago de Chile, CEPAL.

CEPAL (2012b). *The Employment Situation in Latin America and the Caribbean.* Santiago de Chile, CEPAL. Available at www.eclac.cl/ilo.

CEPAL (2013a). *Anuario Estadístico de América Latina y el Caribe*. Santiago de Chile, CEPAL.

CEPAL (2013b). *Social Panorama of Latin America*. Available at www.eclac.cl

Chiavegatto Filho, A.D. et al. (2014). 'Racial disparities in life expectancy in Brazil: Challenges from a multiracial society' [epub ahead of print]. *American Journal of Public Health*.

Cornia, G.A. and Martorano, B. (2010). *Policies of Reducing Income Inequality: Latin America during the last decade*. New York, UNICEF Working Paper.

Cowen T. 2013. *Average is Over*. New York, Dutton

Faerstein, E. (2008). *Race and Health: Some Trends and Challenges*. http://www.epi2008. com.br/apresentacoes/MESA_REDONDA_21_09_15H45_pdf/Eduardo%20Faerstein. pdf (accessed on June 28 2014).

Fishlow, A. (1976). 'Brazilian size distribution of income,' in Foxley, A. (ed.) (1976). *Income Distribution in Latin America*. Cambridge, Cambridge University Press.

Flora, P. (1983/1987). *State, Economy and Society in Western Europe, 1815–1975*. Vols. 1 and 2. Frankfurt and New York, Campus.

Flores-Macías, G. (2012). *After Neoliberalism*. Oxford, Oxford University Press.

Gasparini, L. and Lustig, N. (2011). *The Rise and Fall of Income Inequality in Latin America. ECINEQ Working Paper 2011–213*. New Orleans, Tulane University.

Hills, J. (2004). *Inequality and the State*. Oxford, Oxford University Press.

Huber, E. and Stephens, J. (2012). *Democracy and the Left*. Chicago, University of Chicago Press.

Humboldt, A. v. (1822/1966). *Ensayo politico sobre el Reino de la Nueva España*. Mexico, Editorial Porrua.

Kaelble, H. (2007). *Sozialgeschichte Europas*. München, C.H. Beck.

Kempf, I. (2007). '"Resistiendo al viento": advances y retrocesos en el desarrollo reciente de los derechos de los pueblos indígenas en las Naciones Unidas,' in Martí i Puig, S. (ed.) (2007). *Pueblos indígenas y la política en América Latina*. Barcelona, Fundación CIDOB.

Lustig, N., L. Lopez-Calva, Ortiz-Juarez, E. (2012). *Declining Inequality in Latin America in the 2000s: The Cases of Argentina, Brazil, and Mexico. ECINEQ Working Paper 2012–266*. New Orleans, Tulane University.

Morrisson, C. (2000). 'Historical perspectives on income distribution: The case of Europe,' in Atkinson, Λ.B. and Bourguignon, F. (eds). (2000). *Handbook of Income Distribution*. Vol. 1. Amsterdam, Elsevier.

Noah, T. (2012). *The Great Divergence*. New York, Bloomsbury Press.

OECD (2011). *Divided We Stand*. Paris, OECD.

OECD (2014). *Tax Revenue Statistics in Latin America*. Paris, OECD.

Piketty. T. 2013. *Le capital au XXIe siècle*. Paris, Seuil

Singer, A. (2014). 'Rebellion in Brazil.' *New Left Review,* vol. 85, no. 1, pp. 19–37.

Soares, S.S.D., Foutoura, N.O. and Pinheiro, L. (2007). 'Tendências recentes na escolaridade e no rendimento de negros e brancos,' in Barros, R. Paes de, Foguel, M.N. and Ulyssea, G. (eds). (2007). *Desigualdade de Renda no Brasil: uma análise da queda recente*. Vol. 2, Rio de Janeiro, IPEA.

Therborn, G. (1984). 'Classes and states: Welfare state developments, 1881-1981.' *Studies in Political Economy*, vol. 13, no. 1, pp. 7–41.

Therborn, G. (2004). *Between Sex and Power, Family in the World. 1900–2000*. London, Routledge.

Therborn, G. (2013). *The Killing Fields of Inequality*. Cambridge, Polity.

UNDP 2003 *Human Development Report 2004*. New York, UNDP.

UNDP (2010). *Regional Human Development Report for Latin America and the Caribbean*. New York, UNDP.

UNDP (2013). *Human Development Report 2013*. New York, UNDP.

Weisshof, R. (1976). 'Income distribution and economic growth in Puerto Rico, Argentina and Mexico,' in Foxley, A. (ed.) (1976). *Income Distribution in Latin America*. Cambridge, Cambridge University Press.

PART II
Challenges for Coordinating Economic and Social Policies

Chapter 3

The Limits of Redistributive Policies in Latin America: Complementarities between Economic and Social Protection Systems

Rubén M. Lo Vuolo

Problems of Complementarities between Economic and Social Protection Systems in Latin America

Compared with other regions of the world, Latin America has historically exhibited higher inequality and volatility in economic growth. History tells us that the occasionally improved conditions that benefited the most impoverished sectors during boom periods were worn down by recurring crises. Economic instability is a structural problem in Latin American countries; moreover, social protection systems do not work as effective countercyclical instruments to sustain welfare for the most vulnerable groups.

In spite of recent growth and improvements in social policy coverage and their positive impacts on employment and poverty reduction, these structural features continue to characterize the region. Thus, concerns about the sustainability of recent achievements are justified. Latin American growth is losing strength. The recent phase of economic growth sprang from a very favourable international context: a growing global economy, low interest rates, capital flows, high commodity prices, migrant remittances, etc. Moreover, it is important to remember that the region was recovering from a previous economic recession: when one re-calculates Argentina's performance outside official statistics,[1] the comparison between Latin American growth during 2002–2012 (3.8% annual average) and the previous growth cycle of 1990–1998 (3.4%) does not seem to show a differentiated performance in the second phase (Coremberg, 2013).[2] Looking at the period in which the regime of imports substitution was in force (1950–1980), Latin America grew at an annual rate of 5.5%, a close figure to the present growth rates of most Southeast Asian countries (Ocampo, 2012).

Therefore, two issues remain central in the discussion on social progress and redistribution in Latin America. One touches on the capacity to avoid, manage, and control recurring economic crises. The other refers to the prevailing faith in the sustainability of

---

1   According to official figures, Argentina's rate of growth during 2002–2012 came to an impressive 99%, more than doubling the region's average rate of growth. "However, if we use ARKLEMS GDP estimation, instead, the growth performance of Argentina is substantially lower (71%, nearly 30 points less than the official figures) and lies behind those of Peru and Uruguay" (Coremberg, 2013: p. 7).

2   Between 2002 and 2012, Argentina, Peru and Uruguay led growth rankings. The largest countries in the continent (Brazil and Mexico) grew below the region's average. However, during 1998–2002 Latin America only grew at an annual rate of 1.3%, while Argentina (-18.4%) and Uruguay (-17.7%) showed an impressive net drop in their GDPs, followed by Venezuela and Paraguay (Coremberg, 2013).

the distributional spillover effects of accelerated economic growth on employment, wages and their positive complementarities with social protection systems' coverage and benefits.

Several reasons have been put forth to explain the region's performance in economic volatility and inequality, including colonial heritage, dependency on natural resources, structural limitations on developing dynamic industries and integrating modern and lagging sectors, informal economies, elite preferences, high concentrations of power, political instability, etc. Extended rule by repressive authoritarian regimes is another important factor, as these regimes are associated with a lack of incorporation and higher inequality (Huber et al., 2006). Sustained democracy, especially if coupled with left-wing parties controlling the executive branch, is claimed to account for larger degrees of redistribution in Latin America (Huber and Stephens, 2012). Alongside endogenous elements, the asymmetric and dependent integration of Latin American countries into the global economy and political systems is frequently pointed to.

All these explanations help to understand the issue, but it is unclear which variables have the most influence. In any case, the present-day problems and institutional configurations of Latin American social systems have been shaped by complex historical paths which do not develop through continuous processes, but rather through recurring crises and readjustments. Latin American institutions have been structured and re-structured over time and on multiple occasions by various powerful agents.

These processes of structuring and restructuring occur in different social domains, creating institutional complementarities which help to explain, among other things, the limits of redistributive policies in the region. Here I focus on complementarities between the economic and social protection systems. The hypothesis is that, despite some improvements during the last years, the persistence of non-positive complementarities between the economic and social protection systems explain the difficulty in stabilizing a pattern of growth able to sustain increases in productivity and distribute these increases to the majority of the population in a progressive fashion.

The complementarities between the economic and social protection systems are mainly expressed in the labour market and in fiscal activity. For instance, the heterogeneity of the production regime and its long-standing deficiencies in systemic productivity limit the labour market's potential to function as a solid structure for social integration and social mobility, also, hindering the chances of legitimizing a universal and progressive social protection system. Furthermore, these and other features of the economic regime have forged non-positive complementarities with a stratified social protection system structured by an ethos of social insurance and assistance-conditional programs, as well as with a regressive and unstable tax system where payroll and indirect taxes prevail.

The idea of "institutional complementarities" is widely used in the literature on "varieties of capitalism" to posit the argument that the relations between institutions in different societal domains explain comparative economic advantages shaped by the preferences and behaviour of firms.[3] For instance, in this literature's view, social programs do not just involve costs for firms but also crucial benefits for the productive performance of the labour force. Social policies could favour incentives that support firms' competitive strategies and feed positive synergies between the economic and the social protection system, which contributes to progressive redistribution and thus to legitimizing the social order.

---

3   See the original presentation in Hall and Soskice (2001). Also, see Aguirre and Lo Vuolo (2013), for a recent summary and discussion of this literature in relation to Latin American countries.

Additionally, it is argued that a particular variety of capitalism combines with a particular political system in explaining redistributive outcomes (Iversen and Soskice, 2006).

A controversial claim of this literature states that positive complementarities stimulate institutional path dependency and thus reduce the likelihood of drastic institutional changes. This is the main reason why this literature asserts that the type of capitalism presented across various countries is unlikely to change. Latin America's history offers elements to discuss these and other arguments.

Indeed, some work under the variety of capitalism methodology offers explanations for the perpetuation of non-positive institutional complementarities in Latin American countries. The region is seen as dominated by a "hierarchical" form of capitalism characterized by large family-based economic groups and transnational companies which demand state support but are under no pressure to sustain redistribution and social policies (Schneider, 2009; Schneider and Karcher, 2010; Schneider and Soskice, 2009). In this scenario, firms and governments are not interested in promoting technological innovation, productivity and human skills. Among other things, this explains the persistence of the widespread informal economy.

Among various points of contention,[4] the varieties of capitalism approach have been criticized when applied to Latin America for neglecting the role of the state as promoter of growth and welfare and the role of changing political coalitions in power (Bizberg and Théret, 2012; Boschi, 2011; Sánchez-Ancochea, 2009). The state can break these institutions' path-dependence and lead the way to more autonomous development. Arguably, the idea that the state can change path-dependence and drive new patterns of development is introduced to explain why some "emerging" countries in the region have shown growth and remarkable improvements in social equality over the past decade.

Some arguments around the idea of institutional complementarities bring us back to the founding principles of the "Keynesian Welfare State." The idea is that various kinds of institutional social and economic arrangements enabled the coexistence of high levels of economic growth and employment alongside the pursuit of a relatively egalitarian distribution. The notion that complementarities and "system coordination" shaping the evolution of political economies and mutually reinforcing different subsystems has been widely used to understand problems of performance and adjustment in modern capitalist societies.[5] I will argue that the concepts of institutional complementarities and system integration can help to understand the limits of redistributive policies in Latin America. However, in order to do so, it is imperative to advance more research on these concepts when applied to countries in the region.

Here, the term institutional complementarities refers to theories and policies wherein the economic and social protection systems reinforce each other over time in order to lend mutual stability and positive performance to the social system as a whole in an effort to improve the welfare of the general population. On the one hand, such complementarities depend on the existence of mechanisms through which the economic system secures macroeconomic consistence and stable resources to fund social policies. On the other hand, complementarities depend on the social protection system's ability to legitimize support for the structure of the economic (and political) system and to generate labour force, improving people's autonomy and well-being.

---

4   See a summary of these contentions in Sandbrook et al. (2007: pp. 3–37). Also Aguirre and Lo Vuolo (2013).

5   See Habermas (1973).

My central argument is that these complementarities do not act positively in terms of redistribution and the enforcement of universal rights in Latin America. Even when Latin American countries have changed institutions and policies more frequently and radically than European countries, some structural features remain, reinforcing negative complementarities between the economic and social protection systems. Both systems should be analysed, taking the relationship between them into account.

When examining the domains typically considered for international comparison, one sees that the region is home to a remarkable diversity of macroeconomic policies, production and social protection systems. If studies lump together the experiences of countries with very different histories and involving a variety actors and policies, their specificities are overlooked. This makes it difficult to capture the specific configuration between the state, the market, and the family in conventional variety of capitalism and welfare state regimes' typologies.

Countries in the region are continuously modifying rules and institutions, with macroeconomic policies first on the list. These policies become endogenous to the political economy, not simply external elements to the behaviour of actors. Notwithstanding, even when state power has shown an ability to change policies and break institutional path dependency, certain common features have remained through these changes which pose strong limits on redistribution and inequality.

For instance, the importance of the informal economy, the heterogeneity of the production system, an ethos of social insurance, dilemmas of horizontal solidarity, the hostility of powerful political actors to universal policies, the regressivity and deficiencies of tax systems and an inability to control evasion and verify incomes, etc. Also, the low administrative capacity of the state has reduced its ability to verify the rules of access and the effective needs of claimant/beneficiaries through standardized and impartial procedures. Even when the state has the power to promote changes, it is not independently consolidated, financially secure, or politically stable.

State institutions, mainly those related to sensitive areas of human wellbeing, are more active for certain population groups than for others, lacking the ability (or the interest) to defend and enforce universal social rights for the most vulnerable groups (which might be legally established). Social divisions and social mobility are shaped by institutional membership and, as is well known, institutions plagued with high inequality hamper others in their performance. In general, labour markets and the institutional fiscal set tend to reproduce and even amplify market inequality in Latin America.[6] Also, the welfare of large parts of the population is more dependent on the domestic and communitarian spheres than in more mature welfare state regimes. The advance of conditional cash transfer programs stands as striking evidence of the stratified institutional set in the region: even when beneficiaries consider them a right, the truth of the matter is that they do not represent consolidated social rights but rather political instruments of social administration and control (Lo Vuolo, 2012a).

These limits on redistribution could be amplified when confronted with other socio-economic characteristics of the region. For instance, even those Latin American countries with a "high" human development index not only display comparatively high levels of inequality, but also high demographic dependency, high fertility rates, and high levels of

---

6 This general statement must be qualified for specific cases, such as Costa Rica and other countries with a more "social-democratic" approach to the welfare regime. However, even there it is difficult to sustain past achievements (Martínez Franzoni and Sánchez-Ancochea, 2013).

urbanization (the region shows an important surge of urban dwellers in the last decades). For instance, in most countries in the region, the population has begun to age before the social benefits to the salaried labour force reach universal coverage. Other social risks, like climate change, are not even considered in the debate. In other words, the structure of social risks is changing in the region, but institutional complementarities display old and well-known problems. In the past, economic growth has postponed their emergence, but recurrent crises and adjustment have always reminded us of their presence.

First lesson: The Limits of Redistribution During the ISI Regime

The ripest period for redistribution in the region was likely between the 1950s and 1970s. During this period many Latin American governments followed conceptual principles similar to those of the continental European countries in terms of institutional complementarities between the economic and social protection systems. These principles can be briefly summarized as follows.

First, the implementation of a social protection system was mainly a political decision in terms of creating a "social wage." Resources that covered social policies were considered as part of earned wages and were determined by the evolution of the number of wage earners, wage levels, and payroll taxes. The relative evolution of these variables was likely to follow a sort of virtuous path. At the outset of economic growth, there tends to be a rapid increase in the number of wage-earners; afterwards, the increase takes place at a lower rate. Simultaneously, wage increases are regular and self-sustained. As the number of wage earners and the level of wages increase, social wages rise (and sometimes payroll taxes, too).

The belief was that the expansion of social policies would sustain itself based on an implicit trust in a virtuous circle: social protection increases productivity; productivity increases growth and wages; wages increase growth and social protection. Macroeconomic policies were thus conceived to boost depressed economies and rapidly increase employment. Fiscal and monetary policies sought to preserve full employment, preventing the economies from falling into recessions and seeing a rise in unemployment.

In short, trust in positive complementarities between the economic and the social protection systems were set simultaneously, and relied upon both the economic and the political spheres. From one side, it was claimed that the economic cost associated with social protection could be compensated with the beneficial increase in worker productivity and growth. At the same time, a political commitment was made to shift productivity increases into a stable distribution of wages and benefits, and into an increased participation of social wage in total wage. As in most continental countries in Europe, the social insurance ethos prevailed under the generalized belief that everyone will be able to find a job.

However, the economic aspect did not perform as expected; and the region encountered many obstacles in modernizing lagging sectors and incorporating all the labour force into formal salaried relations. Also, the political commitment lacked a consensus as to how and when to transfer the increases in productivity to social policies benefiting the whole population.

One of the differences between the most redistributive European welfare states and Latin America countries lies in the timing and the institutional design of the political commitment as to the distribution of productivity gains. In Europe, the commitment was made prior to the economic boom of the post Second World War period; in Latin America it was made afterwards, or step by step. While by the 1940s and 1950s the process of legislative development of welfare systems was broadly completed in Europe, the main institutional structure for social protection systems was not well established in many Latin American countries before the growth period of the import substitution regime.

Here we encounter another difference: the "gaps" between the rules and the real outcomes of social protection systems in Latin America (Arza, 2004). In most countries social rights were legally established for all citizens, but in practice only a few groups enjoyed the benefits. Social policies in Latin America were founded on universalistic aims but developed in a fragmented and unequal manner, with severe limitations on the expansion of coverage and the equalizing of benefits (Mesa-Lago, 1978; Lautier, 2006). As a result, distributional conflicts were exacerbated and the state was hampered in its efforts to consolidate a stable funding mechanism for social protection systems.

The informal economy is an important factor in explaining these results. It works as low-cost provider of manpower (and fiscal credit) for employers trying to avoid paying the "political" increase in wages and the costs of the social wage, to which they have not agreed. Also, informal labour relations hobble the process towards decommodification and limit coverage for the large proportions of the population that remain outside the reach of social insurance systems.

Even during the "golden age" of the import substitution model, Latin American economic systems faced enormous difficulties in implementing the universal aim of the social protection systems. The heterogeneous production system and challenges in upgrading technology and substituting the most complex industrial goods put extra pressures on wages (and the informal economy) in the push to increase competitiveness.

Notwithstanding, given the level of growth, the trust in the virtuous circle remained. Poverty was mainly seen as a temporary problem and the social protection system included neither unemployment insurance nor huge income transfer policies for the working poor. Limited social assistance policies often distributed goods and services but not cash transfers.

The limits for growth and redistribution of these dynamics became evident in the 1970s. On multiple occasions, expansionary fiscal and monetary policies initially performed well in terms of growth and employment, but then caused severe problems in the external balance, the fiscal sector, and inflation. Recurrent crises and stop-go economic volatility became frequent. Macroeconomic policies were then dubbed stabilization policies, emphasizing the anti-cyclical function that they were called upon to fulfil. From then on, the region was used as a kind of laboratory where the most extreme recommendations of the so-called Washington Consensus were put into practice.

Second Lesson: No Redistribution for a Healthy Macroeconomic Environment

The Washington Consensus promoted by international financial institutions found a promised land in Latin America, thanks to foreign debt pressures and the need to overcome the macroeconomic instability of previous years. Policy recommendations included a package of pro-market actions, passive monetary policy and severe restraints on fiscal policy, openness to international flows of trade and capital, and several deregulatory measures in the markets of goods, finance and labour. The privatization of social insurance schemes was a key element of the prescription.

Under the Washington Consensus policies, complementarities between the economic and the social protection systems follow the extreme orthodox advice: social policies should not affect healthy labour market incentives and macroeconomics. Increasingly shaky labour relations and an increased tie between contributions and benefits in social policies was the advice given to boost financial markets, growth, workers' efforts, and employment. Accordingly, social protection systems should be built as a modular system tied to each risk pattern[7]. The most vulnerable part of society's increased ability to take risks would stimulate "entrepreneurial spirit" and encourage individuals' efforts to overcome poverty by themselves. In this framework, informal work is explained by workers' myopia in understanding the benefits of being insured, and by the inefficiency of social insurance schemes.

The universalistic aim of social policies was confronted with the argument that it did not work in the best interest of the poor. The goal of social policies is to struggle against poverty; to be effective, it was argued, social policymakers should set aside this universalistic aim and strengthen the relationship between benefits and contributions, preferably through private insurance. The poorest groups would receive residual subsidies by means of social assistance programmes when they proved their need through means tests.

As a result of the Washington Consensus hegemony, Latin American countries started to rely more heavily on market solutions for welfare and on selectivity as the criterion for policy orientation (exclusion from benefits and, in some cases, higher co-payments). These processes led to major reform of public institutions in many countries—even those, like pension systems, which were considered "difficult to reform" in the European case (Lo Vuolo, 2002). Health services experienced indirect privatization as well the growing presence of private or semi-private health insurance systems, leading to problems of skimming and the de-financing of the public service.

Structural economic heterogeneity has intensified during this period, fostering greater labour market segmentation, lowering labour security measures, and reducing labour costs (and purchasing power). Subcontracting part-time work or jobs without contracts, the reduction of formal public employment, the expansion of jobs in microenterprises, domestic service and self-employment, and excessive working hours for some groups were all part of the reconfiguration of labour markets. The results were not those advertised, but rather a downward flexibility of wages in the formal and informal labour market. More people fell out of "normal" work patterns, and we have seen no decline in the size of the informal economy across the region (Tokman, 2007).

In short, instead of solving problems of complementarities between the economic and social protection systems, the Washington Consensus policy package aggravated the non-positive bias. During the 1990s, the Gini index increased in almost every Latin American country (Colombia and Uruguay were the exceptions). At the beginning of this decade open unemployment averaged 9%, showing a marked growing tendency, with peaks of 20% in Argentina and 16% in Uruguay, Colombia and Venezuela. Public employment participation dropped and low productivity services increased.

While insecurity in labour markets, a lack of social security coverage and regressive income distribution become a generalized feature, demands for compensation systems have grown. As a result, the region is seeing a general tendency to set up focalized poverty alleviation schemes, administrated separately and generally tied to unemployment or some test of poverty.

In the wake of promises of sustainable growth, the economic and social situation worsened and deep crises affected many countries, first around 1995–1997 and then

---

7   See Lo Vuolo (2009a) for a discussion of social risk management analysis.

in 2001–2002. The crisis was later magnified by the so-called "flight to quality" effect during the "dot-com" crises in the US, when there was an important capital flight outside Latin America.

The crises and the social effects of the Washington Consensus experiment open the door for new changes. A new phase of economic growth has come to the region, in a favourable international context. Unfortunately, structural problems in the region were not resolved; and new ones emerged as the result of the Washington Consensus.

Third Lesson: Growth and Redistribution Back on the Agenda

The end of the import substitution model and the subsequent frustration with the Washington Consensus in following decades saw increasingly divergent development and international integration paths among Latin American countries (Bizberg and Théret, 2012). Some countries have consolidated more outward-looking and other more inward-looking models; some remain more open liberal economies, while others choose more state-led strategies.

In this divergent scenario, since the end of the economic crises of 2001–02, most Latin American countries (the remarkable exception is Mexico) have experienced an important recovery in GDP levels, which was particularly strong until the global crisis of 2008–09. This new phase of economic growth coincides with the beginning of the commodity price boom in 2002 (petroleum, natural gas, metals, and agricultural products), reinforcing faith in the distributional spillover effects of accelerated economic growth on employment, wages and social protection.

In some countries the favourable international context was accompanied by a rise in domestic demand (minimum wage, public expenses, credit, etc.). In most cases, redistribution from public policies returns to the agenda as a result of economic growth and new social programs. In some countries, measures such as export taxes, subsidies, price controls, and nationalization of public services were put in practice.[8]

The new approach in public policies is sometimes presented as inspired by the so-called Neo-Structuralism approach. Adherents to this approach question the economic orthodox rules of the Washington Consensus, focusing mainly on the macroeconomic unbalances attached to market imperfections in the region and giving a central role to employment and domestic demand management (Bresser-Pereira, 2011). In redistribution, they seem to share the faith in the spillover impacts of accelerated economic growth on employment, wages and welfare. In this sense, their attention continues to be focused on a short and medium-term distributive conflict rather than on the broad-based capacity-building of institutional change (Marques Pereira, 2006; Lo Vuolo, 2009b). The distributional issue is again a dependent variable of a sound macroeconomic policy and growth.

These were not the original precepts of Latin American structural thought. In original structuralism, little distribution is to be expected as a consequence of the spilling-over effect of productivity profits in a growing economy because of the heterogeneity of the production system, the consumption patterns and structural restrictions of the external and

---

8   While the definition of "left-leaning" governments can be controversial, many scholars consider the centrality of redistribution as an evidence of the resurgence of the Latin American left (Levitsky and Roberts, 2011).

fiscal sector.[9] Structural productive heterogeneity and the pattern of specialization in the region limit development and redistribution.

The informal economy has consistently shown itself to not simply be an imperfection of the labour market or the result of the absence or excessive presence of the state. Informality is a key element of the accumulation process in which the expected profit rate is estimated considering the persistence of labour market heterogeneity and fragmentation. The informal economy provides labour, goods and services to the formal economy, lowering its costs. It acts as a permanent buffer for labour market flexibility.

Recent events prove that the original structural concerns are still valid. In spite of recent growth, production systems remain heterogeneous, many low-productivity sectors have been left behind, and economic segmentation has accelerated (CEPAL, 2012a). Even countries with a long industrial tradition, like Brazil, are losing competitiveness in industrial and high-tech sectors (Bruno, 2007; Salama, 2012). Indeed, most of the demand-led growth during recent years came through exports and raising consumption of all social classes, whereas the region continues to show serious deficiencies in investment (levels and structure). This remains a serious shortcoming of Latin America economic regimes, not only because consumption of middle and upper classes drive imports, but also due to increasing demands from capital engaged in producing high-technology products for investment in reproductive capital, labour force skills, and reliable infrastructure.

Growth facilitates incorporation into the labour market; but structural problems in this market remain. When we take a global view of Latin America over the past few decades, we see a tangible increase in both the working-age population and participation rates, but occupation increases at lower rates than the joint evolution of age and participation rates. Most of the new entrants were women, who have the least structural power to negotiate the conditions in which they join the market. Also, growing economic activity rates among women generate a sustained change in household size and composition and reduce the prevalence of male breadwinner/nuclear families.

Consequently, the promise of workers' incorporation into social protection through positive complementarities between growth and employment has once again failed to materialize, not because there is no incorporation to the labour market but mainly because a large part of this incorporation remains fragile and precarious. Difficulties are experienced not only by unemployed and unregistered workers but also by "semiformal" workers, unregistered employees working at formal companies and employees that are only partly registered (for instance, listed as working fewer hours or earning more than they actually do). The gap between formal and informal wages and the spread of informal relations bear witness to the fact that that workers do not choose a given type of labour relation but rather simply accept what society offers them.

In short, even after recent economic growth, problems in the labour market persist. The dual approach that distinguishes between the poor (a small group, targeted for social assistance) and the non-poor with normal secure employments (a large group, covered by social insurance) does not apply. Most people are somewhere in the middle, and therefore the treatment of unemployment as a risk (an event that disrupts a normally stable working situation) is simply not appropriate. A huge area of working poor relies on low and unstable incomes, being excluded from both social insurance and targeted assistance policies. Few people in Latin America do not work at all, and few have stable long-lasting employment. Income insecurity is chronic: income loss is not only frequent but can arrive unexpectedly.

---

9   In this respect, one might recall Celso Furtado's classic work (Furtado, 1965).

Conditional Cash Transfer Programs and Non-Contributory Pensions

Trying to cope with these problems, some Latin American governments have organized huge campaigns to combat poverty through programs endowed with abundant resources that enable a broader coverage and benefit range, including non-monetary components. Venezuela is the paradigmatic case, although similar policies have been carried out in Bolivia, Ecuador, and Nicaragua (Filgueira et al., 2011).

More remarkable is the generalized acceptance and spread in the region of the so-called Conditional Cash Transfer programs (CCTs).[10] These programs have been implemented by most governments, whether they are right-leaning or left-leaning, pro-market or pro-State. Even when every country accounts for its own antecedents and trajectories, the operating rules of these programs show common features: (i) monetary transfers (in some cases complemented with in-kind transfers); (ii) targeting of poor and/or extremely poor households with children and adolescents (some programs do permit household categories without children); (iii) punitive conditionalities linked to school assistance and health checks of both children and adolescents, and for pregnant women; (iv) a preference for transferring the benefit to mothers; (v) the selection of beneficiaries according to geographic priority zones, self-identification, means and/or needs tests, etc.

Formally, CCTs attempt to attain two formally declared objectives. In the short term, they aim to decrease families' income poverty; in the long run they aspire to increase human capital formation in younger generations to improve future employability and break the cycle of inherited income poverty. Such a scheme supposes that the rate of return of fiscal expenditures on conditional income transfer programs would be higher with the transfer directed to the children, and compliance with conditionalities vouched for by their parents (World Bank, 2009).

In practice, CCT programs seek to compensate for the incomplete coverage of one of the oldest social insurance schemes in the region: Family Allowance Programs for formal employees. Parallel to the CCT programs, non-contributive Family Allowance Schemes have spread as well. These programs, generally also targeted at and conditioned to means tests, pay benefits for dependent family members of those people not covered by contributive family allowance schemes.[11]

Other non-contributive programs on the rise in the region are those paying pensions to elderly people (Arza, 2012). Examples include the rural pensions in Brazil (financed through a tax on sales of agricultural production and social security resources), the "Income Dignity" program (*Renta Dignidad*) in Bolivia (non-contributive and universal), and the universal and unconditional pension in Mexico City. Argentina has incorporated many beneficiaries into its pension schemes thanks to a "pension moratorium," which discounts any amount of social security contributions not paid during working life from the pension received.

Critical evaluations of the targeted and conditional income transfer programs themselves point to numerous problems: the arbitrary selection of beneficiaries, interference in people's

---

10   In 2010, the CEPAL databases recognized CCT programs in 18 countries in the region, covering over 25 million households (roughly 113 million people), with an average cost of 0.4% of GDP (Cechini and Madariaga, 2011).

11   Chile, for instance, has the Single Family Subsidy (*Subsidio Único Familiar*) for low-income households that do not have access to contributory family allowances. Uruguay expanded coverage of its contributive family allowances program to include non-contributive benefits; and Argentina provides a non-contributive benefit for unemployed and/or informally employed people with dependent children (Lo Vuolo, 2012b)

lives, political clientelism, the stigmatization of recipients, an inability to achieve universal coverage or act preventively in terms of income poverty, the fomentation of poverty traps and of informality, etc. Moreover, the programs receive criticism since both the means test applied and the benefit level consider the whole family, while compliance with conditionalities in practice becomes the exclusive responsibility of the women (Rodríguez Enríquez, 2012).

Targeting also ends up reducing the demand, through access cost (self-targeting), multiplying horizontal inefficiencies (i.e., part of the target population is covered, while part is not) and vertical inefficiencies, allowing for evasion (i.e. some families are included as poor without actually being poor) (Lavinas, 2012). In practice, the potential to increase human capital formation is uncertain since Latin American countries have no solid mechanisms to guarantee an efficient follow-up on school attendance or visits to health clinics. Conditions for access to cash transfers appear more appropriate for the containment of public spending, especially given that the state falls far short of providing a broad and diversified set of decommodified services in adequate quality and quantity.

Moreover, CCTs do not imply a change in the expenditure scenario, insofar as their spread has been correlated to country size and they represent a minor proportion of social expenditure. Social policies continue to focus on a short and medium-term distributive conflict rather than on broad-based capacity-building and institutional change.

The trend toward the expansion of pension coverage through non-contributory or semi-contributory pension schemes has generated a remarkable improvement in levels of old-age protection (Arza, 2012). However, even when a general consensus regarding the need to complement existing social insurance systems with alternative schemes is in evidence, significant differences remain in the policies adopted. In some countries in which universal pensions have been implemented and/or expanded, progress toward a rights-based strategy for old-age protection seems to be underway.

However, policies differ with regard to their levels of institutionalization. "Policies aiming to create universal protection, if not well institutionalized through stable rules and secure financing can be only short-term achievements" (Arza, 2012); and these policies are more prone to cutbacks and policy reversals. Thus, the limits for redistribution and universal social protection still remain. Failures in the arena of the primary distribution are not counterbalanced by progressive redistribution in the fiscal arena.

Redistribution and fiscal activity

General trends in Latin America social expenditure display the movements of economic and political cycles: adjustment and strong fall in the 1980s, growth in the beginning of the 1990s, deceleration and decrease in the middle of the decade, and a return to growth after 2001–2002.[12] Towards 2007–2008, all countries presented a social expenditure per capita level double or triple that of 1990–1991.

However, the general growth in social expenditure did not eliminate the vast disparities between the countries: countries with higher GDP per capita also dedicate a higher share of total public spending to social expenditures. In 1980, those proportionally spending most were Chile, Uruguay, Argentina, and Brazil; the same countries remain at the top of spending lists around 2008–2009, with the proportions of social spending over total public spending rounding up to 65%. Meanwhile, Central American countries reach average levels

---

12   See CEPAL (2012b); CEPAL (2011); CEPAL (2010).

of 50–55%. In general, countries showing high levels of social expenditure are also those with, inter alia, higher levels of formalization of employment, a social policy administration that covers their entire territory, and higher primary schooling levels.

In those cases where the proportion taxes over the GDP is greater, social expenditure tends to be high but not particularly progressive. In part, this is due to the fact that countries with greater tax revenues tend to be those with higher spending in social security. Spending on pension systems remains the largest component of social expenditure, even in countries which have privatized their public pension systems due to the deficit created by redirecting pension contributions to individual accounts (so-called transition costs).

In comparative terms, average tax burden represents a low percentage of GDP in Latin America: 17.5% of GDP for national and sub-national governments (Corbacho et al., 2013).[13] Most Latin American countries show a tax burden lower than the one expected according to its national income. Guatemala, Mexico, Panama, and Trinidad and Tobago have tax burdens around 10% of GDP; Mexico, notably, shows a tax gap of 11.5 percentage points of GDP. However, the tax burden has increased since the beginning of the 1990s, rising in almost all Latin American countries. Only Mexico, Trinidad and Tobago, and Venezuela, which are oil exporters, show a decrease between 1991–93 and 2008–10. While Latin America's tax burden is low, it is the world region that has seen the greatest increase to this burden over the past two decades.

Moreover, taxes are only a part of total fiscal resources; payroll taxes and non-tax revenues (royalties, public enterprises benefits, etc.) are another important component. Taking into account all fiscal resources, the average burden of fiscal resources increased from 18.6% of GDP to 23.2% between the beginning of the '90s and the end of the 2000s. Taking into account total fiscal resources, the situation of some low-tax burden countries shifts[14] (the commodity boom contributes to this result, as several governments raised export taxes.). In eight countries in the region, fiscal resources coming from this source rose from 3.9% of GDP to 7.9% between 1991–93 and 2008–10. However, for the region as a whole the increase was less significant: from 1.1% to 1.9% in the second half of 2000s.

A low tax burden is a problem for many countries; but another acute problem is a lack of progressivity in the tax structure. The most regressive taxes have seen the greatest increase over recent decades. VAT is the main tax in the region, coming to 6.3% of GDP on average (comparable to developed countries, and even higher in countries like Brazil and Uruguay). Nominal rates of such taxes have increased: VAT jumped, on average, from 13.4% to 15%, and payroll taxes from 19.8% to 21.6% between 1991–93 and 2008–10. Meanwhile, eco-taxes in Latin America are low, and many countries devote significant sums to subsidizing fuel-oil consumption.

By contrast, average import duties fell from 12.9% to 8.8%; maximum levels of nominal income taxes were reduced both for firms and individuals. In general, the main problem lies in personal income taxes; even Brazil, with a high tax burden, shows a low performance in this tax (Cetrángolo and Gómez-Sabaini, 2007).

As for the burden of regressive taxes, another problem in the region is the high volatility of fiscal resources. This volatility has increased with indirect taxes and the importance of resources coming from the external sector; where the economic and fiscal structure is more

---

13 Eastern Europe's tax burden comes to 24.1% of GDP; the 32 non-Latin American OECD member countries show an average of 25.4%.

14 For instance, Bolivia comes to 26.3% of GDP, and Mexico 21.7% (Corbacho et al., 2013).

concentrated in few taxes, the problem looms larger. Additionally, the low burden of fiscal resources in sub-national governments posits an acute problem, as they tend to hold the greatest responsibility for social services and infrastructure.

In short, fiscal income in the region has increased in recent years but still is dominated by consumption taxes, value added taxes, payroll taxes, and, most recently, by revenues stemming from the exploitation of non-renewable resources. This tax structure is fragile and volatile. The changing favourable external environment and the limits of the post-recession accelerated growth in the region make this tax strategy less sustainable in the short and medium run. These and other elements raise serious doubts as to the potential of taxes and transfers to significantly reduce inequality and poverty in the region. Taxing consumption and exports is less painful than building consensus around a more sustainable and progressive fiscal reform.

In spite of these structural problems, recent studies argue that the impact of taxes and transfers are very positive in countries such as Argentina, Brazil and Uruguay, less so in Mexico and little in Bolivia and Peru (Lustig et al., 2013). The alleged reasons are different. For instance, in Brazil and Uruguay, the reduction in disposable income inequality is attributed mainly to the impact of cash transfers. In Peru, low redistribution is said to stem from direct taxes, and solely from cash transfers in Bolivia (which has practically no personal income taxes).[15]

These results should be considered cautiously, because they are strongly dependent on assumptions about how taxes and expenditures ought to be allocated among population groups. Also, countries like Argentina pose serious problems, with a lack of reliable official data and household surveys. Finally, the high volatility of a regressive tax system combined with informal labour markets, low productivity, private and segmented public services, and focalized programs are precisely not the institutional complementarities followed by those countries able to successfully construct sustainable progressive social systems.

On the contrary, other cases show progressive and sustainable revenue collection and government spending on the promotion and even the production of publicly provided, universal services for all citizens (education, health care, day care, elder care, job training programs, temporary employment programs in the public services, after-school programs, maternal and parental leave, etc.). Unfortunately, successful cases of universal social policies are scarce in the region, even when they proved to have a stronger redistributive capacity than segmented-corporatist and even targeted policies alone (Martínez Franzoni and Sánchez-Ancochea, 2013).

After the Washington Consensus experiments and with the persistence of fragmented social protection systems, Latin America presents an unequal financing and provision of public goods, combined with a major presence of market provision of welfare services (in pension systems, health provision, higher education, etc.). The advance of cash transfer programs in the region is not solving the problems of these institutional complementarities. On the contrary, it seems to be working to consolidate a fragmented system with strong limits on redistribution and social mobility.

---

15 When one adds the effect of in-kind transfers (access to free or quasi-free services in education and health), the authors saw a substantially sharper decrease in inequality across all countries, ranging from 24.5%, 23.7%, and 20.2% in Argentina, Brazil, and Uruguay, respectively, to 8.1% in Peru.

Challenges and strategies for redistribution in Latin America

Even after the recent phase of economic growth, Latin American countries continue showing many problems in sustaining progressive distributional spillover effects on employment, wages, and social protection. History has shown that the region has serious difficulties in preventing and controlling recurring economic crises, and the changing international context does not look favourable in the near future. The economic and social protection systems also reinforce each other over time, working to deny mutual stability and positive performance to the social system as a whole in its effort to bring about solid improvements in the welfare of the general population.

The region's growth patterns have not secured macroeconomic consistence or stable resources to fund social policies; the heterogeneity of the production regime and its long-standing deficiencies in systemic productivity have limited the labour market's ability to function as a solid structure in social integration and the legitimation of a more universal and progressive social protection system. At the same time, regressive and unstable tax systems dominated by indirect and payroll taxes face significant difficulties in financing a stratified social protection system organized under an ethos of social insurance and assistance-conditional policies.

The high volatility of a regressive tax system, coupled with a segmented labour market, focalized programs and privatized and segmented markets for public goods, are precisely not the institutional complementarities seen in those countries able to construct sustainable progressive social systems. The need for change and the search for positive complementarities between the economic and social protection systems are prevailing problems across Latin America. Indeed, the changing constellation of social risks and problems of institutional complementarities are also affecting European countries known for their robust social protection regimes, producing a growing duality both in their production structure and their labour markets. These dualities result in a more segmented welfare regime and greater inequality.[16]

New social risks and new concepts of social progress

Inequality, poverty and exclusion are combined with other socioeconomic transformations in Latin America: early demographic transitions, urbanization, female labour market incorporation, exposure to new consumption patterns, informal labour markets, etc. New social risks are also emerging, such as those related to the unequal effects of climate change and the policies promoted to deal with it (Lo Vuolo, 2014). In short, there seems to be a "double injustice": the groups and populations likely to be most harmed by climate change are least responsible for causing it and have the least resources to cope with the consequences (Gough, 2011). Thus, a growing concern centers on the need to "decarbonize the welfare state" (Gough and Meadowcroft, 2011).

Also, it is worth observing that emerging kinds of violence and anomie are directly linked to the globalization of consumerism and the prevailing imagery of "the good life." Recent growth driven by raising consumption was accompanied by serious deficiencies in investment and increased imports for high-income groups, threatening the balance of payment.

---

16   See Palier and Thelen (2010), for an analysis of the cases of France and Germany.

However, the present consumption of the most disadvantaged cannot be postponed and should be an absolute priority in the reformulation of social progress in Latin America.[17] In this sense, social progress ceases to be seen as an ideal to be reached in the long term, in the name of which present consumption of certain basic standards is postponed (Lo Vuolo, 2011). This means that the discussion should include opulence and collective priorities when the costs and benefits of growth and social progress are divvied up. Redistribution is a matter of wealth as well as poverty.

Concepts of social progress should thus be reformulated, taking into account the need to have a solid starting base in the present, a sort of "brake" on the deployment of economic and social forces. Progress would hence cease to be a concept focused exclusively on increases, and incorporate conservative and defensive components such as basic consumption, basic social services, free time, environment, etc. Redistribution is a matter of time as well as money.

In the current global context, the ability to adapt economically is crucial, and policies of risk reduction and alleviation are central to political life. The road ahead is not to pursue the lowest wages or the most lax environmental standards under the "commodity consensus," but to provide good services for a healthy, educated, and therefore productive workforce along with governments able to mediate societal disputes in favour of new paradigms of social progress.

Growth and employment

Latin America's patterns of production include a premature de-industrialization and productive specialization, according to static comparative advantages in sectors that show a feeble capacity for diversification and technological improvements. The technological gap has grown not only in comparison to the dynamic Asian economies, but also against the more developed natural-resource-intensive economies (CEPAL, 2012a). Economic regimes that remain specialized in primary resources present high levels of structural heterogeneity, show a huge informal economy and a highly regressive fiscal system, are not the most suitable economic regimes for sustainable redistribution and universal social protection.

Recent experience in the region shows that a demand-led economy with an employment target is more advisable than supply-side economics. However, accomplishing this aim requires not only a strong commitment from political authorities but also the coordination of the exchange rate and monetary and fiscal policies in order to stabilize effective demand and generate positive incentives for investment (Meade, 1996; Lo Vuolo, 2009b).

However, given current global tendencies and the productive structure and patterns of specialization in the region, employment creation requires multiple integrated policies. Along with macroeconomic policies focused on employment, it is advisable to promote the public sector's role as employer in essential public service areas such as health, education, community service, day care, elder care, job training programs, after school programs, social infrastructure, etc. These activities are all labour intensive and barely dependant on foreign inputs, and could also be part of a strategy of employment creation and labour formalization.

---

17 Here I am not defending any list of consumer goods and services or entering into a debate on "primary goods," "skills," "functionalities," "opportunities" and so on (Sen, 2009: Ch. 10). Instead I simply state that certain basic consumer goods cannot be postponed and are therefore a priority, while the consumer patterns of the most privileged groups are not.

In any case, today growth is not just a measure of economic performance but also a measure of political success. This is true of most capitalist economies, because economic growth creates the illusion that "everybody wins": capitalists receive high profits and workers obtain employment and better salaries. Economic growth is a political project that makes it easier to win elections, manage political conflicts and keep the demands of various social groups latent and controlled. Therefore, questioning the level of economic growth as an indicator of social progress and promoting the inclusion of new dimensions in the evaluation of people's well-being, even when technical foundations are solid, is not an easy task in the region.

An even trickier undertaking is a discussion of the central role of employment and labour markets. However, this has become increasingly necessary in Latin America, where the heterogeneous employment market is a space of economic inequality and social disqualification for a large part of the population. This is exacerbated when the employment relationship becomes a factor in access to social insurance coverage, thus generating an arbitrary selection process for access to universal social rights. In the Latin American case, the lack of social mobility is also explained by the "gaps" between rights established by laws and practice.

Also, inequalities characterize demographic transition processes and the growing trend of women's inclusion in the labour market and as intermediaries of assistance programs. Thus, the discussion on the use of time in a region marked by unpaid work and work outside the market must also present special characteristics. Undoubtedly, the region should move for new policies of maternal and parental leave along with the creation of a national system of personal care.

Social mobility channels continue to be stymied, mainly by the labour market and stratified social protection systems. In societies where social protection systems have broadly expanded, low poverty numbers are coupled with strong intra- and inter-generational mobility. This is true for both European nations and the Latin American countries that have been pioneers in building more universal social protection systems.

The reformulation of the public policy system in line with an alternative vision of social progress must include two unavoidable points: i) all actions which tend to diminish the role of market employment as an intermediary for social rights are in line with progress; ii) all actions which tend to value work outside the market employment, as well as free time, are in line with progress. This leads us to ponder issues such as unconditional income, the presence of institutions which facilitate the reconciliation between work in the labour market and work in the domestic environment, access to health and education systems in conditions of equality, etc.

Social protection systems: Universality, autonomy

Here, the central problem is that Latin American social protection systems are conceived as a means to manage different risks for different population groups, not as a move against the certainty of social vulnerability and low social mobility. After several experiments, the lesson seems clear: building a more universal social protection system cannot be achieved by employing targeting and fragmented institutions but, rather, by making use of universalistic institutions. When sheltered by massive targeted programmes, a collective imagery (legitimacy) and a specialized bureaucracy (technical rationalization) come forth, standing diametrically opposed to the universal nature of benefits and the enforcement of personal autonomy, which constitute the basic nature of social rights.

In this respect, Latin America confirms that one of the fundamental ambivalences of modernity is captured by the twin notion of liberty and discipline in the context of a plurality of modes of socio-political organization (Wagner, 1994; Lo Vuolo, forthcoming). Problems of institutional complementarities emerge when some institutional components improve autonomy for a minor group while others impose discipline and coercion on the vast majority of the population. Such processes of inequality would eventually lead to "crises of incorporation" (Filgueira et al., 2011).

The potential to achieve universal inclusion through separate, targeted and contribution-based schemes is inherently limited. Moreover, effective state enforcement of the duty to work (workfare programs) is difficult in countries with heterogeneous production systems and a large informal economy. The argument that it is the very insecure nature of income assistance that will lead workers to look for formal and more secure jobs does not hold in this scenario. It is equally plausible to argue that the lack of a reliable safety net has induced the preference for informal work, and indeed that the informal sector is thus making up for a broader public policy failure.

The aim of universal social protection systems is to prevent and protect people from social risks, as well as to reduce vulnerability and promote social mobility. Social assistance programmes ought to be the exception, not the rule, for social policies. From this perspective, in Latin America the structure and functioning of social protection systems are not very well captured by concepts such as formal/informal or commodification/decommodification, but call for other criteria such as clientelization and declientelization, universalization and focalization, conditionality and unconditionality.

This clearly expresses the need to look not only at formal rights and benefits received but also at processes to access them. For example, it is not only important to consider how much income people receive, but also the form of access to this income. It is not only relevant to know if health services are provided, but also to know the conditions to access these services.

Universal and unconditional health care and education not only help to create productive employment, but are also central to promoting social mobility, mitigating income inequalities, and fortifying the social cohesion and sense of trust that facilitate high productivity. Thus, they should be universal and complemented by universal (and unconditional) policies to prevent insufficient incomes.

The existing assistance and conditional cash transfer programmes must be re-examined to simplify and unify them into one or few programmes of direct income transfer to the whole population. Latin America shows that more insecure labour relations are, the more flexible and well-funded income maintenance systems must be. Assistance-conditional programs increase individual dependence on the selection criteria applied by the bureaucracy. Social fragmentation is consolidated by discriminating between those who deserve assistance and those who do not. The blame is placed on the individuals (unemployed, poor, unqualified, etc.) and their "inability" to get a formal job in the market. These types of programs also distort political practices, as they enhance the power of the authorities who control the assignment of benefits and favour political clienteles. Furthermore, assistance-targeted and -conditional programmes are highly pro-cyclical and create poverty and employment traps.

Pension systems should continue the tendency to create a base for more universal and unconditional benefits (Goldberg and Lo Vuolo, 2006). Pensions should guarantee a universal and unconditional right to a basic benefit as the first goal, and then complement with social insurance schemes. The basic pillar of pension systems would also have a favourable impact on entry into and exits from the labour market, while offering minimum guarantees that would foster participation in other contributory pillars. For this purpose, contributory pillars should abandon financial capitalization systems in privately administered individual accounts and transform them into pay-as-you-go systems. Experiments with notional accounts should also be considered.

Income sustaining policies should be combined with food sovereignty policies. Public strategies are needed to guarantee popular sectors access to a healthy food consumption pattern.[18] Action is needed in terms of distribution channels; the promotion of self-managed cooperatives, society and community-driven undertakings; education policy intended to improve popular sectors' consumption behaviour, etc.

A tax reform reinforcing the implementation of direct and progressive taxes and reducing pro-cyclical behaviour is needed. Several countries in the region have demonstrated an ability to achieve fiscal surplus when pressured to pay public financial debt; however, the challenge today is to turn this capacity to goals such as changing the tax and expenditure structure inherited from institutional reforms.

In this respect, is worth noting that universal policies of income transfer are also helpful for fiscal reform, especially in income taxes, for two main reasons: (i) they can be integrated as effective fiscal credits with income taxes (Barbeito, 1995); (ii) they legitimize tax reforms, given the low degree of administrative capacity and corruption. Payroll taxes have a limited ability to finance universal social protection systems, mainly in labour markets with structural features like those in Latin American countries. Other taxes should be contemplated in the reforms, such as inheritance, finance, environmental, etc.

The above analysis points to the need to discuss the very concept of social progress and development in the region, placing redistribution at the top of the public agenda. The existing and long lasting institutional complementarities between the economic and social protection systems in Latin America pose a serious limit to redistribution in the region. This is not an issue of technical problems in some programs, but of the very conception of the role of redistribution in a sustainable development project for Latin American countries.

Bibliography

Aguirre, P. (2005). *Estrategias de consumo: qué comen los argentinos que comen.* Buenos Aires/Madrid, Ciepp/Miño y Dávila.

Aguirre, J. and Lo Vuolo, R.M. (2013). *Variedades de Capitalismo. Una aproximación al estudio comparado del capitalismo y sus aplicaciones para América Latina.* Buenos Aires, Ciepp.

Arza, C. (2012). 'Basic pensions in Latin America: Toward a rights-based policy?' in Lo Vuolo, R.M. (ed.) (2012). *Citizen's Income and Welfare Regimes in Latin America. From Cash Transfers to Rights.* New York, Palgrave Macmillan.

Arza, C. (2004). *Distributional Impacts of Social Policy. Pension Regimes in Argentina since c. 1944.* London, London School of Economics and Political Sciences.

Barbeito, A. (1995). 'La integración de los sistemas de transferencias fiscales como instrumento de integración social,' in Lo Vuolo, R.M. (ed.) (2012). *Contra la exclusión. La propuesta del ingreso ciudadano.* Buenos Aires, Miño y Dávila/Ciepp.

---

18   See Aguirre (2005).

Bizberg, I. and Théret, B. (2012). 'La diversidad de los capitalismos latinoamericanos: los casos de Argentina, Brasil y México.' *Noticias de la Regulación*, vol. 61, no. 4, pp. 2–22.

Boschi, R. (2011). *Variedades de Capitalismo, Política e Desenvolvimento na América Latina*. Belo Horizonte, Editora UFMG.

Bresser-Pereira, L.C. (2011). *Structuralist Macroeconomics and the New Developmentalism*. São Paulo, Getulio Vargas Foundation.

Bruno, M. (2007). 'Financiarisation et accumulation du capital productif au Brésil. Les obstacles macroéconomiques à une croissance sutenue.' *Revue Tiers Monde*, vol. 189, no. 1, pp. 65–92.

Cechini, S. and Madariaga, A. (2011). *Programas de transferencias condicionadas. Balance de la experiencia reciente en América Latina y el Caribe*. Cuadernos de la CEPAL, 95. Santiago de Chile, CEPAL

CEPAL (2012a). *Cambio estructural para la igualdad: Una visión integrada del desarrollo*. Santiago de Chile, CEPAL.

CEPAL (2012b). *Panorama Social de América Latina 2011*. Santiago de Chile, CEPAL.

CEPAL (2011). *Panorama Social de América Latina 2010*. Santiago de Chile, CEPAL.

CEPAL (2010). *Panorama Social de América Latina 2009*. Santiago de Chile, CEPAL.

Cetrángolo, O. and Gómez-Sabaini, J.C. (2007). *La tributación directa en América Latina y los desafíos a la imposición sobre la renta*. Santiago de Chile, CEPAL.

Corbacho, A. et al. (2013). *Recaudar no basta. Los impuestos como instrumentos de desarrollo*. Washington, DC, Banco Interamericano de Desarrollo.

Coremberg, A. (2013). *Measuring Argentina's GDP G rowth: Just Stylized Facts*. Buenos Aires, Universidad de Buenos Aires.

Filgueira, F. et al. (2011). 'Shallow states, deep inequalities and the limits of conservative modernization: The politics and policies of incorporation in Latin America,' in M. Blofield, M. (ed.) (2011). *The Great Gap. Inequality and the Politics of Redistribution in Latin America*. University Park, PA, The Pennsylvania State University Press.

Furtado, C. (1965). *Desenvolvimento e Subdesenvolvimento*. São Paulo, Editora Fundo de Cultura.

Goldberg, L. and Lo Vuolo, R.M. (2006). *Falsas Promesas. Sistema de Previsión Social y Régimen de Acumulación*. Buenos Aires/Madrid, Ciepp/Miño y Dávila.

Gough, I. (2011). *Climate Change, Double Injustice and Social Justice. A Case Study of the United Kingdom*. Geneva, UNRISD.

Gough, I. and Meadowcroft, J. (2011). 'Decarbonizing the welfare state,' in Norgaard, R. and Schlosberg, D. (eds.) (2011). *The Oxford Handbook of Climate Change and Society*. Oxford, Oxford University Press.

Habermas, J. (1973). *Problemas de legitimación en el capitalísmo tardío*. Buenos Aires, Amorrortu editores.

Hall, P. and Soskice, D. (2001). *Varieties of Capitalism. The Institutional Foundations of Comparative Advantage*. Oxford, Oxford University Press.

Huber, E. et al. (2006). 'Politics and inequality in Latin America and the Caribbean.' *American Sociological Review*, vol. 71, no. 6, pp. 943–963.

Huber, E. and Stephens, J.D. (2012). *Democracy and the Left. Social Policy and Inequality in Latin America*. Chicago, The University of Chicago Press.

Iversen, T. and Soskice, D. (2006). 'Electoral institutions and the politics of coalitions: Why some democracies redistribute more than others.' *American Political Science Review*, vol. 2, no. 100, pp. 165–181.

Lautier, B. (2006). 'Una protección social mutualista y universal: condición para la eficacia de la lucha contra la pobreza,' in Lo Vuolo, R.M. (ed.) (2006). *La credibilidad social de la política económica en América Latina*. Buenos Aires, Miño y Dávila/Ciepp.

Lavinas, L. (2012). 'Brazil: The lost road to citizen's income,' in Lo Vuolo, R.M. (ed.) (2012). *Citizen's Income and Welfare Regimes in Latin America. From cash transfers to rights*. New York, Palgrave Macmillan.

Levitsky, S. and Roberts, K.M. (2011). *The Resurgence of the Latin American Left*. Baltimore, The John Hopkins University Press.

Lo Vuolo, R.M. (2014). *Cambio climático, políticas ambientales y regímenes de protección social. Visiones para América Latina*. Colección Documentos de Proyecto. Unidad de Cambio Climático de la División de Desarrollo Sostenible y Asentamientos Humanos de la Comisión Económica para América Latina y el Caribe (CEPAL), Proyecto Política Fiscal y Cambio Climático, mayo.

Lo Vuolo, R.M. (Forthcoming) "The limits of autonomy in Latin American social policies: Promoting human capital or social control?" *European Journal of Social Theory*, special issue on "Modernity and capitalism" edited by David Casassas and Peter Wagner, vol. 19, no. 2, 2016.

Lo Vuolo, R.M. (2012a). 'Epilogue,' in Lo Vuolo, R.M. (ed.) (2012). *Citizen's Income and Welfare Regimes in Latin America. From Cash Transfers to Rights*. New York, Palgrave Macmillan.

Lo Vuolo, R.M. (2012b). 'The Argentina "Universal Child Allowance." Not the poor but the unemployed and the informal workers,' in Lo Vuolo, R.M. (ed.) (2012), *Citizen's Income and Welfare Regimes in Latin America. From cash transfers to rights*. New York, Palgrave Macmillan.

Lo Vuolo, R.M. (2011). 'Consideraciones para el debate acerca del progreso social en América Latina,' in Rojas, M. (ed.) (2011). *La Medición del progreso y del Bienestar. Propuestas desde América Latina*. México, DF, Foro Consultivo Científico y Tecnológico.

Lo Vuolo, R.M. (2009a). 'Social exclusion policies and labour markets in Latin America,' in Hujo, K. and McClanahan, S. (eds.) (2009). *Financing Social Policy: Mobilizing Resources for Social Development*. Basingstoke, Palgrave.

Lo Vuolo, R.M. (2009b). *Distribución y crecimiento. Una controversia persistente*. Buenos Aires/Madrid, Ciepp/Miño y Dávila.

Lo Vuolo, R.M. (2002). 'Ideology and the new social security in the Argentine,' in Abel, C. and Lewis, C. (eds.) (2002). *Exclusion and Engagement. Social Policy in Latin America*. London, Institute of Latin American Studies, University of London.

Lustig, N. et al. (2013). 'The Impact of Taxes and Social Spending on Inequality and Poverty in Argentina, Bolivia, Brazil, Mexico, Peru and Uruguay: An Overview.' *CEQ Working Paper No. 13*. CIPR/Tulane University.

Marques Pereira, J. (2006). 'Teoría económica y credibilidad de la política anti-cíclica. La distribución del ingreso y los límites al crecimiento económico,' in Lo Vuolo, R.M. (ed.) (2006). *La credibilidad social de la política económica en América Latina*. Buenos Aires/Madrid, Ciepp/Miño y Dávila.

Martínez Franzoni, J. and Sánchez-Ancochea, D. (2013). 'Can Latin American production regimes complement universalistic welfare regimes? Implications from the Costa Rican case.' *Latin America Research Review*, vol. 48, no. 2, pp. 148–173.

Meade, J.E. (1996). *Full Employment Regained? An Agathotopian Dream*. Cambridge, Cambridge University Press.

Mesa-Lago, C. (1978). *Social Security in Latin America, Pressure Groups, Stratification and Inequality*. Pittsburgh, University of Pittsburg Press.

Ocampo, J.A. (2012). *Let's Be Clear: This Will Not Be Latin America's Decade*. VoxLACEA, http://vox.lacea.org/?q=JoseAntonioOcampo1

Palier, B. and Thelen, K. (2010). 'Institutionalizing dualism: Complementarities and change in France and Germany.' *Politics & Society*, vol. 38, no. 1, pp. 119–148.

Rodríguez Enríquez, C. (2012). 'Should citizen's income become a goal for feminism in Latin America?' in Lo Vuolo, R.M. (ed.) (2012). *Citizen's Income and Welfare Regimes in Latin America. From Cash Transfers to Rights*. New York, Palgrave Macmillan.

Salama, P. (2012). *Les Économies Émergentes Latino-Américaines. Entre Cigales et Fourmis*. Paris, Armand Collin.

Sánchez-Ancochea, D. (2009). 'State, firms and the process of industrial upgrading: Latin America's variety of capitalism and the Costa Rican experience.' *Economy and Society*, vol. 38, no. 1, pp. 62–86.

Sandbrook, R. et al. (2007). *Social Democracy in the Global Periphery. Origins, Challenges, Prospects, Cambridge*. Cambridge University Press.

Schneider, B.R. (2009). 'Hierarchical market economies and varieties of capitalism in Latin America.' *Journal of Latin American Studies*, vol. 41, no. 03, pp. 553–575.

Schneider, B.R. and Karcher, S. (2010). 'Complementarities and continuities in the political economy of labour markets in Latin America.' *Socio-Economic Review*, vol. 8, no. 4, pp. 623–651.

Schneider, B.R. and Soskice, D. (2009). 'Inequality in developedcountries and Latin America: coordinated, liberal and hierarchical systems.' *Economy and Society*, vol. 38, no. 1, pp. 17–52.

Sen, A. (2009). *The Idea of Justice*. London, Penguin Books.

Tokman, V. (2007). *Flexiguridad con informalidad: opciones y restricciones*. Santiago de Chile, CEPAL.

Wagner, P. (1994). *Sociology of Modernity. Liberty and Discipline*. London, Routledge.

World Bank (2009). *Conditional Cash Transfers. Reducing Present and Future Poverty*. Washington, DC, World Bank.

Chapter 4
"Postneoliberalism" and Social Inequalities in the Andes: Reflections and Hypotheses on the Venezuelan, Bolivian, and Ecuadorian Cases

Juan Pablo Pérez Sáinz

Introduction

The text at hand poses a question as to what changes have been wrought under the tenures of *chavismo* in Venezuela, MAS in Bolivia, and the *Revolución Ciudadana* in Ecuador in terms of the distribution and redistribution of the surplus in an attempt to revert the effects of (neo)liberal reforms. A bibliographical overview will provide an answer in the form of two hypotheses: that there have been no significant transformations in the distributive arena, but some in the redistributive sphere; and that these changes go beyond the expansion and consolidation of the conditional cash transfers so dear to (neo)liberalism, as they imply an expansion of basic citizenship, including historically marginalized subaltern sectors as citizens.

Beyond a doubt, the most important event to mark the turn of this century in Latin America has been the so-called "left turn."[1] In a number of Latin American countries, and through electoral processes, governments have come to power that profess the need to overcome (neo) liberalism, with varying degrees of radicalism. Authors sympathetic with these experiments (Sader and Gentili, 2003; Sader, 2008; French, 2009) have hence begun utilizing the term "postneoliberalism," suggesting that the previous order has been definitively overcome. We would regard such a position with skepticism, but neither do we believe that this is simply a redefinition of (neo)liberalism with a more "friendly" face, or behind a "progressive" mask. We would postulate that this is an ambiguous phenomenon, containing as many continuities as it does ruptures. That is, this appears to be a period of transition which may stall out and redefine the (neo)liberal order, but which may also find its consummation in opening the way for a new historical epoch of the development of capitalism in the region.[2] Indeed, we do not have enough historical perspective to make predictions at this point. Hence, we will bracket the term "postneoliberalism" with quotation marks.

This text seeks to explore whether, in this new context, there has been a reduction in the inequalities created by (neo)liberalism via processes of structural adjustments. In this

---

1   The text that follows is a briefer version of the working paper published by desiguALdades.net (Pérez Sáinz, 2014a). I would like to take the opportunity to thank Barbara Fritz and Lena Lavinas for their incisive comments on an early draft.

2   One might also argue that this transition would be in the direction of postcapitalism. But such a scenario would seem quite improbable at the moment.

sense, we are most interested in the inequalities that have made Latin America the least equal region on the planet: to wit, income inequalities. But, as we are looking at inequalities of result here, we would like to shift the analytic focus onto the causes at hand. This implies honing in on surplus inequalities and considering the establishment of the conditions of the generation and distribution of surplus within the primary sphere, comprised of the basic markets. But the analysis must be complemented by a consideration of how this surplus may be redistributed amongst households in the secondary sphere. Our empirical referent examines the three countries that have taken the "postneoliberal" view to its most radical extent: Venezuela with *chavismo*; Bolivia with the Movement for Socialism (MAS); and Ecuador with its *Revolución Ciudadana*.

The distributive, or primary sphere for the surplus, comprises the basic markets, spaces for the exchange of the basic resources of society (labor, land, capital, etc.). In terms of the establishment of conditions for the generation and appropriation of the surplus, one can identify two fields of surplus inequalities: one, of the conditions for labor power exploitation, and another for the conditions for hoarding opportunities for accumulation. In the first, made concrete in the labor market, power is defined in the struggle between work and employment.[3] A field where work predominates is an asymmetric field where capital clearly overpowers labor; a field characterized by employment is one where this asymmetry is relativized and where the power of capital is not quite so overwhelming. In terms of the hoarding of opportunities for accumulation, which occurs in the rest of the basic markets, power is defined by the struggle between closure and opening. A field characterized by closure, where a few proprietors of means of production monopolize the principal opportunities for accumulation, would be clearly asymmetrical. This asymmetry may be eased by efforts toward opening, allowing more proprietors to take part in such opportunities (Pérez Sáinz, 2014b).[4]

For its part, the secondary sphere is one of redistribution, based on social policies that allow the state to redistribute surplus—principally, although not exclusively, through taxation. Beneficiaries tend to be households and their members as individuals. Such policies may take on a number of forms (universality, targeting, etc.), which means that their coverage, the specific kinds of beneficiaries in question, and their content vary with the historical and social context.

In this piece, we pose a number of questions as to the three governments in question: have they brought about significant changes in the distributive sphere in both the fields of surplus inequalities?; have they achieved important transformations in the redistributive sphere?; and, should any of these answers be in the affirmative, how have they done it? We will review an array of texts we consider relevant, seeking to answer these interrogations with hypotheses. A plausible formulation of such hypotheses is the aim of this text.

---

3 We will use this distinction between work and employment as postulated by Castel (1997), in which the latter is work plus rights and guarantees. In Latin America, the primacy of work in the primary-export model of the oligarchical order would not be questioned until the emergence of formal employment, within the model of accumulation based on industrialization and oriented towards the domestic market. Indeed, formal employment meant closing the gap between work and citizenship. But under the (neo)liberal order, formal employment has been questioned; moreover, given the transformations wrought in labor markets, especially via the generalized precariousness of wage relations, work has regained its primacy (Pérez Sáinz, 2012).

4 Agrarian land reforms in Latin America sought to broaden access, although their results were generally quite slim, demonstrating the power of local elites.

Beyond this introduction, the present work is divided into three sections. The first addresses the answers that these three "postneoliberal" governments have offered in response to the transformations in the primary sphere brought about by structural adjustments. There follows a section regarding the changes effected by these governments in the secondary sphere. With all these elements, we will conclude by formulating a pair of hypotheses about the transformations wrought by these governments in the distributive and redistributive spheres.

"Postneoliberal" Answers in the Distributive Sphere

The dynamics of structural adjustments varied amongst these three countries, making it pertinent to sketch out the range of their effects in each case. Venezuela began a process of structural adjustment in 1989, which may be characterized as incomplete, and which failed in its most ambitious objective: establishing new accumulation axes, oriented towards exportation and under the aegis of private capital, alternatives to the guiding forces of oil and state-managed oil rent. That is, this was an attempt to overcome the historical "rentierism" that had characterized the country. This process was questioned violently in two highly tense moments: the "Caracazo" of 1989 and the coup d'état of 1992, led by then-Commander Chávez, who would reach power through electoral means in 1999. His triumph would be the end of the line in the long deterioration of the consensus reached four decades before, which had leaned principally on the distribution of oil rent.[5]

For its part, Bolivia, out of the three cases at hand, had the most profound case of structural adjustment. It focused principally on dismantling the state capitalism born of the revolution of 1952 with processes of privatization in key sectors. This broad-ranging effort was made possible by the restructuring of the political system, leaning on the main political parties, in the so-called *democracia pactada* (pact for democracy), built on a consensus around the (neo)liberal order. But the economic and social exclusion of the majority of society from the benefits of this new model, alongside the opening of political spaces to subaltern (particularly indigenous) sectors, led to a questioning of this consensus. The turn of this century saw an increase and a change in the nature of the social conflict that reached a peak in two "wars": the water war in Cochabamba, and the gas war in El Alto and La Paz. The final act of this process of intense conflict was the electoral triumph of MAS and Evo Morales, an indigenous leader and cocalero union leader.

Ecuador's process of structural adjustment was long and torturous. It came to a climax under the administration of Durán Ballén (1992–1996), which saw the most drastic implementation of (neo)liberal reforms, especially in terms of the financial market. Indeed, the banking sector produced the crisis of 1999 that involved the seizure of private deposits and which would wind up in dollarization, an indelible mark of the country's incorporation into globalization. Opposition from unions, then from the indigenous movement, were the expressions of subaltern resistance to the imposition of (neo)liberal order. But the crisis had a fundamentally political expression in the overthrowing of three presidents. At these moments, especially in the case of the last, middle-class *Sierra* sectors emerged as the protagonists. It was in this period of profound political crisis that Rafael Correa appeared as

---

5   We refer here to the so-called "Punto Fijo Pact" of 1958; there is a generalized consensus, across a number of authors, that it crumbled definitively at the end of the past century.

an electoral option, initially as a dark horse, but who would wind up bringing his *Revolución Ciudadana* project to fruition.

The installation of "postneoliberal" governments in these three countries has meant that some of the transformations wrought by (neo)liberalism have been reversed, while other elements have been carried on. The following table displays the main reactions from these governments to each of the fields of surplus inequalities in each of the three countries considered over the current period.[6]

Table 4.1   "Postneoliberal" interventions in the area of surplus distribution

Fields of surplus inequalities	Venezuela	Bolivia	Ecuador
Conditions of labor power exploitation	Reducing precariousness by increasing public employment	Relative reduction in precariousness	Reduction in precariousness via regulation
	Functional distribution of income unaltered	Sustained increase in real minimum wage	Sustained increase in the real minimum wage
	Conflict with CTV (Confederation of Workers of Venezuela)	Regressive functional distribution of income	"Desectorization" of the labor movement
		Marginalization of labor movement	Criminalization of social protest
Conditions of hoarding opportunities for accumulation of wealth	Recovering control of PDVSA	Negotiated nationalization of the hydrocarbon sector	"Desectorization" of entrepreneurial sectors
	Cooperation with foreign capital in the hydrocarbon sector	Recognition of Aymara business	Monopolistic concentration
	Nationalization in multiple sectors	Conflict with "Media Luna" elites	Very limited land redistribution
	Conflict with Fedecámaras	Modifications to the INRA Law	
	New loyal business organizations		
	Mission Zamora		

In these three countries, (neo)liberalism attempted to impose two great transformations in the area of conditions of exploitation of labor power, although with varying effects and degrees of success: the questioning of formal employment as a referent for occupational modernity, and the precariousness of wage relations.[7]

---

6 We should warn that we are dealing with extremely changeable realities, and our analysis is limited in its condition as the product of secondary sources, mainly bibliographical ones.

7 (Neo)liberalism has brought about four important transformations in this field of surplus inequalities, in the region: beyond the two already mentioned, the configuration of employability as

The first transformation was manifested in two phenomena. On one hand, the processes of structural adjustment—since the very first measures—affected public employment, the core of formal employment. Both Venezuela and Bolivia thus saw a reduction in positions and a freezing of salaries in the public sector. The consequences of these measures were more dramatic in the Bolivian case; the state was a large employer, due to its centrality in the model of accumulation, as has been mentioned (Lander and Fierro, 1996; Ellner, 2009; Arze Vargas, 2004; Wanderley, 2009).[8] On the other hand, the questioning of formal employment had another facet as well: the privatization of social security in the attempt to restore the divide between citizenship and work. This was attempted in Venezuela and Ecuador, although without success (Ellner, 2009; Lander and Navarrete, 2009; Pérez Sáinz, 2014a), but Bolivia saw a drastic and *sui generis* overhauling of social security.[9]

The precariousness of wage relations, meanwhile, manifested itself in three dimensions. First came processes of labor deregulation. Venezuela saw a labor reform at the end of the 1990s that brought about important reductions in social benefits for workers (Ellner, 2009; Lander and Navarrete, 2009).[10] In Bolivia, job stability was undercut, including that of public employees, and the state was unable to intervene in wage negotiations in the private sector, only being able to fix salaries for their employees (Arze Vargas, 2004; Wanderley, 2009).[11] In Ecuador, during the orthodox period of the adjustment, corresponding to the Durán Ballén administration (1992–96), a reform was implemented that included a revision to the Labor Code, seeking to increase labor flexibility (Acosta, 1999). Secondly, private companies deployed strategies for productive restructuring that tended to disempower wage earners. This was the case in Venezuela, which featured a reduction in jobs, strategies for flexibilizing labor, a polarization and reduction in qualified labor, intensification of work, and, obviously, a drop in real salaries (Lander and Fierro, 1996).[12] Ecuador saw the generalization of labor intermediation and hour-based labor contract systems (Rivas, 2008; Viteri, 2008).[13] And, thirdly, as part of the process of rising job precariousness, there came a weakening of union action, a phenomenon we will address later on.

The "postneoliberal" governments in question have attempted to reverse some of these (neo)liberal legacies in the realm of work.[14] One thus must mention, in first place,

---

a (neo)liberal labor utopia, and the emergence of structural unemployment (Pérez Sáinz, 2012). As for this phenomenon, note that the average open urban unemployment rate from 1990 to 1999 in the three countries at hand was 5.1 in Bolivia, 9.4 in Ecuador, and 10.5 in Venezuela (OIT, 2000: Table 6-A). Mention that in the two former countries, emigration had an important role as a mechanism for adjusting the labor market, especially in Ecuador after the 1999 crisis.

8   Hence, "… between 1985 and 1987, the government closed down the majority of its mines, reducing the workforce from 30,000 to around 7,000, and hence demolishing the base of the organized labor movement. It also dismissed 31,000 public service workers by the end of the decade, and 35,000 manufacturing jobs were lost due to economic contraction" (Spronk, 2006: p. 4).

9   The problem of social security will be addressed in the following section.

10   The Organic Labor Law was reformed in 1997, and a (neo)liberal-inspired Organic Law of the Social Security System was passed. But this legal reform of social security was never applied (Méndez, 2008).

11   This labor reform, however, was blocked by the still-valid 1942 Labor Law (Antelo, 2000; Wanderley, 2009).

12   It thus comes as little surprise that salaries, which came to 49.9% of national income in 1982, saw their share fall to 39.1% in 1992 (Lander and Fierro, 1996: Table 6).

13   These strategies were applied in both the private and public sectors (Rivas, 2008).

14   The weight of wage earners in the total of the urban employed, at the start of this century, varies from country to country: 44.5% in Bolivia; 54.6% in Ecuador; and 55.9% in Venezuela

the recovery of public employment, which suggests that the jobs created during this period would not necessarily be marked by precariousness. This phenomenon has been broadest in Venezuela,[15] but in the Bolivian case one should emphasize the greater ease of access for the indigenous workforce into the public sector under the tenure of MAS (Arze Vargas and Gómez, 2013). That is to say, there has been a questioning of the secondary segregation that barred the indigenous from accessing public employment. Secondly, certain measures have tended to move against the precariousness of wage relations: to wit, in the Ecuadorian case, one should mention the 2008 decree from the Constituent Assembly prohibiting complementary services, labor intermediation, and hour-based labor contract systems (Rivas, 2008; Viteri, 2008; Ospina Peralta, 2013). Bolivia's Decree No. 28699 has also driven a tendency towards the elimination of free hiring and labor flexibilization, as imposed by (neo)liberalism. However, the passing of the Investment Law in an attempt to attract foreign capital, permitting free hiring, has called new protective legislation into question (Mayorga and Rodríguez, 2010). These opposing tendencies seem to be reflected in the fact that extreme precariousness has decreased for both manual and office workers, but non-precariousness also fell, thus producing an increase in relative precariousness (Arze Vargas and Gómez, 2013: Table 19).[16] Finally, one must also mention the policies that have driven a sustained increase in the real minimum wage, with positive increases in Bolivia (since 2009) and Ecuador (since 2007), although Venezuela's progress has been halting, especially over recent years, due to the impact of inflation.[17]

However, it would not seem that wage policy in general has empowered workers, at least in the cases of Bolivia and Venezuela. For the latter, Álvarez (2013: Table 5) presents troubling data on the functional distribution of income: the percentage of wages as a share of national income in 2009 was 37.0%, almost identical to the 1997 figure of 36.6%. In the case of Bolivia, meanwhile, Arze Vargas and Gómez (2013: pp. 140–141) have pointed to the fall of wages as a share of national income, from 36% to 25% over the first decade of this century. That is to say that, in terms of the functional distribution of income, the power of wage earners has not changed under *chavismo* and has deteriorated in Bolivia, even under MAS.

This disempowerment is also a reflection of the weakening of workers' collective action in general, and unions in particular. As has already been mentioned, this weakening was forged—with varying degrees of intensity across the three cases—during the period of (neo) liberalism. The most dramatic case was that of the Bolivian Workers' Confederation (COB), probably the greatest victim in the Bolivian structural adjustment (Arze Vargas, 2004; Barr, 2005; Wanderley, 2009). In the Ecuadorian case, the United Workers Front (FUT) tried to oppose stabilization measures in the '80s through a series of national strikes, with uneven success (León and Pérez Sáinz, 1986; Ycaza, 1991) but would lose its leadership role in the early 1990s, ceding to the emerging indigenous movement (Verdesoto Custode, 2013).

(OIT, 2000: statistical annex, Table 6). That is to say that we are obviously dealing with extremely heterogeneous labor markets, as is to be expected of late modernized countries.

15   The weight of public employment in urban occupation went from 14.8% in 2000 to 20.5% in 2012 (OIT, 2013: statistical annex, Table 6).

16   This is an indicator drawn up by CEDLA (Center for the Study of Labor and Agrarian Development), which " ... combines situations of the partial or total absence of job stability with adequate income and access to social security" (Arze Vargas and Gómez, 2013: p. 136).

17   In 2012, indices of the real minimum wage (base 100 in 2000), were as follows: 153.6 in Bolivia; 144.9 in Ecuador; and 113.0 in Venezuela. The unweighted regional average was 137.2 (OIT, 2013: statistical annex, Table 10).

Likewise, the Venezuelan Workers' Confederation (CTV) was hit hard during the '90s by the corruption of its leaders and by its wearing down as a chain of transmission for Acción Democrática (AD) and being set against the appearance of an independent union movement, plus an abrupt drop in union membership (Hellinger, 1996; Roberts, 2003).

In none of the three cases did unions play a leading role in the processes that led to the processes that put these "postneoliberal" governments in power. In Venezuela, the two milestones that preceded Chávez's electoral victory were a spontaneous popular uprising, the so-called "Caracazo," and a coup d'état (Sonntag and Maingón, 1992; Dávila, 2000; López Maya, 2003). Moreover, in this case, the demand for change in the 1990s meant the inclusion of historically marginalized sectors, such as slum dwellers, as opposed to the trend over previous decades of incorporating unionized workers (McCoy, 2010). Chávez's electoral triumphs would thus be explained by massive support from marginalized sectors (Álvarez, 2013).

In Bolivia, the conflict that led MAS to power, and which had its decisive moment during the so-called "gas war," was tied to local movements of peasants and, crucially, indigenous movements (Prada Alcoreza, 2003; Rivero, 2006; García Linera, 2009). With MAS' victory at the polls, these social movements had managed to elevate a political organization born from within them to the heart of power. However, this does not mean that social movements as a whole are represented in the political system, nor that this is necessarily a government of social movements.[18] And in Ecuador, the political crisis reached a peak of conflict in the removal of three presidents and was led by the middle sectors (Pachano, 2005; Ramírez Gallegos, 2005; Verdesoto Custode, 2013). The indigenous movement burst onto the scene during the uprising of 1990; on that note, it is very important to recall that the movement was not characterized by class (peasants) actors, but by peoples and nationalities, with citizenship-related claims (León Trujillo, 1994; Barrera Guarderas, 2001; Sánchez-Parga, 2007; Zamosc, 2007). Through the Confederation of Indigenous Nationalities of Ecuador (CONAIE), it became a central subaltern actor in the social and political arenas. However, this movement entered into crisis as the result of a dual process: on one hand, communal society began to crumble (in the "decommunalization" of indigenous society), and, on the other hand, their integration into the political system via the creation of a political party (*Pachakutik*) was ultimately clientelistic (Sánchez-Parga, 2007). Their participation in the Lucio Gutiérrez administration was the coda for this process.

Back to the union movement, and regarding Venezuela, one must note that the relations between Chávez's administration and the CTV were marked by conflict, especially from 2002–2004, when the confederation placed itself alongside the political and social forces that sought to oust Chávez by any means possible (coup d'état, oil strike, or recall referendum). Concretely speaking, the CTV organized four general strikes, the second of which made the coup d'état possible (Ellner, 2005; López Maya, 2010). Because of this, as Iranzo and Richter (2006) have pointed out, the government has pursued four strategies in opposition to CTV: control from within, control from without, disregard for the confederation as a social actor, and dismantling of the organization from below.[19]

---

18 This second issue is complex, and has been examined from a variety of positions (Stefanoni, 2006; Mayorga, 2009; Tapia, 2009; Anria, 2010; Zuazo, 2010).

19 Later on, the government dialogued with the UNT (National Workers' Union), created in 2003, which saw growth after unions such as the CTV shed members. Iranzo and Richter (2006) have argued that, despite its greater affinity with *chavismo*, this organization has voiced criticisms of the government, as well as being shot through with a number of conflicting currents.

One might also mention that the relations between the government of the *Revolución Ciudadana* and the union movement, as well as with other social movements (indigenous ones in particular) have been characterized by conflict. This administration has been shaped by technocrats and leftist intellectuals who consider themselves the incarnation of the interests of citizens and the nation, above corporate interests (De la Torre, 2010). In this last sense, the *Revolución Ciudadana* has opposed protests and social conflicts, casting its relationships with social actors in terms of "desectorization," a term that seeks to ignore class affiliations and consider all persons as ideally passive citizens. A perverse corollary of this has been the criminalization of social protest, in which workers and indigenous peoples have been seen by the government as potential agents of transgression (Lalander and Ospina Peralta, 2012; Verdesoto Custode, 2013).[20]

Consequently, the weakness of union actors in "postneoliberalism" suggests that the measures favoring wage earners have moved towards a passive brand of empowerment. In general, however, one has the impression that addressing conditions of exploitation of labor power has not been a priority for these governments, and that there have thus been no decisive interventions towards significantly reverting the asymmetry in favor of capital that was imposed by (neo)liberalism.

As for the monopolizing of opportunities for wealth accumulation, these governments have also had to face down a variety of legacies from (neo)liberalism. Three points stand out in this respect. The first has to do with a historical issue: land distribution. While these are all urban societies, significant percentages of the population remain in rural zones, especially in Bolivia and Ecuador. The latter, during the most critical phase of the structural adjustment, passed new land legislation in keeping with (neo)liberal ideology, which, among other things, commercialized communal lands (Barrera Guarderas, 2001; Tuaza Castro, 2011). Bolivia also saw the passage of the INRA Law in 1996 (Ley 1715 del Servicio Nacional de Reforma Agraria), which fit within the World Bank's guidelines for the creation of land markets via the process of determining the legality of land titles and a titling program, known as *saneamiento de tierras*.[21] This was part of an attempt to promote the development of export agriculture, especially in the Santa Cruz region (Molina, 2008; Ormachea Saavedra, 2008).

The responses in "postneoliberal" governments in both countries, in terms of land distributions, have been faltering at best. Ospina Peralta (2013: p. 229) notes that from 2007 to early 2012, only 5,000 hectares had been delivered. Moreover, it would seem that the government had veritably abandoned its redistributive aims, this being one of the factors to generate tension between most of the indigenous movement and Correa's administration (Lalander and Ospina Peralta, 2012). The same has been true in Bolivia, where the great achievement of the reformulation of land legislation under the MAS administration has been

---

20   We should note that Correa, when consolidating his power in 2009, was dealing with weakened social movements. This was the case with the union movement, which was not able to recover the leadership role it had held in the 1980s; only in the 1990s, with the plebiscite proposed by Durán Ballén, did there come a resurgence of organized labor, this time limited to the public sector. The same would be the case with the indigenous movement—CONAIE specifically, with the crisis we have already mentioned. Correa has only driven this weakening further, supporting rival indigenous organizations to show that CONAIE did not have a monopoly on representing the indigenous community (León Trujillo, 2010).

21   As Salazar Lohman (2013) has pointed out, this law included an ethnic element, in keeping with the prevailing multiculturalism of the period, recognizing so-called Original Community Lands (TCO) through Convention 169 of the International Labor Organization (ILO).

the continued granting of land titles to indigenous communities. The principle of fulfilling economic and social functions has been maintained, preserving large-scale property in the hands of private businesses.[22] This has led to the impression that the opportunities for distribution are limited, as they have relied on the results of the so-called *saneamiento*.[23]

Venezuela presents a case of a more radical attempt at land redistribution. Indeed, the new legislation passed in late 2001 was a factor in the most critical period that Chávez's government was forced to face.[24] Governmental action was funneled through Mission Zamora, which sought to eliminate large estates and distribute their land through the so-called *cartas agrarias*, or agrarian deeds, awarded to peasants willing to cultivate them and provided with financial and technical assistance to boost their productivity. From 2003 to 2008, 4,380,147 hectares were distributed, benefiting 101,549 productive units (peasants and cooperatives) and benefiting 110,000 families indirectly (Álvarez, 2009: p. 138). A pillar of this policy was the Fundos Zamoranos, a new sort of unit of farming production, cooperatives formed by all the producers in a given zone. That said, the program's development and consolidation have been quite limited; in 2008, it came to just 2.3% of the terrain used for farming, and employed 0.7% of the agricultural workforce (Hernández, 2009: 90). That is to say that this new productive unit has not managed to guarantee an increase in agricultural output by reducing dependence on food imports (Sanjuán, 2009).

The second issue has to do with the relationship between these "postneoliberal" governments and private capital. This point has two main aspects.

The first involves relations with foreign capital, as structural adjustments implied privatizations that, when it came to key sectors, wound up in foreign hands. The most emblematic case would be Bolivia, as a crucial event in MAS' rise to power was the so-called "gas war." Once elected, they brought about the nationalization of the hydrocarbon sector with the Supreme Decree 28701, dubbed "Héroes del Chaco" in a nationalistic reference to the Chaco War. The decree overturned the conditions imposed by previous administrations and returned to state control, putting increased value on public holdings and increasing revenue intake (Stefanoni, 2006; Velasco Portillo, 2011).[25] However, this measure did not enter into conflict with foreign capital; the increased flexibility of state positions on key issues (specifically in terms of profits and audits on capitalization) have led to what has been dubbed "negotiated nationalization" (Velasco Portillo, 2011).

The same might be said of the Venezuelan case, where the state's relationship with foreign capital in the hydrocarbon sector has been equally harmonious. The 2001 Hydrocarbon Law represented continuity, rather than a rupture (Lander and Navarrete, 2009). Indeed, some critical of *chavismo* have argued that this legislation has provided greater legal security for foreign capital, formalizing the opening of the sector (Arenas, 2010). In this sense,

---

22   Although the Constitution stipulates a limit on the extension of one's rural holdings, capitalist enterprises have managed to evade this by acquiring multiple terrains and leasing lands (Ormachea Saavedra, 2008).

23   It has been estimated that in 2010, just 8.6% of public land was available for distribution (Arze Vargas and Gómez, 2013: p. 90).

24   According to Parker (2008), the act in question was not as radical as it might have seemed, as one of its central objectives was agrifood production. Businesses' fears were rooted in the juridical fragility of the land titling process, and the possibilities it opened for the government to impose its aims.

25   In fiscal terms, one must mention that the creation of a direct tax on hydrocarbons (IDH) (Law 3058, from 2005) inverted the fiscal logic imposed by (neo)liberalism, focused as it was on the imposition of private consumption, and became the most important fiscal measure since the 1990s (Arze Vargas and Gómez, 2013).

Chávez's administration has not evaded the rentier tradition, with its oil policy reproducing past phenomena; there are no glaring differences between "rentier socialism" and the rentier capitalism that preceded it (López Maya and Lander, 2009). The new element in *chavismo*'s oil policy would be its geostrategic use (Mora Contreras, 2009).

In the Ecuadorian case, the Hydrocarbon Reform Law 2006–42 stipulated a renegotiation of oil contracts, from "production-sharing agreements" over oil production to contracts of "provision of services." However, it has been noted that, in the extraction and use of oil, private companies have been allowed to act in violation of constitutional regulations, with the exception becoming the rule and past practices essentially being perpetuated (Acosta, 2011).

While in all three cases the state has seen a larger share of oil and gas revenues, this has not meant a decrease in extractivist activities. Rather, they have been exacerbated by the growth of mining, especially in Bolivia and Ecuador (Arze Vargas and Gómez, 2013; Ospina Peralta, 2013). This deepening has stirred up social conflicts between these "postneoliberal" governments and ecological groups, as well as part of the indigenous movement. Moreover, there has emerged a sharp contradiction between the values of living well, or Vivir Bien/ Buen Vivir (*suma qamaña*/*sumak kawsay*), as enshrined in the constitutions of both Bolivia and Ecuador, and the developmentalist attitudes of these administrations. The case of the highway built through TIPNIS (Indigenous Territory and Isidoro Securé Park) is the most paradigmatic example in the Bolivian case. In Ecuador, meanwhile, extractivism is one of the many issues driving a wedge between the government of the *Revolución Ciudadana* and the indigenous movement (Lalander and Ospina Peralta, 2012).[26]

The second aspect has to do with relationships with domestic businesses. In the Venezuelan case, the key issue was the recovery of Petróleos de Venezuela, S.A. (PDVSA), which had become a transnational and practically autonomous entity thanks to a pact with political and economic elites over previous decades (Lander, 2005; Álvarez, 2013). This process was expanded during the second Caldera administration, which saw the opening and internationalization of the oil industry, essentially sabotaging the quota policy established by OPEC and bringing about a drop in crude prices and the largest drop in Venezuelan oil revenue in its history (Ellner, 2009; Lander and Navarrete, 2009; López Maya, 2009). To borrow Álvarez's (2013) precise turn of phrase, PVDSA had become a "state within the state."

The recovery of this business falls within the second act of the critical period of 2002–2004, namely, the oil strike,[27] which crippled the Venezuelan economy. Controlling it led to the government's firing 18,000 employees, and, more specifically, the majority of its executives and administrative figures (López Maya, 2004: p. 118). The opposition thus lost a key source of financing, which the government moved to use in funding activities that shaped an alternative model.[28] In this vein, one should point to the start of the development of what would be called "missions," social programs designed to aid historically marginalized subaltern sectors, which we will address in the next section.

---

26   In Venezuela, this kind of ecological conflict is generally muffled by a decades-old rentier culture, cropping up in more local cases, as with the resistance of the Yukpa, Bari, and Japrería peoples to the coal mining and growing cattle farming in Sierra de Perijá (Lander, 2013: p. 26).

27   The other two acts were the coup d'état of April 2002 and the recall referendum of August 2004. For an enlightening analysis of this key period for *chavismo*, see López Maya (2004).

28   PDVSA's contribution went from 11.3 million USD in 2000 to 12,161 in 2004 (Álvarez, 2013: Table 1). This gives some idea of the magnitude of what was at stake.

In Arenas' (2009) view, the relationship between the Chávez administration and business has been characterized by four phenomena. The first would be the confrontation with Fedecámaras, the historical association of chambers of commerce,[29] for which the government would wind up withdrawing recognition. Secondly, the government has conducted relations with certain business groups, thus privileging individual negotiations over business organizations, as was the case with the negotiations over joining MERCOSUR. Thirdly, loyal business organizations have emerged, as was the case with Empresarios por Venezuela (Empreven) and the Confederación Nacional de Agricultores y Ganaderos de Venezuela (Confagán). Fourthly, the administration has engaged with foreign capital, leading to the Venezuelan Hydrocarbons Association (AVHI), which brought together the principal foreign businesses active in the hydrocarbon sector.[30]

In the Bolivian case, two phenomena may be highlighted. On one hand, under MAS' tenure, one of the emerging elites comprised urban Aymara entrepreneurs[31] who were able to obtain social recognition (Salman, 2009). Alongside them (if not one and the same) were certain sectors of Aymara businesspeople in Bolivia who became integrated over recent years into global circuits of goods produced in China (Tassi et al., 2012). On the other hand, MAS has had a conflict-ridden relationship with the "Media Luna" elites of the eastern departments of Pando, Beni, Tarija, and, above all, Santa Cruz.[32] The backdrop for this conflict, meanwhile, was the territorial shift of the accumulation axes over recent decades. These axes have shifted from Oruro (its mining industry in decline) and La Paz (unable to establish a new technological basis in keeping with the demands of globalization) to Santa Cruz, with its export-focused agroindustry, and Tarija, with its immense gas reserves (García Linera, 2009).[33]

Finally, in the Ecuadorian case, one might consider Rafael Correa's relations similar to those developed by Chávez: personalized, not corporatized. Behind this would be the previously mentioned "desectorization" policy, which also applies to chambers of commerce. This aside, however, one must recall that the so-called "strategy for transformation of the productive structure" ultimately privileges domestic capital (Minteguiaga, 2012). In this sense, it does not seem that the power of big Ecuadorian capital has been affected. Data from the last Economic Census of Ecuador presented in late 2011 show a high degree of monopolistic concentration (Ospina Peralta, 2013).[34]

---

29   One should recall that Pedro Carmona, president of Fedecámaras, was elected president of the nation in the spurious administration born of the coup d'état of April 2002.

30   In the wake of the coup d'état of April 2002, the subsidiaries of foreign companies came together in AVHI as an entity apart from Fedecámaras and the Cámara Petrolera Venezolana, seeking to distance themselves politically from both (Mora Contreras, 2009).

31   This would be the bourgeosie that Toranzo Roca (1991) dubbed a *burguesía chola*, and which followed a strategy of accumulation that differed from that followed by oligarchical business groups: they did not benefit from state patronage; they defined the scope of their accumulation internally, with no luxury consumption and a focus on ritualistic spending.

32   With MAS in office, this elite would lead a ferocious opposition movement calling for extreme autonomy for the "Media Luna" departments, bordering on secession and including the invention of the concept of the "nación camba," with clear ethnic/racial implications (Molina, 2008).

33   In this sense, one must recall that the elites of Santa Cruz occupied crucial positions in the definition of economic policy, this since 1985, independently of the party coalition in power. With the ascension of MAS, they were displaced from these privileged posts; their fight for autonomy would thus represent a step back from their former pretensions of national hegemony (García Linera, 2009).

34   According to the same author, "... the data are hair-raising: 1% of consulted establishments (5,111 businesses) were responsible for 89.9% of total sales, and 91.5% of the total gross added

In this sense, it is important to note that these governments are not anti-business.[35] Private activity remains the bulk in these countries. In Venezuela, as employment data suggest, the public sector has seen considerable growth, driven by a number of nationalizations over recent years. But, as has been shown in terms of the functional distribution of income, capital has continued bringing in the surplus at levels similar to the period before Chávez's administration. In Bolivia, the private sector generates 70% of the country's GDP (Arze Vargas and Gómez, 2013, Graph 6). And in Ecuador, it must be underscored that the state went from generating 25% of GDP in 2006 to nearly 50% in 2011 (Ospina Peralta, 2013: p. 199). Public spending on infrastructure, however, has come to stand as one of the most important opportunities for private capital to accumulate. Moreover, in this case we have already mentioned the high concentration in the business sector in terms of the generation of added value and control of the domestic market. That is to say, a monopolistic situation persists, guaranteeing a pooling of opportunities for accumulation in the hands of big capital.

The situation might come to change if the strategies posed by these governments should come to pass. Here we refer to the development of new economic models that, in keeping with government discourse, would shape a "postcapitalist" order.[36] In the Venezuelan case, past the critical period of 2002–2004, *chavismo* flowed into "21st Century Socialism." In Bolivia the discussion focuses on "communitarian socialism," while Ecuador's strategy casts itself as an "endogenous, biocentric [model] based on the use of biodiversity services, knowledge, and tourism" (Ospina Peralta, 2013, p. 181).[37] In this sense, apart from the issue of the nature of this kind of activity, what interests us is seeing if there have been significant processes of opening in this field that would create opportunities of accumulation for other economic actors aside from businesses. This leads us to the third issue in the realm of surplus inequalities.

In the case of Venezuela, the so-called social sector of the economy came to 0.5% of GDP in 1998, while ten years later it had risen to just 1.6% (Álvarez, 2009: p. 253). In the Bolivian case, this sector increased its share of GDP, from 2.2% in 2005 to 2.6% in 2010, while the community sector went from 7.2% to 6.3% over the same period (Arze Vargas and Gómez, 2013: Graph 6). As for Ecuador, meanwhile, the solidary economy would focus on agroecology, community tourism, and, above all, credit cooperatives. These latter areas have seen spectacular growth, but only during the period before the current administration (Ospina Peralta, 2013). That is to say, it would seem for the moment that the weight of these "new forms of economy" is quite marginal, and there are no signs of opening in terms of opportunities for accumulation of wealth.

---

value … the earnings of the 55 largest private businesses in the nation went from slightly over 800 million dollars in 2005 to 1,486 [million] in 2007, to 1,645 [million] in 2009, and topped out at 1,641 million in 2011, although the volume of sales continued to grow" (Ospina Peralta, 2013: pp. 230–231).

35   Arditi (2010) considers that one of the traits of the "new left" in Latin America is its lessened hostility towards private property and the market, displaying a tendency towards coexistence.

36   The quotation marks indicate that it does not strike us as obvious that the direction being taken is that of a social order significantly different from capitalism, especially in the Ecuadorian case.

37   This author has emphasized that Correa's vision does not fit within a postcapitalist perspective, but rather references the "communitarian socialism" of the '60s as put forth by Christian democracy. As this author argues, this would be "… a 'paternal capitalism' born of the action of enlightened Christian leaders working towards the common good, despite—as President Correa put it in a recent speech—the generalized cultural 'mediocrity' which lies at the 'root of underdevelopment'" (quotation marks his) (Ospina Peralta, 2013: p. 270).

This being the case, in terms of this field of surplus inequalities, it would not seem that there has been any significant opening of opportunities for accumulation, which would thus continue in the hands of big capital. A generation of new opportunities in terms of "new forms of economy" has become apparent, but they remain quite marginal at the moment.

"Postneoliberal" Answers in the Redistributive Sphere

In the three countries in question, and up through the last year of available information, there has been an increase in public social spending per capita, both generally and across its various components (education, healthcare, and social security), with greater speed in Ecuador but on a larger scale in Venezuela (Pérez Sáinz, 2014a: Table 6).[38] This increase has been going on since 2007 in both Bolivia and Ecuador; in the first case under the already-installed MAS administration, but in the second at the very start of the tenure of the *Revolución Ciudadana*. In Venezuela the growth came in 2004, when the crisis period was winding down in the government's favor, specifically with the recovery of control over PVDSA. In this vein, the important point would be to determine whether this growth has been an index of continuity of (neo)liberal policies, conditional cash transfers in particular, or whether, on the contrary, there has been a rupture. The table below reflects the main measures adopted by these governments.

Table 4.2   **"Postneoliberal" interventions in the area of surplus redistribution**

Areas	Venezuela	Bolivia	Ecuador
Conditional cash transfers		Juancito Pinto Voucher	Human Development Voucher
		Juana Azurduy Voucher	Human Development Credit
Basic citizenship	Increase in social public spending per inhabitant	Increase in social public spending per inhabitant	Increase in social public spending per inhabitant
	Misiones Barrio Adentro, Robinson, and Ribas	National Literacy Plan	
		Post-literacy plan	
Social security	Expansion of the affiliated population	Pensions law	Expansion of the affiliated population
		Maintenance of the individual pension fund system	IESS Bank
		Renta de la Dignidad	

Indeed, the policy of conditional cash transfers has been maintained in the cases of Bolivia and Ecuador; in Venezuela, when this kind of program was first popularized, the Chávez administration was already in power.

---

38   Data from CEPALSTAT.

In the Bolivian case, it was the MAS administration who moved to broaden conditional cash transfers via two programs: the Bono (Voucher) Juancito Pinto, and the Bono (Voucher) Juana Azurduy de Padilla, also known as the mother-child voucher. The former seeks to keep primary-school students in school by providing an annual transfer. The second looks to cut down on maternal mortality by encouraging pregnant women to undergo regular checkups. It was introduced in 52 municipalities and later universalized by the central government for a five-year period (Wanderley, 2009: pp. 80–81; Molyneux and Thomson, 2013: pp. 75–76). Payments on these transfers have increased: 50% from 2006 to 2010 for the Juancito Pinto program, while the Juana Azurduy voucher went up 250% from 2009 to the following year (Arze Vargas and Gómez, 2013: Table 13).

Ecuador, meanwhile, has the Human Development Voucher (BDH). It was preceded by two programs: the 1998 Bono Solidario (Solidary Voucher), which sought to compensate lower-income households for the elimination of electricity and gas subsidies; and the Beca Escolar (Scholarship), implemented around the same period with a transfer of five dollars per child (up to two per household). In 2003, the programs would be fused into the BDH. This kind of program has two traditional components: transfers for children between the ages of 6 and 15 to keep them from leaving school, and attendance at health center checkups for children under the age of six (Ponce, 2013). But the BDH has been joined under the Correa administration by a series of complementary programs: Red de Protección Solidaria (Solidary Protection Network), Cobertura de Protección Familiar (Family Protection Coverage), Bono de Emergencia (Emergency Voucher), and Crédito de Desarrollo Humano (Human Development Credit). The latter, which was a foretaste of the BDH itself, is meant to incentivize self-employment, as well as increasing the incomes of families with fewer resources and guaranteeing their sustenance. This measure has been criticized for reflecting a certain distrust of these sectors, supposedly not worthy of formal credit programs (Enríquez Bermeo, 2013).

This continuity in the use of conditional cash transfers—which has also been the case with other "postneoliberal" governments—has been emphasized by Reygadas and Filgueira (2010), who see a tendency for these programs to remain and grow. These authors doubt that there has been a true break in the case of these governments, which rather reproduce traces of the paternalism and clientelism of previous social policy. This conclusion does not differ much from that of Roberts (2012), who declares that Latin America's "left turn" has produced neither an economic nor a social model in opposition to (neo)liberal thought.

We do not share completely in this opinion, and we believe that the first-generation social policies oriented towards expanding basic citizenship have been more important than the maintenance and expansion of conditional transfers.

In Bolivia, the National Development Plan of 2006 proposed orienting the educational system around two basic points: respect for sociocultural diversity and adaptation to the new productive model (Wanderley, 2009). More concretely, a National Literacy Plan was formulated, as well as the already mentioned Juancito Pinto voucher program. As for the former, over 800,000 people were covered, and in early 2009 the government declared that illiteracy had been eradicated. There followed a post-literacy program to provide primary education to those previously taught to read and write, and for those age 15 and older. By 2009, 52,627 people had been benefited by the program (Mayorga and Rodríguez, 2010: 113). In terms of healthcare, the government's main objective has been gradual access to the system, which incorporates, beyond traditional medicine, all of the population under age 21, women who may be pregnant, giving birth, or lactating, and those suffering from chronic diseases (Wanderley, 2009). That is to say that the public option in terms of healthcare has focused on primary care, while attention at other levels is dependent on the monetary capacity of patients themselves (Arze Vargas and Gómez, 2013).

Ecuador has focused on access to education and healthcare for the most disadvantaged sectors by removing barriers such as annual fees for schooling or medical checkups (Ramírez Gallegos, 2010). An absence of fees, infrastructural improvements, and a doubling of annual checkups (from 14 to 30 million per year) are the achievements in terms of health; in education, meanwhile, the government itself has emphasized greater access to all levels of education for historically marginalized ethnic and social groups (Ospina Peralta, 2013: 215–216). It is important to mention that these initiatives fit with the "desectorization" strategy, a key element in the agenda of the *Revolución Ciudadana* government.[39]

While in the two previous countries one has the impression that the search for the universalization of basic citizenship may be served by expanding coverage and investing in more efficient interventions, the Venezuelan case has seen an attempt at an unprecedented framework: the so-called *misiones* (missions).

These, once again, emerged during the critical period of 2002–2004.[40] Having overcome the coup d'état and recovered control of PDVSA, the government began funding activities meant to frame an alternative model. Chief among them are the so-called missions, covering an extraordinarily broad range of activities, including primary healthcare (Misión Barrio Adentro); food security (Misión Mercal); literacy (the two Misiones Robinson); educational plans (Misión Ribas, Misión Sucre, and other initiatives); and distribution of lands and support to peasants (Misión Zamora) (López Maya, 2004; Lander and Navarrete, 2009). Similarly, Chávez, for the first time, placed social priorities at the forefront of his political strategy (Parker, 2005).[41]

Of all the Venezuelan missions, three focused on education and healthcare merit greater attention. As for the latter, the Misión Barrio Adentro has attempted to create a new model of healthcare more focused on prevention than cure, including 10,000 Cuban professionals brought into aid their Venezuelan colleagues. It has been rolled out over four phases, the first being an attempt at universalizing primary healthcare via the creation of 6,575 health centers for over 16 million people, especially in both urban and rural peripheral areas (Álvarez, 2013: p. 345).[42] This effort has been well received among the population, penetrating into communities not included in the traditional healthcare system and reducing infant mortality to boot (Sanjuán, 2009). In the field of education, the Misión Robinson should be mentioned, as well as Misión Ribas. The former has aimed and managed to eradicate illiteracy, while the latter has attempted to help youth and adult dropouts to complete secondary school and obtain their degrees (Sanjuán, 2009; Álvarez, 2013).[43]

---

39   This implied the February 2009 abolition of the National Office for Bilingual Intercultural Education (DINEIB) which had been a key representative of the indigenous in the state apparatus for decades. In facing down CONAIE, the government accused the agency of corruption and even racism for its lack of consideration of the mestizo and African-descendant population (Tuaza Castro, 2011).

40   Various authors have signaled that the missions were fundamental in generating political support for Chávez during the recall referendum of August 2004 (Penfold-Becerra, 2007; Stefanoni, 2012).

41   Maingón (2004) has argued that social policy under Chávez, during the administration's first four years, posed no breaking point with policy over the last two decades of the past century, keeping up compensatory and assistance-based patterns.

42   The other three phases focused on higher levels of the health system (Álvarez, 2013).

43   Graduates of this mission may continue their college studies thanks to another mission, Misión Sucre. These graduates compete productively with college students; thus, as Ellner (2010) points out, not all those who "lose out" under *chavismo* policy are to be found amongst the elites. In

The missions have displayed a number of weaknesses: a lack of integration into a comprehensive social policy; assistance-focused programs; tensions with existing institutions; the bureaucratization of community participation, etc. On the other hand, however, they have put forth a novel institutional framework favorable to greater flexibility in the application of social policy, and, above all, they have displayed an ability to incorporate historically marginalized subaltern sectors, who have been able to act as true citizens (Sanjuán, 2009). In this sense, the state has emerged as an agent of popular empowerment by promoting these sectors' involvement in solving their own problems (Monedero, 2010). We share in the idea that the inclusion and empowerment achieved thus far, with the human dignity they have provided to these subaltern sectors, constitutes *chavismo*'s greatest strength, consistently underrated or misunderstood by the opposition (McCoy, 2010).

The last dimension in question is the area of social security, pensions in particular. In the Venezuelan case, the country went from 387,007 pensioners in 1998 to 1,289,320 in 2009 (Monedero, 2010: pp. 245–246). In the Ecuadorian case, affiliation to social security rose at the start of the Correa administration, but this tendency stalled out, with perhaps 28.9% of the economically active population (PEA) being affiliated. Its greatest achievement may have been the financial restructuring of the Ecuadorian Institute of Social Security (IESS) and the creation of the Banco del IESS (IESS Bank), which allows for the institution to invest its funds directly, bypassing private banks and playing a key role in financing housing (low-income in particular) and consumption (Ospina Peralta, 2013: p. 218). We should also note that, within the framework of the National System of Inclusion and Social Equity established by Correa's administration, social security represents the upper "floor," where subsidies to the vulnerable population, noncontributory (subsidized) insurance, and semi-contributory insurance make up the lower "floors" (Enríquez Bermeo, 2013: Graph 5).

The most interesting case here is the Bolivian, since the social security system was privatized during the (neo)liberal period. The *sui generis* privatizations carried out in the country meant that the seed capital of the companies affected wound up being managed by the administrators of pension funds; they, through a trusteeship, were meant to provide universal old-age insurance dubbed the "Bono Solidario" (Bonosol). This meant combining privatization with universal-leaning social compensation (Arze Vargas, 2004; Wanderley, 2009). In 2010, under MAS, a new Pensions Law was passed and introduced three important changes regarding (neo)liberal reforms: dropping the retirement age from 65 to 58 years; reduction in the "replacement rate," from 70% to 60% of one's salary; and the creation of a Fondo Solidario (Solidary Fund) with contributions from both work and capital gains (Arze Vargas and Gómez, 2013: 147). Another change included substituting Bonosol with the so-called Renta de la Dignidad (Dignity Pension), which has increased in scale, dropped its age of entry (from 65 to 60), and has achieved nearly universal coverage in its sector (Wanderley, 2009; Arze Vargas and Gómez, 2013).[44] However, for Arze Vargas and Gómez (2013), this new law has not implied a true rupture with previous (neo)liberal reforms, given the maintenance of the principle of individual capitalization, and measures solidary with lower incomes fall to wage-earners, freeing capital from this responsibility.

---

this marginalization of traditional universities lies one of the motives for the student movement's often-belligerent opposition to the administration.

44 In 2012, Renta Dignidad covered 91% of the population over age 65, the highest rate of coverage in Latin America, alongside Argentina (Rofman et al., 2013: p. 59).

One last element that we feel is important to consider is that oil and gas rents play an important role in financing social policies in all three countries. In this sense, the social destination of the money accrued by so-called "progressive neo-extractivism" has important effects in terms of the social and political legitimation of this kind of model, but also generates a vicious cycle, as the social and environmental impacts of such activities demand further compensatory action in the future (Gudynas, 2012). However, one must tread carefully so as to avoid falling into reductionist analyses that attribute undue leadership to "rentierism" and "extractivism" when interpreting the actions of these governments, at least in the cases of Bolivia and Ecuador.[45]

It is thus the case that, unlike the primary sphere, this secondary sphere seems to have been privileged by the three governments in question, which have produced various combinations of an expansion in citizens affiliated to the social security system and the maintenance and expansion of conditional cash transfers as well as, above all, social policies on primary care in both healthcare and education. In other words, it would seem that "postneoliberalism" has, in these three cases, placed its chips on redistribution over distribution, emphasizing the broadening of basic social citizenship.

Conclusions

With the array of reflections developed in the two preceding sections, we may attempt to respond to the questions posed in the introduction. The answers that we put forth here, as already stated, are hypothetical in nature.

"Postneoliberalism" has not set out to return to social citizenship based on formal employment, nor, for the moment, on opening opportunities for the accumulation for smaller property-holders. Our first hypothesis would thus be that the changes brought about in the primary sphere do not seem to be significant, and that this third Rousseauian drive has been rooted in the redistributive sphere.[46] This strikes us as a key aspect of the three cases in question, although it would have to be modified for other "postneoliberal" experiments in the region where unions and the workers' movement are generally more active. (Argentina, Brazil, and Uruguay come to mind.) But the redistributive emphasis present in all three governments examined in this text does not imply pure continuity with (neo)liberal social citizenship. Our second hypothesis is that there came attempts to include subaltern sectors that had been historically marginalized in terms of basic social citizenship, in contrast to (neo)liberalism's move to disguise these groups as simply "poor." We believe that significant processes towards the recognition of basic social rights have taken place, which will not easily be reversed, as these sectors now feel empowered as citizens.

---

45   In the first case, non-extractive fiscal revenue (VAT, customs duties, specific taxes on consumption, etc.) outstripped those from hydrocarbons and mining thanks to increased collection efforts (Arze Vargas and Gómez, 2013). Likewise, in Ecuador, the increase in public spending was not only driven by a greater share in oil rent, thanks to rising prices on the global market, but also by an increased tax-collection capacity and a greater relative weight of direct taxation, to say nothing of the reduction of foreign debt obligations (Ramírez Gallegos, 2010; Ospina Peralta, 2013).

46   The first Rousseauian moment came about during Independence and lasted through the mid-19th century. The second is associated to the development of social citizenship and the growth of formal employment, the product of a model of accumulation oriented towards the domestic market and founded on industrialization. The latter had its clearest expression in populist regimes, but was not limited to them. For more on this, see Pérez Sáinz (2014a).

This last phenomenon would thus represent, in our opinion, the uncontested legacy of "postneoliberalism." On that note, in conclusion, one might recall the testimony of one humble Venezuelan citizen mentioned by Eduardo Galeano, and which Félix Población would later quote on his Blog Bocalle, in the digital newspaper Público, on December 17th, 2012. This citizen declared: " *... I don't want Chávez to go because I don't want to go back to being invisible."*

Bibliography

Acosta, A. (1999). 'El tortuoso e interminable ajuste ecuatoriano.' *Nueva Sociedad*, vol. 161, no. 3, pp. 57–69.

Acosta, A. (2011). 'La reforma a la ley de hidrocarburos y la renegociación de los contratos petroleros.' *La Tendencia*, vol. 11, no, 24, pp. 95–103.

Álvarez, V.R. (2009). *Venezuela: ¿Hacia dónde va el modelo productivo?* Caracas, Centro Internacional Miranda.

Álvarez, V.R. (2013). 'La transición al socialismo de la Revolución Bolivariana. Transiciones logradas y transiciones pendientes,' en Arze, C. et al. (comp.) (2013). *Promesas en su laberinto. Cambios y continuidades en los gobiernos progresistas de América Latina.* La Paz, IEE/CEDLA/CIM.

Anria, S. (2010). 'Bolivia's MAS: Between party and movement,' in Cameron, M.A. and Hershberg, E. (eds.) (2010). *Latin America's Left Turn. Politics, Policies and Trajectories of Change*. Boulder, Lynne Rienner Publishers.

Antelo, E. (2000). 'Políticas de estabilización y de reformas estructurales en Bolivia a partir de 1985.' *Serie Reformas Económicas No. 62.* Santiago de Chile, CEPAL.

Arditi, B. (2010). 'Arguments about the left turns in Latin America: A post-Liberal politics?,' in Cameron, M.A. and Hershberg, E. (eds.) (2010). *Latin Americas's Left Turn. Politics, Policies and Trajectories of Change.* Boulder, Lynne Rienner Publishers.

Arenas, N. (2009). 'Las organizaciones empresariales venezolanas bajo el gobierno de Hugo Chávez (1999–2007). ¿De la sociedad civil nacional a la internacional?' *Cuadernos del Cendes*, vol. 26, no. 71, pp. 1–25.

Arenas, N. (2010). 'La Venezuela de Hugo Chávez: rentismo, populismo y democracia.' *Nueva Sociedad*, vol. 229, no. 5, pp. 76–93.

Arnson, C.J. et al. (comp.) (2009). *La "nueva izquierda" en América Latina: derechos humanos, participación política, y sociedad civi.* Washington, Woodrow Wilson International Center for Scholars.

Arze Vargas, C. (2004). 'Las rebeliones populares de 2003 y la demanda de nacionalización de los hidrocarburos: ¿fin de la era neoliberal en Bolivia?' *Cuadernos del CENDES*, vol. 21, no. 56, pp. 83–103.

Arze Vargas, C. y Gómez, J. (2013). Bolivia: '¿El "proceso de cambio" nos conduce al Vivir Bien?' en Arze, C. et al. (comp.) (2013). *Promesas en su laberinto. Cambios y continuidades en los gobiernos progresistas de América Latina*, La Paz, IEE/CEDLA/CIM.

Arze, C. et al. (comp.) (2013). *Promesas en su laberinto. Cambios y continuidades en los gobiernos progresistas de América Latina*, La Paz, IEE/CEDLA/CIM.

Ayala, M. y Quintero, P. (comp.) (2009). *Diez años de revolución en Venezuela. Historia, balance y perspectivas*. Ituzaingó, Editorial Maipue.

Barr, R.R. (2005). 'Bolivia: Another uncompleted revolution.' *Latin American Politics and Society*, vol. 47, no. 3, pp. 69–90.

Barrera Guarderas, A. (2001). *Acción colectiva y crisis política. El movimiento indígena ecuatoriano en la década de los noventa*, Quito, OSAL/CIUDAD/Abya Yala.

Cameron, M.A. and Hershberg, E. (eds). (2010). *Latin Americas´s Left Turn. Politics, Policies and Trajectories of Change*. Boulder, Lynne Rienner Publishers.

Castel, R. (1997). *La metamorfosis de la cuestión social: una crónica del salariado*. Buenos Aires, Paidós.

Davila, L.R. (2000). 'The rise and fall of populism in Venezuela.' *Bulletin of Latin American Research*, vol. 19, no. 2, pp. 223–238.

De la Torre, C. (2010). 'El gobierno de Rafael Correa: posneoliberalismo, confrontación con los movimientos sociales y democracia plebiscitaria.' *Revista Temas y Debates*, vol. 14, no. 20, pp. 157–172.

Ellner, S. (2005). 'The emergence of a new trade unionism in Venezuela with vestiges of the Ppast.' *Latin American Perspectives*, vol. 32, no. 2, pp. 51–71.

Ellner, S. (2009). 'Las reformas neoliberales y la crisis política venezolana, 1989–1999, antecedentes de la llegada de Hugo Chávez al poder,' en Ayala, M. y Quintero, P. (comp.) (2009). *Diez años de revolución en Venezuela. Historia, balance y perspectivas.* Ituzaingó, Editorial Maipue.

Ellner, S. (2010). 'La primera década del gobierno de Hugo Chávez. Logros y desaciertos.' *Cuadernos del CENDES*, vol. 27, no. 74, pp. 27–50.

Enríquez Bermeo, F. (2013). 'De las Transferencias Monetarias al Sistema Nacional de Inclusión y Equidad Social,' en Ponce, J. et al. (comp.) (2013). *Hacia una reforma del Bono de Desarrollo Humano: Algunas reflexiones.* Quito, Abya Yala/CARE.

French, J.D. (2009). 'Understanding the politics of Latin America's plural lefts (Chávez/ Lula): Social democracy, populism and convergence on the path to a post-neoliberal world.' *Third World Quarterly*, vol. 30, no. 2, pp. 349–370.

García Linera, Á. (2009). *La potencia plebeya. Acción colectiva e identidades indígenas, obreras y populares en Bolivia*. Bogotá, CLACSO/Siglo del Hombre Editores.

Gudynas, E. (2012). 'Estado compensador y nuevos extractivismos. Las ambivalencias del progresismo sudamericano.' *Nueva Sociedad*, vol. 237, no. 1, pp. 128–146.

Hellinger, D. (1996). 'The Causa R and the Nuevo Sindicalismo in Venezuela,' *Latin American Perspectives*, vol. 23, no. 3, pp. 110–131.

Hernández, J.L. (2009). 'Evolución y resultados del sector agroalimentario en la V República.' *Cuadernos del CENDES*, vol. 26, no. 72, pp. 67–100.

Iranzo, C. y Richter, J. (2006). 'La política laboral en la Venezuela de Hugo Chávez Frías.' *Revista Latinoamericana de Estudios del Trabajo*, vol. 11, no. 18, pp. 5–32.

Lalander, R. y Ospina Peralta, P. (2012). 'Movimiento indígena y revolución ciudadana en Ecuador.' *Cuestiones Políticas*, vol. 28, no. 48, pp. 13–50.

Lander, E. (2005). 'Venezuelan social conflict in a global context.' *Latin American Perspectives*, vol. 32, no. 2, pp. 20–38.

Lander, E. (2013). 'Prólogo. Tensiones/contradicciones en torno al extractivismo en los procesos de cambio: Bolivia, Ecuador y Venezuela,' en Arze, C. et al. (comp.) (2013). *Promesas en su laberinto. Cambios y continuidades en los gobiernos progresistas de América Latina.* La Paz, IEE/CEDLA/CIM.

Lander, E. y Fierro, L.A. (1996). 'The impact of neoliberal adjustment in Venezuela, 1989–1993.' *Latin American Perspectives*, vol. 23, no. 3, pp. 50–73.

Lander, E. y Navarrete, P. (2009). 'La política económica de la izquierda latinoamericana en el Gobierno: el caso de la República Bolivariana de Venezuela (1999–2006),' en Ayala, M. y Quintero, P. (comp.) (2009). *Diez años de revolución en Venezuela. Historia, balance y perspectivas*. Ituzaingó, Editorial Maipue.

León Trujillo, J. (1994). *De campesinos a ciudadanos diferentes. El levantamiento indígena*. Quito, CEDIME/Abya-Yala.

León Trujillo, J. (2010). 'Las organizaciones indígenas y el gobierno de Rafael Correa.' *Iconos*, vol. 37, no. 1, pp. 13–23.

León Trujillo, J. y Pérez Sáinz, J.P. (1986). 'Crisis y movimiento sindical en Ecuador: las huelgas nacionales del FUT (1981–1983)' en Verdesoto, L. (comp.) (1986). *Movimientos sociales en el Ecuador*. Quito, CLACSO/ILDIS.

López Maya, M. (2003). 'The Venezuelan 'Caracazo' of 1989: Popular protest and institutional weakness.' *Journal of Latin American Studies*, vol. 35, no. 1, pp. 117–137.

López Maya, M. (2004). 'Venezuela 2001–2004: actores y estrategias.' *Cuadernos del CENDES*, vol. 21, no. 56, pp. 105–128.

López Maya, M. (2009). 'El movimiento bolivariano: ascenso al poder y gobierno hasta 2008,' en Ayala, M. y Quintero, P. (comp.) (2009). *Diez años de revolución en Venezuela. Historia, balance y perspectivas*. Ituzaingó, Editorial Maipue.

López Maya, M. (2010). 'Venezuela: once años de gestión de Hugo Chávez Frías y sus fuerzas bolivarianas (1999–2010).' *Revista Temas y Debates*, vol. 14, no. 20, pp. 197–226.

López Maya, M. y Lander, L.E. (2009). 'El socialismo *rentista* de Venezuela ante la caída de los precios petroleros internacionales.' *Cuadernos del CENDES*, vol. 26, no. 71, pp. 67–87.

Maingón, T. (2004). 'Política social en Venezuela: 1999–2003.' *Cuadernos del CENDES*, vol. 21, no. 55, pp. 47–73.

Mayorga, R.A. (2004). 'Crisis del sistema de partidos políticos en Bolivia: causas y consecuencias.' *Cuadernos del CENDES*, vol. 21, no. 57, pp. 83–114.

Mayorga, F. y Rodríguez, B. (2010). 'Nacionalismo e indigenismo en el gobierno del MAS.' *Revista Temas y Debates*, vol. 14, no. 20, pp. 97–122.

McCoy, J. (2010). 'Venezuela Under Chávez: Beyond liberalism,' en Cameron, M.A. and Hershberg, E. (eds.) (2010). *Latin America's Left Turn. Politics, Policies and Trajectories of Change*. Boulder, Lynne Rienner Publishers.

Méndez, A. (2008). 'Origen, desarrollo, crisis y reforma de la Seguridad Social en Venezuela.' *Serie Diálogo Político*, Caracas, ILDIS.

Minteguiaga, A. (2012). 'Política y políticas sociales en el Ecuador reciente: dificultades asociadas a la salida del ciclo neoliberal.' *Revista Ciencias Sociales*, vol. 135–136, no. 1–2, pp. 45–58.

Molina, F. (2008). 'Bolivia: la geografía de un conflict.' *Nueva Sociedad*, vol. 218, no. 6, pp. 4–13.

Molyneux, M. y Thomson, M. (2013). 'Programas de Transferencias Monetarias Condicionadas y empoderamiento de las mujeres en Perú, Bolivia y Ecuador,' en Ponce, J. et al. (comp.) (2013). *Hacia una reforma del Bono de Desarrollo Humano: Algunas reflexiones*. Quito, Abya Yala/CARE.

Monedero, J.C. (2010). 'Venezuela bolivariana: reinvención del presente y persistencia del pasado.' *Revista Temas y Debates*, vol. 14, no. 20, pp. 229–256.

Mora Contreras, J. (2009). 'Las bases de la política rentista y bolivariana del gobierno de Chávez.' *Opiniones Contrapuestas No. 5,* Cochabamba, Universidad Mayor de San Simón.

OIT (2000). *Panorama laboral. América Latina y el Caribe 2000.* Lima, Organización Internacional del Trabajo.

OIT (2013). *Panorama laboral. América Latina y el Caribe 2013.* Lima, Organización Internacional del Trabajo.

Ormachea Saavedra, E. (2008). ¿Revolución agraria o consolidación de la vía terrateniente? El Gobierno del MAS y las políticas de tierras. La Paz, CEDLA.

Ospina Peralta, P. (2013). 'Estamos haciendo mejor las cosas con el mismo modelo antes que cambiarlo. La revolución ciudadana en Ecuador (2007–2012),' en Arze, C. et al. (comp.) (2013). *Promesas en su laberinto. Cambios y continuidades en los gobiernos progresistas de América Latina.* La Paz, IEE/CEDLA/CIM.

Pachano, S. (2005). 'Ecuador: cuando la inestabilidad se vuelve estable.' *Iconos,* vol. 23, no. 1, pp. 37–44.

Parker, D. (2005). 'Chávez and the Search for an Alternative to Neoliberalism.' *Latin American Perspectives,* vol. 32, no. 2, pp. 39–50.

Parker, D. (2008). 'Chávez y la búsqueda de una seguridad y soberanía alimentarias.' *Revista Venezolana de Economía y Ciencias Sociales,* vol. 14, no. 3, pp. 121–143.

Penfold-Becerra, M. (2007). 'Clientelism and Social Funds: Evidence from Chávez's Misiones.' *Latin American Politics and Society,* vol. 49, no. 4, pp. 63–84.

Pérez Sáinz, J.P. (2014a). 'El tercer momento *rousseauniano* de América Latina. Posneoliberalismo y desigualdades sociales.' *desiguALdades.net Working Paper No. 72,* Berlin, Freie Universität.

Pérez Sáinz, J.P. (2014b). *Mercados y bárbaros. La persistencia de las desigualdades de excedente en América Latina.* San José, FLACSO.

Ponce, J. (2013). El Bono de Desarrollo Humano en Ecuador, en Ponce, J. et al. (comp.) (2013). *Hacia una reforma del Bono de Desarrollo Humano: Algunas reflexiones.* Quito, Abya Yala/CARE.

Ponce, J. et al. (comp.) (2013). *Hacia una reforma del Bono de Desarrollo Humano: Algunas reflexiones.* Quito, Abya Yala/CARE.

Prada Alcoreza, R. (2003). 'Perfiles del movimiento social contemporáneo. El conflicto social y político en Bolivia.' *Observatorio Social de América Latina,* vol. 4, no. 12, pp. 35–46.

Ramírez Gallegos, F. (2005). 'Insurrección, legitimidad y política radical.' *Iconos,* vol. 23, no. 1, pp. 83–92.

Ramírez Gallegos, F. (2010). 'Post-neoliberalismo indócil. Agenda pública y relaciones socio-estatales en el Ecuador de la Revolución Ciudadana.' *Revista Temas y Debates,* vol. 14, no. 20, pp. 175–194.

Reygadas, L. and Filgueira, F. (2010). 'Inequality and the Incorporation Crisis: The Left's Social Policy Toolkit,' in Cameron, M.A. and Hershberg, E. (eds.) (2010). *Latin America's Left Turn. Politics, Policies and Trajectories of Change.* Boulder, Lynne Rienner Publishers.

Rivas, P. (2008). 'La estabilidad laboral que todos dicen defender.' *Actuar en Mundos Plurales,* vol. 2, no. 1, pp. 2–5.

Rivero, M. del C. (2006). *El poder de las luchas sociales. 2003: quiebre del discurso neoliberal.* La Paz, CEDLA.

Roberts, K.M. (2003). 'Social correlates of party system demise and populist resurgence in Venezuela.' *Latin American Politics and Society*, vol. 45, no. 3, pp. 35–57.

Roberts, K.M. (2012). 'The Politics of Inequality and Redistribution in Latin America's Post-Adjustment Era.' *Working Paper No. 2012/08*, Helsinki, UNU-WIDER.

Rofman, R. et al. (comp.) (2013). *Más allá de las Pensiones Contributivas. Catorce experiencias en América Latina*. Buenos Aires, World Bank.

Sader, E. (2008). *Refundar el Estado. Posneoliberalismo en América Latina*. Buenos Aires, Ediciones CTA/CLACSO.

Sader, E. y Gentili, P. (comp.) (2003). *La trama del neoliberalismo. Mercado, crisis y exclusión social*. Buenos Aires, CLACSO.

Salazar Lohman, H. (2013). *La formación histórica del movimiento indígena campesino boliviano. Los vericuetos de una clase construida desde la etnicidad*. Buenos Aires, CLACSO.

Salman, T. (2009). 'Searching for status: New elites in the new Bolivia.' *Revista Europea de Estudios Latinoamericanos y del Caribe/European Review of Latin American and Caribbean Studies*, vol. 86, no. 1, pp. 97–105.

Sánchez-Parga, J. (2007). *El movimiento indígena ecuatoriano. La larga ruta de la comunidad al partido*. Quito, CAAP.

Sanjuán, A.M. (2009). 'La esencia social de la revolución bolivariana en Venezuela: una mirada preliminar sobre sus fortalezas y debilidades,' en Arnson, C.J. et al. (comp.) (2009). *La "nueva izquierda" en América Latina: derechos humanos, participación política, y sociedad civil*. Washington, Woodrow Wilson International Center for Scholars.

Sonntag, H.R. y Maingón, T. (1992). *Venezuela: 4-F 1992. Un análisis sociopolítico*. Caracas, Editorial Nueva Sociedad.

Spronk, S. (2006). 'Roots of Resistance to Urban Water Privatization in Bolivia: The "New Working Class," the Crisis of Neoliberalism, and Public Services.' *Annual Meeting of the Canadian Political Science Association*, York University, Toronto, (June 3).

Stefanoni, P. (2006). 'El nacionalismo indígena en el poder.' *Observatorio Social de América Latina*, vol. 6, no. 19, pp. 37–44.

Stefanoni, P. (2012). 'Posneoliberalismo cuesta arriba. Los modelos de Venezuela, Bolivia y Ecuador a debate.' *Nueva Sociedad*, vol. 239, no. 1, pp. 51–64.

Tapia, L. (2009). 'Representación, participación y democratización en las relaciones Estado- sociedad civil en Bolivia,' en Arnson, C.J. et al. (comp.) (2009). *La "nueva izquierda" en América Latina: derechos humanos, participación política, y sociedad civil*. Washington, Woodrow Wilson International Center for Scholars.

Tassi, Nico et al. (2012). 'El desborde económico popular en Bolivia. Comerciantes aymaras en el mundo global.' *Nueva Sociedad*, vol. 241, no. 1, pp. 93–105.

Toranzo Roca, C.F. (1991). 'A manera de prólogo: burguesía chola y señorialismo conflictuado,' en Mayorga, F. (comp.) (1991). *Max Fernández: la política del silencio. Emergencia y consolidación de la Unidad Cívica Solidaridad*. La Paz, ILDIS/Facultad Ciencias Económicas y Sociología UMSS.

Tuaza Castro, L.A. (2011). *Runakunaka ashka shaikushka shinami rikurinkuna, ña mana tandanakunata munankunachu: la crisis de movimiento indígena ecuatoriano*. Quito, FLACSO.

Velasco Portillo, S.R. (2011). *La nacionalización pactada: una nueva forma de gobernanza sobre el gas boliviano*. Quito, Abya Yala/FLACSO.

Verdesoto, L. (comp.) (1986). *Movimientos sociales en el Ecuador.* Quito, CLACSO/ILDIS.

Verdesoto Custode, L. (2013). *Acteurs et jeux politiques en Equateur 1979–2011,* Thèse de Doctorat. Paris, École des Hautes Études en Sciences Sociales.

Viteri, R. (2008). 'Terciarización e intermediación laboral: un tema crucial y poco claro.' *Actuar en Mundos Plurales,* vol. 1, no. 1, pp. 7–10.

Wanderley, F. (2009). *Crecimiento, empleo y bienestar social ¿Por qué Bolivia es tan desigual?* La Paz, CIDES-UMSA.

Ycaza, P. (1991). *Historia del movimiento obrero ecuatoriano. (De la influencia de la táctica del frente popular a las luchas del FUT). Segunda parte.* Quito, CEDIME/CIUDAD.

Zamosc, L. (2007). 'The Indian Movement and Political Democracy in Ecuador.' *Latin American Politics and Society,* vol. 49, no. 3, pp. 1–34.

Zuazo, M. (2010). '¿Los movimientos sociales en el poder?.' *Nueva Sociedad,* vol. 227, no. 3, pp. 120–135.

Chapter 5

Social Policy and Structural Heterogeneity in Latin America: The Turning Point of the 21st Century[1]

Lena Lavinas and André Simões

"The growing dissemination of modern products in Latin America in no way changes the weakness of the traditional social relations into which these objects are incorporated. How modern a society is has less to do with the objects that are disseminated within it than with the modernness of its institutions and of the relationships on which the design, acquisition, selection, and evaluation of the usefulness of those objects are based" (Fajnzylber, 1990: p. 162)

Introduction

In their correspondence, especially in the year 1942, Beveridge and Keynes (Harris, 1997) forged a partnership that would prove successful over the course of the 20th century, as they contributed reciprocally to the design and theoretical foundations of what would become the model for social regulation par excellence of the Fordist accumulation regime, envisioning not simply its complementarity but rather its efficiency in stemming uncertainty and economic instability, both being sources of deep socioeconomic insecurity for families and individuals, and threats to the system itself.

The Keynesian welfare state (Jessop, 1993) was an exceptional innovation, with its logic rooted in the disassociation between individual welfare and revenue from work or assets, so as to maintain aggregate demand at a satisfactory level in periods of shrinking economic activity and allowing for permanent expansion. A minimum level of income should thus be guaranteed for all, independently of the value of one's work or properties, and it would fall to the state to determine such a level, in addition to the principal responsibility of guaranteeing that all citizens, regardless of class or status, have access to the best possible standard in an array of services judged to be indispensable (Briggs, 1961).

For the first time, a model emerges where social policy is recognized as inseparable from economic policy, and thus an essential instrument in the state's promoting of economic development (Simões, 2012). In the words of Donzelot (1994, apud Palier 2002: p. 194), there emerges a "circular mechanism" characterized by bonds of cooperation and systemic strengthening of the regime of accumulation, not by subordination of the social element to the economic.

---

1   Thanks to Ricardo Bielschowsky, Rubén Lo Vuolo, and Barbara Fritz for critical comments on an early version of this chapter.

We may concisely define this model of regulation via the privileged role granted to social spending, in both sustaining consumption and incentivizing direct job creation. According to Palier (2002), the former use meets the consumption needs of the population (seniors and retired people, the poor, unemployed, and children through universal benefits, etc.) via cash transfers. It thus ensures increasingly dynamic market expansion in times of growth, and may constitute a countercyclical measure during downturns in the cycle. The latter use of social spending uses the provision of universal and decommodified or partially subsidized public services to create jobs in a number of sectors (healthcare, education, daycare, transportation, etc.), which is key in terms of raising work productivity, ideally disseminating this rise throughout the whole system. This job creation, one might add, is not confined to the public sector in terms of direct provision, but also impacts many industrial sectors (pharmaceuticals and R&D, to name a few) that supply the public sector.

This model sought to insert the market into the political and social organization of nations (Polayni, 1944). In other words, the expansion of markets in the postwar period was dictated by the actions of political institutions (national states, in this case) and social institutions (mainly unions and the new regulatory forms adopted within social protection systems), resulting in the formation of development models that reserved a significant portion of the fruits of economic growth for the population itself.

This led to the emergence of various formats of welfare states, all characterized by decommodification (Polanyi, 1944) of the workforce so as to ensure its relative emancipation vis-à-vis the market. Decommodification and deindividualization (Rosanvallon, 2011) were thus the two driving forces in market societies whose extraordinary expansion came alongside a striking reduction in levels of inequality and destitution, in addition to consolidating democratic institutions aimed at heading off risks and uncertainties by ensuring welfare, economic security, and growing social homogenization.

In order to face down the destabilizing machine of expanding capitalism, a form of social regulation with the following essential premises comes to the fore:

1. equal treatment: it overcomes class or status cleavages, making citizenship the foundation for universal access—policies for all (or, in the words of Beveridge, 1942, "a plan all-embracing in scope of persons and needs");
2. the end of the social service state: the welfare state is no longer limited, as it once was (at the time of the Poor Laws or within the limits imposed by the Bismarckian model), to providing a restricted array of services to a specific sector of the population, identified by criteria established a priori;
3. coverage in keeping with contingencies and needs: instead of minimum social standards at a survival level, as in the past, the state is tasked with ensuring protection over the entire life cycle, and guaranteeing a standard of wellbeing compatible with and befitting economic development and its evolution. Hence, rights cannot be circumscribed in "packages."

Two separate modes of social policy, with specific objectives, spread during postwar period in the western economies that were able to install welfare states. They make up one of the poles of the *double movement* (Polanyi, 1944) inherent in the development of capitalism. On one side, cash transfers (contributory or noncontributory); on the other, the provision of decommodified services. While the former would seek to compensate for market failures and smooth consumption over the course of one's life, an array of services in terms of healthcare, education, and housing aimed at leveling out opportunities (Barr, 2012) and promoting equity.

In Latin America, meanwhile, social protection systems were shaped from their start by a regional context of great heterogeneity, although the region was a pioneer in introducing social security programs in the early 20th century, compared to other continents in the developing world (Mesa-Lago 2007). These systems remained incomplete and unrefined, and although the principle of universality was referred to in a very few countries (Argentina, Chile, Uruguay, and Costa Rica), none would get close to the idea of universal coverage until the 1970s. In the rest, the idea of protection remained embryonic and was nearly always the privilege of the elites in the public sector and the military, as well as sectors linked directly to the agro-export model. As for noncontributory benefits (for the poorest), the extremely limited offering failed to crystallize as a right or a state responsibility, and remained restricted, when available, to a very limited group of countries. The better part of the region—with its high levels of informality, low rate of wage employment and the predominance of the effective exclusion of rural and indigenous populations from contributory systems, in many cases—saw starkly reduced coverage.

Such characteristics on their own point to the fragile, nearly nonexistent link between social and economic policy, a state of affairs that predominated over the course of the second phase of Latin American state-led industrialization, commonly referred to as the first wave of developmentalism, with strikingly varied effects across the countries on the continent (Bertola and Ocampo, 2012). While the national-developmentalist state managed to promote a process of capitalist modernization and support for the new urban industrial proletariat after World War II, it did not manage to incorporate the mass of workers on the margin of this new regime of accumulation, marked by wage relations. These masses thus remained largely set apart from incorporation into the market.

The 21st century seems to have finally enshrined a new framework in Latin America for social and economic policy, leading to the advent of mass consumption societies. This phenomenon is made even more relevant by the fact that one of the obstacles to economic and social development in Latin America, in a structuralist vision, lay in the lack of a vigorous domestic market which might, through an import-substitution process, push an increase in industrial productivity and a subsequent rise in average salary, thus engendering a virtuous and permanent cycle of the expansion of production and demand, founded on a dynamic of innovation that might constantly refine the consumption patterns of a mass society.

Residual conditional cash transfer programs and microcredit, alongside specific forms of social regulation, such as the minimum wage, have shown themselves to be, if not completely functional, then at least contemporary with this new "developmentalist strategy," one which has finally discovered social policy. Latin America is recognized today for its success in having incorporated tens of millions of individuals into the consumer market in the span of a few years while contributing to their social inclusion, a feat which stands as extraordinary in the light of the continent's history.

What did structuralist thinking cast as a hindrance to the defense and construction of social policies, and what was the prevailing model of social regulation, redistribution, or framework for incorporating social and economic policy in the administrations that chose to return to a structuralist mode at the turn of this century? If, as Bertola and Ocampo (2012) indicate, Latin America failed to maintain a trajectory of sustainable growth over the course of the 20th century so as to reduce the gap that sets it apart from developed countries in countless respects, might the state's structuralist-driven perspective, with its exclusive focus on economic policy (and with a key emphasis on industrial expansion), have compromised that effort through its inability to associate and coordinate economic and social policy in search of a sustainable dynamic?

A number of authors (Bielschowsky, 2010, 2012; Bresser-Pereira, 2012, Bresser-Pereira and Theuer, 2012; Carneiro, 2012; Cepeda, 2012; and Bastos, 2012) have recognized the resurgence of Latin American structuralist thought in the void left by mediocre performance over the neoliberal era. And, just as happened post-WWII, this turning point has come about amidst a keen crisis in central economies (Carneiro, 2012). The state resumes a leadership role in formulating a national project for development meant to overcome the bottlenecks that continue to block technical advancement, innovation, productive diversification, but now tied to a plan for social inclusion. This would thus be the differential for social-developmentalism (Carneiro, 2012), or, as Bastos (2012) puts it, "distributive developmentalism guided by the state," vis-à-vis seminal structuralist thought: renewed attention on social issues and equity as a constitutive part of the new model of developmentalism, this time included amongst the priorities for state action.

In this chapter, we will examine whether (and how, and in what form) social policy has indeed become a prime, indissociable element of macroeconomic strategies around a return to economic growth on stable, sustainable bases, making redistribution a dynamic factor in the consolidation of market societies around the expansion of demand. Three issues run through the chapter: 1) what model of social inclusion currently holds sway in this new phase of so-called developmentalist strategies?; 2) what role is attributed to the social protection system and social policy *lato sensu* in this dynamic?; and 3) how do economic and social policy fit together in the context of the growth and expansion of the market society?

The chapter is divided into five parts. After this introduction, it will recapitulate the conception of the social element in original structuralist thinking. The third section addresses the first return to social policy in the CEPAL-driven formulation of the 1990s, where the idea of social inclusion first appears, seeking to evaluate whether this point indeed constitutes a reflexive relation between social and economic policy. In the fourth section, there follows an analysis of the content of social policy and its rationale in Latin America's latest phase of growth, taking Brazil as an illustrative case. Finally, a few conclusions close the chapter, addressing the questions formulated around the permanence (or lack thereof) of a missing link in the reflexivity of social policy as a driver of demand in this new phase of development. The objective is to reflect on the prevailing model of social regulation, and consider whether it strengthens universalist principles with the power to make more egalitarian societies possible on our continent.

The Place of the Social in Original Structuralist Thought

Original structuralist thought is, in its essence, not simply a critical alternative to orthodox liberal thought in economy, but rather, principally, a catching-up strategy. In this sense, it casts the state as the driver behind the transformation of the archaic productive structures inadequate to the expansion of capitalism in the developing world, which reproduce asymmetries between the center and the periphery, reproducing underdevelopment (Furtado, 2013 [1961],[1973]; Prebisch, 1949), exacerbating inequalities between industrialized nations and the rest of the world and hamstringing the advance of market societies.[2]

---

2   As Bertola and Ocampo (2012) have demonstrated, the gap in per capita income between Latin America and developed countries only increased from 1950 to 2008.

Latin American structuralism forges a strategy to reduce such inequalities, questioning the place set aside for the periphery (the Ricardian model of comparative advantages and criticism of Joseph Viner's theory of economic development) through the structural transformation of the economy from agro-export to an urban-industrial base (Bielschowsky, 2012).

In this context, which prevailed immediately after the Second World War through the end of the 1980s, the goal was to overcome two dimensions of backwardness through planned state interventions, being the productive specialization of the periphery and its profound structural heterogeneity, thereby strengthening an institutional context (Bertola and Ocampo, 2012; Bielschowsky, 2009) that had received little stimulus for innovation and the dissemination of technical advancement.

The most complete formulation on the challenges of the social from the initial construction of Latin American structuralist thought may perhaps be found in Aníbal Pinto's (2000 [1970]) classic works on the region's structural heterogeneity,[3] one of the great obstacles to the full development of productive forces and capitalist social relations. Structural heterogeneity here refers to the "coexistence of a labor force employed with elevated levels of productivity (not far from those of the great centers), and "normal" levels (that is, at the rate permitted by available techniques), with a labor force of sharply reduced productivity" (Rodríguez, 2009, p. 323), this latter group poorly paid or paid at subsistence wages, leading to the persistence of structural underemployment (elastic labor supply), restricting the growth of the wage bill, which in turn impedes a rise in employment and salaries and tends to concentrate income in the most productive sectors, with extremely limited scope and magnitude. It should be emphasized that structural heterogeneity concerns not only employment, but also the productive structure itself.

In Rodríguez's words, "the image before us is that of economies that see their growth limited, if not impeded, by repeated shortfalls in the expansion of demand for various kinds of consumer goods, which may be decisively related to income distribution profiles marked by high concentration, this linked to the superabundance of labor and consequent limitations on rising salaries" (2009: p. 319). From this angle, the impediment to the advancement of market societies in Latin America lay above all in the absence of mechanisms for expanding consumption, it being constrained by low productivity and the persistent abundance of labor that is rudimentary from a technical point of view. In other words, "the dynamic action [that] operates on the supply side as well as around demand for final consumer goods" (Furtado, 2013 [1961]: p. 118) was not materializing.

Pinto, in refuting dualist theses,[4] recognizes that in central postwar economies, the long-term tendency towards the homogenization of the system through the convergence of productivity levels across sectors was not exclusively the product of market forces or economic policies, but was driven by social policies as well.[5] In his words, this convergence was not "a totally spontaneous or natural tendency" (2000: p. 574 [1970]).

In pointing out that the "capacity to spread or stimulate the modern sector was revealed [in Latin America] to be far less than expected, to say the least" (2000: p. 575

---

3   According to Octavio Rodríguez, the seminal concept was first formulated by Prebisch in his 1948 manifesto. (Heterogeneidad Estructural y Empleo, *Revista de la CEPAL*, special number, 1970).

4   Given our focus on the CEPAL school of thought, we have deliberately not introduced Francisco de Oliveira's lucid, constructive, and vigorous critique of dualist thinking.

5   See, on this, Simões (2012), who describes in his thesis, using Polanyi's contribution, how economic policy is successfully molded to social policy without dominating it. Due to a lack of space, this point cannot be developed here.

[1970]), leading to a deepening of the degree of heterogeneity instead of promoting the homogenization of the global structure, Pinto observes that public spending and social investments that might have compensated by pulling resources from the modern sector to those left on the margins of the benefits of economic growth (the internal periphery, marginalized groups, etc.) did not come through. That is to say, social policy was not integrated into the original structuralist framework, which quite probably strengthened the model's concentration-oriented deviations, while it expanded through "sumptuary" consumption (Pinto, 1970–2000: p. 583) guaranteed to the elites and upper middle classes. The author estimates that, by the late 1960s, 40–50% of the population on the continent was marginalized or not incorporated into the market, excluded in terms of both consumption and occupation.[6] The reproduction of internal peripheries reproduced the subsistence logic without breaking with it, thus compromising the generation of surpluses.

Indeed, original structuralist thought did not press on with its reflection around the need to construct social protection systems as a central element in overcoming the structural heterogeneity characteristic of Latin American economies. What was concretely observed was subordinating social security models created over the first three decades of the 20th century to structuralism's mold, in response to the process of economic modernization that served to shift the axis of capital accumulation towards urban-industrial activities. These models proved incapable of fomenting greater social cohesion and homogeneity.

In broad strokes, the Latin American countries quickest to introduce social protection systems did so in two ways. One path was the result of the democratization of political institutions, where the growing bargaining power of the working class drove the construction of pension and healthcare systems, in a few cases covering the portion of the population outside the labor market. This process was most intense in Uruguay—slightly less so in Chile—where the demands of the large working class found support in a democratic government committed to social development (Huber and Stephens, 2012).

The second form, more present in the Brazilian and Argentine cases, saw social policies used to *coopt* the working class, which was exerting pressure on the authoritarian administrations of Vargas and Perón. Through labor legislation (Mesa-Lago, 2007), centralization of the control and management of the pension system and control of unions and political parties, the populist governments of these two countries began regulating the action of the working class (Fleury, 1994). In both, the institutionalization of social policies came about in an environment characterized by authoritarianism, where citizenship was regulated (Santos, 1979), and conceded only to workers linked to the formal market for urban work, which was quite restricted in many cases.

In not conceiving and formulating social policy as a means for changing social relations, the Latin American developmentalist state displayed severe short-sightedness in its early days, neglecting to acquire the means and mechanisms that might broaden the internal market and homogenize the economic system through homogenizing the social element, also contributing to the incorporation of technical progress on a growing scale through mass consumption. In the structuralists' original terms, the heart of the social lay in addressing the issue of land. Their strategy consisted of redistributing the means of production and land

---

6   In Brazil, as Dedecca (2005) has argued, the absence of social policies that might provide the foundation for solid economic growth in the period largely led to the segmentation of the Brazilian labor market, characterized by high levels of informality and by an excess of labor, factors that were apparently responsible for the "wretched income distribution associated to that development process" (p. 101).

access through agrarian reform so as to destabilize the logic and concentrating mechanisms of landed estates and progressively overcome structural heterogeneity and its crippling effect on the elastic labor supply. This radical proposal sought to promote a degree of land redistribution so as to absorb the labor surplus in agricultural disputes; instead of migrating to cities and lowering the value of urban-industrial labor, the agricultural workforce would be "pared down." The various models of agrarian reform introduced in the region over the course of the 20th century, however, were similarly unable to achieve this (Thorp, 1998).

In our understanding, first-generation structuralist thought read the issue of the social as essentially a "concentration of factors" (land, in this case), which was compromising investment and change in the technological base.

However, we might refer to a perspicacious observation from Pinto that would pass unnoticed even during the reformulation of post-'90 structural thought. To wit, "'consumption financing' takes on equal or greater importance (especially in our countries) than the 'investment financing'" (2000: p. 584 [1970]).

Without continuing in a formulation as to how to incentivize consumption financing beyond salary increases tied to productivity gains, thus ignoring the central role played by social policy in this process, Pinto merely sketches out a solution to the damming of demand. This inversion of the terms of the equation of the model never gained strength among structuralists, only *ex-post*, during the new phase of economic growth of the 2000s. This was the missing link in the structuralist and neo-structuralist models for overcoming the obstacles of persistent structural heterogeneity, promoting the expansion of the market society through social policy, just as expressed in Polanyi (1944).

Not only did structuralist thinking come around slowly to the relevance and centrality of social policy in promoting development, it, in implementing this point with a stark delay, privileged the problem of incorporation into the consumer market in a blow to the genuine logic of equity, thus compromising the goal to overcome Latin America's heterogeneity. Aníbal Pinto's insight would ultimately gain adherence on the margins of the structuralist framework, through both redemocratization, forcing governments to consider the vote of the masses, and the prevalence of the model of social risk management (Holzmann and Jorgensen, 2000) put forth by neoliberalism, remade in the social protection floor (ILO, 2011; Fagnani in this book), where consumers replace citizens (Lavinas, 2013).

Neo-Structuralism and the Restoration of the Social, *Pauvreté Oblige* (Post-1990)

In Rodríguez's (2009) view, structuralist thinking renews itself in the 1990s in incorporating the challenge of equity as raised by Fajnzylber (1990). One might recall that indices of poverty and indigence rose significantly in the region during the critical years of the 1980s. While the proportion of the poor rose from 40.5% in 1980 to 48.4% in 1990, the percentage of the indigent went from 18.6% to 22.6% over the same period. In 1990, Latin America could count the stunning sum of 203 million people living in poverty, as opposed to 136 million ten years before (CEPAL, 2012). The lost decade and the deepening of social issues made it imperative to rethink a development strategy that might include some form of redistribution.

Fajnzylber then argued for a new model of industrialization that would incorporate technical advancement incrementally and promote equity, filling the so-called "empty box" in allowing Latin America to share growth with greater redistribution, just as was the case in the 1970s and '80s in countries such as Portugal, Spain, South Korea, and

Israel, among others. This "new industrialization," as he dubbed it, ought to "bring along with it an improvement in income distribution, [and thus] in standards of social equity" (Rodríguez, 2009: p. 35), the only way to incorporate the bulk of the population into the "new alliance" for development. To this end, it should surmount "the central feature of the process of development in Latin America [which] has been its inadequate adoption of technical progress" (Fajnzylber, 1990) within the productive system, and from there overcome underdevelopment.

Fajnzylber credits the state with the role of associating the increase in productivity to "redistributive patterns that sustain increments of the demand for goods and services, these being compatible with the turnover (sale) of similarly expanding production" (Rodríguez, 2009: p. 36). Only in opening the *black box* of technical advancement and innovation would it be possible to change the social structure and promote development as a complete process (CEPAL, 1990; CEPAL, 2000: p. 10), thus creating inclusion.

The question is, where does social policy fit in this new model, which puts forth and bases itself on equity, not competitiveness (Fajnzylber, 2000: p. 886 [1990])? What shape does it take on, since market expansion is always molded by the characteristics of society (Polanyi, 1944)? In the early structuralist phase, consumption expanded freely, as it was restricted to the peripheral elites who adopted "consumption patterns similar to those in countries where the level of capital accumulation was much higher and impregnated with a culture driven by technical progress" (Furtado, 2013: p. 179 [1973]). Hence, the glaring lack of redistributive mechanisms that might back up a steady trajectory towards surmounting underdevelopment.

Hence Furtado's dubbing such a process "modernization" (2013: p. 180 [1973]): when industrialization stops import substitution so as to meet the demands of more sophisticated consumption patterns, it is done without the corresponding process of capital accumulation and incorporation of technical progress, which would allow for innovation to be internalized by the productive system. This modernization mirrors a larger phenomenon of dependence,[7] which expresses "the persistent disparity between consumption levels (eventually including part of working-class consumption) and capital accumulation in production" (2013: p. 186 [1973]), as well as productivity gains.

Seeking an alternative to the pressure built up by this modernization, incapable of transforming the productive structure or homogenizing keenly unequal Latin American societies, Fajnzylber introduces the themes of equity and social justice, albeit without laying out how to make them into the principle for structuring and coordinating the other goals in his famous sequence.[8] In the 1990 document *Transformação Produtiva com Equidade* [Productive Transformation with Equity], neither does CEPAL explain in detail how such a turn might be produced, rather simply mentioning the need to "improve income distribution" (2000: p. 892 [1990]) and bring industrialization and technical progress to other sectors, agriculture, and services. Some initiatives are launched through the choice of policies that may meet the "imperative of equity" and reorient productive dynamics, the core of them being technical services, training, support for microbusinesses, redrawing tax policy (to

---

7   By dependence, Furtado means the phenomenon in which a country "maintains itself in the position of cultural satellite to central countries in the capitalist system, and finds itself in a phase of capital accumulation far inferior to that of the latter" (2013: p. 184 [1973]).

8   According to the author, economic theory that prioritizes competitiveness to promote growth begins with the former principle and seeks to have equity as its output. In his proposal, the following equation is inverted: equity => austerity (understood as a change in consumption patterns) => growth => competitiveness.

raise savings) and, more generally, "fit social services to the needs of the poorest sectors." In terms of institutional reforms, no reference is ever made to social protection systems as an indispensable pillar for structural transformations focused on reducing the elevated degree of social and productive heterogeneity. The strategy boils down to improving labor input through systems for training, accessible education, adult education, and vocational retraining (CEPAL, 2000: p. 901 [1990]).

Bielschowsky (2009: p. 177; p. 183) recognizes that education and knowledge appear as a prime vector that might ultimately guide changes in the social structure through the expansion of employment and salaries, and thus the wage bill. This is to say that, once again, the raising of work productivity takes on central importance in the neo-structuralist framework, now shot through by a discourse of equity. The latter, as in the seminal phase (1948–1989), is now conceived through the lens of surmounting the structural labor surplus through professional and vocational training.

One can glean from the publications and writings ballasting the strategy for facing down the expanding neoliberal wave, amidst societies' opening up to democracy, that social integration should be fomented through the creation of mid-sized and small microbusinesses, functioning at minimum standards of efficiency. With the defeat of agrarian reform, this new, strongly liberal-hued model has turned to absorbing the labor surplus, an effort now cast in terms of the autonomous worker and micro-business owner in the great cities being swelled by the swift process of urbanization. This effort would apparently lead to the reduction of underemployment and contribute to the expansion of the mass domestic market. In parallel, education, when prioritized, would improve the qualifications of the labor force, backing up an increase in productivity and then in salaries. Bielschowsky (2009: p. 175) also sees mobilization around the return to a democratic order as a path to reconfigure, this time in a virtuous dynamic, the relationship between the structure of supply and demand, previously decentralized (hampering the market society and the wage bill, with consequences not only in terms of concentration of wealth and keen inequality, but also in the reproduction of underdevelopment.)

Social policy as a strong institutional element of an integrated, reflexive, and diverse system of social protection, in the forms that backed up economic growth in the European welfare states and even in the United States,[9] is not proposed in the neo-structuralist framework. According to Rodríguez, once again, "Latin American structuralism tends to consider the state and the sociopolitical relationships that sustain it as key in the search for and choosing of alternatives" (2009: p. 48), thus ruling out a possible, functional mediation of social policy in redesigning social relationships and fomenting development.

The neo-structuralist perspective (Bielschowsky, 2009) finally comes to fruition in the 2000s with the return to and renewed interest in state intervention in the economy, no longer exclusively tied to the expansion and diversification of the industrial sector alone, but also with a more homogenous and broader view of development.

The main novelty of the wave of economic growth post-2003–4 seems to be the fact that mass consumption has finally set in, notably through a rise in employment and salaries and a considerable broadening of credit availability (a new factor in the Latin American context), making the mass domestic market one of the drivers of the return to development. One may thus affirm that the innovation of the 2000s was that "modernization" came to

---

9   The creation of Social Security in 1935, with public social security and unemployment insurance, in addition to other forms of income guarantees through targeted policies. For more on this, see Krugman (2007).

the working classes as well, through the extension of a consumption pattern previously restricted to the lifestyles of the middle classes, such as cars, appliances, electronics, and a number of other goods. Fajnzylber's critical reading of the Latin American development model of the 1980s, cited in the epigraph to this chapter, remains uncomfortably relevant and fits like a glove when introducing the topic of the next section, which addresses the social regulation model in vogue in the region. In his words, in Latin America, "physical objects have been transplanted to a greater extent than the know-how and the institutions required to design, produce, and adapt these objects to local conditions" (1990: p. 20), promoting the "convergence of 'showcase modernness'" (1990: p. 26).

21st-Century Structuralism: Links between Social and Economic Policy?

Latin America in the 21st Century: Growth and incorporation into the market

The 2000s saw an important watershed across Latin America, especially after 2003, when the region entered a promising phase of strong economic recovery, with an average GDP growth rate around 4.1% from 2004–2013, as opposed to an average of 2.7% from 1984–2003 (IMF, 2014). In addition to riding the wave of rising commodity prices worldwide, given its abundance of natural resources, Latin America also moved to consolidate its macroeconomic and institutional fundamentals (Bellefontaine and Rharrab, 2014), further favoring a successful recovery out of the crisis.

Another characteristic of this clear bounce-back is the increasingly intense advance of the service sector, which came to 64% of regional GDP in 2013. Regional industry remains lacking, hit hard by international competition and reduced competitiveness, given the resilience of low productivity levels in the manufacturing sector, which was even more severely struck by the effects of exchange rate appreciation.

The most influential factor in growth is family consumption—which comes to 2/3 of Latin America's GDP—in a reflection of the increase in employment, salaries, and credit. According to Bellefontaine & Rharrab, "between 2004 and 2013, 85% of regional growth has come from the accumulation of production factors, labor in particular. The great contribution from labor input, which has been constant over the past 20 years, may be explained by the rise of the working-age population, an increase in their participation in the job market, the drop in unemployment, and an improvement in human capital" (2013: p. 23).

Indeed, between 2003 and 2012, the urban unemployment rate fell from 11.1% to 6.4% in Latin America (CEPAL/ILO, 2014: p. 28), a noteworthy performance, although this downward trend has favored women less, with a rate of 7.4% as opposed to 5.4% for men. Employment rates went up, as did the gross employment rate.[10] In parallel, informality saw a slight dip and went from an approximate rate of 50% in 2003 to 46.7% in 2012 (CEPALSTAT)[11], leading to a broadening of formalized wage labor and the presence of entrepreneurs in the employed population (CEPAL, 2014: p. 140). Even so, informality remains a registered trademark of the region.

---

10   The gross employment rate rose 5.7% from 2003–2010, off a negative figure (-0.6%) from the previous period (1991–1998) (CEPAL, 2012: p. 206).

11   According to the OIT (2013), informality rates (for non-agricultural work) oscillated across Latin America and the Caribbean, from 40% in Uruguay to 75% in the Plurinational State of Bolivia.

In terms of productivity, today's bottlenecks were already seen as problems in the 1950s (see Bielschowsky 2015 in this book). Apparent labor productivity (GDP/ employed population) grew 1.6% p.a. from 2002–2012, reverting the poor showing of the period 1990–2002 (0.1%). However, the agricultural sector[12]—characterized by low productivity—would see the greatest productivity gains of the turn of the century: an increase of 47% from 2002–2011, against just 9% for the manufacturing sector over the same period (CEPAL, 2014: p. 147–148). Product per employee in the high-productivity sector[13] was, in 2011, 5.8 times that of its low-productivity counterpart. In 2002, the ratio was just a bit higher, at 6.4 times. This means that the challenge of social and productive heterogeneity persists, and continues to undermine the creation of a more integrated and converging dynamic with the dissemination of a more equitable pattern of growth. The low-productivity sector, which includes agriculture, commerce, and services, still accounted for 65% of employment in the region in 2011, as opposed to 69% in 2002. Likewise, its size as a percentage of regional GDP remained practically unaltered during the period, around 40% (CEPAL, 2014).

In a recent study that examined seven Latin American countries,[14] Bielschowsky et alii (2013) confirm this trend, estimating that from 1950 to 1980, total productivity grew, on average, 2.4% p.a., led by industry, with an annual growth rate of 3.2%. In contrast, the recent period of 1980–2005 saw total productivity rise just 0.1% p.a. in the region, this time with agriculture at the fore (2.4% p.a.). Labor productivity in industry, across this sampling of countries, showed mediocre growth (0.8% p.a.). The service sector, meanwhile, saw a negative figure (-0.8%). By way of comparison, Asia (six countries),[15] average labor productivity across all sectors rose 2.9% p.a. over the same period, with sectorial performance of 3.7% p.a. in industry, 2.6% p.a. in agriculture, and 1.5% in services.

The absence of a solution for challenges around labor productivity in Latin America is thus patently apparent, with persistent profound structural heterogeneity, given the hypertrophy of the low-productivity tertiary sector (Bielschowsky, 2013). The rebound of economic activity, with a rise in employment, remuneration, and the advance of formalization did not manage to derail this endogenous, structural mechanism for reproducing the region's inequalities.

As has been amply stated, the minimum wage, with a strong and long-standing institutional framework in the region,[16] becomes a key instrument within the equation for stimulating consumption and a prime instrument for social policy in the hands of the state. According to CEPAL (2014), the real minimum wage went from $158 in 2002 to $298 in 2011, with a little leg up from the exchange rate appreciation prevalent in the region during the period. The rise in the national minimum remuneration, which spreads gains to workers beyond the growth of labor productivity, stands as the principal mechanism for primary distribution, via the labor market.

---

12   A similar diagnosis to that of Lora and Pagés (2011), in which, compared to the rest of the world, labor productivity in Latin America only performed favorably in agriculture, with practically zero growth in the service sector and improvements below the international average in industry.

13   According to CEPAL (2014), this category includes financial services, electricity, mining, real estate, and business services.

14   To wit, Argentina, Brazil, Chile, Mexico, Venezuela, Colombia, and Peru.

15   Here, China, India, South Korea, Thailand, the Philippines, and Indonesia.

16   On this, see CEPAL (2014), with a detailed analysis of the policy for real increases in the minimum wage in Latin America starting in the early 2000s (pp. 152–160), and its impact on reducing inequalities.

A number of authors (Lavinas, 2013a; Inchauste et al., 2012), as well as CEPAL (2012) dovetail in recognizing that the pivotal factor in reducing poverty in Latin America over the past decade was the growth in employment. In CEPAL's view, new opportunities in the labor market can explain ¾ of the drop in poverty in the region over the 2000s, with the relevant rate dropping to 27.9% in 2013 (164 million people below the poverty line),[17] as against 43.9% in 2002 (CEPAL, 2013). Interpretations also converge on the point that wage inequality is notably correlated to real gains in the minimum wage.[18]

Meanwhile, conditional cash transfer programs continue to spread, pushing towards incorporation into the market. In little-integrated areas, where a subsistence-oriented mode of social reproduction still persists—for example, in the regions and countries where indigenous communities or small-scale farmers dominate—and for a contingent of tens of millions of the poor and excluded on urban peripheries, with an income deficit that generates negative externalities and restricts solid market functioning, these programs provide, more than basic support, a definitive link with the commodification of a number of areas of life. Nearly all Latin American countries have now adopted conditional cash transfer programs, which are low-cost and have weak institutional backing,[19] but considerable visibility (Lavinas, 2013).

Although social spending has risen from 2002 to 2013, going from 15.2% to 19.2% of the region's GDP (CEPAL, 2013), the area most privileged in this respect has been monetary transfers (around 2/3 of social spending), to the detriment of spending on healthcare, education, housing, and sanitation, which have grown more slowly. Over two decades (1991–2011), while contributory and noncontributory cash transfers rose 3.16% in real terms, healthcare spending rose 1.22%, education 1.9%, and housing just 0.99%. In 2011, deficits in healthcare coverage were high (affecting 1/3 of formal workers and 57% of informal workers, according to the 2013 Social Panorama), just as a considerable percentage of workers did not contribute to social insurance (44.6% of salaried workers and 87.6% of autonomous workers).

This spending profile has thus prioritized correcting market failures instead of stimulating social homogenization, through policies to equalize access to decommodified services, which would certainly bear a much higher cost and demand serious and consequential tax reform, engaged with creating a more far-reaching standard of redistribution.

It thus seems relevant to affirm that, in the 21st century, the role played by social policies in Latin America harbors significant differences from the virtuous role displayed in European countries during the postwar period. The first difference has to do with the timid growth of investment in social infrastructure, the demand for which tends to rise as demographic factors—such as an aging population, a new profile of family arrangements, the lengthening of the educational process for growing contingents of the population—as well as factors intrinsic to the process of capitalist modernization and the broadening of the

---

17   One might note that the poverty line adopted in Latin American countries generally follows the World Bank's guidelines: US$2.25/day, with the indigence line at US$1.25/day.

18   CEPAL (2014) recognizes "that minimum wages have an impact across the distribution (lighthouse effect) and that real increases have had an equalizing effect on distribution" (p. 152), demonstrating how the ratio of minimum wage/average and mean salary saw increases in the majority of Latin American countries from 2003–2012, sometimes spectacularly so, as was the case with Argentina and Uruguay.

19   In no Latin American country do these conditional cash transfer programs stand as a right. They may be eliminated or modified by a decision from the central or federal executive branch at any time.

consumer market have pressed for an increase in the provision of public services. Here, the public sector clearly cedes ground to the privatization of a growing array of services, healthcare being the most paradigmatic case, although hardly the only one.[20]

If income rises and the public provision of services continues to register deficits in provision, both in terms of quality and quantity, the advance of private provision is naturally incentivized, with the support of new financial services such as insurance, credit, and private pension funds. The latter have seen strong segmentation, increasingly meeting the needs of all income brackets, although still unable to guarantee ideal coverage or security against risks and uncertainties. The Brazilian case, as discussed in the next section, will illustrate this dynamic.

Another difference in the profile and structure of the prevailing model of social regulation vis-à-vis the more redistributive model implemented in European countries lies in the absence of linkages in the formation of a virtuous circle between production and mass consumption, with the weakest tie being not only low productivity levels, but also low investment rates, which, despite a rising trend over the decade, have consistently fallen short of the levels necessary to drive more active, sustained growth. The investment rate stands at 23% of the regional GDP (Bellefontaine and Rharrab, 2014). If we consider the investment rates of the countries with the largest economies, such as Argentina, Chile, Brazil, Uruguay, and Mexico, only Chile saw investments at 25.6% of GDP[21] in 2012.

Finally, one might recall the strong expansion of credit in the region, which, on average, rose from 31% of GDP in 2004 to 38.5% in 2011 (annual growth rate of 9%).[22] As Hansen and Sulla (2013) indicate, credit to families accelerated much faster than corporate credit, with emphasis on consumer credit, followed by housing loans. Consequently, the role of credit in driving innovation, disseminating it throughout the productive structure and promoting the concentration of capital indispensable for economic development, seems to have been left aside as the leading tendency in the expansion of credit and financial markets on the Latin American continent.

We argue that the Brazilian case is extremely illustrative of this strategy of stimulating consumption through expanded access to the credit market and the appropriation of social policy to guarantee the growth of domestic demand from a perspective of monetization and commodification instead of strengthening and consolidating social protection systems. Despite a few important counter-reforms, such as i) the re-nationalization of Argentine pensions in 2008; ii) the creation of a basic solidary pension, public retirement funds for poor seniors who did not contribute to social security, as was the case in Chile (2008); and iii) Renta Dignidad, in Bolivia, a public universal pension scheme, or the resilience of Social Security in Brazil (see Fagnani's chapter in this collection) amidst pushes to dismantle its financial architecture (Lavinas, 2014; Fagnani and Vaz, 2013), it is clear that social protection systems remain either unfinished or at risk, as they lack an equally essential

---

20 Due to a lack of space, we will simply cite a few examples that show that families' private spending (out of pocket and private insurance) holds the greatest weight in the region. In the case of Colombia and El Salvador, such spending represents 45–49% of total spending on healthcare. In Brazil, Mexico, Peru, and Uruguay, meanwhile, the private portion of healthcare spending varies between 54% and 63% (data for 2009 to 2011), tending to trend upward (Sanchez, 2014). Universal public healthcare has not been a part of the redistribution of welfare on the continent.

21 For a parallel, recall that the Asian countries had investment rates lower to Latin American ones in the 1960s, and saw them rise steadily starting in the 1970s.

22 This dynamic varied significantly from country to country. Brazil, Paraguay, and Venezuela stand out over this period as the countries with the swiftest expansion of credit.

dimension of social policy, being the provision of universal public services to the whole of the population, swimming against the tide of commodification and the conditionalities that regulate and restrict access to assistance programs.

A "fractured" paradigm is thus implemented; instead of promoting the decommodification of the workforce, it incentivizes commodification all the way down (Fraser, 2012), subordinating social policy to economic policy, the former understood simply as a multiplier to foment growth and the expansion of the domestic market in the short term.

Brazil as Illustration of the Model of Commodification of Social Policy

The ideas from this new cycle of growth have not moved away from the liberal field, although they have shifted somewhat in relation to the policies in place over the course of the 1990s (especially in the need for exchange rate devaluation and a raise in salaries). The heart of the proposals revolved around the urgency of expanding markets, with the state tasked with guaranteeing macroeconomic stability by controlling relative prices. In this model, redistributive issues would be secondary, without taking on crucial importance in pushing growth, although Brazil—in this sense a mirror of Latin America—saw a reduction in its levels of inequality and poverty post-2000, swimming against the tide of the trend in developed countries (see Therborn's chapter in this collection).

Since then, successive administrations[23] have put greater emphasis on a tripod of policies for stimulating domestic demand—increases in social spending, especially cash transfers; a policy of raising the real minimum wage; and expansion of personal credit, all this set against a panorama of growth with increased employment. This model, which Carneiro (2012) and Bastos (2012) have called social developmentalism, seeks to solve a series of structural bottlenecks via the expansion of the domestic consumer market, chief among its aims a greater diversification of the productive sector, which would drive a rise in productivity levels so as to overcome severe social and productive heterogeneity.

In broad strokes, social developmentalism may be defined as a model that includes something close to one of the principal ideas of original structuralism—to wit, an emphasis on the growth of the mass consumer market—but, unlike the first wave, it includes the social dimension of market incorporation as a central pillar in Brazilian developmental strategy rather than simply focusing on supply.

In other words, the development of productive forces, seen by structuralism as the principal means for national development, is driven in new developmentalism by a series of policies focused on incorporating the population into the consumer market.

Though it does not provide a defined theoretical framework, comprising rather an array of practical initiatives rooted in a political base with powerful social appeal (Carneiro, 2012), new developmentalism does not set out to break with the primacy of the market. In fact, the group of policies that characterize it seek to expand mercantile relations through the broadening of consumption of goods and services of all kinds across all levels of society.

---

23 Here we are referring essentially to the second Lula administration, post-2006, and the Dilma administration (begun in 2011).

It has been estimated that between 2003 and 2012, 18.7 million formal jobs[24] were created in Brazil, while average labor income[25] saw a real increase on the order of 30% over the same period (Lavinas, 2014). The unemployment rate, meanwhile, fell from 12.4% in 2003 to 5.4% in 2013 (IBGE, PME). Not even this could cut the rate of informality at the pace expected, stalling at a still-elevated level of 42%.

In analyzing the policy tripod mentioned above, it becomes evident that social spending increases as a portion of GDP, reaching 23.5% in 2011. As in Latin America as a whole, the bulk of this spending comes in the form of direct cash transfers (15% of GDP or 2/3 of social spending), predominating in terms of in-kind modalities (Lavinas, 2013a; see Hermann and Gentil's chapter in this collection) for the same year. If one considers federal social spending alone for the period 2000–2010, a similar trend emerges: direct cash transfers[26] represented 69% in 2010, almost identical to the 2000 figure (68.8%) (IPEA, 2012).[27]

As for the minimum wage, its real value practically doubled between 2001 and 2013[28] (see chapters by Saboia 2015, and Hermann and Gentil, in this collection). It was responsible for 75% of the reduction in wage inequalities over the decade (*Valor Econômico* 2014). Since the minimum wage is a peg for the social security floor,[29] it also allowed pension and retirement funds to have a significant impact on the drop in the Gini index, which fell from 0.593 in 2001 to 0.529 in 2011, where it stabilized.

More jobs and rising labor income led to the broadening of work remuneration as a portion of GDP, when measured through the lens of income, revealing increased labor input in the composition of national product. From 2000 to 2009—the last year of the series made available by IBGE's System of National Accounts—the wage bill went from 46.7% to 50.6% (Hallak Neto, 2013). This meant that in Brazil, family consumption, which oscillated around 60% from 2003–2012 (see, on this, Hermann and Gentil in this collection), drove economic growth forward.

Finally, one might look to the behavior of credit, which broadened stunningly over the decade, soaring from 22% of GDP in 2001 to 56.5% in December 2013 (BACEN, 2014). By the end of 2013, free credit came to 56.6% of the total volume of credit. This led to an explosion in sales, which more than doubled in volume from 2003 to 2014 (IBGE, Pesquisa Mensal de Comércio). Input from family income consequently rose over the course of the decade, going from 18.3% to 45.5% from 2005 to 2014 (Figure 5.1), growing faster than average income.

Such spectacular progress should be seen in a context of creating new forms of credit[30] meant to resolve inefficiencies around access to financial markets, especially related to

---

24   RAIS—CAGED, Ministério do Trabalho.

25   Estimated in 2013 at R$2,000.00 per month (constant values), while they had stood at R$1,494.00 (constant values), US$909 and US$680, respectively.

26   Contributory pension benefits, and also assistance benefits.

27   Within the rubric of direct cash transfers, only the Benefício a Servidores Públicos Federais (Benefit for Federal Civil Servants) saw a steady drop as a percentage of spending from 1995 on (IPEA, 2012).

28   In January 2014, the minimum wage stood at R$724.00 or US$330 per month.

29   2/3 of retirement and pension funds in Brazil, for a total of 21 million in monthly benefits, are set at the minimum wage.

30   Two types of lines of credit have grown significantly since late 2003. One is consigned loans for formal workers and civil servants, instituted in December 2003 under the first Lula administration. In September 2004, they would be extended to retirees and pensioners under the general social welfare policy. In the so-called *Personal Loan With Payroll Discount*, the value of repayment installments is compulsorily and directly taken from salaries or benefits, and interest rates charged by banks or

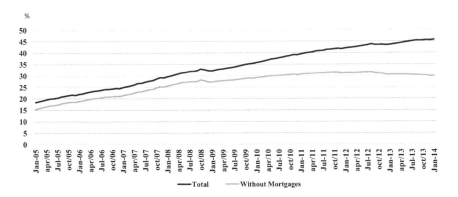

Figure 5.1   Household debt level* Brazil (2005–13)

Source: Banco Central do Brasil.

* In relation to income accumulated over past twelve months.

high interest rates—which, albeit sinking over the past decade, and although inflation has remained under the limit of the current target (6.5%), still rank among the highest in the world. This evidently penalizes family income seriously, but does not hamper consumption, which is pushed on principally by the extension of repayment terms. Figure 5.2 shows the evolution of interest rates on individual loans, demonstrating that the credit supply is strongly segmented. For those with some kind of collateral, such as pension funds or a permanent position (civil servant or formally employed stable worker), consigned credit[31] guarantees lower rates, around 30% p.a. For the rest, being workers and people in more vulnerable and unstable situations, without collateral, rates on personal credit—especially for financing consumption—can be triple that, with rising figures that vary from 75% to 95% p.a.

In terms of hopes for changes in the productive structure and for a rise in labor productivity, the situation is quite different. Indeed, the Brazil of the 2000s still displays relatively low productivity levels. Figure 5.3 shows that the three sectors where productivity[32] rose significantly were agriculture and animal husbandry, extractive industries, and commerce, with the former two undoubtedly spurred by the commodities boom over the course of this decade, with prices trending strongly upwards. The sector most favored by job creation, meanwhile, service, saw the sharpest fall in productivity (-4.2%), followed by industry (-2.8%). For these sectors, the growth in employed personnel exceeded value added.

These data suggest that, despite a record number of formal jobs being created, Brazil did not attain greater homogeneity in its productive structure.

But what might have favored a strong rise in productivity in the agriculture and animal husbandry sector, for example? Our hypothesis is that, beyond a considerable rise

---

financial or credit institutions are lower than market levels, as these borrowers offer collateral. The maximum period for paying off this kind of loan is 72 months. Such loans to individuals fall under the category of free credit. The other kind of loan that saw considerable growth, but under the category of directed credit, was microcredit, which includes personal credit and has taken in growing numbers of the poorest and most vulnerable groups, contributing to finance consumption (Soares, 2014).

    31   According to BACEN, as of December 2013, consigned credit represented 28.9% of personal credit.

    32   Productivity was calculated using the ratio between added value and employed personnel in each sector of economic activity.

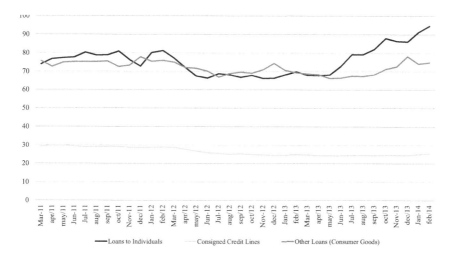

Figure 5.2   Average interest rate—loans to individuals (2011–2013)
Source: Banco Central do Brasil

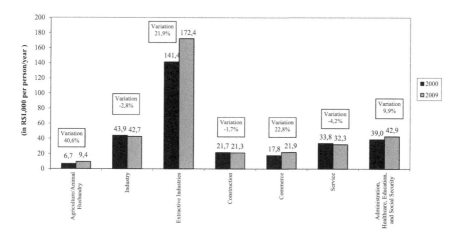

Figure 5.3   Productivity rate* by sectors of economic activity Brazil—2002/2009
Source: Own elaboration based on data from IBGE - Sistema de *Contas Nacionais
            do Brasil.*
Note: *2002 figures were inflated to 2009 prices, using the GDP deflator.

in commodity valuations, a given framework for social and economic policy contributed
to paring down the workforce surplus. On one hand, poverty-fighting policies, via cash
transfer programs, wound up taking their beneficiaries out of the job market or reducing the
pressure that they exerted, thus diminishing severely low-productivity underemployment.[33]

---

33   From 2000 to 2009, agricultural employment as a portion of the Brazilian occupational
structure fell from 22.3% to 17.3% (IBGE, 2014). In absolute terms, there was a reduction of 4.7% in

In the absence of agrarian reform, which lost steam over the course of Lula's two terms and now the Dilma administration, it fell to social poverty-fighting policy to guarantee monetary minimums through the Bolsa Família Program and rural welfare, ensuring incorporation into the consumer market. On the other hand, the national minimum wage aided in homogenizing the lower limit of labor remuneration (through the increase in the minimum wage), while political decisions from the federal executive branch elevated the poorest sectors' propensity to consume, thus raising demand. With the reduction in the labor surplus, which had been holding back an increase in the base salary, not only could the lower limit be raised, but the average salary could rise as well.

It is plausible to suppose that social protection, a minor player, and one nearly absent in the previous phases of economic growth, has been successful as a strategy to foment demand and the expansion of the mass market at the turn of the 21st century, compensating in some measure for the absence in productivity gains that ought to have been observed throughout the productive structure in the wake of growth. The goal of market incorporation implies a guarantee of income, this being a prominent framework in social policy in Brazil as well as Latin America as a whole, during this phase of economic recovery marked by the predominance of governments recognized as center-left.

With this, the country's notorious dynamic insufficiency—to wit, the persistence of structural underemployment, which hinders development—is partially addressed, not by increments in productivity spread throughout the economy, with substantive transformations in the productive structure and employment (both lacking, for example, in the key industrial sector), but via institutional changes in the reproduction of the most vulnerable, least-qualified groups, now either placed outside the job market or concentrated in the service sector.

Our hypothesis is that Brazil's recent return to growth was made possible by a certain sort of social regulation, which prioritizes programs and policies that feature income guarantees, alongside the real increase in the minimum wage and the elimination of barriers to the financial market. Other, not less relevant aspects also came into play, such as tax exemption policy, which was called in to compensate for standing structural problems with a not-entirely-successful attempt at remedying Brazil's low competitiveness domestically and abroad (Cordilha, 2014). Social policy thus becomes the mechanism par excellence in the search for a short-term solution for part of the structural underemployment of the low-productivity workforce, reducing its supply on the job market but guaranteeing it as a presence on the consumer market. It does not, however, address the issue of structural heterogeneity, which continues to generate profound inequalities.

Bielschowsky indicates that one of the potential drivers for Brazilian development in the long term of the so-called social-developmentalist phase (post-2006) might be production and mass consumption,[34] as they allow for "a virtuous integration between growth and an improvement in income distribution" (2012: p. 739). But, while chains were undeniably struck away on the consumption side, production displays a less than virtuous dynamic. Figure 5.4, taken from Cordilha (2014), demonstrates not only a fall in the manufacturing industry's input in terms of total value added to the economy from 1996 to 2011, but also reveals, on the external front, "signs of Brazil's strengthening as an exporter of raw materials, given growing dependence on the exportation of non-industrial and low-tech

---

the population employed in this sector, while added value grew 34% over the same period—hence the significant increase in productivity, as shown in Graph 3.

34   The other two factors would be the use of natural resources and investments in infrastructure.

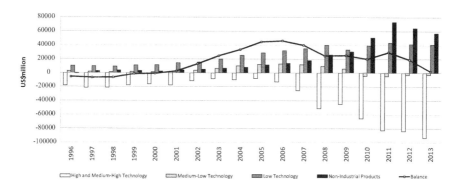

Figure 5.4   Balance of trade by technological intensity, Brazil—1996–2013
Source: SECEX/MDIC. Own elaboration, using information from Cordilha (2014).
*According to OECD classification utilized by SECEX/MDIC.

goods to sustain Brazilian surpluses, alongside a loss of competitiveness in industrial goods, with greater deficits around products of higher technological intensity" (p. 3). The growing importation of manufactured goods may be seen in Brazil's 11-place leap in just seven years on the international ranking of the largest importers, from 31st place in 2005 to 20th in 2012 (IEDI). One should also recall another factor pushing the expansion of mass consumption domestically, which contributed to putting pressure on imports—the prolonged overvaluation of the Real (Singer, 2012), to the detriment of the manufacturing sector, compensated by ample tax exemptions that wound up hobbling Social Security's budget[35] and any chance of broadening the scope of universal policies such as healthcare.

Without a doubt, the past decade has brought decisive government regulatory action (Furtado, 1987: p. 207), through social policy. However, the fractures in the model of social regulation, dominated by a specific kind of policy, have made it possible to drive the mass consumer market without adequately addressing the persistent bottleneck of structural heterogeneity. This would mean tackling grave problems and long-standing gaps in policy, including agrarian reform (to reduce the concentration of property), the universalization of access to quality healthcare and education, and equalizing well-being, to say nothing of tax reform (to reduce the concentration of income and wealth). If, as Furtado has put it (1987: p. 210), the importance placed on non-economic factors in the interpretation of underdevelopment justifies the label "structuralist," then one may conclude that structuralist thought has finally incorporated social policy into its framework, being a non-economic dimension of the reproduction of life. It is social policy that alters the social structure. But, in recent cases, it has done so oriented almost exclusively towards the incorporating

---

35 A number of authors (Fagnani and Vaz, Fagnani, Cordilha) have called attention to the fact that tax exemptions, particularly via the suspension of employers' contributions to social security, puts the Social Security budget at risk; once in surplus, it may begin incurring deficits. After the 2008–9 crisis, the Brazilian government moved to expand these payroll exemptions, favoring around 50 fairly uncompetitive sectors. Once a temporary measure, it is set to become permanent starting in 2015. According to Treasury estimates, quoted by Cordilha (2014), such exemptions may come to R$21.6 billion or US$ 10 billion in 2014, a figure slightly higher than total annual spending on the poverty-fighting Bolsa Família Program.

previously excluded groups into the consumer market, not prioritizing social inclusion. Herein lies its liberal slant.

The issue at center stage in the structuralist paradigm, the elevation of productivity, is thus tabled.

While in the first generation of structuralist thought the key missing link lay in ignorance of the role of social policy in promoting growth in the middle and long term, this phase of development seems to be lacking in its ignorance of the systemic role of social policy in adequately and effectively addressing the challenge of productivity and equity in the long term, through the promotion of universal and unconditional programs that seek to strengthen mechanisms for increasing social homogeneity, reducing differentials in education, healthcare, well-being, and hence productivity as well. For Furtado, underdevelopment means a disparity between the consumption levels of significant groups of a country's population (1972). It seems evident that such differentials in consumption patterns are increasingly shifting away from durable consumer goods (cars, electronics, or large home appliances), and towards access to often indispensable goods such as water and basic sanitation, and others, such as education and healthcare, that may truly open up opportunities and equalize living conditions and well-being.

In the decade of the return to growth, while consumption boomed, the percentage of households with adequate infrastructure—sanitation, trash collection, and treated water—went from 53.6% in 2001 to 61.8% in 2011. This means that more than a third of Brazilian homes fall short of a decent standard of living. In the case of the lowest-income households—up to half a minimum wage per month—48% still lacked adequate sanitation (IBGE, 2012). The progression of certain other goods, meanwhile, with individualized access mediated by the market, has seen a sharp upward bend. This is the case with cell phones, for example, which are now present in practically 90% of Brazilian households, as opposed to 31% in 2001. The percentages of homes with computers (12.5% in 2001 and 42.9% in 2011) and washing machines (33.6% in 2001 and 51% in 2011) also rose notably.

In a study by the Brazilian Institute of Geography and Statistics (IBGE, 2012), based on a methodology developed by Mexico's Consejo Nacional de Evaluación de la Política de Desarrollo Social—CONEVAL, the population was divided into vulnerable groups, a designation determined not only by income, but other indicators as well that point to the existence of deficits in the population's access to a range of services that are indispensable in social reproduction. First and foremost, the proportion of vulnerable citizens as classified by income[36] and social service deficits[37] still takes in 22.4% of Brazilian, although 34.2% are not affected by either kind of vulnerability. The most interesting factor, however, is that the proportion of the population falling under simply income poverty is 7.4%, while 36% are made vulnerable by some kind of social service deficit. This reveals two things: the first is that the incidence of vulnerability through social service deficits is greater than vulnerability through income poverty alone, and the second is that most people under the latter category also display some social service deficit.

---

36   To calculate income poverty, the study employed a relative measure: the proportion of people earning income below 60% of the median.

37   Social service deficits were defined by a series of indicators, summarized under the following headings: a) educational lag; b) physical characteristics of the household; c) access to basic services; d) access to social security.

As public health suffers from chronic underfinancing in Brazil (Bahia, 2013), despite having the resources of the Social Security budget to better meet demand, private provision advances—while remaining inaccessible to the vast majority of the population. In Brazil, a country with a public, universal, free healthcare system, a victory from the era of redemocratization enshrined in the 1988 Constitution, private spending on healthcare outstrips public. While the former comes to 5.5% of GDP, the second stands at 4%. Moreover, ¼ of the population has private healthcare plans and that figure has only grown along with family incomes,[38] stimulated by tax exemptions.

Likewise, 35% of Brazilian workers did not finish primary school, which becomes an important factor in stubbornly low work productivity. This deficit is mirrored at other educational levels; just 54.4% of 15- to 17-year-olds were enrolled in high school. This explains why, in 2012, only 51.8% of 19-year-olds had graduated high school (INEP). As for higher education, and in spite of university quota programs meant to include ethnic and racial minorities (see Sergio Costa's chapter in this collection), 80% of college students attend private colleges, access to which is generally made possible by student loans obtained via the financial market.

Many performance indicators could be called up on the subject of educational quality, such as the country's clearly unsatisfactory PISA results. Just one figure is enough to shock on this account, however, related to adequate school infrastructure as defined in the PNE (National Education Plan), being access to: treated water and basic sanitation, electricity, high-speed internet, handicapped accessibility, libraries, spaces for sports practice, access to cultural goods and art, and science-related equipment and laboratories. While in 2009, 3.06% of Brazilian schools met those criteria, by 2013 the figure was virtually identical: 4.2% (MEC/Inep/Deed). That is to say, over nearly a decade of growth, crucial investments in social infrastructure did not keep up.

Castro (2013) has estimated the distributive effect of public goods such as healthcare and education, as well as cash transfers. He observes that in the current situation, "increased spending on public healthcare and education generate extremely positive developments, in terms of both growth and income distribution" (2013: p. 130). Targeted transfers, meanwhile (Bolsa Família and BPC) had a smaller impact on growth and slightly more on the drop in inequality. This is a clear indicator that while the current pattern of social spending, mostly focused on cash transfers, may stimulate the domestic market, it contributes less to feeding a virtuous dynamic of long-term economic growth and facilitating the rise of locally produced value added.

We argue that the financing model for mass consumption, adopted in Brazil with relative success under the second Lula administration and under Dilma and meant to stimulate the domestic market and keep the economy functioning closer to its potential by driving job creation, broadened the integration of low-income sectors—and even the poorest—into the market. This integration was also facilitated by consumer credit in its various forms (Minha Casa Melhor[39] and Crédito Caixa Fácil are just two such programs). The extension of the

---

38   According to data from the 2008–2009 Family Budget Survey (POF), the richest families (the highest 10% by income), devoted 42.3% of their monthly spending on healthcare in paying for private plans, on average, while the poorest families (40% of the tail end of the distribution) spent an average of 7%. This tendency is flipped in the case of expenses on medicine, which take up nothing less than 74.2% of monthly health-related spending for the poorest families and 33.6% in the health budgets of the richest families (IBGE, 2012).

39   In June 2013, the federal government launched an exclusive financing line on furniture and household appliances for beneficiaries of the house-purchasing program Minha Casa, Minha Vida.

credit market to the poorest and most destitute classes, with terms strictly regulated by the federal government, is doubtless a novelty and fills an important role in the democratization of consumption. However, this model of social regulation does not promote a process of social homogenization that might overcome profound, inequality-reproducing cleavages. It does remove barriers to integration into the market, but does not facilitate convergence to a standard of well-being increasingly shared by all. The model of market incorporation cannot support a solid and sustainable standard for social inclusion, a middle- or long-term path to the solution for the bottlenecks imposed by the permanence of profound social and productive heterogeneity.

By Way of Conclusion

It is no coincidence that the first strategy for broadening and strengthening capital markets in Latin America consisted of the privatization of public funds, sustaining the regional transition, in the 1990s, from pay-as-you-go systems to capitalization systems (Mesa-Lago, 2009; Lavinas, 2013). This attempt failed in part, and public pay-as-you-go systems had to be reintroduced.

The other strategy for expanding financialization came through the expansion of mass consumption through consumer credit for the most vulnerable, previously excluded groups. Conditional cash transfer programs came to be tied to this logic of market extension, stimulating links between the poorest groups and the financial sector through credit, insurance, and microcredit (Lavinas, 2013; Soares, 2014). In the absence of collateral, a steady (albeit small) income backed by the government opens up opportunities to grow mass consumption through credit, the newest forms of which seek to include groups only recently incorporated into the market. Magnitude guarantees scale. The deficit in the provision of free public services in terms of both quality and quantity, segmenting the market and exacerbating government shortfalls, has driven citizens to credit and insurance markets in search of security. This dynamic produces some negative externalities, such as the increase in family debt, and elevated interest rates drive financial capital gains in turn.

Instead of an expansion in the supply of public goods that equalize opportunities and well-being, what we have seen is the commodification of all aspects of life, under the hegemony of the capital market (private insurance and credit for any sort of misfortune). Only decommodification restricts the functioning of the financial market and its deleterious effects, especially in terms of the reproduction of inequalities. To substitute public goods with private provision is thus to restrict the scope of what ought to be decommodified; and this route will certainly not make us more equal.

Nor will it allow for a successful addressing of the problem of structural heterogeneity, which mirrors deficits in universalization. Fajnzylber's declaration at the start of this chapter obliges us to reflect on the recent trajectories of Latin American governments that used social policy to incentivize market incorporation, scorning true social catching-up—something

---

The expectation is that 3.7 million families will be benefited, for a total of R$18.7 billion. The credit line offers up to R$5,000 per beneficiary. The interest rate is 5% per year, with a repayment term of 48 months. Families will be provided a magnetic Minha Casa Melhor card and given up to 12 months to spend their credit.

only possible when equity-promoting policies are truly a priority on government agendas and within institutions, with a real effect on the distribution of social spending.

This chapter shows that the greatest advances of the decade of the return to growth in Latin America came in the labor market. The decoupling of well-being and income or assets as parameters of true social protection remains incomplete, in part because social protection systems, despite some progress, remain equally incomplete and threatened by weak institutional frameworks.

The vulnerable are guaranteed a level of minimum income defined by extremely low poverty and indigence lines, while in terms of social services and basic rights (where supply and coverage remain deficient and insufficient), they are forced towards the market, thus reducing the already-clipped scope of the public sphere.

We consider Fanjzylber and Furtado's line of argument penetrating and incontrovertible in its indication that both the spread of modern products and the generalization of consumption patterns on industrial goods, once a class differential, has little or no impact on the precarious nature of social relations and regional levels of inequality. What differentiates social protection systems in their classical form is precisely how they combine income guarantees with the unconditional universalization of rights and access. It is no accident that greater consumption and market incorporation sans any commitment to the larger decommodification of services and the deindividualization of the right of access cannot overcome our profound and persistent heterogeneity. But this seems to be of little consequence to those who exalt mass consumer society in Latin America while failing to place us on a sustainable trajectory towards overcoming our asymmetries.

Bibliography

BACEN, Séries temporais, dados sobre crédito.

Bahia, L. (2013). 'Financeirização e restrição de coberturas: estratégias recentes de expansão das empresas e seguros de saúde no Brasil,' in Cohn, A (org.) (2013). *Saúde, Cidadania e Desenvolvimento*. Rio de Janeiro, Centro Internacional Celso Furtado.

Barr, N. (2012). *Economics of the Welfare State*. Oxford, Oxford University Press.

Bastos, P.P. (2012). 'A Economia Política do Novo-Desenvolvimentismo e do Social Desenvolvimentismo.' *Economia e Sociedade*, vol. 21, no. 4, pp. 779–810.

Bellefontaine S. and Rharrab T. (2014). 'Amérique Latine: trajectoires divergentes.' *BNB-Paribas Eco-Conjoncture No. 5*, Paris, Paribas.

Bertola, L. and Ocampo, J.A. (2012). *The Economic Development of Latin America Since Independence*. Oxford, Oxford University Press.

Beveridge, W. (1942). The Beveridge Report, *Report of the Inter-Departmental Committee on Social Insurance and Allied Services*. London, Inter-Departmental Committee on Social Insurance and Allied Services.

Bielschowsky, R. et al. (2013). 'Visão de conjunto,' in Bielschowsky, R. (org.) (2013). *Padrões de Desenvolvimento Econômico (1950–2008). América Latina, Ásia e Rússia*. Brasilia, CGEE.

Bielschowsky R. (2012) Estratégia de desenvolvimento e as três frentes de expansão no Brasil: um desenho conceitual. *Economia e Sociedade*, Campinas, v. 21, Número Especial, pp. 729–747, dez. 2012.

Bielschowsky R. (2010) Sesenta años de la Cepal—Textos seleccionados del decenio 1998–2008. Ricardo Bielschowsky compilador. Santiago de Chile: Siglo XXI y CEPAL.

Bielschowsky, R. (2009). 'Sesenta años de la CEPAL: estructuralismo y neoestructuralismo.' *Revista de la CEPAL,* vol. 97, no. 1, pp. 173–194.

Bielschowsky, R. (org.) (1990). *Cinquenta anos de pensamento na CEPAL.* Rio de Janeiro, CEPAL/COFECON/Record.

Bresser-Pereira, L. (2012). 'Do Antigo ao Novo Desenvolvimentismo na América Latina,' in Delorme Prado, L.C. (org.) (2012). *Desenvolvimento Econômico e Crise.* Rio de Janeiro, Contraponto Editora.

Bresser-Pereira, L. and Theuer, D. (2012). 'Um Novo Estado Novo-Desenvolvimentista na América Latina?' *Economia e Sociedade,* vol. 21, no. 4, pp. 811–829.

Briggs, A. (1961). 'The welfare state in historical perspectives.' *European Journal of Sociology,* vol. 2, no. 2, pp. 221–258.

Carneiro, R. (2012). 'Velhos e Novos Desenvolvimentismos.' *Economia e Sociedade,* vol. 21, no. 4, pp. 749–778.

Castro, J.A. (2013). 'Saúde e Desenvolvimento no Brasil,' in *Saúde, Cidadania e Desenvolvimento,* in Cohn, A. (org.) (2013). *Saúde, Cidadania e Desenvolvimento.* Rio de Janeiro, Centro Internacional Celso Furtado.

CEPAL/ILO (2014). *The Employment Situation in Latin America and the Caribbean.* May 2014, Santiago de Chile, CEPAL.

CEPAL (2013). *Social Panorama of Latin America.* Santiago de Chile, CEPAL.

CEPAL (2012). *Structural Change for Equality. An Integrated Approach to Development.* Santiago de Chile, CEPAL.

CEPAL (2000). *Anuario Estadístico de América Latina y el Caribe.* Santiago de Chile.

CEPAL (1990). 'Transformação Produtiva com Equidade,' in Bielschowsky, R. (org.) (1990). *Cinquenta anos de pensamento na CEPAL.* Rio de Janeiro, CEPAL/COFECON/Record.

Cepeda, V. (2012). 'Inclusão, Democracia e Novo Desenvolvimentismo: um balanço histórico.' *Estudos Avançados,* vol. 26, no. 75, pp. 77–90.

Cohn, A. (org.) (2013). *Saúde, Cidadania e Desenvolvimento.* Rio de Janeiro, Centro Internacional Celso Furtado.

Cordilha, A.C. (2014). *Desoneração da Folha de Pagamentos para "Competitividade Espúria"?* [Online] Plataforma Política Social, Disponível em https:// plataformapoliticasocial2.files.wordpress.com/2014/06/ana-cordilha-competitividade-espuria-da-dfp-jul_14.pdf> (Accessed 10/08/2014).

Dedecca, C. (2005). 'Notas sobre a Evolução do Mercado de Trabalho no Brasil.' *Revista de Economia Política,* vol. 25, no. 97, pp. 94–111.

Delorme Prado, L.C. (org.) (2012). *Desenvolvimento Econômico e Crise.* Rio de Janeiro, Contraponto Editora.

CEPAL (2014). *Compacts for Equality: Towards a Sustainable Future.* Santiago de Chile, CEPAL.

Fagnani, E. and Vaz, F.T. (2014). 'Previdência e Seguridade Social: velhos mitos e novos desafios,' in Fonseca, A. e Fagnani, E. (orgs.) (2014). *Políticas Sociais, Desenvolvimento e Cidadania.* São Paulo, Fundação Perseu Abramo.

Fajnzylber, F. (1990). 'Industrialization in Latin America: From the "Black Box" to the "Empty Box."' *Cuadernos de la CEPAL,* No. 60, Santiago de Chile, CEPAL.

Fleury, S. (1994). 'A montagem do padrão de Seguridade Social na América Latina,' in Fleury, S. (org.) (1994). *Estado sem cidadãos*: seguridade social na América Latina [online]. Rio de Janeiro, Editora Fiocruz.

Fleury, S. (org.) (1994). *Estado sem cidadãos*: seguridade social na América Latina [online]. Rio de Janeiro, Editora Fiocruz.

Fonseca, A. and Fagnani, E. (orgs.) (2014). *Políticas Sociais, Desenvolvimento e Cidadania.* São Paulo, Fundação Perseu Abramo.

Fraser, N. (2012). 'Can Society be Commodities all the Way Down? Polanyian Reflections on Capitalist Crisis.' *FMSH Working Paper No. 18,* Paris, Fondation Maison des Sciences de l'Homme & Collège d'Etudes Mondiales.

Furtado, C. (1961). 'Elementos de uma Teoria do Subdesenvolvimento,' in Freire, R. (ed.) (2013). *Celso Furtado. Essencial.* Rio de Janeiro, Penguin-Cia das Letras.

Furtado, C. (1973). 'Subdesenvolvimento e Dependência: as conexões fundamentais,' in Freire, R. (ed.) (2013). *Celso Furtado. Essencial.* Rio de Janeiro, Penguin-Cia das Letras.

Furtado, C. (1972). 'O subdesenvolvimento revisitado,' in Freire, R. (ed.) (2013). *Celso Furtado. Essencial.* Rio de Janeiro, Penguin-Cia das Letras.

Furtado, C. (1987). 'Underdevelopment: To conform or reform,' in Meier, G. (ed.) (1987). *Pioneers in Development.* Oxford, Oxford University Press.

Hallak, J. (2013). *A Distribuição Funcional da Renda e a Economia não Observada no âmbito do Sistema de Contas Nacionais do Brasil.* Doctoral Dissertation, Universidade Federal do Rio de Janeiro.

Hansen, N-J. and Sulla, O. (2013). 'El crecimiento del credito en America Latina: desarrollo financiero o boom crediticio?' *Revista Estudios Economicos,* vol. 25, no. 1, pp. 51–80.

Harris, J. (1997). *William Beveridge, a Biography.* Oxford, Oxford University Press.

Holzmann, R. and Jorgensen, S. (2000). 'Social Risk Management: A New Conceptual Framework for Social Protection, and Beyond.' *Social Protection Discussion Paper No. 0006,* Washington, DC, World Bank.

Huber, E. and Stephens, J. (2012). *Democracy and the Left. Social Policy and Inequality in Latin America.* Chicago, Chicago University Press.

IBGE. System of National Accounts.

IBGE (2012). 'Síntese de Indicadores Sociais: uma análise das condições de vida da população brasileira.' *Estudos e Pesquisas No. 29,* São Paulo, IBGE.

IBGE. PME—PNAD—POF. Several years.

ILO (2011). *Social Protection Floor for a Fair and Inclusive Globalization.* Geneva, ILO.

IMF (2014). Global Economic Outlook.

Inchauste, G. et al. (2012). 'When Job Earnings are behind Poverty Reduction.' *Economic Premise No. 97,* Washington, DC, World Bank.

INEP (2014). *Observatório do Programa Nacional de Educação.* Brasília, MEC/Inep/ Deed. http://www.observatoriodopne.org.br.

IPEA (2012). 'Gasto Social Federal: prioridade macroeconômica no período 1995–2010.' *Nota Técnica No. 9,* Brasília, IPEA.

Jessop, B. (1993). 'Towards a Schumpeterian workfare state? Preliminary remarks on post-Fordist political economy.' *Studies in Political Economy,* vol. 40, no. 1, pp.7–40.

Krugman, P. (2007). *The Conscience of a Liberal.* New York, Norton.

Lavinas, L. (2014). Brazil: 'A New Path to Equality?' *Paper presented at the Brazil Initiative Seminar "Brazil: From dictatorship to democracy (1964–2014)."* Providence, April 10–12, 2014. Brown University.

Lavinas, L. (2013). '21st Century Welfare century ,.' *New Left Review,* vol. 84, no. 6, pp. 5–40.

Lavinas, L. (2013a). 'Latin America. Anti-Poverty Schemes instead of Social Protection.' *desiguALdades Working Paper No. 51,* Berlin, Freie Universität.

Lora E. y Pagés C. (2011). América Latina: cara a cara con la productividad. *Finanzas & Desarrollo*, marzo de 2011, pp. 16–19.

Meier, G. (ed.) (1987). *Pioneers in Development.* Oxford, Oxford University Press.

Mesa-Lago, C. (2007). *As Reformas de Previdência na América Latina e seus Impactos nos Princípios da Seguridade Social.* Brasília, Ministério da Previdência Social.

Mesa-Lago, C. (2009). *World Crisis Effects on Social Security in Latin America and the Caribbean: Lessons and Policies.* London, Institute for the Study of the Americas.

OIT (2013). La Transición de la Economia Informal a la Economia Formal. Informe V Conferencia Internacional del Trabajo, 103a. Reunión 2013, Geneva.

Palier, B. (2002). *Gouverner la Sécurité Sociale.* Paris, PUF.

Peres, L. (2014). 'A Política do Novo Mínimo,' quoting Prof. Naercio Menezes *Valor Econômico,* 18 July, A6.

Pinto, A. (1970). 'Naturaleza e implicaciones de la "heterogeneidad estructural" de la América Latina.' *El Trimestre Económico*, vol. 37, no. 1, pp. 83–100.

Polanyi, K. (1944). *The Great Transformation.* Boston, Beacon Press.

Prebisch, R. (1949). *O desenvolvimento econômico da América Latina e alguns de seus principais problemas,* in Bielschowsky, R. (org.) (1990). *Cinquenta anos de pensamento na CEPAL.* Rio de Janeiro, CEPAL/COFECON/Record.

Rodriguez, O. (2009). *O Estruturalismo Latino-Americano.* Rio de Janeiro, Civilização Brasileira/CEPAL.

Rosanvallon, P. (2011). *La Société des Egaux.* Paris, Seuil.

Santos, W.G. (1979). *Cidadania e Justiça. A Política Social na Ordem Brasileira.* Rio de Janeiro, Campus Ltda.

Sanchez, D.D. (2014). 'Consumo Efectivo de los Hogares en Salud.' *Serie Estudios Estadisticos No. 83,* Santiago de Chile/Washington, DC, CEPAL/OMS.

Simões, A. (2012) *A Centralidade das Políticas Sociais no Capitalismo: uma análise do caso britânico (1945–2010).* Doctoral Dissertation, Universidade Federal do Rio de Janeiro.

Singer, A. (2012). *Os Sentidos do Lulismo. Reforma Gradual e Pacto Conservador.* São Paulo, Companhia das Letras.

Soares, C.M. (2014). *O microcrédito como instrumento de proteção social: uma análise comparativa de Brasil e Bolívia.* Master's Thesis, Universidade Federal do Rio de Janeiro.

Thorp, R. (1998). *Progress, Poverty and Exclusion. An Economic History of Latin America in the 20th Century.* Washington, IADB.

Chapter 6
Macroeconomic Constraints and Limits on Social Spending: An Analysis of the Period 2003–2012 in Brazil

Jennifer Hermann and Denise L. Gentil

Introduction

The administration of Luiz Inácio Lula da Silva (2003–10) marked a turning point in Brazilian social policy, largely maintained under President Dilma Rousseff (2011–14). After nearly two decades of being relegated to second place (if not last) in terms of government priorities, social policy took on a centrality never before seen in Brazil, albeit sharing the stage with a permanent price-stabilizing policy. This change took place as early as the first year of the Lula administration, with the launch of the Fome Zero (Zero Hunger) Program, a series of integrated initiatives from the federal government, aimed at increasing food access and reducing poverty. In 2004 the policy was joined by Bolsa Família, a minimum-income program, which became the most emblematic manifestation of social policy's change in status in Brazil. Another landmark of the Lula and Dilma administrations has been policy devoted to a real increase in the minimum wage.[1]

The advances born of this directional change in Brazilian economic policy are widely recognized, and may be seen in indicators of income, employment, and access to consumer goods on the part of the low-income population, prime beneficiaries of social programs. On a macroeconomic level, however, a few limitations of the model begin to come into focus after a few years.

On one hand, social policy manifests itself in a tendency towards an increase in federal spending, especially on "transfers" (nonrefundable expenses). Though positive from a social point of view, this tendency runs up against fiscal limits, as social spending competes with other categories in a budget which is doubly limited: by the obvious difficulty in continued revenue expansion, and by its subjection to the model of goals for the primary budget surplus, instituted in 1999 under the administration of Fernando Henrique Cardoso and maintained under Lula and Dilma.

On the other hand, one must recognize that any reduction in poverty and income inequality—the raison d'être of social policy—depends, if only in part, on the level of social spending itself, and even the ways in which it is allocated. An important part of this process is constrained by the macroeconomic environment in which social policies are implemented. This involves all of the government's other economic actions—which

---

1 The period also includes social programs in health, education, credit, and housing, among others. One might note, however, that the Lula administration also passed a reform of Social Insurance which made it more difficult for workers to access their retirement benefits, thus going against the tide of social policy.

may broaden or restrict the space for social policy in the public budget—as well as the economy's performance in general. Beyond influencing the distributive powers of social policies, this environment defines the economy's capacity to create autonomous alternatives for income generation, or "exit doors" for assistance programs—that is, formal, qualified jobs fundamental for improving income distribution as a whole.

The distributive effects of social spending are thus ruled by two heavy constraints: a) the specific institutional framework of each program (target population, conditions for the inclusion or exclusion of beneficiaries, volume of resources applied, among other factors); b) the macroeconomic environment in which said social spending is inserted. This chapter seeks to focus on the latter constraint, with its central objective being a discussion of the *model of macroeconomic policy* employed during the Lula and Dilma administrations (with a focus on the fiscal sector) and its contribution to the distributive effects of its social spending programs.

The chapter will continue for five more sections. Section 2 discusses the principal macroeconomic channels of influence by which public spending affects income distribution. This analysis is theoretically grounded in a Keynesian focus on fiscal policy, which indicates three possible macroeconomic effects of public spending: the *multiplier* effect, which acts on families' consumption—being thus directly related to social policy spending and its distributive impacts; and the *crowding-out* and *crowding-in* effects, which act on private investments, with an indirect influence on the distributive effects of social spending. Sections 3 and 4 provide general descriptions of the model of macroeconomic policy and spending policy, respectively, employed by the Lula and Dilma administrations. Section 5 summarizes the possible channels of influence that these policies may have had on the distributive effectiveness of social policy. Section 6 concludes the chapter.

The Macroeconomics of Public Spending and its Distributive Effects

Public spending in the Keynesian Model

The cornerstone of macroeconomic Keynesian theory is the Principle of Effective Demand (Keynes, 1936: Ch. 3), which dictates that productive activity, responsible for income generation in its various forms (wages, profits, taxes, etc.), is determined by spending (effective demand) by agents—families, businesses, and the government:[2]

[1] $Y = f(C, I, G, NX)$

where Y = aggregate output (Gross Domestic Product—GDP); C = household consumption; I = private investment; G = consolidated public spending (federal, state, and municipal governments, and state-owned enterprises); NX = net external demand (exports minus imports); $f'C, f'I, f'G, f'NX > 0$.

From a Keynesian approach, public spending's first channel of influence over the functional and personal distribution of aggregate income flows from its capacity to *generate* a part of it. In principle, the greater G is, the greater the effective demand, and, ceteris paribus, the greater the income distributed amongst wages, profits, taxes, etc. Apart from this "scale

---

2   For the theoretical basis for the Principle of Effective Demand, see Keynes (1936, 1937, and 1973), Minsky (1975), and Carvalho (1992), among others.

effect," public spending may stimulate private spending in consumption and investment. The former characterizes the multiplier effect of public spending; the latter reflects the *crowding-in* (expansive) and *crowding-out* (restrictive) effects on private investments.

The distributive effects associated to these channels of influence for social spending are also constrained by the specificities of the spending policy in two areas: a) the allocation of G amongst the expenditure categories common to the public sector: consumption, investment; transfers; and financial expenditures (in the service of the public debt); b) its *financing structure*, which the character of the tax burden and the public debt financing G at each cycle. The next subsections will analyze each of these effects and constraints.

Public spending and consumption: The multiplier effect

The multiplier effect on autonomous expenses stems from the positive influence exerted by income, independent of origin, on families' consumption; since, from a Keynesian approach:

[2] $C = c.(1-t).Y,$

where c = marginal propensity to consume; t = the tax burden of the economy; $0 < c < 1; 0 < t < 1$; and, thus, $0 < c.(1-t) < 1$.

As Y also responds positively to increases in C, the multiplier acts through successive decreasing increases in Y and C, which, once summed up, produce a total increase in income, represented as:[3]

[3] $k = dY/dG = 1/[1-c.(1-t)]$

In open economies, a part of this increase in consumption will be satisfied by imports, reducing the multiplier effect to:

[4] $k = dY/dG = 1/[1-c.(1-t) + m]$

where m = the import coefficient of the economy (Froyen, 2001, Ch. 5).

In short, the multiplier effect of G (as with any other autonomous spending) is increased by the propensity to consume and restricted by the tax burden and the import coefficient. Among these constraints, the tax burden is the only variable within economic policy—fiscal policy, as is public spending. As such, it may in theory be administered in coordination with spending policy, so as to potentiate its macroeconomic and distributive effects. The propensity to consume and the import coefficient are structural and parametric variables for fiscal policy, which (alongside other elements) define the macroeconomic environment into which public expenditure policy is inserted.

In addition to cultural factors, the propensity to consume reflects two structural forces (Keynes, 1936: Ch. 9–10): the country's income pattern, as measured by income per capita: the lower the historical level of aggregate and per capita income, the greater the propensity to consume tends to be; and b) the pattern of personal distribution of income in the country: generally, the worse this appears (the greater the concentration), the greater the propensity

---

3   For a formal demonstration of the Keynesian multiplier, see Hermann (1988).

to consume, because, in this case, the relative weight of the low-income population is increased within GDP. The propensity to consume is thus unlikely to act as a restriction on the distributive effectiveness of public expenditure policies, as its macroeconomic effect is favored in the poorest and most socially unequal economies—precisely those most in need of such policies.

The import coefficient, meanwhile, tends to act perversely in such economies—which, on the international stage, are placed in the category of developing nations. One of the defining characteristics of this international position is technological underdevelopment in relation to countries with higher income (Furtado, 1986), reflected in a chronic difficulty to compete in the domestic market (as well as abroad), especially (but not exclusively) in relation to high-value-added products. Given this state of affairs, and unless policies restricting imports are in place, lower-income economies tend to operate with a high import coefficient. Moreover, this coefficient tends to develop procyclical behavior, increasing precisely when aggregate demand is expanding most rapidly. Thus, although the propensity to consume contributes to increasing the multiplier effect of public spending in these cases, much of it will be neutralized by the increase in imports.

The contradictory effects between the variables that determine the magnitude of the multiplier point to the importance of previously mentioned specificities within spending policy.

As regards the allocation of G, the role of the propensity to consume would indicate transfers as the item of greatest distributive impact, as they directly affect the low-income population. The restrictive role of the import coefficient, however, suggests that any public expenditure policy strongly concentrated in transfers will have little efficacy in distributive, macroeconomic, or even fiscal terms. This form of government action tends to worsen the country's position externally, reinforcing its condition as a "less developed country," and thus the need to maintain or even increase fiscal expenditures with transfers. Transfer expenditures would thus ideally be a part of a broader policy of economic development also covering consumer spending and government investment, aimed at bettering the country's position in the international market—via industrial policy, foreign trade, and public investments in infrastructure, health, and education, among other sectors.

At the other end of the spectrum from transfers, one finds spending on interest on the public debt. These expenditures, destined for rentiers—savers and financial institutions that hold part of the debt on the market—with a lower propensity to consume, have a regressive distributive effect and do not contribute positively to the multiplier effect of public spending.

In terms of financing G, it is difficult to indicate an "ideal" structure from a distributive point of view, since both taxation and public debt (which originates interest expenditures) have unfavorable distributive effects. These effects, however, may be attenuated by the type of taxation, allocation of spending, and monetary policy (which affects the cost of the public debt, through interest rate policies).

In the case of taxation, its influence on the multiplier effect is favored by the combination of a progressive tax structure with a redistributive allocation of spending: an increased burden on the higher-income strata, with this revenue allocated to policies targeting the least fortunate classes, can directly increase the propensity to consume and the multiplier effect of public expenditures. As for the debt, if the government's borrowing allows it to sustain or even increase public spending on programs that benefit income redistribution, the unfavorable distributive effects on consumption will be attenuated. Moreover, as an integral (and important) part of the asset market, the public debt also influences the distributive effectiveness of public spending via its effects on interest rates. These, which are the source of the *crowding out* effect, analyzed below, depend in part on monetary policy.

Public spending and investment: The crowding-in and crowding-out effects

The *crowding-in* and *crowding-out* effects (respectively CIE and COE) illustrate the possible influence of public spending on two determinants of aggregate investment, from a Keynesian approach: the long-term expectations that guide the decision to invest, synthesized in what Keynes called the "marginal efficiency of capital" (the rate of return expected on an investment); and interest rates, which, serving as a financial or opportunity cost, compete with the marginal efficiency of capital, limiting or favoring investments.

The CIE comes about when public spending favorably affects long-term expectations, inducing an expansion in private investment—which represents the central goal of fiscal policy from a Keynesian approach. To this end, the direct stimulus provided by public spending in the short term (measured by the multiplier effect) is less important than the signal that public expenditures send to companies, indicating the behavior of aggregate demand in the future. For the CIE, thus, allocation is more crucial than the magnitude of the expenditure.

The allocation pattern that most contributes to the CIE coincides, in part, with that which increases the multiplier effect of G. Among the non-financial government expenses, public investment—especially in terms of expanding and modernizing productive and urban infrastructure—is most likely to generate a CIE. Social expenditures, especially on education and health, can also contribute to this process, although with less visible effects in the short term.

In addition to the linkage effects on other sectors, public investment contributes to reduce production and transaction costs in the economy, thereby generating improvements in measures of productivity and possibly inflation as well. Social spending also tends to favor labor productivity, given the improvement in the education and qualifications of the labor force, as well as improvements in the workers' general health conditions. With these effects in mind, social expenditures can be taken rather as a special kind of public investment—and not a simple running expense—since, in the long term, they contribute to increase the productive capacity of the economy.

The distributive effects associated to the CIE are, quite clearly, beneficial. The expansion of private and public investments directly elevates aggregate income; moreover, the possible fall in prices and/or inflation that follows a reduction in costs and an increase in productivity, meanwhile, benefits everyone, but especially the least fortunate classes, who dedicate a larger portion of their income to purchasing essential goods and services. This increase in productivity may even have an indirect beneficial effect on the functional distribution of income, with positive effects also possible on personal distribution as well. As productivity rises, so does room for raising nominal wages (constrained by workers' bargaining power, of course), without a corresponding increase in prices—which attenuate or even neutralize the effect of real wage increases.[4]

An adequate allocation of public spending is a necessary condition, but not sufficient to provoke the CIE. The long-term expectations that constrain private investments are also influenced by conditions external to fiscal or social government policy. An unfavorable

---

4 When coupled with greater productivity, an increase in salaries does not squeeze profit margins, and thus does not induce companies to correct prices.

macroeconomic environment (be it domestic or international), for example, reduces the probability and magnitude of a CIE on two fronts: through a negative influence on the expected rate of return, and through a probable increase in interest rates, associated to the higher preference for liquidity that generally accompanies such periods. This latter factor characterizes one of the possible causes of the COE.

The COE is defined by precisely such a retraction in private investment, caused by a rise in interest rates following an increase in public spending. Thus, the first condition for the COE is that the rise in G be, at least in part, financed by issuing public debt—and therefore accompanied by the creation or expansion of the government deficit. The financing of this deficit will result in the COE if the debt issued by the government provokes (or demands) a rise in the interest rates. Two scenarios may lead to this effect: a) relative shortage of currency; or b) high preference for liquidity.[5]

The former characterizes a certain lack of coordination between fiscal policy (expansionary) and monetary policy (contractionary), which obviously ought to be avoided. A high preference for liquidity is the money-market reflection of an unfavorable macroeconomic environment, which already induces a decrease in private investment on its own. In this scenario, a rise in interest rates is quite probable, but it is difficult to tell which part of the fall in investments is due to this, and which is directly motivated by the deterioration of expectations.

The Model of Macroeconomic Policy under the Lula and Dilma Administrations (2003–2012)

Short-term macroeconomic policy

While President Lula began his first term in 2003 with considerable political/electoral capital, he was given relatively little space in terms of economic policy. On one hand, there was the "cursed legacy" left by the two terms of President Fernando Henrique Cardoso (FHC, 1995–2002): inflation back in the double digits (the Broad Consumer Price Index, or IPCA, at 12.5% in 2002), troubling external restrictions, weak growth, and a rise in social debt, among other difficulties. Moreover, in Lula's "Letter to the Brazilian People," released during the electoral campaign in response to an uptick in his perceived "riskiness"—which, in addition to directly threatening his election, exacerbated the macroeconomic situation—the then-candidate had sworn to carry on existing macroeconomic policy.

We do not seek to discuss the possible ways in which this difficult situation might have been addressed.[6] For our purposes, it is simply important to note that the first Lula administration was, indeed, characterized by the continuation of the orthodox model of macroeconomic policy, instituted in Brazil during the 2nd FHC administration. This model, as we know, rests on three pillars: a) a floating exchange rate; b) an inflation targeting regime (ITR) for monetary policy, in which the base interest rate is defined by the Central Bank in an attempt to meet a set level of inflation; c) a primary budget surplus regime

---

5   A third possible scenario is the market's rejection of government bonds. This, however, is an extreme and atypical situation, generally in the wake of some recent episode of default on the public debt.

6   For interesting interpretations in this vein, see the articles that comprise the collection organized by Paula (2003).

(seeking to control the public debt stock) for fiscal policy, also guided, since 2000, by the Fiscal Responsibility Act.

This model of macroeconomic policy was maintained, in its essence, throughout the 2003–2012 period. The short-term macroeconomic management under the first Lula administration followed a clearly conservative bent, characterized by high interest rates and primary budget surpluses, prioritizing the economy's return to price stability (Table 6.1). The restrictive effects expected of this policy contrast with the GDP indicators from this period: they show a constant trend towards a return to growth starting in 2004 and only interrupted in 2009 by the effects of the international crisis begun in the American economy the year before.

Brazil's growth from 2004–08 may be explained, essentially, by the positive influence of the international climate, which created a series of effects that would prove beneficial for the Brazilian economy. Starting in 2003, the return to global economic growth and the flow of capital in the international market raised external demand and the prices of commodities being exported by Brazil. This favored an improvement in the country's external accounts and, combined with a policy of high interest rates (although lower than those during the second FHC administration), also improved stability in exchange rates and inflation. Under these circumstances, the return to growth in Brazil was led by exports and investment (Table 6.2). Another factor contributing to investment between 2004–08 was the fact that, from the 2nd Lula administration on, macroeconomic policy had been increasingly designed from a less conservative (or "more Keynesian") standpoint. Finally, the combination of greater economic growth with greater monetary stability (considering prices, interest, and the exchange rate) contributed to an improvement in public finances, reducing the share and the financial cost of the "indexed" debt, the nominal deficit, and the public debt/GDP ratio.

In late 2008, the American financial crisis and its spreading effects, especially on European countries, interrupted the "boom" of the world market from 2004–08. The year 2009 was marked by a severe decrease in liquidity, commerce, and international economic growth. In Brazil, in contrast to all episodes of external turbulence since the 1980s, the ripple effect was modest this time: in the midst of the deep global recession set off by the crisis, the deceleration in economic growth in Brazil from 2009 on may be considered a satisfactory performance.

The Brazilian economy's greater resistance to the 2008 crisis reflected a combination of factors (Carvalho and Souza, 2009; Gentil and Maringoni, 2009): a) the Brazilian financial system's low involvement with external assets and liabilities; b) the fact that, by this period, growth in Brazil was already more dependent on domestic demand than the external market (Table 6.2); c) broad anticyclical efforts by the government, using the conventional instruments of fiscal and monetary policy as well as an expansion in public credit, supported by large capital contributions from the National Treasury to the three largest federal banks in the country: the Brazilian Development Bank (BNDES), Banco do Brasil (BB), and Caixa Econômica Federal (CEF).

Macro-developmentalist policy

The intense use of public credit in Brazil in the post-external crisis period was not an isolated policy, nor a strictly anticyclical one. Federal banks played a central role in the developmentalist policies of the Lula and Dilma administrations. From the list of the social programs supported by federal banks, one might point to the Consigned Credit and

Table 6.1   Brazil: Selected macroeconomic indicators—2002–2012—annual averages

Brazil: Selected Macroeconomic Indicators

2002-2012 - Annual Averages

Period	GDP Real Growth (%)	Inflation (IPCA) (%)	Real Interest Rate[1] (%)	Public Account (% GDP) NFSP[2] Nominal	Primary	Debt Service	Net Public Debt	Tax Burden
2002	2.7	12.5	5.9	4.5	-3.2	7.7	60.4	32.4
2003	1.1	9.3	12.8	5.2	-3.3	8.5	54.8	31.9
2004-08	4.8	5.4	9.1	3.0	-3.5	6.5	46.1	34.1
2009-10	3.4	5.1	4.5	2.9	-2.4	5.2	40.6	33.7
2011-12	1.8	6.2	3.4	2.5	-2.7	5.3	35.8	n.a.

Brazil: Selected Macroeconomic Indicators

2002-2012 - Annual Averages

Period	External Accounts US$ Milhões Reserves[3]	Balance of Payments[4]	Capital Account	Current Account	Exchange Rate[5] (R$/US$)
2002	37,823	302	8,004	-7,637	2.92
2003	49,296	8,496	5,111	4,177	3.08
2004-08	115,942	25,517	23,550	2,533	2.26
2009-10	263,814	47,876	85,606	-35,788	1.88
2011-12	365,313	40,064	92,571	-53,360	1.85

Source: Ipeadata (accessed Oct 2013).

IPCA = Wide Consumer Price Index.

SELIC rate = basic (or market money) rate in Brazil.

1. Accumulated SELIC rate during the year, deflated by IPCA.

2. NFSP = Consolidated public sector borrowing requirements (w/o exchange rate depreciation). Negative sign indicates primary budget surplus.

3. Concept of international liquidity. Data from December 2013.

4. Differences between the surplus of the balance of payments and the sum of the capital and checking current accounts are due to "errors and omissions."

5. Average yearly tax (sales). Annual average sale taxes.

Table 6.2 Real growth and GDP composition by components of aggregate demand—2003–2012

Real Growth and GDP Composition by Components of Aggregate Demand 2003-2012

Year	Real Growth (%)						Share in the GNP (%)				
	Consumption of		GFCF	Exports	Imports	GDP	Consumption of		GFCF	Exports	Imports
	Households	Government					Households	Government			
2003	-0.8	1.2	-4.6	10.4	-1.6	1.1	61.9	19.3	15.3	15.0	12.1
2004	3.8	4.1	9.1	15.3	14.4	5.7	59.8	19.2	16.1	16.4	12.5
2005	4.5	2.3	3.6	9.3	8.5	3.2	60.3	19.9	15.9	15.1	11.5
2006	5.2	2.6	9.8	5.0	18.5	4.0	60.3	20.0	16.4	14.4	11.5
2007	6.1	5.1	13.9	6.2	19.9	6.1	59.9	20.3	17.4	13.4	11.8
2008	5.7	3.2	13.6	0.6	15.4	5.2	58.9	20.2	19.1	13.7	13.5
2009	4.2	3.9	-6.7	-10.2	-11.5	-0.6	61.1	21.2	18.1	11.0	11.1
2010	7.0	3.3	21.9	11.5	36.2	7.5	59.6	21.2	19.5	10.9	11.9
2011	4.1	1.9	4.7	4.5	9.8	2.7	60.3	20.7	19.3	11.9	12.6
2012	3.0	3.2	-4.0	0.5	0.2	0.9	62.3	21.5	18.2	12.6	14.0

Source: IBGE, National Accounts 2000 / Annual, via Ipeadata. Accessed: Oct/2013.
GFCF = Gross Fixed Capital Formation.

Microcredit initiatives, created in 2003 and led on the market, respectively, by the BB and the Bank of the Brazilian Northeast (BNB); and the My House, My Life Program (MCMV), created in 2008 and principally financed by CEF. MCMV labels itself a mixture of social program and a production-sector program, envisioning the construction (by private companies) and acquisition (by low-income consumers) of low-income housing, supported by special lines of credit from CEF (subsidized on the acquisition side).

In terms of programs to stimulate investments, 2004 saw the launch of the Industrial, Technological, and Foreign Trade Policy (PITCE-MDIC, 2007). Through PITCE, government programs supporting exports were integrated into programs that supported industrial development, with a focus on sectors with a high capacity for innovation, in a larger effort to increase competitiveness abroad (Carvalho Jr., 2005).[7] The BNDES participated directly in formulating PITCE, alongside other government agencies, and stands as one of its principal public supplier of credit.

During Lula's second administration, three other government programs relied on the BNDES as their primary public financing support: the Growth Acceleration Program (PAC, 2007); the Productive Development Program (PDP, 2008); and the Investment Sustainability Program (PSI, 2009). The PAC is a bold, lasting program of public and private investments in productive and urban infrastructure (transport and energy in particular). The PDP is a program of industrial policy, like PITCE, designed to broaden private investment and its exports by stimulating R&D and the exporting activity of micro- and small enterprises. The PSI was an emergency measure created in 2009 as part of the government's anticyclical efforts during the crisis abroad. Originally meant to run through June of 2010, but successively extended through (at least) December 2013, the Program consists of special lines of credit from the BNDES (quickly approved and at lower interest rates) for the same sectors prioritized under the PDP.[8]

Spending Policy of the Lula and Dilma Administrations (2003–2012)

As described in previous sections, the federal government's spending policy was broadly used in the 2003–2012 period in order to boost the domestic market—through an increase in consumption and government investment—and increase the workability of redistributive public policies—via a real increase in the minimum wage and income transfers to families. Under this heading, we will analyze four main categories of public spending: consumption, investment, income transfers, and interest.

Government consumption

The data show that government consumption varied little when measured as a percentage of GDP during the period 2003–2012 (Table 6.2). The cost of maintaining the machinery of government, as released in the IBGE National Accounts, includes the wages for federal, state, and municipal civil servants, purchases of goods and services by the three branches of

---

7   PITCE prioritized pharmaceuticals, semiconductors, software, and capital goods.

8   The PAC is coordinated by the Ministry of Finance and the PDP by the Ministry of Development, Industry, and Commerce. Relevant information may be found at these agencies' websites (www.fazenda.gov.br/pac and www.mdic.gov.br/pdp, respectively). The PSI is managed by the BNDES itself, and information may be found at the bank's website: www.bndes.gov.br/psi.

government, and the depreciation of fixed capital. One sees that government consumption remained stable, hovering on average around 19.8% of GDP from 2003–2008. In 2009, as a strategy in the face of the crisis, government consumption jumps to 21.2% of GDP and then falls 0.5 percentage points of GDP as a result of the contractionary fiscal movement in 2011, with a cut in the purchase of goods and services meant to maintain public administrations. The strong deceleration in the economy surprised the government, forcing it back to a focus on consumption as a form of reaction. 2012 thus saw government consumption rise again, to 21.5% of GDP. Wages paid to civil servants, however, have been in decline as a percentage of GDP since September 2009 (IPEA, 2012).

Government consumption, although stable as a percentage of GDP, reveals an average growth rate of 5% in the 2001–2011 period when analyzed in terms of absolute deflated values (Santos, 2012). The expansion of this variable increases income, favors growth, and helps maintain education, health, social assistance, justice, public security, urban transportation, and other sectors that guarantee an array of public services essential to the population. Gobetti and Orair (2010) and Santos (2012) have noted, however, the low dynamism of so-called intermediate federal consumption (total consumption expenditures of federal government, excluding servants wages). This would be the result of the federal government's progressive reluctance to directly contract services in health and education, transferring a growing sum of resources so that these services might be carried out by the states and municipalities—thus increasing expenses on "intergovernmental transfers."

In this vein, Gobetti and Orair (2010) reference the increase in transfers to the Unified Health System (SUS) from 2001 to 2011, the Basic Health Care Package and the Family Health Program, Pharmaceutical Assistance, Health Surveillance, AIDS Prevention, Mobile First Aid Service (SAMU), complements to the Development Fund for Basic Education and Development of Teaching (FUNDEF) and Primary and Secondary Education Maintenance and Development Fund (FUNDEB), school meals, the Money Straight to Schools Program (PDDE), and school transport. The authors show that intergovernmental transfers for health and education grew in real terms at a high average rate of approximately 10.7% p.a. As mentioned previously, the government's aggregate consumption measured through national accounts grew at an average rate of 5% p.a. between 2001 and 2011. By cross-referencing this information, one may conclude that a significant part of that consumption was dedicated to maintaining two sectors (health and education) that attend to the basic needs of the neediest, supporting them through federal transfers to other levels of government.

To sum up the expansionary and redistributive mechanism, wage expenses and intermediate consumption at the federal and state levels have been relatively stable from 2003–2011 when measured as a percentage of GDP, with a tendency for low dynamism for federal data. However, expenditures on municipal consumption reveal another dynamic. In terms of percentages of GDP, they increased roughly 0.5% between 2002 and 2010. This behavior may be explained by transfers of resources linked to health and education from the federal and state government to municipalities, as previously mentioned. Santos (2012) affirms that municipal expenses on health and education represented 1.3% of GDP in 2002 and rose to occupy 2.1% by 2010.

Since the execution of health and education programs raised expenses on wages, as the vast majority of expenditures in these two sectors go to paying public professionals, the impact on the economy begins with households' consumption. The high propensity to consume, given that wages in these sectors are traditionally low, elevates the multiplier effect of municipal spending and injects dynamism into the local economy. In addition, government purchases rise, as intermediate consumption to municipal governments grows. This is not merely a matter of creating demand, however. An array of public services is generated that may sow abilities and skill sets in individuals and social groups, making them more productive, setting off effects on productivity of aggregate labor force and thus improving employees' income.

Public investment

From 2004 to 2008, the Brazilian economy underwent a period of rising investment in industry and infrastructure, driven by worldwide demand, which affected the steel, paper, cellulose, and mining industries, and was accompanied by an expansion in domestic credit and capital markets. By 2008, the investment cycle had grown beyond exporting sectors, also taking in those focused on the domestic market and infrastructure (Puga et al., 2010). With the deterioration of the international scenario in the 2009 crisis, this movement was interrupted. Nevertheless, in 2010 the internal market, pushed on by expansionist macroeconomic policy, managed to compensate for the weak performance of external demand. In the two-year period 2011–2012, however, investments did not manage to recover their former vigor—see Table 6.2.

Brazilian fiscal policy would seem to be an exemplifying mechanism for "crowding-in." Government consumption did not need to fall so make public investment grow from 2003–12, and both drove the expansion of private investment, although from 2011–12 the latter was less active.

The high level of public goods and services being offered through government consumption brought with it the necessity to maintain and renew facilities such as schools, hospitals, health centers, etc., which further increased government investment and induced growth in a number of branches of the private sector. In addition to this driving mechanism, fiscal strategy turned to the infrastructure and logistical constructions included in the PAC, petroleum investments in the pre-salt layer, and the various projects meant to prepare the country for global events such as the World Cup and Olympics, to such an extent that one may state that, from 2006 on, growth was progressively led by household and government consumption, and by public investment.

Indeed, the Brazilian economy's gross fixed capital formation (GFCF) rose in the period being examined, going from 15.3% of GDP in 2003 to 18.2% in 2012, having reached 19.5% in 2010 (Table 6.2). It is important to note that GFCF rose at an average rate of 6.4% p.a. from 2005–2012, far outstripping the GDP growth rate in this period, inverting a tendency towards low growth (an average of 1% a.a.). It is worth repeating that since 2009, the investment rate has maintained a slower and less stable rhythm, with the exception of 2010; in 2012, it saw a swift fall of 4% (Table 6.2), settling at 18.1% of GDP.

Santos (2012), Orair and Gobetti (2010), and Orair (2011) clarify the magnitude of public investment in the national economy, resolving long-standing methodological problems of distortions, inconsistencies, and a lack of information.[9] Working off of these

---

9   Federal investments are considered to be those carried out directly by the federal government, its capital transfers to states and municipalities, and the investments of federal state-run companies. In terms of a source of data on federal investments, the cited authors use the information from SIAFI (programmatic functional classification), and used DEST's Budget of State-Run Company Investments for the state-run firms. The data on public investment correspond to the effective sums paid each

authors, if one adds up federal, state, municipal, and federal state-owned enterprises investments, it becomes evident that government investments grew progressively, moving from around 2.5% of GDP in 2004 to 4.7% of GDP by late 2010 (Gobetti, 2010). This movement was temporarily interrupted by a hefty reduction in this variable, driven by the 0.4% fall in federal investment in the year 2011 (Ministério da Fazenda, 2012: p. 28), partly a consequence of the restrictive macroeconomic policy that followed the rapid expansion of 2010.

Table 6.3 presents disaggregated data on investments by government and federal state-owned companies. The following relevant trends become evident: a) there was a return to public investment after 2005, led by infrastructural interventions; b) investments by federal state-owned enterprises expanded rapidly, especially those of the Petrobrás Group, which came to represent 54% of all government investments; these investments grew, influenced by an increase in the production of petroleum and gas through large-scale Petrobrás initiatives (the construction of refineries in Pernambuco, Maranhão, Ceará, and Rio de Janeiro) and the start of petroleum extraction from the pre-salt layer in 2008; c) federal investments in transport infrastructure (highways above all) and federal state-owned companies' investments in electricity tripled between 2005 and 2011 (going from R$ 6.8 bn to R$ 20.5 bn); and, d) federal investments in health and education quintupled, with a total sum going from R$1,2 bn in 2005 to R$ 7,1 bn in 2011.

One important aspect of this period is that growth of government investment in infrastructure operates simultaneously with a trend towards the spread of concessions (privatization in some cases) for airports, highways, railways, ports, electricity, and high-speed trains, and auctions in the oil and gas sector. The terms of these concessions varied, but in general they provided conditions favorable to private investment, involving subsidized resources from the BNDES. The State creates spaces for private capital in order to generate a new cycle of sustainable economic growth. Thus, despite possible problems related to the specific terms of these concessions, State action through this channel contributes to generate a crowding-in effect.

One might note that the design of the expansionary cycle supported by consumption and public investment is reaffirmed by Petrobrás' withdrawal of the calculations for the federal primary budget surplus goal in 2008, with Eletrobrás following suit in 2009. This new flexibility in fiscal policy seems to reflect a change in direction for the government, however timid (since the measure does not affect the whole of public investments), in the sense of strengthening the role of the State in the planning and guidance of the economy. The primary budget surplus was reduced from 2009 onward, remaining around 2.5% of GDP, on average, from 2009–12, a level befitting the lower growth rates of the post-global crisis phase, as compared to the 3.5% of GDP primary budget surplus of the 2004–08 phase (Table 6.3).

---

year, including payments on the current budget plus effective payments on sums from previous years (excluding the sums yet to be paid and still not processed). The choice to opt for these data was led by the greater precision of this methodology, which generates data closer to reality than IBGE's National Accounts; the latter tend to produce overestimates, among other reasons, for including in the federal level's GFCF the still-pending sums to be paid (that is, expenses that are undertaken and not paid, and which may never be paid or only come through in later years).

Public Investment in Brazil - Government and State-Owned Enterprises 2005-2011 (Current in R$ Million)

Year	2005	2006	2007	2008	2009	2010	2011
Economic Infrastructure	**23,410**	**27,102**	**34,157**	**48,024**	**67,635**	**83,911**	**80,403**
Petrobrás Group	16,567	18,050	24,066	36,264	51,204	63,211	59,859
Eletrobrás Group	3,208	3,204	3,104	3,878	5,212	5,279	5,157
Transport Sector	3,635	5,848	6,986	7,882	11,219	15,421	15,387
Infraero and Air Transport	566	1,165	1,006	995	1,105	1,306	1,567
Highway Transport	2,593	4,111	4,994	5,107	7,817	10,260	11,212
Railway Transport	236	335	508	923	994	2,549	1,558
Ports and Waterway Transport	240	236	478	857	1,303	1,306	1,050
Other Investments	**8,718**	**11,528**	**14,318**	**20,877**	**24,332**	**33,335**	**30,373**
State-Owned Enterprises - Financial Sector	1268	1034	1114	1691	2015	2463	2209
State-Owned Enterprises - Other Sectors	406	391	401	398	803	739	646
Government	7,044	10,103	12,803	18,788	21,514	30,132	27,518
Urban and Sanitation Infrastructure	594	1,679	2,359	5,341	5,247	5,353	4,922
Hydric Infrastructure	401	482	559	965	1,749	2,201	1,500
Education and Health Infrastructure	1,225	1,870	2,130	3,124	3,868	7,109	7,060
Other - non-classified	4,824	6,073	7,755	9,359	10,650	15,470	14,036
Total Federal Public Investments	**32,127**	**38,630**	**48,475**	**68,901**	**91,967**	**117,246**	**110,776**
Total in % of GDP	**1.6**	**1.6**	**1.8**	**2.3**	**2.8**	**3.1**	**2.7**

Source: Elaborated by Santos (2012) based on updated data from Orair and Gobbet (2010).

Table 6.3   Public investment in Brazil—Government and State-owned enterprises 2005–2011 (current R$ million)

Public Spending on Income Transfers

Social spending and its direct effects on income

One of the defining characteristics of fiscal policy from 2003–2012 lies in the importance taken on by income transfer expenditure. Social Security Transfers and Subsidies (known as TAPS) are, in the IBGE national accounts' definition, public resources meant for the private sector, with no equivalent counterpart, and which do not weigh in the government's offering of public goods and services.

The study of the impact of income transfers as a strategic element of the Brazilian economy's new pattern of growth may create a number of connections, as indicated in Section 2. The first connection, between autonomous spending in the social sector and the level of economic activity, is decisive in directly driving household consumption. The elevated magnitude of this spending and its trend towards monetary income for a population with a high propensity to consume (needy seniors, pensioners, the sick, accident victims, low-income households, and the unemployed) transformed it into an important autonomous component of aggregate demand, influencing the rhythm of economic growth over the past decade and creating a powerful domestic mass consumer market.

The second connection is drawn between income transfers and incentive to private investment—capital formation, in other words. And the most important reason for this, as Keynes (1936) pointed out, is that capital is not a self-sufficient entity, existing independently of consumption, and any bolstering of the propensity to consume, which may be considered a permanent phenomenon, bolsters the demand for capital.

The third connection is formed between income transfers and the reduction of poverty and social inequality. This was likely one of the most important characteristics of the 2000s—when, according to CEPAL, a period of growth was accompanied by income distribution for the first time in the economic history of Brazil and South America as a whole (CEPAL, 2010; 2012).

First of all, it is convenient to clarify the definition of income transfers. According to Santos (2012), TAPS comprise nine items: 1) benefits from the General Social Security Regime (RGPS); 2) the TAPS paid by state and municipal governments to retired public servants; 3) federal payments to retired federal public servants; 4) withdrawals from the Employment Time Guarantee Fund (FGTS); 5) expenses on unemployment insurance and wage bonuses, financed by the Workers' Support Fund (FAT); 6) benefits associated to the Organic Law of Social Assistance (LOAS); 7) public transfers made to private nonprofit institutions (TIPSFL); 8) benefit payments from the Bolsa Família Program; and 9) subsidies to the private sector.

The TAPS data used in Table 6.4 correspond to the figures from IBGE's National Accounts from 2003–2009, and calculations by Santos (2012) for the same period, as well as projections for 2010 and 2011. The information shows a slight ascendant tendency for TAPS, which rose from a level of 14.5 of GDP in 2003 to 14.95% in 2011. In 2009, in an effort to compensate for the slowdown of the domestic economy in the face of the global crisis, TAPS grew to 15.21% of GDP. In recent years, TAPS seem to have leveled out at around 15% of GDP.

What is truly relevant is that the composition of TAPS has changed; transfers sent directly to lower-income households have taken on greater weight. As may be seen in Table 6.4, expenses on benefits from the Organic Law of Social Assistance (LOAS), along with Bolsa Família Program and benefits financed with resources from FAT (unemployment

Evolution of TAPS in Brazil (% of GDP) - 2002-2011

Year	Retirements and Pensions of Federal Civil Servants	RGPS	FAT	LOAS	FGTS	Bolsa Família Program	Retirements and Pensions of State and Municipal Civil Servants	TIPSFL	Subsidies to Private Sector	Errors and Omissions (2)	TOTAL (1)
2002	2.1	6.0	0.5	0.2	1.3	0.1	2.7	0.4	0.2	0.5	14.1
2003	2.2	6.3	0.5	0.3	1.2	0.1	2.6	0.4	0.2	0.8	14.6
2004	2.1	6.5	0.5	0.4	1.1	0.2	2.5	0.5	0.1	0.3	14.1
2005	2.0	6.8	0.6	0.4	1.2	0.3	2.4	0.5	0.2	0.1	14.5
2006	2.0	7.0	0.7	0.5	1.3	0.3	2.4	0.5	0.2	0.1	14.9
2007	2.0	7.0	0.7	0.5	1.4	0.3	2.4	0.5	0.2	-0.2	14.8
2008	2.0	6.6	0.7	0.5	1.4	0.4	2.3	0.5	0.1	-0.1	14.4
2009	2.1	6.9	0.9	0.6	1.5	0.4	2.4	0.6	0.2	-0.3	15.2
2010	1.9	6.8	0.8	0.6	1.3	0.4	2.2	0.6	n.d.	n.d.	14.8
2011	1.9	6.8	0.8	0.6	1.4	0.4	n.d.	0.6	n.d.	n.d.	15.0

Source: Santos (2012), based on data from: Banco Central do Brasil, Caixa Econômica Federal, Execução Orçamentária dos Estados e Municípios (STN), Finanças do Brasil (STN), IBGE, Base SIGABRASIL, Resultado Fiscal do Governo Central (STN), Contas Nacionais (IBGE), SIAFI/STN.

TAPS = Social Security Transfers and Subsidies to the Private Sector.
RGPS = General Social Security Regime.
FAT = Workers' Support Fund.
LOAS = Organic Law of Social Assistance.
FGTS = Employment Time Guarantee Fund.
TIPSFL = Transfers to Private Nonprofit Institutions.

Table 6.4   Evolution of TAPS in Brazil (% GDP)—2002–2011

insurance and wage bonuses) were expanded. Smaller but significant increases were seen in retirement benefits, pensions, and other benefits from the General Social Security Regime (RGPS). Meanwhile, FGTS withdrawals and subsidies to companies remained stable over the past decade; and transfers to federal, state, and municipal public servants fell (columns 2 and 8 of Table 6.4).

The real increase in the minimum wage had a strong impact on benefits' rise in value, given the legal connection between them, which contributes to increasing the disposable income of those who request State aid (IPEA, 2010, p. 63). The benefits from LOAS are equivalent to a minimum wage, as are benefits financed by FAT resources (unemployment benefits and wages bonuses), and nearly 60% of the welfare benefits offered by RGPS. The policy of increasing the purchasing power of the minimum wage explains much of the expansion of TAPS during the period at hand.

The rise in expenses on transfers was also tied to a growth in coverage. In 2002, there were 20,752,506 active recipients of welfare benefits. By 2011, this figure had grown to 28,909,419 an increase of around 40%, with 8,156,913 more recipients included. As for the value of these benefits, one sees that in 2002 it came to R$ 6,871 million, whereas by 2011 it had risen to R$ 23,154 million, a nominal increase of 237% (RGPS Historical Database). According to Fagnani (2012), current coverage extends to over 110 million people, including indirect beneficiaries (family members).

TAPS did, indeed, grow and positively affect personal income distribution. In targeting a broad swath of the population, with lower income and an elevated propensity to consume, they offer a potent multiplier effect on GDP and income. Simulations run by Silveira et al. (2011) for the period 2008–2009 (Table 6.5) demonstrate that spending on social policy principally alter the income of the segment with least purchasing power (1st quintile). The original earnings of this sector (prior to State intervention) came to just 1.0% of total income. After retirement benefits, pensions, support, Bolsa Família Program, unemployment insurance and other benefits, the percentage rose to 2.4%. But income after government transfers, when added to social spending on education and health and deducted from indirect and direct taxes, rises to around 4.2% of total income for the 20% poorest, a higher sum than the original income (without State intervention). The same table also shows that the second quintile has attained a notably higher income after government intervention, from an original level of 4.6% to a new high of 7.2% of total income after transfers and health and education spending.

Another recent study, this by IPEA, introduced important results in the move to capture the effects of government spending on economic growth (GDP) and household income (IPEA, 2010). The study in question simulated shocks in a number of types of autonomous spending and reconstructed the economic cycle, using the National accounts and a Social Accounting Matrix for Brazil in the year 2006. It concluded that, in 2006, the average multiplier effect of autonomous spending in general (investment, exports, and government spending) was 1.57—that is, for every R$ 1.00 spent, sent abroad or spent by the government, an additional R$1.57 of GDP would be generated. As for aggregate household income, which is a more appropriate income concept for measuring well-being, the average multiplier of autonomous spending is 1.17—that is, for every new 1% of GDP in investments, exports, or government spending, households would see their income increase, on average, by 1.17%.

The use of the IPEA methodology mentioned above (2010) allowed for a better understanding of the specific multiplier effect exerted by social spending on GDP, and on income over the course of the economic cycle; it indicated that the shock of a hypothetical

Per Capita Distribution of Nominal Household Income, by Income Strata (2009)

Statistics	Income Share of Each Quintile (%)				
	Original Income (1)	Initial Income (2)	Disposable Income (3)	Post-Tax Income (4)	Final Income (5)
1st Quintile	1.0	2.4	2.6	2.2	4.2
2nd Quintile	4.6	5.9	6.2	5.7	7.2
3rd Quintile	9.4	10.4	10.9	10.3	10.4
4th Quintile	18.1	18.3	18.8	18.3	14.7
5th Quintile	67.0	63.0	61.6	63.5	63.5
Gini Coeficient (%)	64.3	59.1	57.6	59.8	50.0
Average (R$ - January 2009)	596.5	733.0	662.4	561.6	663.5

Source: Silveira et.al. (2011). Apud Castro, 2013.

(1) Original income earning from labor, sells, interests, rents, grants, etc (before State intervention).
(2) Initial income = original income plus retirements, pensions, social assistance transfers, unemployment insurance, etc.
(3) Disposable income = initial income minus income taxes.
(4) Post-tax income = disposable income minus indirect taxes.
(5) Final income = post-tax income plus education and health spending.

Table 6.5   Per capita distribution of nominal household income, by income strata (2009)

increase of 1% in GDP on social spending would bring a multiplier of approximately 1.37. However, certain sectors of social spending hold significantly higher GDP multipliers than others. For example, education and health have the greatest multipliers of GDP (1.85 and 1.70, respectively), while expenses on Bolsa Família Program brought a multiplier of 1.44, the Continued Payment Benefits (BPC) came to 1.38, and welfare benefits from RGPS came to 1.23.[10] Moreover, the study shows that spending on social programs is just as important for GDP growth than commodity exports, which have a multiplier of 1.40.

The IPEA study in question (2010) indicates that the effect of social spending on household income is more relevant than its effect on GDP. A one-percentage increase of GDP in social spending raises household income by 1.85%, on average. In this case, income transfers have a heftier impact on household income when compared to other social spending; expenses on Bolsa Família Program, BPC, and RGPS have a multiplier effect of 2.25, 2.20, and 2.10, respectively, while the multiplier of education spending is 1.67, with 1.44 for health.

The flip side: Social spending and tax collection

Another important result of the same IPEA study (2010) speaks to the effect of social spending on the growth of revenue from taxes, fees, and social contributions, given their positive impact on household and firms' incomes. The social accounting matrix revealed that 56% of the value of social spending returns to the Treasury in the form of taxes and social contributions, after passing through the entire process of income multiplication generated by those very expenditures. Thus, the multiplier effect in subsequent exercises guarantees a tax return to the government, letting social spending finance itself in future.

Without a doubt, the improvement in income distribution born of social policies—and, above all, from the expansion of the labor market—had a positive effect on the contributive capacity of a population previously excluded from the system. The post-2004 landscape marked the start of a period of much steeper growth in the collection of social contributions that finance Social Security, corroborating the thesis that the Brazilian social protection system becomes financially viable when fiscal policies of raising social spending kick off the process of boosting aggregate demand; later, and consequentially, revenue from social contributions rises, allowing the policy of progressive spending to continue.

Studies like those by Orair (2012) and Santos and Costa (2008) identify the specificity of the change in the tax burden after 2004, a period that saw greater tax breaks alongside a rise in the gross tax burden, from 31.7% of GDP in 2003 to 35.3% in 2011. The authors claim that the rise in the tax/GDP ratio sprang from the increase in income from labor and profits, bases for taxation and social contributions which grew faster than GDP.

According to Orair (2012), tax revenues from labor income expanded with the increased formalization of the labor market after 2004. The regressive nature of the tax system was only exacerbated. Personal income taxes, payroll taxes, and social contributions rose as a percentage of GDP, from 9.5% in 2002 to 10.6% in 2007; after the economy's slowdown, they rose again to a high-water mark of 12.2% in mid-2012. The increases provoked by these taxes came to nearly three-quarters of the total growth in the tax burden over the

---

10   As the IPEA author clarifies (2010), the lower GDP multiplier for income-transfer expenses is tied to the lower number of times that the resource circulates in the economy, as indicated by the Social Accounting Matrix and National Accounts. Education spending, on the other hand, circulates more in the economy than a direct income transfer to families.

period 2002–2012. Of the 3.5% increase in the total tax burden, 2.6% came from taxes on labor income, and 0.9% from taxes on profits. The main source of funds for welfare, the Social Contribution to the General Social Security Regime (RGPS) grew at an average rate of 13.9% p.a. from 2004–2009, tracking along with the average increase of 13.2% p.a. in wages.

The other sources of revenue meant to finance social security—the Social Contribution on Net Profits (CSLL) and the Contribution for Social Security Financing (COFINS)—also saw significant growth from 2002–2012, which only increased after 2004. COFINS grew 1.7 p.p. above GDP over the whole period, while CSLL grew 0.6 p.p. Although the Provisional Contribution on Financial Flows (CPMF), created to finance the social security system in Brazil, was eliminated in 2007, collections for the social security system continued to expand.

It has become clear that, while the government has managed to balance revenues and expenditures on the social side, the multiplier and redistributive effects of this policy, while significant, become limited by the weight and regressive nature of the tax burden.

Public expenditures on interest payments

Expenditures on interest payments contribute little to GDP growth, and plenty to the concentration of wealth.

In 2003, public spending on interest payments reached the high mark of 8.5% of GDP; but this has been followed by a continual tendency towards a fall in this indicator, which has stabilized around, on average, 5.25% of GDP from 2009–12 (Table 6.1). Historically, public sector expenditures on debt service have grown sharply in periods of severe currency turbulence—notably in 1999, 2002, and 2003—but the international financial crisis that struck the country in the last trimester of 2008 did not lead to a rise in interest rates. Unlike previous critical periods, the federal government reacted by pulling back both on monetary policy (in reducing the base interest rate) as well as fiscal policy (reducing the primary surplus).

One might note that this behavior—and, along with it, the reduction in the government's financial expenses—was facilitated by a long-standing policy initiated in 2004, meant to change the management of the federal public debt. Since then, the debt indexed to the most volatile variables in the market—exchange and interest rates—has been gradually substituted by pre-fixed debt, or inflation-indexed debt (indexed to IPCA). Given the favorable outcome for the Brazilian economy post-2004, this management strategy seems to have proved itself less onerous for the public sector, as well as making government financial expenditures more predictable and manageable.

Macroeconomic Constraints on Social Policy: Synthesizing Trends under the Lula and Dilma Administrations

Theoretical analyses have shown that, from a Keynesian approach, the distributive effectiveness of social policies rises along with the macroeconomic impact of public spending as a *whole*—not just on social expenditures—given the combination of three effects: the multiplier effect, which acts on household consumption, and the crowding in and crowding out effects (CIE and COE), which act on private investment. These effects, meanwhile, are constrained by a broad array of variables, both structural and macroeconomic, as well as the nature of fiscal policy regarding two elements: the allocation framework and the financing of public spending.

In analyzing these constraints, one may argue that the redistributive effects of social policies tend to be amplified by the following conditions: a) the higher the total level of public spending; b) the higher the propensity to consume of the groups being benefited by public spending; c) the lighter the tax burden; d) the lower the economy's propensity to import; e) the greater the prevailing degree of confidence (or optimism) in the economy; f) the lower the prevailing interest rates on the domestic asset market. The latter two act favorably on the CIE and COE, magnifying the first and containing the second. The rest contribute to increase the multiplier effect of public spending.

As for spending allocation, we return to the necessity to reconcile social policies based on income transfers (with a high multiplier effect, given their direct beneficiaries' high propensity to consume) with a broader and more consistent policy of economic development. In step with the reduction of poverty and income inequality, it is key to attenuate the economic underdevelopment of the nation itself, which underscores the need for income-transfer policies. This calls for a public spending structure with more space for expenditures on investments (in infrastructure and public services, among other sectors) and even government consumption to allow for permanent programs to support research, innovation, education, etc. Given the government's budgetary restrictions, as set by the tax burden and its borrowing capacity, a policy along these lines would require some degree of sacrifice on the part of "strictly social" policy—and hence its multiplier effect as well—in the short term. In a longer view, however, this tack tends to increase the distributive effectiveness of public spending through the crowding-in effect.

As for how to structure the financing of these expenditures, it is difficult to point to an "ideal" structure, given a clear tradeoff between two viable sources. On one hand, the lighter the tax burden, the greater the multiplier effect of spending—which, in principle, would favor its redistributive effect and possibly the CIE as well. On the other hand, a lower taxation level may restrict the government's ability to implement social policies, in limiting the total amount of spending possible. This limit may be attenuated by borrowing, a resource potentially restricted by the COE.

As shown, unlike the multiplier and crowding-in effects, the crowding-out effect depends less on the specific conditions around public spending policy —the sum of G, its allocation, or even, to a certain extent, the magnitude of the deficit to be financed. The same level of spending and deficit that produces a COE in a period of monetary tightening and/or of high liquidity preference would not produce this effect in a more favorable environment. In short, the COE is not a direct consequence *of the deficit*, nor of the spending itself, but rather a possibility influenced by the monetary environment in which the deficit is being financed. This environment is regulated by monetary policy, and not by fiscal measures. As such, an occasional reduction in the distributive effectiveness of a given public expenditure policy resulting from the crowding-out effect ought to be more appropriated attributed to a lack of coordination between this policy and monetary policy.

Having considered all these conditions, an analysis of the Brazilian case shows that, in the field of macroeconomic policy, a defining characteristic of the Lula and Dilma administrations has been the conciliation of an orthodox (non-Keynesian) model of macroeconomic policy with the use of developmentalist policies (generally attuned to a Keynesian approach), which had been banned from any prescription for State action in Brazil since the early 1990s.

The reigning conservatism in the management of fiscal and monetary policy, though weakening over the course of the 2nd Lula administration, certainly operated as a brake on what might have been the greater distributive impact of the Lula and Dilma administrations' social policies, by virtue of three macroeconomic effects: a) restricting the multiplier effect of public spending through a moderate increase in the tax burden, linked to a rise in the regressivity of its distribution between wages and profits; b) restricting its crowding-in effect, apparently confirmed by the stability of the economy's investment rate, hovering around a pitiful 16% of GDP before 2006, and its moderate climb to 18% from 2007–12, which was a period of a greater expansion in public investment; c) favoring the crowding-out effect, given restrictions on liquidity generated by policies under Lula's first administration that kept real interest rates high.

On the other hand, the developmentalist bent of this "hybrid" model of macroeconomic policy lessened the restrictive effects on social policy's distributive effectiveness, which was imposed by the conservatism of fiscal and monetary policy. In addition to the emphasis on social programs, the developmentalist policy pursued under Lula and Dilma was guided by a return to public investment, not just from the public administration itself but also through federal state-owned companies; by programs meant to stimulate private investment and innovation, with a strong boost for federal public credit, especially through the BNDES; by policies of "financial inclusion," such as consigned credit, microcredit, and housing credit, all led by federal banks (the BB, BNB, and CEF, respectively); and by the policy of a continual real increase in the minimum wage. At the same time, these policies contributed to increasing the multiplier and crowding-in effects of public spending, partially compensating for fiscal and monetary restrictions.

Though generally beneficial for economic development, this policy strategy seems to have been relatively inefficient in terms of promoting a significant change in the conditions of external competitiveness, and thus in the country's position on the international commercial stage as a whole. From the perspective of the macroeconomic and distributive effects of the public expenditures at the base of this developmentalist policy, it is important to note that, in addition to increasing domestic income, it must be able to keep this income from flowing out via imports, which reduce its multiplier effect and possibly the CIE as well. Table 6.2 demonstrates that this was not the case in Brazil from 2003–12, a period in which imports grew, on the whole, at a higher rate than GDP, as well as household and government consumption and investment. The only exceptions were the years 2003 and 2009, which saw a sharp deceleration in economic activity domestically and abroad. If this strategy of foreign positioning is maintained, a large part of the developmentalist efforts of the Lula and Dilma years will be for naught.

Finally, a disaggregated analysis of public spending shows that, while restricted by the policy of high primary budget surpluses during the period, public expenditures also served a compensatory and largely favorable function in the redistribution of income, given the following: a) though stable as a proportion of GDP, total public spending expanded in absolute terms over the course of the whole period; b) the expansion of government consumption was led by health and education; c) public investment grew significantly, both in absolute terms and as a percentage of GDP—that is to say that this investment expanded, on average, at a higher rate than the economy as a whole; d) expenditures on transfers rose little in relation to GDP, but their composition was altered to favor income redistribution—that is, reoriented towards the lower income levels; e) expenditures toward interest on the public debt tended to decrease during the period, while remaining a major restriction on nonfinancial public-sector expenditures.

Conclusion

Having noted that social policy is not created in a vacuum, but rather as a subset of fiscal policy and hence of macroeconomic policy as well (which are also ruled by other goals), this chapter analyzed the nature of these constraints in Brazil during the years 2003–2012, seeking to evaluate their possible contribution to the redistributive effectiveness of social spending under the Lula and Dilma administrations.

Without failing to acknowledge the successes of the Lula and Dilma administrations' spending policies, one must conclude that, in spite of the rising significance of expenditures on income in Brazil, and despite the fall in inequality, income distribution remains brutally unequal: 63.5% of all income is still in the hands of the 20% wealthiest in the country (data from 2009). Reconciling greater economic growth with lower income inequality demands that government spending policies address income distribution more fully. To this end, two strategies are crucial: a) raising per capita social spending, increasing the number of income transfer beneficiaries and universalizing the services offered by the State; b) attenuating, insofar as possible, the structural, fiscal, and monetary restrictions on the distributive effectiveness of public spending policy, particularly the propensity to import, the regressive tax system, and the policy of high interest rates—which, beyond the crowding-out effect, impedes a more notable reduction in the government's financial expenditures.

Tax policy, for example, had room to be less conservative, given the continuous fall in the net public debt and the prevailing greater economic growth, which favored an increase in government revenues. Tax breaks could have been broader, and distributive adjustments in the burden could have been deeper.

Monetary policy also had the opportunity to be less restrictive. The period 2003–12 was marked by ample liquidity and low interest rates on the international market, sparking a strong influx of capital to Brazil (FDI and portfolio investment), the accumulation of international reserves, and an appreciation of the exchange rate, which favored control of inflation. Under the Lula and Dilma administrations, monetary policy ran in opposition to fiscal policy, limiting its distributive effects. It is no coincidence that its results in terms of economic growth and income distribution pale in comparison to the sharp rise in public spending. In short, the Brazilian economy's solid fundamentals during the period indicated that it would have been possible to stimulate greater growth and income distribution under current fiscal policy.

Facing the problem of social inequalities in Brazil will undoubtedly demand actions that go beyond social spending policy. Overcoming the centuries-old social wounds that have followed the evolution of the Brazilian economy calls for an active, prolonged, and systematic policy of spending over a variety of sectors and State functions, the final extent of which must be driven by the goal of full employment. In turn, income redistribution policy will demand changes in the tax structure, inverting the direction of the tax burden so that workers and the needy do not carry the weight of a more progressive social spending policy. A more incisive framework for taxing high profits, large estates, speculative earnings, and financial wealth has become quite a political liability in recent years. Taxation and spending must be coordinated and complementary so that active fiscal policy's redistributive efforts are not simply limited to spending, hampered in its efficacy by the staggeringly regressive tax burden.

Bibliography

ANFIP (org.) (2009). *Crise Financeira Mundial: impactos sociais e no mercado de trabalho*. Brasília, Fundação ANFIP.

Carvalho Jr, A.M. (2005). 'A Política Industrial e o BNDES.' *Revista do BNDES*, vol. 12, no. 23, pp. 17–28.

Carvalho, F.J. Cardim de (1992). *Mr. Keynes and the Post-Keynesians*. Cheltenham, Edward Elgar.

Castro, J.A. (2012). 'Política social e desenvolvimento no Brasil.' *Economia e Sociedade*, vol. 21, no. 3, pp. 1011–1042.

Castro, J.A. (2013). *Política social, distribuição de renda e crescimento económico*. São Paulo, Fundação Perseu Abramo/mimeo.

CEPAL (2012). *Cambio Estructural para la Igualdade. Uma visión integrada del desarrollo*. San Salvador, CEPAL, www.cepal.org/publicaciones.

CEPAL (2010). *La Hora de la Igualdad. Brechas por cerrar, caminos por abrir*. Brasília, CEPAL, http://www.eclac.cl

Costa Neto, Y.C. da (2004). *Bancos Oficiais no Brasil: origem e aspectos de seu desenvolvimento*. Brasília, Banco Central do Brasil.

Froyen, R.T. (2001). *Macroeconomia*. São Paulo, Ed. Saraiva.

Furtado, C. (1986). *Teoria e Política do Desenvolvimento Econômico*. São Paulo, Nova Cultural.

Gentil, D.L. e Maringoni, G. (2009). 'Crise econômica e condicionantes internos e externos,' in ANFIP (org.) (2009). *Crise Financeira Mundial: impactos sociais e no mercado de trabalho*. Brasília, Fundação ANFIP.

Gobetti, S. (2006). *Estimativa dos Investimentos Públicos*. Brasília, ESAF.

Gobetti, S. (2010). *Qual é a real taxa de investimento público no Brasil?* Nota Técnica, Brasília, IPEA/Dimac.

Gobetti, S. e Orair, R.O. (2010). 'Classificação e análise das despesas públicas federáis pela ótica macroeconômica (2002–2009).' *Texto para discussão No. 1485*, Brasília, IPEA.

Hermann, J. (1988). 'O processo multiplicador: uma visão alternative.' *XVI Encontro Nacional de Economia da ANPEC*. Belo Horizonte, Dec 5–7, 1988, pp. 49–66.

Hermann, J. (2004). 'O Trade Off do Crescimento no Brasil nos Anos 1990–2000: análise crítica e alternativas de política monetária.' *Revista Econômica*, vol. 6, no. 2, pp. 261–289.

IPEA (2013). *Carta de Conjuntura No. 20*, setembro. Brasília, IPEA.

IPEA (2010). 'Efeitos econômicos do gasto social no Brasil,' in *Perspectiva da política social no Brasil, Livro 8*. Brasília, IPEA.

Keynes, J.M. (1936). *The General Theory of Employment, Interest and Money*. London, Macmillan.

Keynes, J.M. (1937). 'The General Theory of Employment.' *Quarterly Journal of Economics*, vol. 51, no. 2, pp. 209–223.

Keynes, J.M. (1973). *A Monetary Theory of Production. The Collected Writings of John Maynard Keynes, vol. 13*. London, Macmillan.

Ministério do Desenvolvimento, Indústria e Comércio Exterior (2007). *Política Industrial contará com R$ 15,05 bilhões em recursos* [Online], Brasília, Ministério do Desenvolvimento, Indústria e Comércio Exterior, Available at www.mdic.gov.br (Accessed 1 December 2007).

Ministério da Fazenda (2012). *Economia Brasileira em Perspectiva, 17° Edição* [Online], Brasília, Ministério da Fazenda. Available at www.fazenda.gov.br/publicações (Accessed December 1, 2012).

Minsky, P.H. (1975). *John Maynard Keynes.* New York, Columbia University Press.

Orair, R. (2012). *Carga Tributária 2002—2012: estimação e análise dos determinantes da evolução recente* [Online], Brasília, Tesouro Nacional, Available at https://www.tesouro.fazenda.gov.br/pt/premio-tesouro-nacional/xvii-premio-2012-trabalhos-selecionados (Accessed 6 August 2014).

Orair, R. e Gobetti, S. (2010). 'Retomada do investimento público federal no Brasil e a política fiscal: em busca de um novo paradigma,' in IPEA (org.) (2010). *Brasil em Desenvolvimento: Estado, planejamento e políticas públicas.* Brasília, IPEA.

Paula, J.A. de (org.) (2003). *A Economia Política da Mudança: os desafios e os equívocos do início do governo Lula.* Belo Horizonte, Autêntica.

Pivetti, M. (2006). 'The 'Principle of Scarcity,' Pension Policy and Growth.' *Review of Political Economy*, vol. 18, no. 3, pp. 295–299.

Santos, C.H. (2012). *Um Panorama Macroeconômico das Finanças Públicas 2004–2011.* Brasília, IPEA.

Santos, C.H. e Costa, F.R. (2008). 'Uma metodologia de estimação da carga tributária bruta brasileira em bases trimestrais.' *Economia Aplicada*, vol. 12, no. 4, pp. 581–606.

Silveira, F.G. et al. (2011). 'Qual o impacto da Tributação e dos Gastos Públicos Sociais na distribuição de renda do Brasil? Observando os dois lados da moeda,' in Ribeiro, J.A. et al. (org.) (2011). *Progressividade da tributação e desoneração da folha de pagamentos: elementos para reflexão.* Brasília, IPEA/Sindifisco/DIEESE.

Chapter 7
Structuralist Reflections on Current Latin American Development

Ricardo Bielschowsky

Introduction

This chapter seeks to contribute to the debate on current development in Latin America. While hardly aspiring to present definitive answers, it represents a framework for formulating questions, inspired by CEPAL's classical structuralist approach.

After nearly a quarter century of reduced growth, Latin America's economy is finally growing again, hitting an average rate of GDP growth of 3.9% per year (CEPAL). Expansion held at around 5% per year from 2004–2008, recalling the high points of the era of industrialization. Growth was interrupted by the international crisis of 2009 and only resumed at a slower annual pace, around 4%, from 2010–2013; this rate was highest in the resource-rich region of South America, which saw a considerable improvement in terms of trade driven by Chinese importations, as opposed to the nations in the zone significantly poorer in resources and more dependent on the United States: Mexico, the rest of Central America, and the Caribbean.

Practically the whole of this period also saw a reduction in unemployment, improved salaries, and a fall in poverty indices—with the necessary qualifications for country-to-country differences, of course. Not less importantly, these years saw a surprising deconcentration of income, breaking with a distributive rigidity that had stood for several decades; although insufficient to break the region out of its status as the worst for distribution in the world, the reduction in Gini coefficients was significant (over 5 percentage points).

The most common question inspired by the current state of the economy, especially in the case of South America, is what may happen when this favorable phase, driven by the international prices of raw materials, comes to an end. Insufficient productive diversification, low industrial growth and considerable deficits in the balance of trade of industrial goods were recently accompanied by broadening deindustrialization (begun in the 1980s and 1990s), and, in some countries, the "reprimarization" of exports (return to major dependence on primary exports) and relatively reduced investment levels, both generally and specifically in terms of infrastructure, raised eyebrows as to the use made of this period to establish a systemic competitive and productive edge (CEPAL, 2012).

At the same time, in the social sphere, important advances in the labor market—with employment and salaries high, a few advances in terms of social protection, greater aid to the poorest and an improvement in income distribution—stand alongside at least two worrisome tendencies. Firstly, the fall in unemployment has been attained through low-quality positions, resulting in low labor productivity. Secondly, not only has the region seen scanty progress in terms of urban social infrastructure (low urban mobility, a lack of adequate sanitation systems and other insufficiencies in housing conditions, etc. persist), but the principle of universal social protection, as Lavinas (2013) points out, has also been defeated by growing commodification, as in the cases of health and education.

At the moment there seems to be great perplexity as to the answers to these and other problems, with the debate fragmented and disjointed. All signs point to the persistence of a somewhat confused ideological climate, without leadership or clear developmentalist references, and plagued by resistance from neoliberal ideology—which, although weakened, has continued far longer than the resounding failure of its application in the 1990s might suggest.

This chapter positions itself on developmentalist, heterodox ground. It takes concrete inspiration from the Brazilian case but also poses questions that, with certain provisos, may apply to many countries in Latin America.

This is the signal for the traditional warning employed by those who analyze the region: it is, as everyone knows, heterogeneous. While the countries of Latin America (exceptions aside) share high rates of poverty, a strong concentration of property and income, and, especially in South America, an abundance of natural resources, they also display widely varying sizes, degrees of modernity, and social and productive structures, as well as a variety of institutions and state purviews. The exercise of comprehending and analyzing current tendencies and attempting to extrapolate development strategies for the region as a whole is inevitably given to errors and imprecisions. One must be cautious, especially so because the potential power and the demands of state interventions involve functions and mechanisms that are specific to each of the region's countries, in several of their concrete aspects.

At some point, agendas for development must be made specific for each country, and it is then that analysis faces a special challenge. In heterodox camps, when analysts critical of the mainstream examine the past three and a half decades, their most common conclusion is the defense of "more state action," in both the social and the economic arenas. But those who defend this point of view are faced with a problem which is hardly trivial. During the period of industrialization, which came to a close in the early 1980s, while it was argued that the state is key to guaranteeing market efficiency and making structural transformation possible, a clear economic strategy was defended in tandem: industrialization. The recent return to the idea of the need for state action in social and economic development, alongside the gradual weakening of neoliberal hegemony, points to a question that has not yet been adequately addressed: more state action, but for which domestic development projects, duly differentiated from country to country?

This chapter amounts to a methodological exercise around the construction of an agenda for reflecting on this and other issues related to the current state of Latin American development. The aim at hand is to help formulate questions. The chapter's structure comprises three "structuralist pieces," conceived independently in other papers by the author. With a few additions and subtractions, they are summarized, tied together, and presented as a whole here.

The chapter is divided in three sections, apart from this introduction and the conclusion. Section 2 presents CEPAL's original structuralist analytical framework, and its modern form (cf. Bielschowsky, 2009). It is argued that structuralism, over 60 years after its conception, remains a powerful instrument with which to conceive of the developmental problems faced by Latin America, as attested to by the quality of CEPALian works from the contemporary "neostructuralist" period, begun in the 1990s and applied to the period of greater commercial and financial openness.[1] An important proviso must be noted, however:

---

    1 By way of example, consult the reports published from the periods of biennial sessions. A collection of the most relevant texts published by CEPAL from 1998–2008 may be found in

to wit, neostructuralism has ignored one of CEPAL's most relevant classical elements, namely the concept of "patterns" or "styles" of development.

Section 3 is inspired by an article that uses the Brazilian case to illustrate the analytic strength of this very concept, via an attempt to identify the pattern and strategy behind current Brazilian development (Bielschowsky, 2012). It is argued that, taking the place of the driving forces behind the economy (these being from 1930–1980 investment drivers linked to industrialization and urbanization), today sees three drivers for investment in operation, tied to three expanding fronts in the Brazilian economy: mass consumption, natural resources, and infrastructure. There follows a reflection on the social aspect of current Brazilian development, as linked to the economy.

The fourth section continues where the other two left off, and formulates a structuralist line of questioning as to the current pattern of Brazilian development, extending it to the rest of Latin America—with the necessary provisos about undue generalizations.[2]

The Classical Structuralist Approach and its Current State

With all due adaptations and updates, the original analytical framework of structuralism, as introduced by Raúl Prebisch at CEPAL, remains valid for examining the current state of Latin America.

This is the case, one might note, for reasons that are less than encouraging: though there has been social and economic progress since Prebisch (1949, [1951] 1973)[3] and other great partners in CEPALian theorization, such as Celso Furtado (1959, 1961, 1969), Aníbal Pinto (1965, 1970), Osvaldo Sunkel (1958, 1970), and Medina Echavarría (1963) analyzed the region in the 1950s and 1960s, underdevelopment is a long way from being overcome.

Prebisch's original structuralist analysis has three elements.[4] They define the underdevelopment of the Latin American "periphery" by contrast, holding up the socioeconomic structures prevalent in the "center":

1. Low diversity in production and exports, which brings external vulnerability and thus imposes structural limits on growth, stemming from the structural inequality in the balance of payments. This was true in the 1950s and holds true in the 2010s, with diversity either low or at least "insufficient" for the purposes of sustaining growth in the medium or long term. One has only to note that the region's balance of trade is increasingly weighted towards deficits in terms of goods and services of high technological density—the very area with the greatest dynamism in world consumption and commerce.

2. Structural heterogeneity in production, with abundant work availability and low average productivity, producing, as its "mirror image," poor income distribution and social heterogeneity, accompanied by the concentration of property. This was true in the 1950s, and remains the case today.

Bielschowsky (2010).

2   This reflection was presented by the author at a conference in Rio de Janeiro in October 2013: the "desiguALdades" Project from the Freie Universität Berlin, organized by Professors Barbara Fritz and Lena Lavinas.

3   Prebisch's initial trilogy in CEPAL, written in 1949 and 1950, includes the inaugural 1949 edition of Estudio Económico (see CEPAL,1951).

4   Cf. Rodrigues (1981), as regards the first two.

3. Hobbled states with insufficient tax revenue and inadequate entrepreneurial capacity, creating a dysfunctional institutional backdrop for investment and technical progress, and driving the tendency towards a low propensity to invest and innovate. With few exceptions in the area of tax revenue, and with provisos as to the profound differences between the countries of the region, this characterization remains valid for Latin America today.

This identification of Latin American underdevelopment and analysis of "center-periphery" relationships framed the formulation of CEPAL's theses in the 1950s and 60s, such as the deterioration in terms of trade, the asymmetry between a high propensity to import and low export elasticity (leading to a structural imbalance in the balance of payments), structural inflation, a tendency towards long-term underemployment, technological and financial dependence, and "styles" of development.[5]

It is no challenge to confirm the continued urgency of this inaugural characterization of underdevelopment, and its related theses. The risk of undoing recent improvements in the terms of trade lies behind countless analyses that reject deindustrialization and "reprimarization"; and the regrettable memory of countless episodes of external shocks—which have grown more frequent since the financial opening of the 1990s, thanks to the volatility of financial flows—serves to underscore the continued relevance of both the thesis of structural inequalities in the balance of payments as well as of the existence of non-monetary causes for inflation. This is no less true in the cases of predictions of continued underemployment—the abundance of manpower and the precarious state of labor relations have borne out the pessimistic forecasts of the past—and theories pointing to the region's technological and financial dependency. Latin America is still far from shaking its "peripheral condition" and staking out long-term autonomy in order to grow.

Structuralist thought in its current "neostructuralist" incarnation is an adaptation of the classical model that seeks to analyze peripheral conditions in the context of the new regulatory framework introduced by neoliberal reforms. Its current form, as seen in CEPAL's primary documents produced since the early 1990s, has a few improvements and a few shortcomings in relation to its classical forebear.

The main steps forwards here are the inclusion of the topic of environmental sustainability (for example, CEPAL, 2000); increased attention to macroeconomic problems (for example, CEPAL, 1995 and 2002) and the issue of education (for example, CEPAL, 1992); as well as, under the clear inaugural influence of Fajnzylber (1983), the area of technological innovation (for example, CEPAL, 1990 and 2012). No less important was the (tardy) inclusion of the issue of social protection and the rights of citizenship, in the 2000s (for example, CEPAL 2000 and 2006).[6]

The model, however, also introduced two (interrelated) steps back. First, there is little attention paid to investment—the principal raison d'être for economic developmentalist ideology in CEPAL's first decades, during which the political objective of the agency was

---

5   Later on, in the early 1980s, Sunkel, 1981, was equally prescient in addressing the issue of environmental sustainability from a structuralist perspective, calling attention to the "dominant" and "ascendant" nature of the destructive pattern of production and consumption prevailing in the socioeconomic processes of the region.

6   The matter of distribution, present in CEPAL texts since the 1960s, limited its approach to poverty and the concentration of income as stemming from the condition of the labor market, ignoring issues of social protection (welfare, education, health, housing, etc.). My thanks go to Lena Lavinas (I.E.-UFRJ) for her pertinent critical observation in this case.

to lend speed and efficiency to the process of accumulating industrial capital. This neglect has come despite the fact that fixed investment remains by far the principal vehicle of technical progress, and that in Latin America, increases in productivity and competitiveness are rarely brought via innovations not tied to new equipment. Secondly, the neostructuralist framework lacks a notion of national patterns and strategies for development, in which an analysis of the process of investment—and its principal determinations—is central.[7]

The way to recover this idea of patterns of development is to identify the current drivers of investment in Latin America, and see what is happening with them. In the period of industrialization, investment was led by industrial expansion and the infrastructure that served it, including the infrastructural framework formed as a consequence of concomitant urbanization. What fronts of expansion may be found in Latin American economies today?

Brazilian Development: Pattern and Strategy

In the case of Brazil, I sought to answer the question above with a sketch of what I believe to be the country's new pattern of development.[8]

Economic and social evolution over the past decade in Brazil have been good to the country's population, giving hope and force to social pressure for a reduction in poverty levels and the concentration of property, income, power, and access to the rights of citizenship—which, despite important recent advances, persist markedly in Brazilian society.

The era of state-led Brazilian industrialization (1930–1980) produced developmentalist thought dedicated to the project of the structural transformation of the economy, from agro-export to urban-industrial. What is current developmentalist thought doing now?

A counterpoint with the older style of developmentalism may help to qualify the question. To this end, three of the previous model's characteristics will be recalled here.

First, it was argued that the state is necessary to lend efficiency to the market economy and make structural economic transformations possible. Albeit simplifying, one might say that this principle is broadly shared by modern developmentalist thought.

Secondly, the old model supported a clear economic strategy: industrialization. Hence the question—what strategy is being supported now?

Thirdly, two strains of thought on social transformation—conservative and progressive developmentalism—were facing off. The victory of the former was first secured by rigid structures of power and domination, then consummated by the 1964 military coup and elevated to hegemonic status over the course of multiple military governments. The latter, which sought social inclusion through work and popular sharing in the fruits of the technical progress created by industrialization, stayed in the political fight for a more just society

---

7   Gerschenkron (1962) is, of course, the most important point of reference in the discussion of "patterns of growth." Another pertinent source of inspiration is CEPAL's historical-structural approach. The intellectual production of many CEPALians, such as Aníbal Pinto (1965; 1970), Celso Furtado (1959; 1961; 1969), and Maria da Conceição Tavares (1964; 1971) is based on the concept of patterns, styles, or models of growth, as indicated by Bielschowsky (1998). The first issue of the CEPAL Review, in 1976, included three articles discussing the concept of "styles of development," from economist Aníbal Pinto (1976) and sociologists Graciarena (1976) and Wolfe (1976). On this topic, see also Sainz and Calcagno (1992).

8   This section is a slightly modified version of a brief article published in 2012, in Portuguese, on the site of the "Plataforma Política Social" network (www.plataformasocial.net.br), which is, in turn, based on Bielschowsky (2012).

even post-1964, eventually being rewarded with the return to democracy and the 1988 constitution, which confers broad rights to citizenship. The question, again: what strategy is being pursued by current developmentalist strategy in the social arena?

As for the first of the two questions—that is, a strategy for the economic arena—my diagnosis of recent developments and the outlook for the future is that, despite macroeconomic policies that have been often unfavorable to growth and almost always unfavorable to competitiveness, in addition to an exceedingly modest performance over the past three years (2011–2013), the country entered a new era in the mid-2000s.

The Brazilian economy's logic of expansion saw the inauguration of three fronts for expansion, or three "investment drivers," the combination of which contains considerable potential dynamism in the long term: an internal market of mass production and consumption, infrastructure (productive and social), and natural resources.[9]

This is not trivial. If we consider that a development strategy is the design of the deliberate enactment, by governments and social actors, of a viable and desirable pattern of development, then we may say that we are looking at possibilities for defining and affirming a promising strategy in the economic field, ones not seen since 1980, when half a century of growth and technical progress via industrialization came to an end. After over two decades of stagnation and dead ends, recent years have seen the emergence of a viable pattern of structural transformations conducive to development, centered on the aforementioned triad of investment drivers.

The strength of these drivers is externally dependent on the evolution of the Chinese economy and the development of the international crisis; and internally dependent on the strategy and policies to be followed, especially when it comes to adding two "turbines" to these three motors—namely, technological innovation and the broadening of internal production chains—and an increase in investment rates.

This article does not examine the advances or shortfalls in the planning and execution of governmental policies in terms of taking advantage of the potential of existing growth. There would be both positive and negative aspects of note, but they would exceed the scope of this text.

One may simply say that an inadequate approach to these three investment drivers will mean wasting the enormous potential for growth in productivity, income, and employment that they represent. There is the risk, for example, that the framework of leaning on an "enclave" form of export-focused agribusiness may spread, that investments in infrastructure may be made with principally imported capital goods, or—worst of all—that growth may occur without industrial diversification and expansion, and in the context of a continued "reprimarization" of exports.

For that matter, it may be prudent to warn that the model is unlikely to stand if the situation is one of mass consumption in Brazil and mass production in China—mass production and consumption must both be in effect domestically. The continued unsatisfactory performance of the manufacturing sector is a waste of a prime space for the production and creation of income and employment, which offers not only potential gains in productivity and competitiveness by virtue of the scale of mass production and innovation, but also may serve to generate independent sectors that, if adequately managed, will make it possible to

---

9   In a recent study (Bielschowsky et al., 2014), it was shown that the period 2004–2008 saw simultaneous expansions in investments on these three fronts, at nearly identical speeds, surprisingly enough, each at around 10% per annum, on average.

bypass the possibility of the balance of payments hampering growth, a recurring feature of Brazilian economic history.

There is enormous room to be potentially staked out by governmental policies that maximize incipient forces and oppose obstructions to domestic development. Developmentalist thought, in order to ensure growth and competitiveness in this new stage, must go far beyond the necessary macroeconomics—which have wrongly dominated the debate on development in Brazil—and include the sphere of productive transformation via investment and innovation.[10]

I will now move to two comments on the relationship between the economic and social arenas. They serve to show that, despite the fact that new developmentalism has a way to go in terms of assimilating this relationship, the historical context for advances is promising. I would concur with the assertion by Eduardo Fagnani, coordinator of the "Plataforma Política Social" network, in a message recently sent to participants in the network: "The principal hypothesis I have labored under is that this improvement in welfare is the product of forays into this new model of developmentalism that has broadened the convergence between economic and social objectives."[11] The two comments that follow will demonstrate my affinity with this proposition.

The first has to do with a relatively obvious connection between the economic and social dimensions of development, which is comprised of both. As has been recognized, mass consumption has been a decisive element in recent economic expansion, and was the product of a significant increase in wages and transfers (for which the increase in the minimum wage was decisive), a rise in popularly available credit, a drop in the relative prices of wage goods, and a strengthening of social welfare (Bolsa Família, etc.).

Not all scholars of government policy are aware that the strategy for growth along with income redistribution via production and mass consumption was clearly spelled out in Lula's 2002 platform and highlighted by the administration in its 2004–2007 "Multiannual Plan," which was approved in 2003 (Brasil, 2003). Of course, what has happened since then is nothing more than the first step on the long path to following the proposal that Celso Furtado (1969) and other progressive intellectuals and politicians made more than forty years ago, urging a change in the model of concentrated income and elite consumption to deconcentrated income and mass consumption.

The second comment addresses a point that may be much more controversial. Beyond the fact of an improvement in income distribution and a substantial drop in poverty indices, and a significant increase in occupation and the formalization of work relations to boot, what can be said of the attention paid to the rights of citizenship, as expressed in the 1988 Constitution?

Fagnani is, once again, correct in his summary of the issue when he says that, since the introduction of the Constitution, Brazilian society has been home to opposing tendencies that express a tension between "small state" and "welfare state" models. The former gained strength from 1990 to 2002 under neoliberalism; the second attempted a shaky comeback

---

10 This observation stands in terms of a certain neglect of these spheres by "new developmentalism," an expression coined by Bresser-Pereira to describe a group of economists critical of the macroeconomics dedicated to stabilization and less attentive to the damage done to industrial competitiveness by elevated exchange and interest rates. The first new-developmentalist essays date from the mid-2000s. See, for example, Sicsú et al. (2005) and Bresser-Pereira (2010).

11 See at www.plataformasocial.net.br.

in the first years of Lula's administration (2003–2005), and seems to have made more significant progress since then.

On one hand, one can, for example, turn up indications that the immense concentration of property has not been broken up, the pressures exerted by and the advance of privatization and commodification over social policies have only increased (across health, education, culture, security, etc.), little progress has been made in terms of urban mobility and sanitation, and the federal pact has been weakened.

On the other hand, one can also display evidence of advances in terms of the strengthening of a fundamental part of social protection policies—i.e., growing formalization of the labor market and the establishment of a policy to raise the minimum wage that led to close to a doubling in real values from 2003 to 2013. Although they have been quite slow, there have been clear advances in policies covering education, security, food, and unemployment insurance. Initiatives such as these, in a universal vein, were carried out in solidarity with the fight against poverty and extreme indigence.

The coexistence of contradictory trends ought to come as no surprise: this is a period of the clash between market individualism, born of neoliberalism, and a defense of the principles of solidarity and rights as expressed in the 1988 Constitution. The clear identification of a desirable and viable strategy for development, in which economic and societal progress are integrated, will strengthen the political and ideological dispute on the side of a vision of full citizenship.

A victory in this arena will depend on many factors, among them the progress and results of the distributive conflict in the labor market, which may tend to worsen. This leads me to a final comment, speaking of a new Brazilian dilemma: the fact that the country has managed to combine a decade-long virtuous increase in employment and salaries with a simultaneous, alarmingly slender increase in productivity.

All signs seem to indicate that improvements in distribution and an increase in the salaries of the poorest sectors of society are now sparking an important change in the profile of the expansion in demand and, thus, in the expansion of employment as well—analogous to Furtado's (1969) prediction in the 1960s as to what would happen in industry if an improvement in distribution were to take place. Current tendencies appear to be leaning towards a broadening of labor-intensive services, which display much lower productivity in relation to sectors with middling and high-intensity focus on capital and a qualified workforce.

Meanwhile, this process does not seem to be inflating costs, which may occur following businesses' reactions to salary hikes that outpace productivity—perhaps because initial profit margins were quite high. In the middle term, the solutions that capitalism tends to offer for this problem are mediated by technical progress that reduces reliance on manpower. And in the long term, with well-functioning national states, improvements in infrastructure and the education system also work in favor of productivity, soothing the distributive conflict.

In the short term, should inflationary pressures on costs be confirmed, the best way out is the formation of pacts between workers and employers in terms of "wage policies." The negotiations set for 2015 in the Brazilian Congress on the maintenance or modification of the rule determining an increase in the minimum wage present themselves as an extremely favorable opportunity.

One thing, however, is certain: despite conservative affirmations to the contrary, manpower in Brazil remains far from scarce. Subsistence farmers, household employees, and street vendors abound, as well as those working in a considerable number of other occupations that may, in relatively short periods, be transferred to modern sectors of

Brazil's economy with significant increases in net income, either attenuating or completely eliminating the eventual inflationary pressures. In other words, the Brazilian economy is still far from absolute full employment, which continues to limit potential output expansion; and there is still considerable space within which to increase average productivity through the transfer of underemployed workers to more modern sectors.

Structuralist Interrogations of the Current Model of Brazilian Development, with Generalizations as to Latin America

This section brings together questions drawn from the structuralist approach to Latin American underdevelopment, previously discussed in section 2 (insufficient production diversity, structural heterogeneity, and institutional inadequacy) with the notions of patterns of development and fronts of expansion that may be applicable to Brazil today, as discussed in section 3 (natural resources, infrastructure, and mass consumption), extending these, whenever appropriate, to other countries in the region.

At this point, I may as well repeat an important caveat. This sidesteps the fact that, in comparison to South America, the countries of Central America and the Caribbean are for the most part poorer in natural resources and are much more closely tied to tendencies in the American economy—the "maquiladoras," for example, tourism, and remittances from immigrants in the USA. This is also the case with Mexico, with the exception of its petroleum.[12]

Structuralist analysis is no less valid in the case of these economies than with their South American counterparts, but their cases must be analyzed as a separate bloc. This is not done here, which means that the procedure which will be followed here is extremely simplifying.

Persistence of low and/or inadequate production diversity?

Among the three fronts for expansion in the Brazilian economy, two seem to hold for a considerable number of countries in the region: i.e., natural resources and infrastructure (general and residential), the latter made possible in many countries by their very wealth in terms of natural resources. The same is not true for the expansion front linked to mass production and consumption; besides Brazil, which has been increasing the dynamism of its economy this way, Mexico and Argentina—given the greater relative size of their economies and their greater production diversity—are the only nations with the potential to follow suit. Moreover, in the case of Mexico, Central America, and the Caribbean, as already observed, natural resources have not had the same dynamic effect as in South America. Instead, when American demand heats up, expansion may occur through maquiladora-related industries.

These differences aside, the point I would like to highlight here is that all the fronts of expansion currently in action in Latin American economies seem unlinked from the construction of new production chains and relevant innovative processes (CEPAL, 2012). This is not only true for segments of high technological intensity, but also for a significant part of the manufacturing industry—which is only growing slowly—in part influenced by the strong uptick in demand through popular consumption, driven by wage increases and distributive improvements. One might note, incidentally, that in a number of countries,

---

12   In this vein, see the excellent book by Bértola and Ocampo (2012), covering 200 years of the economic history of Latin America, chapters 4 and 5.

macroeconomic policies focused on controlling inflation through high interest rates and the appreciation of the exchange rate have conspired against investments in the manufacturing industry.

Meeting this important increase in popular consumption over the past decade seems to be a task limited to agriculture in general and the provision of services, especially those with a low concentration of capital and knowledge, which operate at low levels of productivity. This recent trend has a highly laudable offshoot, namely, considerable job creation. These occupations, however low their productivity may be, have the virtue of absorbing manpower in subsistence activities, elevating the average productivity of the working population. But this presents various problems as well, not the least being that this trend does not solve the classical structuralist issue of the provision of a domestic offering of tradable goods with international competitiveness. Not promoting diversity in production and exports holds back technical progress and any potential rise in productivity, increases external vulnerability and continues exposing the region to the permanent threat of the return of instability, which may be an especially grave one should there came a sharp fall in commodity prices.

Perhaps the most troubling matter is the treatment being given to natural resources, an old front for the accumulation of capital dating back to the colonial period, reinvigorated in this "Sino-centric era" of the world economy. The main question here is: is there adequate "governance of natural resources"?[13] The reply does not seem to be affirmative.

The first issue to be observed has to do with the wasted opportunity to develop domestic production chains and technological capacities in the extraction of natural resources. On one hand, there are cases that point towards favorable advances in this field, such as Petrobras; on the other hand, however, it should be no difficult task to identify a good number of cases in which resource extraction hews closer to the old "enclave" model of mining, with the difference here being that this may be happening even in agribusiness, due to the intense mechanization of the industry over recent decades. The neglect of productive diversification includes the fact that the valorization of exported natural resources has driven up the exchange rate, affecting the competitiveness of the manufacturing industry and the rest of the tradable sector; for a considerable period this was shored up, of course, by the vigorous influx of short-term capital attracted by high interest rates and the financial market's sense of trust in the solvency of countries exporting natural resource-based products.

There are at least three other issues related to the use of the natural resources to be administered in the name of economic and social development, in addition to production diversification: royalties and taxes, environmental control, and access for foreign capital. I will return to this point later on, when we examine the issue of institutional inadequacies.

Persistence of structural heterogeneity?

Evidence abounds that the period of recent growth has brought significant social improvements, with persistently falling unemployment, increased wages, a strong decline in poverty and indigence rates, and an important reduction in income concentration. Nevertheless, despite these advances, the region is still far from having overcome structural

---

13   This expression has been employed by CEPAL of late, inspired by its current executive secretary, Alícia Bárcena. See, for example, CEPAL (2013).

and productive heterogeneity; it has not changed the convergence of abundant manpower, low average productivity, and concentrated property. Underdevelopment, in other words, has not budged. Marked social heterogeneity is the mirror image of productive heterogeneity and the concentration of property.

The good news that may be drawn from recent trends is that, at least in Brazil's case—but possibly also for other Latin American countries—some signs point to the beginning of a reduction in the relative abundance of manpower, even in the lowest-qualified brackets, which increases workers' bargaining power in general. This is a consequence of the fact that the labor supply has been expanding much more slowly, tied to the reality that the improvement in distribution seems to be changing the characteristics of consumption and production, driving them towards extremely manpower-intensive services.

One might note that, given the expansion of employment in services, there have emerged ways around the problem of low income elasticity in the generation of direct jobs in activities tied to natural resources (mining and highly mechanized agriculture), as well as the problem presented by the fact that infrastructure investments tend to be increasingly detached from locally produced capital goods, the end result being a low accelerator and multiplier effect on employment in the economy.

Should these tendencies be confirmed, this would point towards a virtuous movement, strengthening the labor market and pressing it toward better wages and working conditions. At the same time, as I observed earlier, slow gains in productivity may lead to a worsening of the distributive conflict and potential cost-inflation problems, provoked by companies translating wage increases that outstrip productivity into higher prices.

Investigating the need for policies to deal with the considerable sectors of the population that operate on low productivity would certainly include a long list of items. For example, although there are no systematic measures of what has been happening in terms of agrarian reform, it does not seem that any significant progress has been made in this field—nor, it should be noted, in terms of addressing the concentration of land ownership or the titling of property for the residents of low-income urban communities. At the same time, one might wonder to what extent the current upswing has made governments more attentive to supporting family agriculture, small and medium-sized urban businesses, microcredit or autonomous workers, to the education and training of human resources in general and average technical education, etc. A systematic evaluation of figures in these areas might well indicate progress.

At the same time, it is clear that little or nothing has happened within the tax system to improve income distribution; in general, it seems to have remained profoundly regressive, and, in practice, has been a growing force in the perverse fragmentation of the quality of services, as is the case with tax breaks for private health and education providers.[14]

Serious concerns also persist in terms of the fiscal space left for social protection, especially when considering the inclusion of workers who remain in the limbo of informality—this being a full half of the workforce, engaged in a significant number of economies. Revenues have improved in countries with abundant natural resources, but across the region as a whole, the volume of resources is too low to compensate for the enormous contingent of the workforce operating in these conditions by absorbing them into more effective social protection schemes.

---

14   Individual income tax code in Brazil allows for one to deduct from their taxable income sums spent on the education and health of contributors and their dependents, up to a certain level.

Persistence of institutional inadequacy?

In the classical thought of the 1950s, the general backwardness of the region's national states (then linked to the exporting tradition), plus a lack of entrepreneurial ability to carry on the process of industrialization, represented an institutional state of affairs unlikely to foment investment and technical progress. The solution would be the reorganization of state institutions in order to make "state-led industrialization" possible.[15]

Times have changed. State apparatuses are more advanced than they were then, large multinationals have come to the region—including in industry—and national economic groups have formed, some of them on a truly large scale. Even so, considering what is necessary to efficiently put a strong development project in motion, it would be no exaggeration to say that the region still suffers from institutional inadequacy in many senses. The state that would be required to carry out strategies for production diversification and social homogenization is a far cry from what we see now, and the list of inadequacies is long. To list some examples:

1. With a few exceptions, tax revenues are low;
2. Tax collection systems are regressive, further contributing to the unequal distribution of income;
3. Few countries can boast minimally comprehensive, integrated social protection systems;
4. Governments' ability to execute investments in infrastructure, be it directly or through private-public partnerships, is considerably reduced;
5. Institutional ability to control the market in privatized infrastructure sectors is low;
6. Domestic firms are too small in scope to face down global competition and technical progress (relative scarcity of "global players");
7. Domestic innovation systems are relatively weak;
8. Financial systems are incomplete, lacking long-term capital markets, and thus ill-suited to serve in financing fixed investment and innovation;
9. Institutions regulating the environment lack the power and the ability to intervene in cases of adverse natural consequences resulting from the actions of economic agents;
10. The countries in the region are unprepared or politically unmotivated in terms of exercising proper governance of their natural resources.

As for the last point, as I noted previously, Latin America has not seen a trend in the direction of furnishing intensive activities in natural resources with domestic production chains and technological capacities. The shaky governance of natural resources is also plagued by at least three other problems.

Firstly, attention must be paid to the growing pressure on the environment. It would be a mistake to wait for an international consensus on environmental policy; regulatory policies must be put into practice within autonomous domestic spheres.

Secondly, the state has not been adequately absorbing the extraordinary revenues from the activities based on the management of natural resources. Royalties and taxes must be raised so as to finance strategic development goals (both economic and social) and avoid a concentration of income; another key move would be to control exports by large firms in order to avoid transfer pricing schemes.

---

15   This expression is used by Bértola and Ocampo (2012).

Last, but not least, foreign land ownership and/or foreign access to petroleum/ gas and other natural resources are on the rise. There has been no collective response from the countries of Latin America in order to establish conditions for foreign investors in natural resources, which serves to weaken the bargaining position of each individual nation.

The moment to face down this monumental array of developmentalist tasks has not passed; China and other countries will likely be seeking access to Latin American natural resources for some time yet. Given vast Chinese and Asian dependence on said resources, one might imagine considerable maneuvering room to impose conditions. Strengthening the Latin American position in these negotiations would be much facilitated if isolated and uncoordinated attempts were substituted by a collective pact setting minimum demands.

Until this comes to pass, questions remain in the air. For example: isn't Latin America selling itself on the cheap to the Chinese? Is the region hastening the end of the boom by granting unlimited access to this and other countries? Why not study and imitate the ways in which the United States, Europe, Japan, and China have historically dealt with foreign investments in their natural resources, thus gleaning lessons to benefit the region as a whole?

By Way of Conclusion

This chapter has featured three structuralist reflections, focused on analytical formulations as to the current state of the process of Latin American development. In the first, the principal elements of classical structuralism were reviewed, with the argument that they remain valid for the analysis of conditions in Latin America today.

In the second, the current Brazilian case was discussed via the use of a key concept in the structuralist tradition, i.e. patterns of development. It was argued that the effort to make the economy more dynamic in the long term hangs on the ability to "govern" the areas characterized as three fronts of expansion currently operating in the economy—mass consumption, natural resources and infrastructure—and bring out their potential through policies of investment in production chains and innovation.

The third reflection incorporated elements from the first two in order to formulate relevant questions as to the current status of Latin American development. Emphasis went to the Brazilian case, but reflections were extended to the whole of the region.

One final reflection may be in order, by way of a conclusion. Economic development is growth with structural transformation. The golden rule in formulating a specific development agenda for each country is to identify its most desirable, viable development pattern, based on ongoing historical trends, and draw up a strategy in order to "govern" them.

This is no easy task; each country will inevitably have its own particular strategy, hinging on the combination of three dimensions: the scope of its resources (natural, infrastructural, manpower, "knowledge," etc.); the size of its market and its ability to insert itself into the international market via commerce; and its capacity to coordinate and intensify investment decisions by both the state and businesses, including the way in which macroeconomic policy is administered.

This is a subject that has not been plumbed sufficiently in the case of the vast majority of Latin American nations, thus forming a promising avenue for future research. Such task should ideally be accompanied by the structuralist analytic framework discussed here.

Bibliography

Bértola, L. and Ocampo, J.A. (2012). *The Economic Development of Latin America since Independence.* Oxford, Oxford University Press.

Bielschowsky, R. (1998). 'Cincuenta años del pensamiento de la CEPAL: una reseña,' *Cincuenta Años de Pensamiento en la CEPAL.* Santiago de Chile, CEPAL.

Bielschowsky, R. (2009). 'Sixty years of CEPAL: Structuralism and neostructuralism.' *CEPAL Review,* vol. 97, no. 1, pp. 171–192.

Bielschowsky, R. (comp.) (2010). *Sesenta años de la CEPAL—textos selecionados del decênio 1998–2008.* Buenos Aires, Siglo Veintiuno.

Bielschowsky, R. (2012).'Estratégia de desenvolvimento e as três frentes de expansão no Brasil: um desenho conceitual.' *Economia e Sociedade,* vol. 21, n. 1, pp. 729–747.

Bielschowsky, R. et al. (2014). *Evolução dos investimentos nas três frentes de expansão da economia brasileira na década de 2000.* Rio de Janeiro, IPEA.

Brasil (2003). *Plano Plurianual 2004–2007.* Brasília, MPOG.

Bresser-Pereira, L.C. (2010). *Novo desenvolvimentismo: uma proposta para a economia do Brasil.* São Paulo, Nueva Sociedad.

CEPAL (1951). Estudio Económico de America Latina, *CEPAL Working Paper No. E/ CN, 12/164/Rev.1.* New York, UNO.

CEPAL (1990). 'Transformación productiva con equidad: la tarea prioritaria del desarrollo de América Latina y el Caribe en los años noventa,' *CEPAL Working Paper No. LC/ G.1601-P.* Santiago de Chile, CEPAL.

CEPAL (1992). 'Educación y conocimiento: eje de la transformación productiva con equidad,' *CEPAL Working Paper No. LC/G.1702/Rev.2-P.* Santiago de Chile, CEPAL.

CEPAL (1995). 'América Latina y el Caribe: políticas para mejorar la inserción en la economía mundial,' *CEPAL Working Paper No. LC/G.1800/Rev.1-P.* Santiago de Chile, CEPAL.

CEPAL (2000). 'Equidad, desarrollo y ciudadanía,' *CEPAL Working Paper No. LC/G.2071/ Rev.1-P.* Santiago de Chile, CEPAL.

CEPAL (2002). 'Globalización y desarrollo,' *CEPAL Working Paper No. LC/G.2157 SES.29/3.* Santiago de Chile, CEPAL.

CEPAL (2006). 'La protección social de cara al futuro: acceso, financiamiento y solidariedad,' *CEPAL Working Paper No. LC/G.2294 SES 31/3.* Santiago de Chile, CEPAL.

CEPAL (2012). 'Cambio Estructural para la Igualdad, una visión integrada del desarrollo,' *CEPAL Working Paper No. LC/G.2524 SES.34/3.* Santiago de Chile, CEPAL.

CEPAL (2013). 'Recursos naturales: situación y tendencias para una agenda de desarrollo regional en América Latina y el Caribe,' *CEPAL Working Paper No. LC/L.3748.* Santiago de Chile, CEPAL.

Echavarría, J.M. (1963). 'Consideraciones sociológicas sobre el desarrollo económico de América Latina,' *CEPAL Working Paper No. E/CN.12/646.* Santiago de Chile, CEPAL.

Fajnzylber, F. (1983). *La industrialización trunca de América Latina.* México, DF, Editorial Nueva Imagen.

Furtado, C. (1959). *Formação econômica do Brasil.* Rio de Janeiro, Fundo de Cultura.

Furtado, C. (1961). *Desenvolvimento e subdesenvolvimento.* Rio de Janeiro, Fundo de Cultura.

Furtado, C. (1969). 'Desarrollo y estancamiento en América Latina: un enfoque estructuralista.' *Investigación Económica*, vol. 29, no. 113, pp. 43–73.

Gerschenkron, A. (1962). *Economic Backwardness in Historical Perspective.* New York, Frederick A Praeger.

Graciarena, J. (1976). 'Poder y estilos de desarrollo: una perspectiva heterodoxa.' *CEPAL Review,* vol. 1, no. 1, pp. 173–193.

Lavinas, L. (2013). 'The XXI century welfare.' *New Left Review,* 84, page 4–40.

Pinto, A. (1965). 'La concentración del progreso técnico y de sus frutos en el desarrollo de América Latina.' *El Trimestre Económico*, vol. 32, no.1, pp. 3–69.

Pinto, A. (1970). 'Naturaleza e implicaciones de la "heterogeneidad estructural" de la América Latina.' *El Trimestre Económico,* vol. 37, no. 1, pp. 83–100.

Pinto, A. (1976). 'Notas sobre los estilos de desarrollo en América Latina.' *Revista de la CEPAL,* vol. 1, no. 1, pp. 99–130.

Prebisch, R. (1949). 'El desarrollo económico de América Latina y algunos de sus principales problemas.' *CEPAL Working Paper No. E/CN.12/89,* Santiago de Chile, CEPAL.

Prebisch, R. [1951] (1973). *Problemas teóricos y prácticos del crecimiento económico.* Santiago de Chile, CEPAL.

Rodriguez, O. (1981). *La teoría del subdesarrollo de la CEPAL.* México, DF, Siglo XXI.

Saínz, P. and Calcagno, A. (1992). 'In search of another form of development.' *CEPAL Review,* vol. 48, no. 1, pp. 7–41.

Sicsú, J. et al. (2005). *Novo desenvolvimenismo: um projeto nacional de desenvolvimento com equidade social.* Rio de Janeiro, Manolo.

Sunkel, O. (1958). 'La inflación chilena: un enfoque heterodoxo.' *El Trimestre Económico*, vol. 25, no. 4, pp. 570–599.

Sunkel, O. (1970). 'Desarrollo, subdesarrollo, dependencia, marginación y desigualdades espaciales: hacia un enfoque totalizante,' *Revista Latinoamericana de Estudios Urbanos Regionales No. 1,* CIDU/CLACSO. Santiago de Chile.

Sunkel, O. (1981). 'La interacción entre los estilos de desarrollo y medio ambiente en la América Latina,' in Sunkel, O. y Gligo, N. (comp.) (1981). *Estilos de desarrollo y medio ambiente en la América Latina.* México, DF, Fondo de Cultura Económica.

Tavares, M. da C. (1964). 'Auge y declinación del proceso de sustitución de importaciones en el Brasil.' *Boletín Económico de América Latina*, vol. 1, no. 1, pp. 1–63.

Tavares, M. da C. y Serra, J. (1971). 'Más allá del estancamiento.' *El Trimestre Económico*, vol. 38, no. 4, pp. 905–950.

Wolfe, M. (1976). 'Enfoques del desarrollo: de quién y hacia qué?' *Revista de la CEPAL*, vol. 1, no. 1, pp. 129–172.

Chapter 8

Macroeconomics, the Job Market, and Income Distribution in Brazil over the Recent Past: Progress, Regression, and Challenges

João Saboia[1]

Introduction

For decades, Brazil has been known as one of the countries with the worst income distributions in the world. From the 1970s to the 1990s, the Gini index for household income distribution per capita oscillated systematically around 0.6, an extremely high level reached by just a few countries. Starting in the early 2000s, however, income inequality in Brazil took a new turn.[2]

A combination of economic and social policies led to a process of reducing income inequality, which has now lasted for over a decade. Though the Bolsa Família Program[3] is the best-known example of this, social policy developed over recent years as a whole is much broader, benefiting millions of Brazilians at the base of the income pyramid. At the same time, the job market has undergone an extremely favorable period, with considerable job and income creation.

The Workers' Party has held the Presidency of the Republic since 2003, first with President Lula, for two terms (2003/2010), then with his successor Dilma Rousseff (2011/2014). The continuity of a single party in power over a long period, with social issues as a clear priority, allowed for the development of policies without significant breaks, as is generally the case when power is transferred to the opposition. This brought about a clear process of social ascension.

At first in 2009, during the international crisis, and then after 2011, Brazil underwent a clear economic deceleration; this, as of now, does not seem to have affected the process of the improvement in income distribution, although it does pose serious risks for its continuation over the coming years. How long will it be possible to keep up the improvement in income distribution in a country that began growing just around 2% per year in the triennial period 2011/2013, and which does not look to change, economically

---

1   The author thanks Pilar Picon, Giovanna Loiola, and Rodrigo Bazzanella for their help in the collection and processing of the empirical material used in this text, realized with the help of a scientific research fellowship from CNPq and UFRJ.

2   The improvement in income distribution (personal or household) began at the turn of the 2000s. The functional distribution of income (capital x labor), however, only began to improve midway through the decade.

3   The Bolsa Família Program transfers resources to around 14 million families with household income per capita up to R$154 (close to US$50), at an approximate cost of 0.5% of GDP.

speaking, in the short term? Will the job market continue displaying favorable results over the coming years, benefiting the redistributive process? What trajectory might the economy take for the country to return to growth and income to continue to be redistributed without greater inflationary pressures? These and other questions will have to be addressed and discussed farther along.

This introduction will be followed by a brief macroeconomic panorama of the past few years, then a discussion on the recent evolution of the job market and income distribution. The next section seeks to understand how the job market has behaved so positively, contributing to improvements in income distribution, while economic growth has been relatively mediocre over most of the period analyzed. The challenges to be faced in the process of ensuring the continuity of this positive trend are also discussed. Lastly, broad conclusions are presented.

A Summary of the Macroeconomic Situation

Starting in the past decade, the Brazilian macroeconomics saw its share of ups and downs. The 2000s began with slow growth that lasted until the start of the Lula administration, in 2003. The next quinquennial brought a vigorous recovery, which came to a close in 2008 with the effects of the international crisis. Despite measures meant to stimulate consumption in 2009, the result was a drop in GDP that year. In 2010, the economy began recovering again, displaying its best growth rate in the decade and hitting 7.5%. Since then, its evolution has been quite unfavorable, with an average growth rate of 2% per year for the triennial 2011/2013 and no growth in 2014.

There are a number of reasons for the performance described above. Over the period 2004/2008, the Brazilian economy benefited with the favorable turn in the international economy, which was also growing at high rates, leading to ever-higher prices for exported commodities and to the entry of capital into the country. On the other hand, the population's increased spending power fed back into the economy through the growth in familial consumption. With the crisis of 2008, this situation changed starkly. The recent persistence of relatively high inflation rates has led authorities to set interest rates at extremely high levels, attracting the entry of speculative capital and bumping up the exchange rate. The negative effects of this on public accounts and the balance of trade were inevitable. Moreover, despite efforts to jump-start the economy after 2009 with tax breaks on production and payrolls, GDP would only resume considerable growth in 2010, decelerating rapidly shortly thereafter.

Since the late 1990s Brazil has used a series of inflation targets, which are announced in advance. In recent years, the goal has been 4.5% per year, with a tolerance limit of up to 6.5%. Since 2010, however, inflation has hovered quite close to the upper limit of the target. In 2013, for example, inflation hit 5.9%. This led to the adoption of inflation-fighting economic policy measures, basically via raising securities interest rates, the final result of which is a negative impact on economic growth.

On the external economic front, enormous surpluses in the balance of trade (exports/ imports) up until the middle of the past decade fell to nearly nothing by 2013. The 2006 surplus of US$46 billion would drop to just US$2.6 billion in 2013. The nation's current account—which covers all exchanges with the exterior, including goods, services, and income—which came to a surplus of 1.8% of GDP in 2004, has thus turned steeply into the red (-3.7% of GDP in 2013), sparking concerns about how long (and how much) it would continue to be financed by external resources. Consequently, the external debt has grown.

One of the standing difficulties in the return to growth has been the low investment rate, currently around 18% of GDP. According to IMF data for 2012, the majority of the countries in Latin America displays investment rates significantly higher than Brazil's, such as, for example, Argentina and Colombia (24%), Mexico and Chile (25%), Venezuela (26%), and Peru (27%). Both private and public investments have stalled at levels considered insufficient to sustain the country. For the economy to grow again without inflationary pressure, it would be necessary to raise the investment rate considerably so as to attain figures similar to those exhibited by Brazil's neighbors on the continent.

Current expectations as to the future of the Brazilian economy over the coming years are hardly favorable, with no predictions for a large-scale change in terms of a return to growth similar to 2004/2008 in the immediate future. These circumstances, however, may be modified if the international situation improves and the country manages to overcome the conjunction of obstacles it now faces.[4]

The difficulties for the near future of the Brazilian economy fall into several groups. Internally, inflation remains high, tugged upwards by the price of food and services in general. Administered prices have been controlled, but at some point they will have to be readjusted. With the job market still buzzing, pressure for a bump in salaries will likely remain, with effects on prices. The recent depreciation of the BRL has led to, among other things, pressure on the prices of imported products and raw materials, which also feeds back into inflation. This, in turn, brings pressure on monetary policy, leading to a rise in interest rates and stagnant economic growth. Still on the internal front, low investment rates represent new difficulties in terms of economic growth without inflationary pressures. The alternative would be to utilize expansionist fiscal policy alongside an increase in public spending, but this is made unfeasible by the need to generate primary budget surpluses to pay off interest on the public debt, thus avoiding an increase in the ratio between public debt and GDP.

On the external front, the greatest challenge at hand is certainly the current account deficit, which has attained worrisome levels.[5] Despite exchange rate devaluation over the past two years, exports have not reacted favorably, nor have imports fallen—which would be a positive influence on the balance of trade, where Brazil obtained fairly positive results in the middle of the past decade. The services and income account (travel, equipment rentals, royalties, remittance of profits, interest on loans, etc.), has traditionally run negative, and it seems unlikely that considerable improvements are forthcoming in the short term. Therefore, in the best-case scenario, the current account will continue to present a similar level of deficit over the coming years. While, on the one hand, the country's international reserves represent a sort of buffer against speculative attacks on the Brazilian currency, they also represent an enormous cost, given the difference between internal and external interest rates.[6] Of course, if the international situation changes favorably, the country's external accounts can improve along with international commerce and an increase in commodity

---

4   For recent and broadly pessimistic analyses of the Brazilian economy, see, for example, Bonelli and Pinheiro (2013); Giambagi and Pinheiro (2012); Fishlow (2011) and Gonçalves (2013), among others.

5   The current account includes the balance of trade, services, and revenue. 2013 ended on a deficit of US$81.37 billion.

6   The country's international reserves hit US$375.79 billion at the end of 2013.

prices, with the possibility of favorable effects on the balance of trade and the current account. Unfortunately, the international economy has been very slow to recover, giving no clear indications of its trajectory.

In sum, the macroeconomic situation for the short and middle term for the Brazilian economy is worrisome.

The Behavior of the Job Market [7]

In this section, we will sum up the evolution of the job market, from the economic recovery in 2004 to the slowing-down of the past few years, closing out the analysis in 2013. Finally, there will be a concise index illustrating the favorable behavior of the job market over the period.

Along with the improvement in the economy over the quinquennial 2004/2008, the unemployment rate fell steeply over the period, from just over 12% in 2003 to 8% in 2008 (Figure 8.1). Despite recent economic deceleration (with the exception of 2010), the unemployment rate continued falling over recent years, closing out 2013 with the lowest figure in its historical series (5.4%). This apparent contradiction will be discussed farther on in the text.

One of the most striking recent events in the Brazilian job market was the exceptional growth of the minimum wage.[8] The importance of the minimum wage transcends the job market itself, in that it also represents the minimum value for Brazil's general social welfare system, distributed to over 16 million people. It is also used in official social assistance

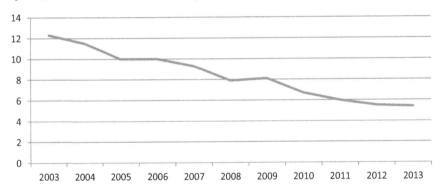

Figure 8.1   Unemployment rate—2003–2013 (in %)
Source: PME/IBGE.

---

7   The data from the job market for this section were taken from the Monthly Employment Survey (PME) by IBGE, which covers the metropolitan regions of Rio de Janeiro, São Paulo, Porto Alegre, Belo Horizonte, Salvador, and Recife, thus representing the reality of the principal metropolitan areas in the nation.

8   The minimum wage was instituted in Brazil in 1940. At first varied by region, with a single national level introduced in 1984. It serves as a reference for the formal sector of the economy, being the minimum salary to be paid to a worker for a 44-hour workweek. In 2014, the minimum wage was set at R$724 per month (around US$320).

payments, pegged as the value of the Continued Cash Benefit paid out to around 4 million senior citizens and the disabled poor.

The growth of the minimum wage was the result of a more favorable political situation, oriented towards improving the life conditions of the poorest part of the population, which allowed for the development of a number of social programs like Bolsa Família. Over the last decade and a half, the minimum wage was systematically readjusted above inflation, leading to its growth in real terms; it increased 75% over the period[9] (Figure 8.2). Starting in 2009, the rules for the evolution of the minimum wage were legally defined with annual readjustments following the inflation over the past 12 months (INPC), plus the growth rate of the economy (variation of GDP), with a two-year lag.[10] This rule will stay in place until the end of 2015, when it is due for reevaluation.

The growth of the minimum wage was mirrored in the average compensation earned by the employed population, which also saw an increase in real terms starting in 2005[11] (Figure 8.2). The considerable job creation in recent years, then, was accompanied by an increase in the average salary and the mass of salaries as a whole, feeding back into the population's spending power. Another contributor to the rise in the average salary was the drop in unemployment over the period, driving the negotiation of higher salaries within the job market.

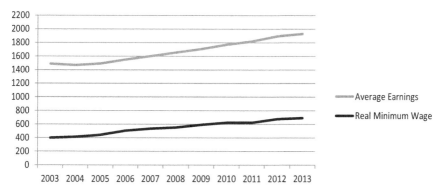

Figure 8.2   Minimum wage and real average compensation 2003–2013 (in R$ as of December 2013)
Source: PME/IBGE and IPEADATA.

The Brazilian job market, however, remains characterized by a high rate of informality—this despite the recent trend towards the increasing formalization of work relations. Formal employment, with official documentation signed by employers, went from being a minority before 2009 to comprising the majority by 2010.[12] While in 2003 just 44% of occupied citizens were working formal jobs, in 2013 55% were formally

---

9   The deflator used to calculate the real minimum wage is the National Index of Consumer Prices (INPC).

10   The two-year delay is due to the fact that when the minimum wage is readjusted at the start of each year, the GDP growth rate for the previous year has not yet been calculated.

11   The deflator used to calculate real average compensation is also the INPC.

12   According to data from the Annual Social Information Report (RAIS) from the Ministry of Labor and Employment, around 18 million formal jobs were created in the country from 2004 to 2012.

employed. This is the end result of a combination of factors. On one hand, society itself began placing greater importance on workers' rights, the flouting of which often leads to suits in Labor Court, usually won by employees. On the other hand, the government stepped up oversight on companies in order to ensure compliance with labor legislation.[13] Finally, the improvement in the job market observed over the period bumped workers' bargaining power, giving them the opportunity to choose better posts compliant with labor legislation.

The education level of the Brazilian workforce is admittedly very low, with negative consequences on work productivity. The best jobs demand a minimum education equivalent to a secondary school degree (11 years of study), or, preferentially, a college degree. This encourages young workers to delay their entry into the workforce and stay longer in school. One piece of evidence for this is the percentage of young people in the Brazilian job market, which has steadily declined. As a consequence, the past few years have seen a significant rise in the education level of the country's workforce.[14] The percentage of workers with high school degrees went from 47% in 2003 to 64% in 2013.

Beyond the variables highlighted above, a number of others may be utilized in confirming the recent improvement so far observed in the Brazilian job market. Saboia and Kubrusly (2014) suggested an index to measure the quality of the job market, based on nine variables and a methodology inspired by the UN's Human Development Index. The index varies from 0 to 1; the larger the figure, the higher the quality of the job market.

The data gleaned from the Monthly Employment Survey gave rise to an array of variables meant to address the complexity of the Brazilian job market. Given the quantity of information produced by this data source, only a few variables were chosen. The criterion employed was the decision to opt for a relatively small number of variables able to represent the various dimensions of the job market. The structure of the correlation matrix between the selected variables demonstrated that the correlations between them are relatively strong, displaying the expected signs.

The selected variables fall into three groups. Each includes a variable considered the principal reference point in the group, and two complementary variables that provide additional information. They are presented below. The first to be listed in each group is the variable considered the principal, and the rest are complementary.

a. Unemployment Variables
   - Unemployment Rate;
   - Long-Term Unemployment (percentage of unemployed 12 months or longer without work);
   - Unemployment of Heads of Household (percentage of heads of household, either men or women, among the unemployed).
b. Income Variables
   - Real Average Income (of employed persons);
   - Undercompensation (percentage of workers who receive less than the hourly minimum wage per work hour);

---

13   See Simão (2009).

14   Despite the growth in average education in terms of years studied, the matter of the low quality of the education being provided remains on the agenda. According to the Program for International Student Assessment (PISA), Brazil's results have improved but are still quite poor compared to other countries. In 2012, for example, Brazil came in 58th place out of 65 participating nations.

- Inequality (relationship between formal and informal employment compensation in the private sector).
c. Insertion Variables
    - Formality (percentage of employees that are formally registered);
    - Underemployment (percentage of underemployed due to insufficient hours, willing to work more);
    - Education (percentage of employed with 11 or more years of study).

In the case of the unemployment variables, the most basic piece of information is the unemployment rate, as discussed above, standing as of the most important macroeconomic variables for a given country. The complementary variables incorporate elements that may aggravate unemployment—to wit, its duration and the presence of heads of household among the unemployed. Long-term unemployment is certainly very important; in removing an individual from the day-to-day experience of economic activity, he or she may lose touch and find it increasingly difficult to return to work. As for unemployed heads of household (men or women), it was sought to emphasize unemployment in their case, which normally hits familial income harder.

The principal statistic for income is indisputably the average salary received on the job market, which has grown considerably over the period, as already indicated. In measuring inequality and low compensation, two complementary variables were incorporated. The measurement for inequality examined the relationship between the average income of those employed in formal (formally registered employees in the private sector) and informal positions (unregistered employees in the private sector). In order to confirm the importance of undercompensation on the job market, the reference point was the value of the minimum wage, plus the percentage of employed persons receiving less than the hourly minimum wage.

Recognizing the importance of the issue of informality in the Brazilian job market and the fact that a great number of the employed find themselves in precarious situations, the basic criterion for measuring insertion was the percentage of those occupied who are formally registered, representing the typical situation for participation in the formal sector of the economy, as already discussed. Underemployment represents an undesirable situation in that it indicates the underuse of the potential of a country's available workforce. The measure for data on underemployment was the percentage of people working fewer than 40 hours a week, though willing and available to work more. The last complementary variable is enormously important, as that the level of education of the Brazilian people is notoriously low. On the other hand, education is tied to work productivity. To measure the education level of the working population, the analysis turned to the percentage of workers with at least a high school education, representing the minimum level for an improved insertion into the Brazilian job market.

Of the nine variables considered in the analysis, only undercompensation did not contribute positively to the rise in the index over the period, due to the considerable growth of the minimum wage. Of the rest, the greatest positive contribution came from the unemployment rate, average compensation, formality, and education. The first three contribute heavily, being considered principal variables and thus exerting greater weight in the calculation of the index. As for education, although it was considered a complementary variable with less weight than the others, its strong positive contribution was a consequence of the steep growth in workers' average education over the period. The result of the index's calculation is, of course, to confirm that there was a great leap in the quality of the job market after 2004, with deceleration coming only at the end of the period, especially in 2013; this may be attributed to the economy's poor performance that year (Figure 8.3).

As the PME's data cover six metropolitan regions, the index utilized allows us to differentiate between them. As was to be expected, there are enormous differences, especially when comparing the more developed regions of the South and Southeast to developmentally delayed areas in the Northeast. São Paulo stands out with the highest results on the index, with slightly under 0.9 in 2013. Rio de Janeiro, Porto Alegre, and São Paulo were all around 0.8; the situation is far worse in Recife and Salvador, with indices close to 0.6. In any case, all of them saw a clear trend towards a rise in the index over the period.[15]

One may thus conclude that the job market had a notable performance over the period 2003/2013, far better than could have been expected, given the behavior of the Brazilian economy over those years.

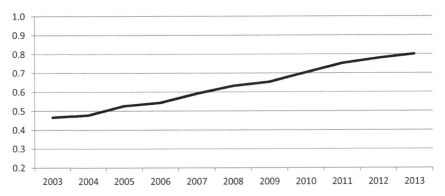

Figure 8.3   Quality index for the labor market—2003/2013
Source: Author's processing , based on PME/IBGE data.

The improvement in income distribution

Brazil has an extremely unequal income distribution, falling among the countries with the greatest levels of income inequality in the world. Whatever the angle—personal income; family income; household income; regional income, etc.—the results show enormous disparities in income.

Over the past few years, however, there has been a considerable improvement, as may be seen, for example, through the sharp drop in the Gini index (which fell from 0.596 in 2001 to 0.530 in 2012).[16] There is a consensus among Brazilian specialists that the reduction in income inequalities is principally linked to the improvement in the job market. The minimum wage has also contributed, be it as remuneration within the job market itself

---

15   Although analysis in this section has limited itself to using PME data, covering only six metropolitan regions in the country, other sources of data, such as the Annual Social Information Report (RAIS), the General Registry of Employed and Unemployed (CAGED), and the National Household Sample Survey (PNAD) confirm the solid performance of the job market over the period analyzed across the country.

16   The Gini index runs from 0 to 1. The lower the figure, the less unequal the income distribution.

or via the fact that the vast majority of pensions and official retirement benefits are pegged to the minimum wage. According to estimates by the author, 75% of the fall in the Gini index for the distribution of household income per capita over the period 2009/2012 might be explained by the action of the minimum wage on the job market, in welfare, and in social assistance.[17]

Moreover, there has come recognition of the important role played by Brazilian income-transfer programs such as Bolsa Família, with an unquestionable contribution to reducing income inequality and poverty. According to Lavinas (2013), 15% of the improvement in income distribution over recent years may be traced to the Bolsa Família and 25% to pensions and official retirement benefits affected by the rise in the minimum wage, with the rest of the improvement being the exclusive result of the income generated on the job market. Despite the recent reduction in inequality, the still-high Gini index leaves no doubt as to the fact that income distribution in Brazil remains very unequal.[18]

Income distribution may also be analyzed through the lens of the functional distribution of income, which demonstrates how earnings are distributed according to gains from capital and work. This focus is not commonly used in Brazil, due to the delay in obtaining estimates from the national accounts in terms of earnings.

The functional distribution of income in Brazil is also quite unequal by international standards. Starting in 2005, however, it began improving significantly, with a rise in the share of compensation for workers, a result in keeping with the improvement in the job market observed over the period being analyzed[19] (Figure 8.4). Given the vigorous growth of average earnings for the employed population starting in the middle of the last decade, any other result in terms of the functional distribution of income would come as a surprise.

Hallak Neto (2013) has developed a methodology for updating the functional distribution of income, which indicates the continuation of this positive trend. According to the author, in 2011, the share of workers' earnings in GDP must have hit something around 43.6%, while the gross operating surplus would come to 32.9%.

In short, one may state that income distribution in Brazil remains characterized by glaring inequalities, but that substantial improvements were observed as of the past decade, the results of favorable job market behavior, the substantial rise in the minimum wage, and the social policy initiative of income transfers for the poorest in society, recently implemented by the government.

A contradiction in appearance only

The simultaneous existence of relatively low economic growth alongside extremely positive behavior from the job market (and in terms of income distribution) over recent years has sparked a variety of questions as to how such a result was possible.[20]

Over the period 2004/2008, the economy behaved satisfactorily, with GDP growing close to 5% per year. The improvement in the job market would thus be, to an extent,

---

17 See Filgueiras (2014).

18 For a discussion of the causes of the improvement in income distribution in Brazil, see the collection by Barros et al. (2007), and Lavinas (2013).

19 The year 2009 was the last with data available on the functional distribution of income, when this text was drawn up. The four elements of functional income distribution presented in Graph 12 are: employee compensation; gross operating surplus (EOB), mixed income; and taxes on production and importation (ILPI).

20 See, for example, Barboza (2014).

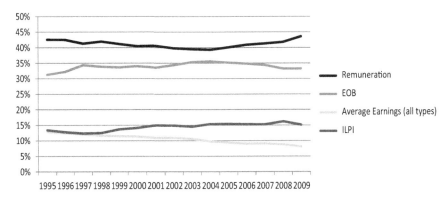

Figure 8.4   Respective shares of GDP components through the lens of income—1995/2009

Source: National Account Systems/IBGE.

compatible with the economic growth observed. 2009 was an extremely negative year for the economy. While the unemployment rate stopped falling that year, the other job market variables, such as average compensation and formalization, remained favorable. According to data from the Ministry of Labor and Employment (MTE), there was a net creation of formal jobs in 2009. In 2010, the economy once again displayed positive indicators, with strong GDP growth (7.5%). It would only be natural, therefore, for the job market to continue improving that year.

For the period 2011/2013, however, the economy grew, on average, just 2% per year. It was thus expected that the job market would backslide or at least stop improving. Nevertheless, it continued displaying favorable results, as discussed above. In 2013, for example, 730 thousand new formal jobs were created, according to the MTE.

One must return to some of the policies implemented by the current administration in the attempt to minimize the impact of the international crisis on the Brazilian economy; these favored the job market over recent years. Tax exemptions introduced in 2009 were principally oriented towards reducing taxes on automobiles and durable consumer goods, especially heavy appliances (refrigerators, stoves, washing machines, etc.). More recently, the rates for welfare contributions were reduced for several sectors of the economy (see the article by Fagnani in this collection). Instead of falling on the payroll, they were instead calculated by companies' billings, in some cases seeing a considerable drop. Nor can one neglect to mention the measures meant to favor credit in general and the reduction of interest rates, which helped to bolster the economy in recent years.

Our interpretation for the apparent contradiction between low economic growth and strong job creation over the recent period may be extrapolated from an examination of the tertiary sector (commerce and services), where productivity levels and salaries tend to be lower. Job creation in Brazil has become increasingly concentrated in the tertiary sector, which is perfectly compatible with a situation of sluggish economic growth.

According to Bonelli and Fontes (2013), the growth of productivity in Brazil's service sector over the period 2000/2008 was negative (-1.7% per year). On the other hand, the productivity of the Brazilian service sector in 2008 came to just 26% of that found in the United States. Such figures lead to a huge capacity for job creation in the tertiary sector. Such jobs, as a rule, are characterized by low productivity and compensation.

According to the National Register of Employed and Unemployed (CAGED), for the triennial 2011/2013, three out of every four jobs created in the formal sector of the economy came in the tertiary sector, with two in services and one in commerce. The trend in the tertiary sector has been to create low-salaried posts. In the case of commerce, for example, this triennial only saw the creation of jobs with compensation up to 1.5 minimum wages (MW). In the service sector the situation is a bit better, and the net creation of jobs often hits 2MW, except for teaching and medical services, where the positive generation of jobs may attain compensation of up to 5MW.

Another issue that has frequently provoked questions about the Brazilian job market is the increased spending on unemployment insurance at a time when the unemployment rate has been falling steadily. There are two basic explanations for this. Firstly, the minimum value for unemployment insurance is pegged to the minimum wage, and the vast majority of beneficiaries receive exactly one minimum wage. The growth of the minimum wage, then, as seen over this period, leads to increased spending on unemployment insurance. Secondly, the considerable growth of formal employment has also contributed, in that workers must belong to the formal sector in order to be eligible for unemployment insurance.

As for increased salaries at a time of low growth for productivity and the economy, the backdrop that may shed some light on the matter is the very policy designed to raise the minimum wage, linked to workers' increased bargaining power, given the low unemployment rate. Thus, sluggish economic growth has not impeded a rise in the average salary.

This process, of course, cannot go on indefinitely. As the unemployment rate is already quite low, it cannot keep falling much farther. Thinking in the middle and long term, it will be crucial for the economy to start growing again in order to ensure increased productivity in general and labor productivity in particular.[21]

The need for increased growth in terms of labor productivity will be made starker over the coming years, the reason being ongoing demographic changes in Brazil. The so-called "demographic bonus," a drop in the percentage of children and the elderly in comparison to the adult population (ages 15–64), will last until the middle of the next decade. At that point, population aging will begin to invert this effect; an increase in labor productivity will then become even more crucial in ensuring the continuity of this process of economic growth. [22]

There are at least two ways of elevating productivity. Firstly, by continuing the ongoing growth in workers' education and improving the quality of the country's education. This is a long-term process; it calls for a greater percentage of students to continue on to college, as well as the strengthening of technical education, as of yet markedly underdeveloped in Brazil.[23] Moreover, the state must interfere directly in primary and secondary school systems, which are of abysmally poor quality in the majority of the country's 5,565 municipalities.

Secondly, a rise in the investment rate will be crucial, leading to a modernization of industrial assets and increased innovation, and thus a bump in the economy's levels of productivity. This is another great challenge that does not depend solely on the public sector. The BNDES has made a great effort on this front, offering an enormous volume of

---

21   As for the issue of the recent low growth of productivity and the need for it to be strengthened in order for the economy to return to growth in the long term, see Bonelli and Fontes (2013).

22   For more on the demographic bonus, see Alves (2013).

23   The government has recently attempted to increase participation in technical education via the National Program for Access to Technical Education and Employment (PRONATEC), created in 2011 with the aim of increasing the array of courses in professional and technical education. That said, secondary school is still not obligatory in Brazil today.

resources at subsidized rates in order to drive the development of the nation's infrastructure. Such an effort must be complemented by the creation of an environment propitious for the creation of positive expectations, driving new private investment in the economy.

If this does not materialize, the result may be the stagnation of the economy and a return to the inflationary process with all its associated consequences, including a possible reversion of the current trend towards the reduction of income inequalities in Brazil.

Conclusion

The improvement in income distribution in Brazil is not an exclusively Brazilian event, having been seen in a number of Latin American countries (as may be seen in Therborn's article in this collection) and noted in progress over the course of the past decade. What may constitute a differentiating element for the country, however, is that the same effect came about during a period of relatively low economic growth. Moreover, surprisingly, income distribution continued improving even through the past few years, when the economy clearly decelerated.

It was argued in this text that the reduction in income inequalities was intimately tied to the favorable performance of the job market through the final triennial of the period being analyzed. Employment rates continued growing considerably, driven by the tertiary sector, where productivity and salaries are generally lower.

Given the official policy of raising the minimum wage, which has a direct impact on the formal sector of the economy and an indirect effect on the informal sector, the base of the salary structure saw growth that favored an improvement in income distribution. Simultaneously, the growth in social programs such as Bolsa Família drove income transfers to the poorest sectors of the population, collaborating to complement the process of reducing income inequality and poverty.

A few challenges have emerged in the attempt to maintain the current trend towards improved distribution, with two points to be highlighted. Firstly, the urgent need to improve the quality of public schools and broaden education in general, including a focus on technical schools. Secondly, the necessity of renewed investment so as to increase economic productivity and allow the country to grow again. The country must modernize itself in technological terms, that is, while the working population must increase its productivity.

These would be minimum conditions for the country to start growing again at reasonable rates and thus continue the ongoing process of income distribution. If they should not be met, attempts at a return to economic growth will come up against significant obstacles, potentially bringing great frustrations for society.

Bibliography

Alves, J.E. (2013). 'O Bônus Demográfico no Brasil.' *Jornal dos Economistas,* vol. 292, no. 11, pp. 3–5.
Barboza, R. de M. (2014). 'PIB e Desemprego no Brasil.' *Valor Econômico,* 16 January, p. 20.
Barros, R.P. et al. (orgs.) (2007). *Desigualdade de Renda no Brasil: uma análise da queda recente.* Brasília, IPEA.

Bonelli, R. e Fontes, J. (2013). 'O Desafio Brasileiro no Longo Prazo,' in Bonelli, R. e Pinheiro, A.C. (orgs.) (2013). *Ensaios IBRE de Economia Brasileira.* Rio de Janeiro, IBRE-FGV.

Bonelli, R. e Pinheiro, A.C. (orgs.) (2013). *Ensaios IBRE de Economia Brasileira.* Rio de Janeiro, IBRE-FGV.

Filgueiras, S. (2014). 'O Dilema do Salário Mínimo,' *Brasil Econômico.* Brasília, 12 May, p. 12.

Fishlow, A. (2011). *O Novo Brasil—as conquistas políticas, econômicas, sociais e nas relações internacionais.* São Paulo, Saint Paul Ed.

Giambiagi, F. and Pinheiro, A.C. (2012). *Além da Euforia: riscos e lacunas do modelo brasileiro de desenvolvimento,* Rio de Janeiro, Elsevier.

Gonçalves, R. (2013). *Desenvolvimento às Avessas—Verdade, Má-fé e Ilusão no Atual Modelo Brasileiro de Desenvolvimento.* Rio de Janeiro, LTC.

Hallak Neto, J. (2013). *A Distribuição Funcional da Renda e a Economia não Observada no Âmbito do Sistema de Contas Nacionais do Brasil*, Ph.D. thesis. Rio de Janeiro, Instituto de Economia, UFRJ.

Lavinas, L. (2013). '21st century welfare.' *New Left Review,* vol. 84, no. 6, pp. 5–40.

Saboia, J. and Kubrusly, L.S. (2014). Indicadores para o Mercado de Trabalho Metropolitano no Brasil. Texto para Discussão 021, Rio de Janeiro, Instituto de Economia, UFRJ.

Simão, A. (2009). 'Sistema de Vigilância e Fiscalização do Trabalho no Brasil: efeitos sobre a expansão do emprego formal no período 1999–2007,' *Boletim Mercado de Trabalho—Conjuntura e Análise n° 39.* Rio de Janeiro, IPEA.

PART III
Widening Political, Social and Fiscal Space: Which Outcomes for Redistribution?

Chapter 9
Volatility, Inequality, and the
Quality of Public Finances in Latin America

Juan Pablo Jiménez and Isabel López Azcúnaga

Introduction

Over the past decade, Latin America underwent an unprecedented period of economic growth, consolidation of public accounts and reductions in inequality. The region faced the external shock of the years 2008–2009 with such an improved situation, in contrast with the historical behaviour that the region has displayed during other crises, a demonstration of the advances made in macroeconomic management and fiscal policy in recent years.

However, this improvement in public finances has not always translated into an adequate supply of public goods and services, both in terms of quality and prioritization. The region continues to face many challenges in this area. The need to address the growing number of social demands related to the low quality of public provision should be coordinated with the importance of maintaining sound public accounts in order to face possible future macroeconomic shocks in a sound manner.

The aim of this chapter is to review the relationship between macro fiscal and micro budgetary policies, in the light of some of the basic characteristics of the region: its limited fiscal space, high volatility generated by macroeconomic shocks, and large inequalities, both personal and territorial. The chapter aims to understand what has happened and provide a comprehensive body of knowledge to determine how fiscal policy should address future challenges.

In this vein, we will first describe various important issues related to inequality in Latin America and those features that are relevant for fiscal policy as well as some new indicators about income concentration. Secondly, we will analyse the evolution of fiscal space and the future challenges of fiscal policy, focusing on both revenues and expenditures. Regarding fiscal revenues, we will consider its evolution, composition and reforms over time; as for public spending, we will analyse one of its most important elements from the point of view of the scope of this work: rigidities and management, efficiency and quality, being aspects that define and characterize the potential of fiscal policy in the region. Finally, main conclusions and future challenges will be presented.

Inequality and Income Concentration in Latin America

Over the last decade, inequality has decreased in the majority of the countries in Latin America. This historic shift was largely the result of unprecedented, steady economic growth and an increase in public spending—mainly through conditional cash transfer programs—that targeted the most vulnerable sectors of the population.

Inequality is a multidimensional concept. In this chapter we focus on the inequality of income distribution, particularly those aspects that are relevant from the standpoint of fiscal policy.

Nevertheless, income inequality is still extremely high in the region. With a Gini coefficient of 0.50, the region of Latin America and the Caribbean remains the most unequal in the world. Moreover, inequality in the region has some distinctive features that shape the way fiscal policy can affect income distribution. Among the factors that shape the relationship between inequality and fiscal policy, either because they limit governments' ability to generate resources or because they reveal a need for redistributive policies, we can highlight the following: (i) high distribution inequality, with a high concentration of income in the top decile, (ii) significant disparities between jurisdictions within a country, (iii) high levels of poverty and destitution, and (iv) the large size of the informal economy.[1]

However, doubts are raised concerning the accuracy of these figures. Amarante and Jiménez (2014) raise concerns about whether the exclusion of the top income bracket may understate total inequality or limit understanding of the dynamics of inequality. In order to confront its limitations it is important to analyse both the indicators used to reflect inequality, and the sources of information being employed. As for indicators, and in the attempt to address the problem of the high concentration of income in the top decile, indicators other than the Gini coefficient are becoming increasingly relevant. Apart from the most familiar 20/20 or 10/10 ratios[2], another relevant yardstick is the Palma ratio[3], defined as the ratio of the richest 10% of the population's share of gross national income divided by the share of the poorest 40%. The Palma ratio addresses the Gini index's oversensitivity to changes in the middle of the distribution and insensitivity to changes at the top and bottom, and therefore more accurately reflects income inequality's economic impact on society as a whole.

Regarding sources of information, a major limitation is household surveys' difficulty in accurately capturing high incomes. It may be a problem of truncation (a lower presence of richer households) or understatement (especially capital income). A possible solution is the reconstruction of high incomes from tax administrations tabulated or microdata. This source of information has allowed the development of a line of research based on the reconstruction of high earnings with a historical perspective (Piketty, 2003; Atkinson et al., 2011).

In the case of the region, Alvaredo (2010b) and Alvaredo and Londoño (2013) calculate a corrected Gini index based on income from household surveys to incorporate information from low income tax records. In their work, they analyze this information for Argentina and Colombia, respectively, showing the evolution of the uptake of the high-income group and its impact on the overall distribution. There has also been recent work on Uruguay with the same methodology (Burdín et al., 2014). The results of these three studies show very interesting information regarding the concentration of high income in the region compared to data on the rest of the world. Around 2005, the top 1% brought in 19.7% of total income in Colombia and 15.8% in Argentina. In comparative terms, this uptake is relatively high, similar for example to U.S. levels (Figure 9.1). In Uruguay, one of the countries with the lowest level of inequality in the region, the uptake of the top 1% is considerably lower,

---

1   See Jiménez and López Azcúnaga (2013) for a more detailed discussion.

2   The 20:20 or 20/20 ratio compares how much richer the top 20% of populations are to the bottom 20% of a given population; this can be more revealing of the actual impact of inequality in a population, as it reduces the effect on the statistics of outliers at the top and bottom and prevents the middle 60% from statistically obscuring inequality that is otherwise obvious in the field. The measure is used for the United Nations Development Programme on Human Development Indicators.

3   See Palma (2011).

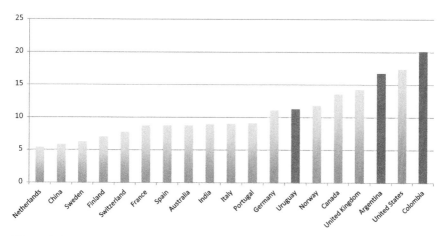

Figure 9.1   Share of total income of the richest 1% (around 2005)
*Data for Uruguay are for 2009.
Source: Amarante, Verónica and Jiménez, Juan Pablo (2014) based on Atkinson et al. (2011) and Burdín et al (2014) (for Uruguay).

coming to 11.3% of total revenue in 2007, but still above most of the countries included in Atkinson et al. (2011).

The Gini index, once corrected by incorporating information from the top 1% through tax data, is considerably higher in all cases (Argentina in particular) than that which comes from household surveys in the three-country region (see Figure 9.2). However, the evolution of both indexes is similar.

Amarante and Jiménez (2014) conclude that analysis of the richest groups that combines tax information from affidavits with the data obtained through the traditional household surveys can be very useful. However, in the case of Latin America, this type of study is fairly recent or quite scarce. Further analysis is needed. This should include new studies from improving existing information incorporating new analysis tools, such as adjustments for underreporting of income or data from sworn tax declarations.

Furthermore, and related to the next section, there remains an unresolved debate in the region: what path should tax reform take in order to increase the share of revenue from the higher income sectors?

Fiscal Space in Latin America: Challenges Ahead and the Need for Reform

The dimension of fiscal policy space available to the government to meet its objectives is a function of three key determinants: the amount of resources available, the number of independent instruments at hand to fulfil objectives, and the degree of competition among different policies in the use of resources and tools (Fanelli and Jiménez, 2009, p. 40).

This definition of fiscal space, unlike other definitions such as that from Heller (2005), for whom "in its broadest sense, fiscal space can be defined as the availability of budgetary room that allows a government to provide resources for a weekend desired, without prejudice to the sustainability of the government financial position"; or the IMF definition reflected in Ostry et al. (2010), that "the fiscal gap is the difference between the current

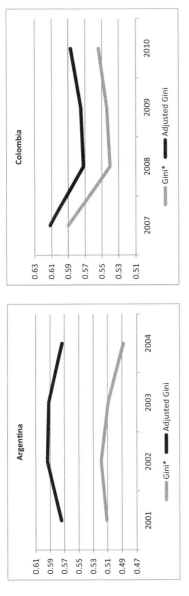

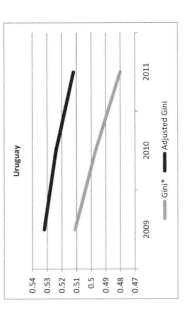

Figure 9.2   Gini index and Gini index adjusted by tax data

Source: Amarante, Verónica and Jiménez, Juan Pablo (2014) based on Alvaredo (2010a), Alvaredo and Londoño (2013) and Burdín et al (2014).

OBS: Gini denotes the Gini coefficient of individual income based on national surveys. Adjusted Gini: the Gini coefficient is corrected with the top 1% income share.

level of public debt and the debt limit implied by the historical record of the country of fiscal adjustment," proposes a broader coverage. Firstly, it is assumed that a government can have different competing objectives (e.g., stabilization against redistribution—or, even within the stabilization target, efforts can be directed toward growth or sustainability). Secondly, it also includes factors such as the distribution of functions between different levels of government that will undoubtedly affect the fiscal space available.

Historically, Latin America has shown a deficit in its fiscal accounts. In the region the tax burden has been largely insufficient to finance public spending. Figure 9.1 shows that solvency problems have left a narrow space for fiscal policy. Over the period 1950–2012, on average, the region shows a negative budget balance, except for the years 2006 and 2007.

However, this historical trend was altered in the period between 2002 and 2008. In this period the macro fiscal situation of the region showed a strong recovery, displaying, for the first time, GDP growth, an external current account surplus, and a fiscal surplus. Moreover, inequality declined between 2003 and 2011. According to ECLAC, the gap between extreme quintiles of the distribution was reduced in 15 out of 18 countries and the Gini index fell by at least 5% in 13 countries. This unprecedented period, in which the region not only saw growth at sustained rates but also a reduction in inequality, broke the so-called "empty box,"[4] presenting a new and unfamiliar scenario in the region.

The economic boom that began in 2002 was accompanied by a sound macroeconomic policy giving countries with the opportunity to increase their reserves and reduce their public debt. As shown in Figure 9.3, international reserves began to increase at significant levels from 2003 on and, despite the international crisis of 2008, have continued to grow to this day.

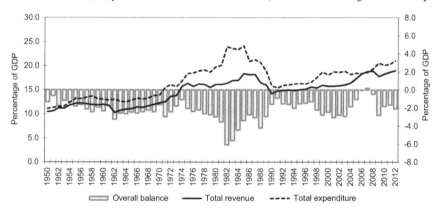

Overall balance ▬▬ Total revenue ▬ ▬ Total expenditure

Figure 9.3   Latin America (19 countries): Total revenue, total expenditure and overall balance, Central Government (as percentage of GDP, simple average)

Source: Own elaboration with data provided by CEPAL (2014b).

_____

4   Almost two decades ago, an economist at ECLAC, Fernando Fajnzylber developed a simple but profound idea. He built a crosstab to classify Latin American countries according to their performance in terms of concentration of income and growth rates (Fajnzylber, 1989). The result was that only one of the boxes of the table remained empty, one where high growth rates combined with lower levels of inequality. Since then, the idea of the "empty box" is used as a metaphor for the deficiencies of the region in growth and income distribution, which remains a challenge for analysts and policymakers.

The greatest strength of public finances was expressed in a significant reduction in the total debt of the nonfinancial public sector as a percentage of GDP, from average values near 60% of GDP in 2003 to only 33% in 2012[5]. Moreover, this debt reduction allowed to change their composition, with an extension of debt maturity, greater participation of fixed rate debt, increased resident participation in their possession and a growing burden of debt in local currency (from 2010, the share of domestic debt in total public debt exceeds that of external debt) (CEPAL, 2013). However, note that this debt reduction, as well as the increase in international reserves, has been very heterogeneous not only between countries but also between sub-regions.

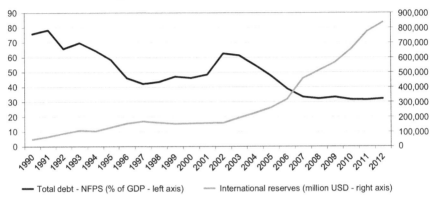

— Total debt - NFPS (% of GDP - left axis)   — International reserves (million USD - right axis)

Figure 9.4   Latin America (19 countries): NFPS total debt and international reserves

Source: Own elaboration with data provided by CEPAL (2014b).
NFPS: Non Financial Public Sector.

This greater macroeconomic strength allowed several countries in the region to adopt countercyclical policies during the crisis. While fiscal policy in Latin America has traditionally been characterized as procyclical[6], recent studies point to a change in this area. In an interesting article, Frankel et al. (2011) analyze changes in fiscal policy in developing countries in recent years. The authors, based on the analysis by Kaminsky et al. (2004), compare the cyclicality of public spending over 1960–1999 and 2000–2009. This last period shows numerous developing countries (Bolivia, Costa Rica, Chile, Brazil, Paraguay and El Salvador) in which tax policy had a largely countercyclical character. The authors attribute this development to some improvement in the quality of institutions and the increase in savings capacity derived from the preceding cycle.

In terms of fiscal institutions, the introduction of fiscal rules by some countries in the region stands out among the novel aspects of the last decade. These rules are instruments that can help steer fiscal policy towards greater sustainability, contributing to macroeconomic stability. Fiscal rules can be classified by their main instrument: budget balance rules

---

5   Data from ECLAC (2013a).
6   See, among others, Gavin and Perotti (1997); Kaminsky et al. (2004); Talvi and Végh (2005) and Alesina et al. (2008).

(e.g. primary surplus, current balance) and spending and/or debt rules (e.g. limits or caps on their growth or size).[7]

In Argentina all levels of government have been obliged to balance revenues and expenditures. Furthermore, primary spending cannot grow faster than the GDP; and borrowing limits have been set at sub-national level. In the case of Brazil, the government has set numerical targets for budget balance, spending and debt. Chile—which is a paradigmatic case—established a structural balance rule which consists, in broad strokes, of a public spending budget that takes into account "structural income" that would be obtained under various medium-term scenarios, sans cyclical components. Peru has established ceilings on budget deficits and debt growth. Mexico set a rule on current equilibrium and is the only Latin American country which has put into effect a fiscal rule that include thresholds for fiscal revenues. In Central America, Panama emphasizes fixed budget deficit ceilings, and a target ratio of debt/GDP.

However, as Ocampo and Vos (2008) argue, rules-based policies tend to work well in normal circumstances, but with the changing economic structures (both the supply side and demand) they may lose relevance or become overly rigid. In addition, since the risks and uncertainties for the economy may be non-stationary, i.e., the transitional changes may permanently alter the trajectory of key macroeconomic variables in times of stress or crisis, some discretion is necessary to articulate policies in order to minimize the risk of huge macroeconomic losses.[8]

Fiscal revenues: The need of reform

As seen before, another salient feature of this improvement in fiscal performance is expressed in the growth of tax revenue. Fiscal revenue (including social security) rose 39% from 1990–92 to 2010–12. This increase was driven primarily by (i) growth in the level of activity, (ii) an increase in the prices of export products, which represent a significant percentage of total revenues in some countries, and (iii) improvements in tax administration, which resulted in reduced levels of tax evasion.

It is important to analyse the role of fiscal reforms in this tax revenue increase. Gómez Sabaini and Rossignolo (2014, forthcoming) argue that the factors behind the increase in tax collections is due to passive policies—that is, assuming invariance on discretionary aliquots and extent of the taxable base, rather than active discretionary policies such as rate increases or expansions of tax bases. As far as passive policies, the authors contend that there are two ways in which the public sector can increase the levying of income tax passively: (i) increasing the tax base: if the untaxed minimum levels and rates do not vary, an increase of taxable income increases the tax levying; and (ii) through an increase in the concentration of income.

However, there have been two important waves of tax reform in Latin America. In the 1980s, due to the severe episodes of high inflation in several countries that made it

---

7   See ECLAC (2011), for a classification of fiscal rules applied in the region during 2000–2010.

8   In connection with the implementation of fiscal rules at the subnational level, see Grambi and Manoel (2012), where fiscal rules are analyzed at the subnational level for four countries in the region (Colombia, Mexico, Argentina and Brazil). This chapter argues that many countries seek to establish fiscal rules for subnational governments as a solution to weakly defined institutional arrangements. The authors conclude, despite the methodological difficulties of analysis in assessing the causal impact of the introduction of fiscal rules for sub-national level in the countries in the sample, the rules are not effective even when the level of compliance, as is the case of Colombia, is quite high.

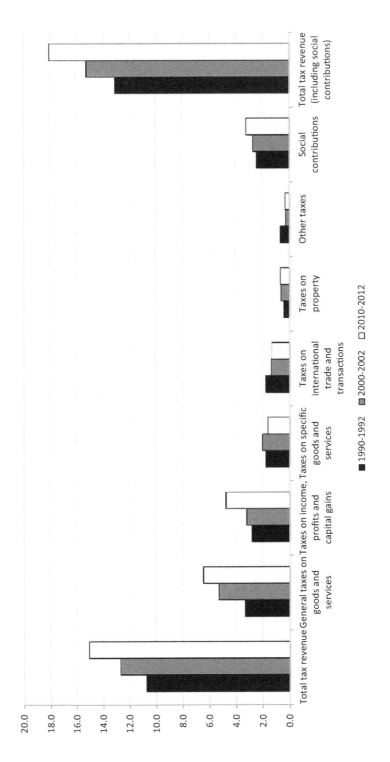

Figure 9.5 **Evolution of revenue structure in Latin America, 1990–92, 1999–02 and 2010–12 (as percentage of GDP)**
Source: Own elaboration with data provided by CEPAL (2014b).

advisable to restore fiscal balance and avoid monetary financing of the fiscal deficit, and the adoption of policies to release the international trade that implied the reduction of tariffs on imports, countries were obliged to pass tax reforms that could both cover the deficit and restore the hole left by the lower revenues due to the reduction of the trade revenues (Lora, 2007).

The new objectives of tax policy became economic efficiency (and by implication the reduction of the efficiency costs of direct taxes), horizontal equity, and revenue adequacy (Cornia et al., 2011; see also Valdés in this volume). To reach these goals, countries had to widen their tax base, rationalize the tax structure, and simplify tax administration. During this "fiscal revolution," redistribution of income became a secondary goal of tax design (Mahon, 2009, p. 4).

Those reforms led to several changes in the tax structure, the most important being a reduction in international trade, social contributions, and individual income taxes and a significant increase of the VAT.

These changes in the tax structure led to important differences in the impact on income distribution. Different authors have pointed to those impacts, all of them agreeing on an effect in terms of decreased progressivity. While Cornia (2010) reveals that the fall in the ratio of direct to indirect taxes significantly raised the Gini coefficient of the distribution of disposable income, Morley (2000) notes that after the tax changes of the 1990s, the burden of taxation fell on the middle and lower classes. Chu et al. (2004) come to similar conclusions, affirming that the decline in tax/GDP and the reduced contribution of direct taxes correlated with the rise in inequality observed over the 1980s and 1990s. One of the positive impacts of those reforms was, as indicated by Mahon (2011), that although the reforms did not aim to promote vertical equity and were regressive in their outcome, they left behind a more capable administration.

The second wave of reforms began during the last decade, when several Latin American policy makers thought that economic orthodoxy would not yield optimal solutions to national economic problems. Inequality started to became a crucial issue in the region. Within this framework, redistribution once again became a primary goal of tax design (Cornia et al., 2011).

New tax reforms were introduced, producing different outcomes in the tax structure. As can be seen in Figure 9.5, there was a significant increase in income and capital gains (68%), a reduction of the share of regressive selective taxes and a further reduction of the share of tax revenue on international trade, while the share of wealth taxes, other taxes and social security contributions was left broadly unchanged.

Over recent years the taxation of income and wealth underwent numerous changes in the region. One of the most prominent, because of its significance and because of the political process involved, was the 2007 tax reform in Uruguay. In this case, low and distortionary taxes were removed, the consumption burden was reduced (reducing the VAT rates and eliminating the COFIS, designed as a wholesaler VAT with a cascade effect), the individual income tax was reintroduced with a wide coverage of taxable income, and taxes on business income were consolidated (Rius, 2012).

In other countries, such as in Ecuador (2008) and Chile (2012), reforms of the income tax were pushed through in the effort to inaugurate a more progressive taxation system; their real effect, however, remains in doubt (Cornia et al., 2011). In 2008, the Mexican government introduced the IETU (*Impuesto Empresarial de Tasa Única*), a minimum tax which aims at strengthening CIT. collection. Peru, in turn, modified the income tax on physical persons in 2009, shifting from a global and progressive tax schedule for all incomes to a dual system inspired by the Scandinavian model.[9]

Most governments also eliminated or reduced a long list of exemptions, deductions and tax holidays which had been introduced in the 1980s and 1990s to attract foreign investments. Evaluations of the impact of these tax incentives showed that in most cases the benefits generated were minimal. These exemptions were thus reduced so that the revenue loss they entailed fell to 1.53 of GDP in 2009 (Cornia et al., 2011).

However, the tax systems in the region still have multiple features that impede proper performance in terms of solvency, efficiency and equity, which should be highlighted: (i) a low and volatile tax burden, (ii) a tax structure skewed towards regressive taxes and (iii) a narrow tax base characterized by high levels of evasion and extensive use of tax expenditures.[10]

These factors characterize the tax structure in the region, not only limiting the ability of tax policy to meet its objectives, but also making it more vulnerable to cycles of both the level of activity and prices of exportable products.

Reform is fundamental in order to cope with future challenges in social spending. And the challenge of dealing with the high concentration of income in the top decile is, without any doubt, one of the most important features shaping not only the impact of fiscal policy on income distribution, but also the very political economy that determines the feasibility and realization of the design and implementation of the kind of reforms needed. Moreover, and as shown in Jiménez and Solimano (2012) an important part of the concentration of income distribution across countries and over time is not in the top 10 percent or the top 5 percent of the distribution, but in the top percentile, or the top 0.1 percent. The argument against raising taxes on top incomes and the very rich (or lowering them as it has been the trend in many advanced and developing countries in recent decades) is that in a market economy, they comprise an engine of economic growth through their role in capital accumulation and innovation. Lowering the return on these activities would just diminish effort and wealth creation, as the argument goes. The issue is controversial for various reasons. On one hand, it is not clear that top incomes are simply the legitimate reward to the effort and talent deployed in competitive markets. But on the other hand, political connections, social background, favorable tax and regulatory treatment are all factors that also contribute to amassing big fortunes.

This debate is on the table in most public finances circles. The IMF (2014), in its very recent Fiscal Monitor, warns that tax systems around the world have become steadily less progressive since the early 1980s, arguing that they now rely more on indirect taxes, which are generally less progressive than direct taxes; and within the latter, the progressivity of the personal income tax has declined, reflecting most notably steep cuts in top marginal tax rates. Relating to this diagnosis, the IMF concludes that the overall fairness of the fiscal system should be assessed in terms of taxes and spending combined. And although most redistribution takes place through the latter, taxation at the top has emerged with renewed force as a major concern over the last few years.

Public expenditure: Challenges ahead

Public expenditure has had an important role in reducing inequality in the region (Gasparini et al., 2009; López-Calva and Lustig, 2010; and ECLAC, 2011); it has increased

---

9   For a more detailed description of recent income tax reforms, see CEPAL (2014).
10 See Jiménez and López (2013) for a more detailed discussion.

significantly, and the share of social spending in the total public expenditure is now bigger than a decade before. However, over decades, fiscal policy's emphasis on solvency resulted this objective dominating the other two, and marked a significant deterioration in the quality of management and public expenditure.[11] The definition of quality in public finances chosen in this chapter characterizes as efficient expenditure that which has positive effects on economic growth, employment and equity.

According to ECLAC, "the concept of quality encompasses the elements of public finances to ensure effective and efficient use of public resources, with the objectives of raising the growth potential of the economy and to ensure increasing levels of equitable distribution" (ECLAC, 2012: p. 33).

One way to try to operationalize this definition is through the graphic illustration of the relationship between efficiency and expenditure. The European Commission (2002) studied the contributions of the different types of expenditure to efficiency, resulting in four categories in which there are two types of expenditure, whose relationship with efficiency is almost linear: interest payments (category 1) which always negatively affect growth and employment; and education, R&D, public investment, healthcare, and active labour-market policies (category 4), which are positive expenditures for growth. However, old age and survivor pensions, employee compensation, and collective consumption (category 2) represent efficient costs up to a certain range, because in excessive proportions they can have negative effects on savings, investment and growth. Similarly, unemployment benefits and other social protection expenditures (category 3) increase macroeconomic efficiency, insofar as they boost women's participation rates and the employment of persons excluded from the market. This third category must reach a minimum bar for their impact on growth and employment to be positive, but as in the case of category 2, there is a threshold beyond which efficiency decreases.[12]

This decomposition is useful for three purposes (ILPES/ECLAC, 2012): (i) it emphasizes a nonlinear relationship between spending and its macroeconomic effects, (ii) proposes a more illustrative classification of economic and functional differentiation, (iii) and can be used as a sequence of medium-term drift that improves the quality of public spending. Then in the light of this limited framework, recent trends in the evolution of expenditure will be analyzed in order to shed light on the status of the region today, the challenges presented and what capabilities exist to solve them.

Analyzing in more detail the evolution of the economic composition of spending (Figure 9.6), we can see the most obvious patterns. A six-percentage point increase in total spending is observed, rising from 15% of GDP in 1990 to 21% in 2012. Current expenditure increased significantly between 1995 and 2001, resulting in a further increase in 2008 and 2009. Interest expenses are relatively stable from 1990 to 2003, at which time they begin to fall as a result of a declining stock of debt and interest rates. Capital expenditures maintain a slight but steady increase during the period, with the most significant increase during the 2008 crisis.

In terms of composition, the most important aspect in Latin America is the increasing participation of capital expenditure and the decline of interest payments on the public debt. In Latin America, the simple average of public capital expenditures for 20 countries increased from 17% to 20% of total expenditure between 1990–96 and 2010–12, while

---

11   For a detailed analysis of the relationship between the macro demands and loss of quality of the public budget in the case of Brazil, see Rezende (2009).

12   See ILPES/ECLAC (2012), and European Commission (2002) for further analysis.

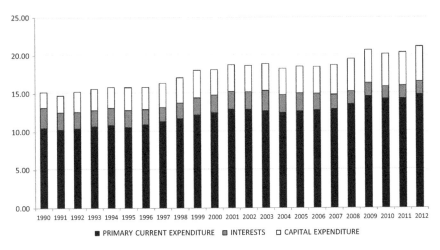

**Figure 9.6   Latin America (19 countries): Central Government
           Expenditure, 1990–2012**

Source: Own elaboration with data provided by CEPAL (2014b).

interest payments decreased by 6 percentage points, from 14% to 8%. The primary current expenditure remained stable, representing 69% in 1990–1996 and 70% in 2010–2012.

These developments notwithstanding, the recovery of public investment remains a pending issue in the region. Public spending as a percentage of GDP represented 6.7% in 1980, declining to a minimum of 3.7% in 2003–2004; since then, it has increased and represented 3.7% of GDP in 2010. Fiscal consolidation during the 1980s and 1990s translated into a sharp decline in public investment, with a consequent negative impact on medium-term growth.

Regarding the functional classification of expenditure, one might well mention the increased social spending in most countries of the region, rising from 45% of the total on average to 63% in Latin America between 2010 and 2011. In recent years, fiscal policies have led to a growing sustainability of public social spending, which has risen from 9.4% to 15.3% of GDP, on average, in the region. The priority given to public social expenditure made it such that, during the crisis, countercyclical responses in the field of social spending were more agile, demonstrating that these expenditures are an essential part of macroeconomic stabilization policies and poverty reduction (CEPAL, 2013b).

Figure 9.7 highlights the sharp increases in countries that already had high social spending in 1990 (Cuba, Argentina, Brazil, Uruguay and Costa Rica). However, there are still many countries in which social spending is still less than 12% of GDP (Mexico, Paraguay, Honduras, Panama, Peru, Ecuador, Guatemala and Dominican Republic).

According to ECLAC (2013) and regarding the evolution of social sector spending, social security and assistance stand as the fastest growers, representing more than half (3.16%) of all the increase of social spending (6.76%) from 1992 to 2011. On average, according to ECLAC data for 2009, social spending goes to education (36%), social security (33%), health (23%) and housing and other (10%). However, just as with all indicators at the aggregate level in the region, the gap between countries in the region is significant.

All these changes in the composition of spending were made possible, among other reasons, because of the increased fiscal space left by the reduction of debt in the region.

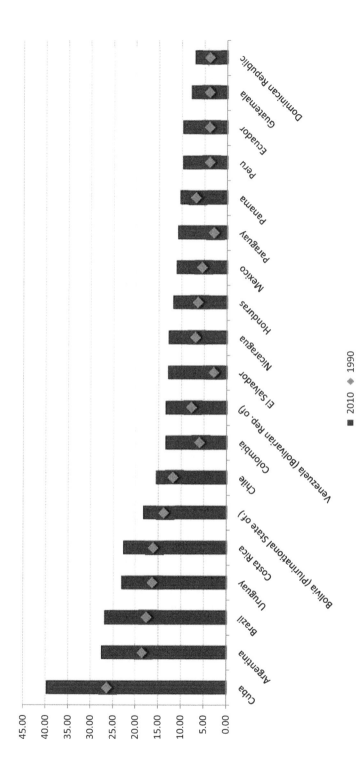

Figure 9.7 **Latin America (19 countries): Social spending, 2010 and 1990**
Source: Own elaboration with data provided by CEPAL (2014b).

Historically, the weight of public debt as a proportion of GDP and the interest payment resulting from this high level of debt have represented a recurring financial constraint on economic growth in Latin America and the Caribbean over previous decades, deteriorating growth expectations and increasing the financial cost of the more expensive projects of public and private investment (ECLAC, 2013).

Given increasing social demands, efficiency in social public spending remains an important challenge in the region. ECLAC (2014) has analyzed efficiency in both, health and educational expenditure. Conclusions about the region are quite similar for both kind of expenditures: the increase have been very relevant (public spending on health has increased from 2.6% of GDP in the early nineties to 3.9% of GDP in 2010–2011, while public expenditure on education went from 2.9% in 1991–1992 to 5% of GDP in 2009–2010); (ii) Latin America, on average, falls at an intermediate level amongst the different regions of the world; (iii) the public share of total health expenditure is 50%, while in Europe, Central Asia and East Asia it is 70%; and (iv) both, health and educational indicators have improved significantly.

However, as pointed by ECLAC (2014), the efficiency of this kind of expenditure is around 80%, meaning that the same results could be achieved while spending 20% less.

Finally, it is key to stop on the analysis of one of the most significant features, fiscal rigidities. Fiscal rigidities are essentially institutional constraints that limit one's ability to change the level or structure of public budgets in a specified period. Their existence is often seen as having two sides: one negative, associated with the limitations on fiscal policy action; and one positive, which relates inflexibility with the need for an institutional framework to help achieve fiscal policy objectives (Cetrángolo and Jiménez, 2009).

Fiscal rigidities can be classified in two large groups: those rigidities stemming from spending policy and those derived from the allocation of tax revenues[13]. In Figure 9.8, levels of expenditure inflexibility[14] are shown for seven countries in the region. Except in the case of Guatemala, expenditure rigidities exceeded 80% of the universe of costs considered. It also shows that three countries in the Andean region recorded the highest percentage of expenditure inflexibility. However, attention should be drawn to the inappropriateness of comparing such indicators, which are not covered by uniform criteria (Cetrángolo and Jiménez, 2009).

The evolution of the business cycle is highly linked to the evolution of the number of fiscal rigidities. During periods of crisis, the establishment of budget rigidities is more the product of severe disputes over financial resources in periods of heavy budget cuts, rather than the result of an appropriate financial design. However, in the context of economic growth—and hence with revenue increasing—the discussion over budget rigidities will relate to the difficulties they pose to meet new objectives, as noted above. It is expected that there is an acceptable consensus on the content and nature of these rigidities, in order to help building a new fiscal pact that comprises both political and social arrangements. Otherwise, such rigidities are a clear reflection of the dispute of interests between different sectors or groups of power around the direction of fiscal policy and government agendas.

---

13   However, as Cetrángolo and Jiménez (2009) pointed out, there are an important number of hybrid situations where expenditure rigidity is manifested through the earmarking of tax revenues.

14   All components should be considered as "inflexible" if their inclusion in the budget is not subject to the discretion of political authorities in the short term. For more details about this definition see Cetrángolo and Jiménez (2009).

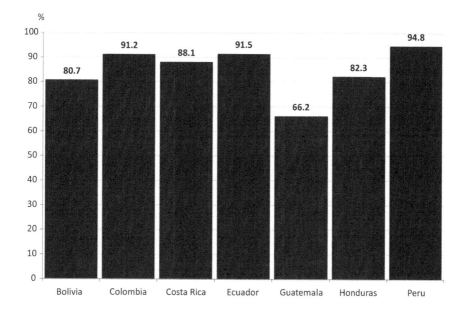

Figure 9.8   Latin America, selected countries: Expenditure inflexibility (2006)
Source: Cetrángolo, Oscar y Jiménez, Juan Pablo (2009).

While it is important to know the degree of flexibility of the budget, it is more important to inquire about the types of rigidities that present a problem, their origins and justifications, and their contribution to democratic debate (Cetrángolo and Jiménez, 2009).

Thus, the degree of relevance of different rigidities of fiscal policy should be evaluated in light of their priorities and requirements. These necessarily change over time, just as social values and priorities are in flux. For this reason, the public budget will contain many components that reflect past agreements and decisions, and one may find specific cases of tax assignments responding to questions that no longer have the same "importance" than they did in the past, and are not a reflection of the current budget debate.

Concluding Remarks and Future Challenges

Traditionally the public finances of the countries of Latin America have observed a significantly reduced fiscal space, linked to scarce tax resources, weak policy instruments and high degree of competition among competing objectives.

Over the last decade, a combination of institutional changes with a sharp increase in tax revenue through improved tax administration, increased prices of exportable products and growth in economic activity, provided fiscal policy with better conditions to face the demands of macroeconomic stabilization challenges.

However, high vulnerabilities on the revenue side coupled with significant rigidities in public spending have hampered this improvement in public accounts in the effort to improve quality in the provision of public goods and services.

Given the multiple social demands that governments in the region face in terms of more efficient and equitable public intervention, along with the resurgence of a macro-economically uncertain situation for developing countries, an agenda for improvement in management and public provision should prioritize proper articulation of the different objectives of public finances, conducting reforms leading to the expansion of fiscal space, improving budgetary institutions and strengthening of coordination mechanisms between different policies across sectors and different levels of government.

Bibliography

Alesina, A. et al. (2008). 'Why is fiscal policy often procyclical?' *Journal of the European Economic Association*, vol. 6, no. 5, pp. 1006–1036.

Amarante, V. and Jiménez, J.P. (2014). *Desigualdad, concentración del ingreso y tributación sobre las altas rentas,* Santiago de Chile, CEPAL (forthcoming).

Atkinson, A. et al. (2011). 'Top incomes in the long run of history.' *Journal of Economic Literature,* vol. 49, no. 1, pp. 3–71.

Alvaredo, F. (2010). 'The rich in Argentina over the twentieth Century 1932–2004,' in Atkinson, A. and Piketty, T. (eds.) (2010). *Top Incomes over the Twentieth Century.* Oxford: Oxford University Press.

Alvaredo, F. and Londoño, J. (2013). *High Incomes and Personal Taxation in a Developing Economy: Colombia 1993–2010.* New York, mimeo.

Burdin, G. et al. (2014). *Desigualdad y altos ingresos en Uruguay: Un análisis en base a registros tributarios y encuestas de hogares para el período 2009–2011,* forthcoming

Cetrángolo, O. and Jiménez, J.P. (comp.) (2009), 'Rigideces y espacios fiscales en América Latina,' *CEPAL Working Paper No. LC/W.269.* Santiago de Chile, CEPAL.

Chu, K. et al. (2004). 'Income Distribution and Tax and Government Social Spending Policies in Developing Countries,' *IMF Working Paper No. 00/62.* Washington, DC, International Monetary Fund.

Cornia, G.A. (2010). 'Income distribution under Latin America's new left regimes.' *Journal of Human Development and Capabilities,* vol. 11, no. 1, pp. 85–114.

Cornia, G.A. et al. (2011). 'A New Fiscal Pact, Tax Policy and Income Inequality. Latin America during the last decade,' *Working Paper No. 2011/70.* Helsinki, UNU-WIDER.

CEPAL (2011). 'Estudio Económico de América Latina y el Caribe 2010–2011,' *CEPAL Working Paper No. LC/G.2506-P.* Santiago de Chile, CEPAL.

CEPAL (2012). 'Cambio estructural para la igualdad: Una visión integrada del desarrollo,' *CEPAL Working Paper No. LC/G.2524 SES.34/3.* Santiago de Chile: CEPAL.

CEPAL (2013). 'Estudio Económico de América Latina y el Caribe 2013: Tres décadas de crecimiento desigual e inestable,' *CEPAL Working Paper No. LC/G.2574-P.* Santiago de Chile, CEPAL.

CEPAL (2013b). 'Social Panorama of Latin America,' *CEPAL Working Paper No. LC/G.2580.* Santiago de Chile, CEPAL.

CEPAL (2014).'Panorama Fiscal de América Latina y el Caribe 2014: Hacia una mayor calidad de las finanzas públicas,' *CEPAL Working Paper No. LC/L.3726.* Santiago de Chile, CEPAL.

CEPAL (2014b). CEPALSTAT. Bases de Datos y Publicaciones Estadísticas, Santiago de Chile, en: http://estadisticas.cepal.org/cepalstat/WEB_CEPALSTAT/Portada. asp?idioma=i (Consultado: 15/01/2014).

European Commission (2002). 'Public Finances in EMU—2002,' *European Economy, Reports and Studies no. 3*. Brussels, European Commission.

Fajnzylber, F. (1989). 'Industrialización en América Latina: de la 'caja negra' al 'casillero vacío': comparación de patrones contemporáneos de industrialización,' *CEPAL Working Paper No. LC/G.1534/Rev.1-P 60*. Santiago de Chile, CEPAL.

Fanelli, J.M. and Jiménez, J.P. (2009). 'Crisis, volatilidad y política fiscal en América Latina,' in Kacef, O. and Jiménez, J.P. (comp.) (2009). *Políticas macroeconómicas en tiempos de crisis: opciones y perspectivas*. Santiago de Chile, CEPAL.

Frankel, J.A. et al. (2011). 'On Graduating on Fiscal Procyclicality,' *NBER Working Paper 17169*. Cambridge, MA, National Bureau of Economic Research.

Gasparini/Cruces/Tornarolli (2009). 'Recent trends in income inequality in Latin America,' *ECINEQ Working Paper 2009-132*, http://www.ecineq.org/milano/WP/ECINEQ2009-132.pdf

Gavin, M. and Perotti, R. (1997). 'Fiscal policy in Latin America.' *NBER Macroeconomics Annual*, vol. 12, no. 1, pp. 11–61.

Gómez Sabaíni, J.C. and Rossignolo, D. (2014). *La tributación sobre las altas rentas en América Latina*, forthcoming.

Heller, P. (2005). 'Understanding Fiscal Space,' *IMF Policy Discussion Paper No. PDP 05/4*. Washington, DC, International Monetary Fund.

ILPES/CEPAL (2012). 'Panorama de la gestión pública en América Latina. En la hora de la igualdad,' *CEPAL Working Paper No. LC/W.426*. Santiago de Chile, CEPAL.

IMF [International Monetary Fund] (2014): Fiscal Policy and Income Inequality. IMF Policy Paper, Washington DC, www.imf.org/external/np/pp/eng/2014/012314.pdf

Kaminsky, G.L. et al. (2004). 'When it Rains it pPours: Pro-cyclical Capital Flows and Macroeconomic Policies,' *NBER Working Paper No. 10780*. Cambridge, MA, National Bureau for Economic Research.

Jiménez, J.P. and López Azcúnaga, I. (2012). '¿Disminución de la Desigualdad en América Latina? El rol de la política fiscal,' *desiguALdades.net Working Paper No. 33*. Berlin, Freie Universität.

Jiménez, J.P. and Solimano, A. (2012). 'Elites Económicas, Desigualdad y Tributación,' *Serie Macroeconomía para el Desarrollo 126*. Santiago de Chile, CEPAL.

López-Calva, L.F. and Lustig, N. (2010). 'Explaining the decline in inequality in Latin America: Technological change, educational upgrading, and democracy,' in López-Calva, L.F. and Lustig, N. (eds.) (2010). *Declining Inequality in Latin America: A Decade of Progress?* New York, United Nations Development Program and Washington, DC, Brookins Institutions Press.

Lora, E. (2007). *The State of State Reform in Latin America*. Palo Alto, IABD, Stanford University Press.

Mahon, J.E. (2009). 'Tax Reforms and Income Distribution in Latin America,' *XXVIII Congress of the Latin American Studies Association*. Rio de Janeiro, 11–14 June.

Mahon, J.E. (2011). 'Tax Incidence and Tax Reforms in Latin America,' *Update on the Americas*. Washington, DC, Woodrow Wilson Center.

Manoel, A., and V. Grembi (2012). Fiscal rules for sub-national governments? Evidence from Latin America," in G. Brosio and J. P. Jiménez (eds.), *Decentralization and Reforms in Latin America: Improving Intergovernmental Relations*, Chapter 12. Northampton: Edward Elgar

Morley, S.A. (2000). 'Distribution and Growth in Latin America in an Era of Structural Reform,' *Conference on Poverty and Inequality in Developing Countries: A Policy*

Dialogue on the Effects of Globalization. OECD Development Centre, Paris, 30 November-1 December.

Ocampo, J.A. and Vos, R. (2008). 'El margen para las políticas y el cambio de paradigma en la instrumentación de las políticas macroeconómicas en países en desarrollo,' *BIS Papers No. 36.* Basel, Bank for International Settlements.

Ostry, J.D. et al. (2010). 'Fiscal Space,' *IMF Staff Position Note No. SPN/10/11.* Washington, DC, International Monetary Fund.

Palma, J.G. (2011). 'Homogenous middles vs. heterogenous tails, and the end of the "inverted-u": It's all about the share of the rich.' *Development and Change,* vol. 42, no. 1, pp. 87–153.

Piketty, T. (2003). 'Income inequality in France, 1901–1998.' *Journal of Political Economy,* vol. 111, no. 5, pp. 1004–42.

Rezende, F. (2009). 'Planejamento no Brasil: auge, declínio e caminos para a reconstrução,' *Escritorio no Brasil.* Brasilia, CEPAL.

Rius, A. (2012). 'La reforma tributaria uruguaya de 2006: Algunas consideraciones de economía política y corportamental,' *Conference Tributación y crecimiento con equidad,* Santiago de Chile, CEPAL, 13–14 August 2012.

Talvi, E. and Végh, C.A. (2005). 'Tax base variability and procyclicality of fiscal policy.' *Journal of Development Economics*, vol. 78, no. 1, pp. 156–190.

Chapter 10

Is Tax Policy Becoming More Pro-equity in the Region? Five Case Studies of Commodity-dependent Economies

Maria Fernanda Valdés

Introduction

In his master work, Richard Musgrave (1959) identified three fundamental objectives of tax and transfers systems: they should ensure an efficient allocation of resources, a stable economy with full employment, and a desirable level of income distribution. This work seeks to assess the redistributive role played by tax policy over the last two decades in Latin America, using the case studies of Argentina, Chile, Colombia, Mexico and Peru.

Evaluating the performance of Latin American tax policies in reference to their distributive role is a valuable exercise. Latin America has continually held the dubious honor of being the most unequal region in the world (UNDP, 2010). However, reductions in inequality over the last decade[1]—precisely when inequality rose elsewhere in the world—aroused curiosity as to how a region that had been so flagrantly unequal, probably since before independence (Sokoloff and Robinson, 2004), could suddenly change course. The reasons pointed out for this change have been multiple, ranging from more pro-equity policies such as public expenditure to changes in labor markets and plain good luck.[2] So far, only a few have inquired as to whether the authorities' use of taxation has differed from the periods of high inequality in the 1990s to the period of declining inequality over the last ten years.[3] If tax policy is becoming more pro-equity, it is more likely to contribute to the sustainability of the decline in inequality.

Determining whether tax policy has become pro-equity over time is an analytical challenge, but also an empirical one. It is an analytical challenge because it implies investigating redistribution through taxation, an idea that has been out of vogue for 40 years. It is also an empirical challenge because in economies as dependent on commodities as Latin American economies, it is difficult to differentiate which changes in tax variables (such as level of revenue or tax structures) are the result of discretionary tax policy and the authorities' fiscal efforts, and which are the result of cycles in commodity prices and pure good luck. With these challenges in mind, the remainder of this chapter is organized as follows: Section 1 assesses how the distributive role of tax policy has changed over time

---

1   See Birdsall et al. (2011), and Lopez-Calva and Lustig (2010).

2   Cornia (2012) and Birdsall et al. (2011) provide a good summary of the reasons behind the improvements. For a critical assessment of changes in social policy in the latest decades see Lavinas (2013).

3   Tanzi (2013), Jiménez and Lopez Azcúnaga (2013) and Cornia et al. (2012) have inquired along similar lines.

in a way that justifies using taxation as a possible explanation of changes in inequality. Section 2 elaborates the analytical framework for analyzing the distributive role of tax policy over time; in practical terms, it shows where to look and which variables to use in analyzing this distributive role over time. Here, I explain why I find that a crucial factor in assessing discretionary tax policy is to analyze structural tax variables instead of regular ones. Section 3 shows the case studies of Argentina, Chile, Colombia, Mexico and Peru and the redistributive role played by tax policy in the 1990–2010 period. The last section presents my conclusions.

The Redistributive Role of Taxation in a Historical Perspective

A study on the distributive role of taxation over time must start by emphasizing that taxation does indeed have a redistributive role to play and can explain changes in inequality. If taxation had no role to play in inequality, the very concept of a "pro-equity tax policy" would be misleading. Therefore, I would like to start with a discussion of how the redistributive role of taxation has changed over time in Latin America and elsewhere. I have identified three general historical paradigms regarding the redistributive role of inequality.

The first paradigm of the distributive role of taxation dates back to the postwar period and the emergence of public finance theory. As explained by Bird (2003), the possibility of changing inequality patterns through taxation was a highly shared belief in the postwar period. It was a reflection of a general optimism which maintained that all perceived ills could be fixed through state action. It is no coincidence that the role of taxes in redistribution emerged exactly when the function of redistribution was returned to the state (Musgrave, 1959).

Musgrave offered insights into two different roles of fiscal policy and taxation on distribution, a distinction that is very much in use today.[4] The first role of taxation is that of modifying the primary distribution. Although he did not use the term "primary distribution" himself, he described this as the "distribution of income and wealth [that] … depends on the distribution of factor endowments … [and] … the prices they fetch in the market" (Musgrave and Musgrave, 1979, p. 11). Taxation accomplishes this function by collecting money, which will later be spent on strengthening human capital through education, health care, sanitation programs, and other social programs. Tax policy thus becomes a factor that contributes to the formation of human capital and thus affects primary distribution. The second role is that of modifying secondary distribution (understood as the distribution after taking taxation into account). This role is accomplished when taxation reshapes after-tax income structures. Taxation is capable of producing this reshaping through what Musgrave and Thin (1948) called the progression of tax systems. Progressive tax systems place the higher burden of the tax on high-income segments, which is meant to change post-tax distribution.

As is documented by Bird (2003), Bird and Zolt (2005) and Tanzi (2013), the optimism of the postwar era was also reflected in Latin America. The dominant Latin American development paradigm, as found in early CEPAL thinking, followed this trend. This was made clear by the paramount importance placed on the distributive role of the state and the instrument of taxation. The ability of taxes to redistribute was unquestioned. In fact, the main recommendation was that Latin American countries, in order to develop, had to

---

4   See for instance the documents of Gómez-Sabaini (2006) and CEPAL (2010).

"learn to tax" (Kaldor, 1963). Learning to tax, for Kaldor, meant collecting more money to finance a developmental state and collecting more progressively to redistribute income and wealth. Note that, according to Kaldor, both objectives could be obtained in the same way: progressive and high income tax rates could increase revenue and create redistribution. As a result of this way of thinking, most early tax missions in Latin America advised policymakers to replace regressive taxes on consumption (tariffs, export taxes, excise taxes, and general sales taxes) with progressive taxes on income.

At the end of the 1970s, this optimism faded as Latin American economies began to slow; and as the continent entered the "Lost Decade" of financial crisis, *the second paradigm* regarding the redistributive role of taxation emerged. Experts started to doubt taxation's potential as a redistributive tool. The new mantra of the epoch was that redistribution could be achieved most effectively through social spending and not through taxation. According to Zee (2004), two interdependent factors may explain this changed perception. Firstly, new evidence from incidence studies showed that the effectiveness of taxation in altering post-tax distribution was limited in most countries and particularly in Latin America, where the progressivity of taxation has been extremely low, while the real effect of taxation on after-tax Gini has been negligible.

The second reason for the change in perception was theoretical. The development of the Optimal Tax Theory (OTT) emerged as *the* economic methodology for assessing the best system to maximize the welfare of societies. In terms of the structure of the tax systems, the normative OTT results from these initial analysis of Mirrless (1976), Tuomala (1990) and others, even with egalitarian motivations, seldom pointed to progressive tax structures (Slemrod, 1994).

The idea that taxation was not among the most important factors for explaining inequality remained prevalent for almost 40 years. This idea has been recently challenged, however, and we are now at the cusp of *the third paradigm* concerning the redistributive role of taxation. This change of paradigm coincides with economists and other social scientists' concern over the spectacular rise in inequality in developed countries (particularly English-speaking countries) over the last 40 years. Preoccupations with inequality in the developed world became more acute after the crisis of 2008, when some notable academics blamed this increase on inequality for the global financial crisis (Stiglitz, 2012).

The new paradigm moves to assert that taxation is—and has always been—a relevant aspect in explaining inequality. The redistributive role of taxation has thus become a primary element in new studies on inequality. Probably the most prominent exponent of this paradigm is Thomas Piketty, who has incorporated these ideas into his recent book *Capital in the Twenty-first Century* (2014), *as well as in other coauthored works* (Alvaredo et al., 2013; Piketty et al., 2011; Piketty and Saez, 2006).

The new paradigm brings back the redistributive role of taxation on two fronts. Firstly, on an empirical level, the works already mentioned prove quite convincingly that taxation does, in effect, explain changes on inequality over time and among countries. This research was intrigued by the fact that most the theories of skill-biased technological change and globalization cannot explain why the US and other English-speaking countries experienced increases in inequality while other high-income globalized countries with similar technological and productivity developments have gone through different patterns of income inequality; the studies use the variable of taxation to explain differences among and within countries over time. They prove that the evolution of top tax rates is strongly negatively correlated to changes in pre-tax income concentration. Secondly, at the theoretical level, their work, and that of other renowned economists such as Diamond and Saez (2011), have modified certain assumptions around and shortcomings of the initial OTT models and have come to state that the optimal tax system is, in fact, a progressive tax system, and not a flat system, as the initial models of the 1970s claimed.

The new paradigm is gaining adepts. At the international level, just as an example, the UNCTAD dedicated a whole section in its 2012 Trade and Development Report to the redistributive effect of tax policy. Moreover, quite recently, the IMF (2014) recognized that taxation is relevant in explaining inequality –something they had not fully accepted previously, one might note.

In Latin America, the redistributive role of taxation has gained a new appeal and more studies are focusing on the tax system as a factor to explain inequality in the region. This is the case with the works of Mahon (2011), Jiménez et al. (2012), Cornia et al (2012), among many others. In the practical arena, the work of Fairfield (2013) taken a step forward into enumerating possible strategies to make tax systems in the region more equalizing. Additionally, as was laid out by Juan Pablo Jimenez and Isabel López Azcúnaga (see section III), there has been interest in obtaining more precise estimations of the concentration of income at the top and the effective tax rates that the people on the top pay—an interest that is only conceivable within the new paradigm.

How to assess the distributive role of tax policy over long time periods

The new paradigm discussed above accentuates the importance of the redistributive role of taxation, thus assuring that the concept of "pro-equity tax policy" is a relevant and workable one. Some years ago, the term "pro-equity tax policy" would have attracted considerable skepticism.

This section delves deeper into this concept, particularly as to which factors and variables one should observe to determine whether tax policy has become more pro-equity over time. This work uses a framework consisting of three factors and finds that tax policy is more pro-equity when it is directed towards a) collecting more, b) collecting more progressively, and c) collecting more counter-cyclically.

A tax policy that increases tax collection is pro-equity for the reason that the more a tax system collects, the more resources there will be to redistribute. Likewise, a tax policy that makes the system more progressive is a pro-equity tax policy, since it changes the burden of taxation to obtain a more even distribution. A tax policy that is counter-cyclical (a policy that reduces taxes during bad times or/and increases taxes in good times, furthermore) tends to be pro-equity, while a pro-cyclical tax policy (a policy that increases taxes in bad times or/and reduces taxes in good times) is at odds with equality. This is so because, firstly, abrupt increases of taxes during bad times in the form of austerity measures tend to fall heavily on the poorest (Woo et al., 2013), especially in regions such as Latin America that tend to have regressive tax systems. Secondly, if we take into account that, according to a study by Mahon (2011), Latin American states have reacted to economic turbulence by increasing their reliance on regressive taxation, we may expect an even more negative effect on distribution. Finally, one of the macroeconomic effects of pro-cyclical tax policy is that it is destabilizing and tends to accentuate economic cycles and create volatility. Volatility and crises have been repeatedly proven to contribute to the creation and recreation of inequalities (Breen and García-Peñalosa, 2005; Baldacci et al., 2002; Calderon and Levy-Yeyati, 2009; Atkinson and Morelli, 2011; Lustig et al., 2000). Therefore, a pro-cyclical tax policy, through its effects on the real economy, categorically aggravates the inequality situation.

In exploring the collecting effort of tax policy, I will use the same variable as Engel et al. (1998), Goñi et al. (2011) and Mahon (2011): the share of tax revenues in GDP. For measuring the progressivity effort, I will use the ratio of personal income tax (PIT) revenues over total revenues (excluding PIT) as a *proxy* for progressivity. The reason for choosing this ratio is that, according to the studies done on the subject (Goñi et al., 2011; Cetrángolo and Gómez Sabaini, 2007), the PIT is the *only* progressive tax in most Latin American economies; therefore, changes in this ratio may indicate efforts to change the progressivity of tax systems. Finally, cyclicality will be analyzed in the standard way: looking at the share of tax revenues in GDP in comparison with the economic cycle.

There is an additional and novel adjustment that this work will introduce to all tax variables: instead of using current tax variables it will use structural tax variables[5]. Structural tax variables are the same variables adjusted for the effects of economic cycles and other cycles affecting the economy. In this study, structural variables are additionally adjusted for the effect of commodity price cycles. Structural tax variables can be interpreted as the tax variables that would exist if prices of commodities were at their long-term value and the economy were running at its potential.

The reason for adding these variables is that the main interest of this work is discretionary tax policy,[6] as opposed to merely tax results or non-discretionary tax policy. Structural variables have traditionally been used to reflect discretionary policy (Blanchard, 1990), grounded in the assumption that, once the effect of the cycle and other variables such as the price of commodities are excluded, changes in structural values must be motivated by tax policy of one kind or another.

I consider that using structural variables is key for studying a region such as Latin America, whose tax systems have historically been so dependent on commodity sectors (Jiménez and Tromben, 2006). Furthermore, the use of structural variables is essential when analyzing the period that this work wants to evaluate, namely 1990–2010. During the initial years of this period, largely until 2003, prices of commodities were stable and low. After 2003 there began a commodity boom, in which commodity prices increased exponentially and achieved historically unprecedented values. Structural tax variables help to correct for this asymmetry. Without this adjustment, the period of extraordinarily high commodity prices will falsely imply increased tax efforts by the authorities. It should never be forgotten that changes in the tax burden do not always mean changes in tax efforts: when additional tax revenues can be explained by changes in commodity prices, one should not praise governments for their extra fiscal efforts. Furthermore, this adjustment is also mandatory for any assessment of cyclicality; tax variables are so intimately bound to the economic cycle and commodity cycles that only by adjusting for these effects can one actually observe the cyclicality of tax policy.

The Case Studies of Five Commodity-Dependent Economies: Argentina, Chile, Colombia, Mexico, and Peru

In order to assess whether the authorities' use of taxation has been more pro-equity in the period of declining inequality compared to the period of high inequality in the 1990s, this

---

5   The methodology for transforming current tax variables into structural tax variables is described in detail in my PhD dissertation (Valdés, 2015).

6   From now on, I will use the term "tax policy" to refer "to discretionary tax policy."

section takes case studies of the five biggest Latin American countries that are dependent on *one* commodity product.[7] The motive for choosing countries reliant on one commodity is that, in order to construct structural tax revenue variables, the identification of a single product is mandatory. Countries with more diversified economies are not suitable for the construction of structural tax revenue variables.

The five case studies analyzed are: Argentina, with 25.6% of its exports comprising soybeans and derivatives; Chile, with 53% of its exports in copper; Colombia and Mexico with 40.7% and 38.3% of their exports, respectively, consisting of crude petroleum and petroleum products; and Peru, with 25% of its exports being copper.[8]

The fact that these five countries have export sectors dependent on commodities is meant to reflect an aspect particularly relevant to this work, namely that these countries' tax systems are also very dependent on commodity sectors revenues, and thus especially susceptible to commodity prices. The reason why the participation of commodities on exports was used for the case selection, rather than the importance of tax revenues coming from commodity sectors in total tax revenues, is the lack of data on the latter.

For the five case studies I have prepared a primary approximation to measure the dependency of tax systems on commodity related tax revenues. Using official data and some imputation techniques,[9] I have constructed a dataset of tax revenues related to commodity sectors for the five cases at hand, and the results are presented in Table 10.1. It is evident that, indeed, the five countries with high participation of commodities in exports also have high degrees of dependency on revenues from commodities. Furthermore, with the exception of Mexico,[10] the average share of tax revenue from the commodity sector has increased considerably. The country with the highest increase was Argentina, where the percentage of total tax revenues coming from commodity sectors multiplied tenfold from the 1990s to the 2000s. The second largest increase was in Chile, where total average tax revenues tripled compared to the average in the 1990s. In Colombia this value doubled, and in Peru it increased by 3 percentage points. It is important to mention that comparison among countries is more problematic due to different methods and imputations.

Table 10.1   Participation of taxes from commodity sectors in total tax revenues, selected countries

Years	Argentina	Chile	Colombia	Mexico	Peru
1990–2000	1.33%	6.85%	4.35%	12.23%	13.08%
2000–2010	11.90%	14.45%	8.71%	9.92%	16.21%

Source: Own calculations based on Valdés (2015).

---

7   The definition of dependency here encompasses countries with at least 25% of exports focused on a single product. Venezuela was on the list of the biggest commodity-dependent countries, but was discarded, as it lacks information on tax revenues.

8   The rate of participation of exports is taken from CEPALSTAT for the year 2010.

9   See Valdés (2014) for an explanation of the data and the methods used to construct this dataset.

10   The Special Tax on Production and Services IEPS paid by PEMEX to the state becomes a subsidy whenever the difference between the price of production and the market price is too high. Therefore in the period after 2003, tax revenues from the IEPS were actually negative.

The data shown in Table 10.1 serves to demonstrate the importance of commodity markets for these countries' tax systems, but, more relevantly, serves to prove that the use of structural variables that adjusts for commodity prices is necessary in order to analyze the tax performance of these countries over time.

Now, in accordance with the previous discussion, tax policy will be assessed in reference to the revenue collection effort, the progressivity effort, and cyclicality.

Revenue collection effort of tax policy

In order to assess the effort of authorities to increase collection, Figure 10.1 shows total tax revenues as a percentage of GDP for each country. Each figure has two lines: the observable tax share, which is total revenues divided by GDP; and the structural share, which is tax revenues adjusted for the cycle and the most important commodity of each country as a share of potential GDP. The structural tax line is the one that describes discretionary tax policy.

Figure 10.1 shows that, looking only at the observable shares, it is evident that all countries increased tax collection over the 20 years analyzed. Argentina and Colombia are the stars of revenue collection increases in the sample. Argentina, remarkably, increased its tax revenues year after year. In 1990 Argentina was collecting 11.9% of its GDP in taxes; 20 years later this value had more than doubled to 26.4%. In the case of Colombia, there is a dramatic and constant increase in tax collection. At the beginning of the 1990s, observable tax collection represented 8.3% of GDP, making Colombia the lowest collector of the sample. From then on, Colombia steadily increased tax receipts to 16.2% in 2007. From 2008 onwards, there was a reduction of the tax share, falling back to around 15% by 2010. In total, during the two decades analyzed, Colombia not only increased its collection by approx. 7 percentage points, but in the 2010s, it was also no longer the lowest collector, having outstripped Peru and Mexico.

Chile and Peru increased their tax revenues in the period by around 4 percentage points. At the beginning of the 1990s, Chilean authorities were collecting 13.4% of GDP in taxes, while at the end of the 2010s this value had reached 17.2%. In contrast to Argentina and Colombia, Chilean tax revenues have not increased continuously. Tax revenues as a percentage of GDP have increased in two particular periods, in the first three years of the sample (1990–1993) and in the four years before the crisis of 2009 (2004–2008); in this latest period, collection peaked in 2008, when collection was as high as 18.9% of GDP. After this period a strong decrease in collection was experienced. Over the other years analyzed, tax revenues have remained rather constant. In Peru, the share of taxes as a part of GDP increased from 12.1% to 15.6%. There was a particular period of revenue expansion in Peru, from 2003 to 2008. The last country in terms of revenue increases was Mexico. In 1990 Mexico was collecting 10,2% of its GDP in taxes, 20 years latter this value had very slightly increased to 10,3%. In 2010 Mexico was the lowest revenue collector of my sample.

Hence, it is clear that tax revenues increased in the case studies, but the interest of this analysis does not lie in tax revenues but in discretionary tax policy. Moreover, this work seeks to uncover a possible policy shift in taxation.

To assess discretionary tax policy, one has to look at the structural line. Figure 10.1 shows that once the effect of the cycle and commodity prices is taken into account, the increase is more modest in all cases, indicating that the increase of tax revenues seen in the latest 20 years were not completely based on discretionary tax policy, but also resulted

Figure 10.1   Total tax revenue as a percentage of GDP, selected countries
Source: Own calculations based on Valdés (2014).

from the commodity boom and positive cyclical stance. Comparing the collection at the beginning of the 1990s to circumstances in 2010, it is evident that Argentina and Colombia are the countries with more intense revenue-increasing discretionary tax policy; adjusting for the cycle and commodities, they increased tax revenues by 11 and 5 percentage points respectively. The third country with considerable revenue-increasing discretionary tax policy was Chile, with an increase in 3 percentage points, followed by Mexico with no increase and then Peru, which saw the value of the collection fall by one percentage point over the period since 1998.

In order to ascertain whether there was a change in the way countries have used tax policy in the period when inequality was increasing compared to the period when inequality was decreasing- which is, by the way, the objective of this work- one needs to identify the year when inequality started to change. Cornia et al. (2012), chose year 2000 as the point when inequality started to change in all countries. They call the period post-2000 the years of the "new fiscal pact." In step with the work of Cornia et al., I will use the term "the new fiscal pact years" throughout this chapter to refer to the years of inequality reduction. Contrary to Cornia et al., I decided to select a country-dependent turning-point year based on data on inequality from the Sedlac-Worldbank database, which shows that 2003 was the year when inequality started to decrease in Argentina and Peru, in Colombia inequality started to decline in 2002, and 2000 was the turning-point years for Mexico and Chile.

Table 10.2 shows the average tax revenue growth of the five selected countries, but now I have separated the two periods to allow for a comparison. If there were a policy shift, one would expect a different average structural tax revenue growth in both periods. After looking at Table 10.2, the average growth value of the structural tax revenues clearly indicates three identifiable experiences. The first experience was that of Chile, Colombia and Mexico, where discretionary tax policy was on average more revenue-increasing in the first period than in in the period of "the new fiscal pact." The second experience is that of Peru where discretionary tax policy in the first period bent markedly towards fewer revenues, while in the second period tax policy was slightly oriented towards increasing revenue. Lastly, there is the experience of Argentina where discretionary tax policy was equally revenue increasing in both periods.

Table 10.2   **Average tax revenue growth, selected countries**

		Observable	Structural
Argentina	1992–2002	2.2%	3.1%
	2003–2010	5.6%	3.1%
Chile	1991–1999	2.2%	2.3%
	2000–2010	0.5%	0.5%
Colombia	1994–2001	3.7%	4.3%
	2002–2010	1.4%	1.0%
Mexico	1991–1999	0.6%	0.5%
	2000–2010	-0.4%	-0.4%
Peru	1999–2002	-2.9%	-4.3%
	2003–2010	2.5%	0.8%

Source: Own calculations based on Valdés (2015).

Table 10.2 also indicates clearly that the increase in the observable revenue collection in the period of the "new fiscal pact" was, in the majority of cases, inflated by the effect of increasing prices of commodity and a positive cyclical stance. Discretionary tax policy can only partially explain the increased collection under the new fiscal pact.

Progressivity Effort of Tax Policy

This section looks to examine how taxation has changed the progressivity of the tax system over time. In the previous section I proposed a proxy for progressivity. In the strictest sense, this proxy equals the ratio of structural PIT tax revenues over the structural tax revenues of the rest of the tax categories. The economic interpretation of this index is the participation of progressive taxes over regressive taxes, once adjusted for the cycle and prices of commodities. The change of this proxy value will be interpreted as a change in discretionary tax policy, such that an increase in this variable indicates a tax policy towards more progressivity of the tax system, while a decrease can be interpreted as the opposite.

Figure 10.2 shows the calculated progressivity index. In general terms, according to this index, the country with the highest average proxy value in the period was Mexico, with a variable average value of 0.33—indicating that, considering an economy running at its trend and prices of commodity at their long-term value, there are, on average, 0.33 Mexican pesos of tax revenues coming from progressive taxes for every peso coming from regressive taxes. The next country is Peru, with an average ratio of 0.13, followed by Chile and Argentina with ratios of 0.08 and 0.06 respectively; finally, the country with the lowest value is Colombia, where the ratio of progressive taxation was, on average, just 0.01.

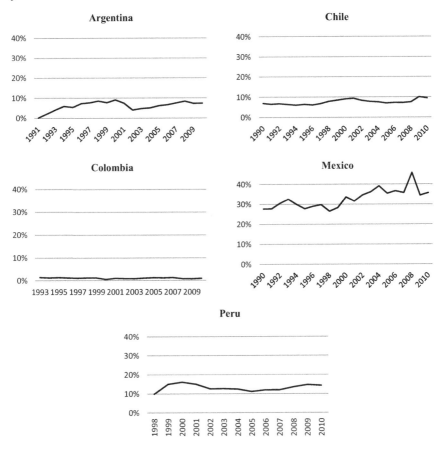

Figure 10.2   Progressivity index (structural PIT revenues / total structural revenues excluding PIT), selected countries

Source: Own calculations based on Valdés (2014).

Some caution should exist around any attempt to derive conclusions from the above data, as the degree of progressivity/regressivity of said progressive/regressive taxes varies significantly among countries. To say that, for instance, the Mexican tax system is more progressive than the Colombian, would be a misleading take on the data. It is true that the Mexican tax system collects more from progressive taxes, but Mexican progressive taxes could be less progressive than Colombian progressive taxes. In other words, a tax such as the PIT could be progressive in all countries, but there are different levels of progressivity; in some countries PIT could be highly progressive, while just slightly progressive in others. I do not account for these differences in degree in this work. Accordingly, I focus on changes in the proxy in each country over time, and not on comparing countries.

Figure 10.2 also illustrates the direction of tax policy in terms of progressivity over the period analyzed. With the sole exception of Colombia, all countries pursued discretionary tax policy that changed the tax system towards greater progressivity. Comparing the proxy in the beginning of the series with the last year of the series, the country that increased its progressivity index most radically was Argentina, which tripled the value. The second position goes to Peru, which increased its progressivity by 44%, then Chile, with a 37% bump, followed by the case of Mexico, with a 29% increase. Lastly we find the case of Colombia, which actually reduced its progressivity index by 34%.

What I want to assess now is whether there has been a policy shift regarding progressivity in recent years. To fulfill this objective, I will duplicate the exercise from the previous section and compare the average growth of the progressivity index in the two periods: the years when inequality was increasing, and the years of the new fiscal pact. Table 10.3 above shows the results of the average growth of the proxy. The structural proxy shows that two countries did indeed pursue more progressivity-oriented (or at least less regressive) tax policy during the years of the "new fiscal pact." This was the case with Argentina and Colombia. Argentinean policy changed towards regressivity during the 1992–2002 period, but it then turned to progressivity during the subsequent period. The case of Colombia is different in the sense that during the period of 1994–2002 tax policy changed the tax system towards more regressivity, shifting towards a less regressive –but still regressive-tax

Table 10.3   Progressivity index growth, selected countries

		Structural
Argentina	1994–2002	-0.10%
	2003–2010	7.6%
Chile	1991–1999	2.2%
	2003–2010	1.0%
Colombia	1994–2001	-4.1%
	2002–2010	-0.9%
Mexico	1991–1999	2.0%
	2002–2010	0.6%
Peru	1999–2002	6.3%
	2003–2010	1.6%

Source: Own calculations based on Valdés (2014).

model in the second period. In the cases of Mexico, Chile and Peru, it is evident that the policy shift was towards less progressivity. In all cases discretionary tax policy tended to make the system more progressive in both periods, but in the second period it became less noticeably progressive.

Cyclicality of tax policy

To address the cyclical stance of tax policy, I have calculated the correlation coefficient of the cyclical component of the GDP with the structural tax revenues as a percentage of GDP for each country. Figure 10.3, Panel A illustrates the results from that correlation, showing that Argentina and Colombia pursued a pro-cyclical tax policy during the years analyzed, Chile and Peru pursued a counter-cyclical tax policy, and Mexico's policy was more acyclical as the correlation of the output gap with the structural tax revenues is positive, but very close to zero.

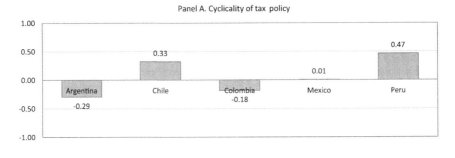

Panel A. Cyclicality of tax policy

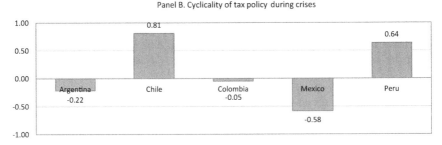

Panel B. Cyclicality of tax policy during crises

Figure 10.3   Correlation analysis, selected countries
Source: Own calculations based on Valdés (2014).

I have indicated above how relevant it is to look at times of crises in the Latin American case to understand the relationship between taxation and inequality; for this reason, I have replicated the exercise only for times of crises. I used the definition of crises from Vegh and Vuletin (2013; 2014), and crisis years can be found in Annex 1.

Figure 10.4, Panel B shows the correlation coefficient of the cyclical GDP with the structural revenues only in times of crises. The figure shows that Argentina, Mexico and Colombia followed pro-cyclical tax policy, pursuing revenue-increasing discretionary tax policy in times of crises. Chile and Peru, on the other hand, moved toward counter-cyclical tax policy in times of crises.

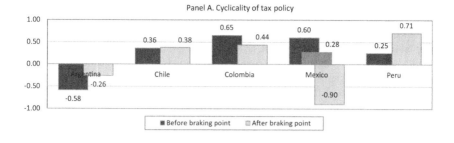

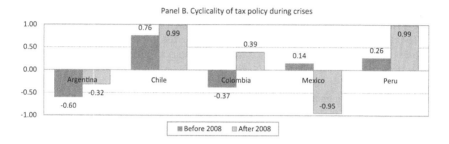

Figure 10.4 **Correlation analysis (policy shift assessment), selected countries**
Source: Own calculations based on Valdés (2014).

Now I would like to evaluate whether there has been a policy shift in the cyclicality of tax policy in the case study countries. I decided to select the turning-point year of each country individually, depending on the year when a new economic cycle started. Annex 2 shows the business cycles of each countries and the selection of the turning-point year. The turning point for Argentina and Chile is 2003; for Colombia, it is 1999; Mexico has two turning points, 1995 and 2003; and the turning point year for Peru was 2001.

I evaluate a possible policy shift regarding two aspects: a policy shift in cyclicality and a policy shift in cyclicality in times of crisis. Regarding a policy shift in cyclicality, Figure 10.4, Panel A shows that it is possible to make out a policy shift in all countries analyzed. The direction of the policy shift varies, however, depending on the case. Argentina's tax policy was pro-cyclical in the first period, moving towards less pro-cyclicality in the latter period. In the cases of Chile and Peru, tax policy was countercyclical and became more countercyclical over time (although the change was very modest in the case of Chile). Colombia pursued countercyclical tax policy until 1999, and a less countercyclical policy afterwards. Mexico was the only case where tax policy was counter-cyclical in the 1990s and became pro-cyclical in the more recent period.

Regarding the question as to whether tax policy reacted differently in the crises of the 1990s and the beginning of the 2000s in comparison to the latest crisis of 2008, Figure 10.4, Panel B shows that indeed, there was a change in the way countries reacted to the crisis of 2008 as compared to crises of the past. In general, all countries pursued a more countercyclical tax policy during the 2008 crisis, or at least less pro-cyclical. The only exception was Mexico, which responded counter-cyclically to the tequila crisis but pro-cyclically to the 2008 crisis.

Conclusions

The objective of this study was to assess whether Latin American tax policy has become more pro-equity over the course of the last 20 years. Particularly, I wanted to see whether the authorities' use of taxation has differed from the periods of high inequality in the 1990s to the period of declining inequality over the last ten years. To answer these questions I used the case studies of the five biggest single-commodity-dependent economies in the region: Argentina, Chile, Colombia, Mexico, and Peru. Venezuela was excluded due to a lack of available data. I compared tax policy of the two periods, examining whether or not tax policy in these countries were oriented towards collecting more, collecting more progressively, and collecting more counter-cyclically. I used structural tax revenues adjusted for commodity prices and the economic cycle, as these are variables that better describe discretionary tax policy.

The results from the empirical analysis are summarized in Table 10.4. In general terms, *the first conclusion* that we can derive from the empirical investigation is that country experiences in relation to taxation are very heterogeneous; thus, the questions this work looks to answer have to be addressed in a country-by-country basis. There is no country where one can sustain unambiguously that tax policy has become more pro-equity.

Table 10.4   Summary of the empirical results

	Was tax policy directed towards more collection in the years of the new fiscal pact?	Was tax policy directed towards more progressivity in the years of the new fiscal pact?	Did tax policy become more counter-cyclical?
Argentina	no	yes	yes
Chile	no	no	yes
Colombia	no	yes	no
Mexico	no	no	no
Peru	yes	no	yes

There is however one country where tax policy categorically became less pro-equity: Mexico. Mexico's tax policy in the 1990s was slightly revenue-increasing and became revenue-decreasing in the period of the "new fiscal pact." In terms of progressivity, taxation tended to make the system more progressive in both periods, but less so in the latter period than in the former. Mexico had a counter-cyclical tax policy at the beginning of the 1990s, but in the 2000s tax policy turned strongly pro-cyclical. The pro-cyclicality of the latest period was also evident in its policy response to the crisis of 2008, which was pro-cyclical, in contrast to the counter-cyclical reaction to the tequila crisis of the mid-1990s.

There is no clear-cut answer to the question of whether Argentina, Chile, Colombia and Peru tax policies have become more pro-equity; these countries had improvements in some aspects and relapses in others. Colombian tax policy tended to make the system more progressive in the period of the "new fiscal pact" as compared to the previous period, when taxation tended to make the system more regressive; but the policies of the 1990s, which were countercyclical and increasing-revenue-oriented, became less so after the 2000s. Chile's tax policy improved slightly in its cyclicality over the years, but its tax policy was less revenue-increasing and tended to make the system less progressive in the period of the "new fiscal pact." Peruvian tax policy became more revenue-increasing and more counter-cyclical over time, but there was no policy shift towards greater progressivity. Argentina pursued a more progressive tax policy and a more countercyclical tax policy in the period of the "new fiscal pact." Furthermore, in comparison to the reaction to the crises of the 1990s and the crises of the beginning of the 2000, Argentina reacted in a less pro-cyclical way to the crisis of 2008. However, there was no policy shift towards a more revenue-increasing tax policy.

From the experiences of these countries we can derive *a second conclusion*: discretionary tax policy was not categorically supporting the decline in inequality seen in these countries over recent years. In the case of Mexico, the reduction in inequality was not achieved with the help of tax policy, but in spite of it. On the whole, if we want to find a policy explanation for the decline in inequality experienced in the latest years, we may very well need to look somewhere else. The ways that these countries have used the tools of tax policy, although varying in certain aspects, do not seem to be considerably superior to the methods of the 1990s, a period when inequality was increasing.

Bibliography

Alvaredo, F. et al. (2013). 'The Top 1 Percent in International and Historical Perspective,' *Working Paper No. 19075*. Cambridge, MA, National Bureau of Economic Research.

Atkinson, A.B. and Morelli, S. (2011). 'Economic Crises and Inequality,' *Human Development Research Papers (2009 to present)*. New York, HDRP/UNDP, http://ideas.repec.org/p/hdr/papers/hdrp-2011-06.html.

Baldacci, E. et al. (2002). 'Financial crises, poverty, and income distribution.' *Finance & Development*. vol. 39, no. 2, pp. 24–27.

Bird, R.M. (2003). 'Taxation in Latin America: Reflections on Sustainability and the Balance Between Equity and Efficiency,' *ITB Paper No. 0306*. Toronto, Institute for International Business.

Bird, R.M. and Zolt, E.M. (2005). 'Redistribution via Taxation: The Limited Role of the Personal Income Tax in Developing Countries,' *SSRN Scholarly Paper ID 804704*. Rochester, NY, Social Science Research Network, http://papers.ssrn.com/abstract=804704.

Birdsall, N. et al. (2011). 'Declining Inequality in Latin America: Some Economics, Some Politics,' *Working Paper No. 1120*. New Orleans, Tulane University, Department of Economics, http://ideas.repec.org/p/tul/wpaper/1120.html.

Blanchard, O.J. (1990). 'Suggestions for a New Set of Fiscal Indicators,' *OECD Economics Department Working Paper No. 79*. Paris, OECD, http://ideas.repec.org/p/oec/ecoaaa/79-en.html.

Breen, R. and García-Peñalosa, C. (2005). 'Income inequality and macroeconomic volatility: An empirical investigation.' *Review of Development Economics,* vol. 9, no. 3, pp. 380–398.

Calderon, C. and Levy-Yeyati, E. (2009). *Zooming in from Aggregate Volatility to Income Distribution*. Washington, DC, World Bank.

CEPAL (2010). *Estudio Económico de América Latina y El Caribe 2009–2010: El Impacto Distributivo de Las Políticas Públicas*. Santiago de Chile, CEPAL.

Cetrángolo, O. and Gómez Sabaini, J. (2007). *La tributación directa en América Latina y los desafíos a la imposición sobre la renta*. Santiago de Chile, CEPAL.

Cornia, G.A. (2012). 'Income distribution under Latin America's new left regimes,' in van der Hoeven, R. (ed.) (2012). *Employment, Inequality and Globalization: A Continuous Concern.* London, Routledge.

Cornia, G.A. et al. (2012). 'A New Fiscal Pact, Tax Policy Changes and Income Inequality,' *Working Paper No. 03/2012.* Firenze, Università degli Studi di Firenze, Dipartimento di Scienze per l'Economia e l'Impresa.

Diamond, P.A. and Saez, E. (2011). 'The Case for a Progressive Tax: From Basic Research to Policy Recommendations,' *CESifo Working Paper No. 3548.* München, CESifo Group.

Engel, E. et al. (1998). 'Taxes and Income Distribution in Chile: Some Unpleasant Redistributive Arithmetic,' *Working Paper No. 6828.* Cambridge, MA, National Bureau of Economic Research.

Fairfield, T. (2013). 'Going where the money is: Strategies for taxing economic elites in unequal democracies.' *World Development,* vol. 47, no. 7, pp. 42–57.

Gómez Sabaini, J.C. (2006). *Cohesión Social, Equidad y Tributación: Analisis y Perspectivas para América Latina.* New York, United Nations.

Goñi, E. et al. (2011). 'Fiscal redistribution and income inequality in Latin America.' *World Development,* vol. 39, no. 9, pp. 1558–69.

International Monetary Fund (2014). 'Fiscal policy and income inequality,' *Policy Paper.* Washington, DC, International Monetary Fund.

Jiménez, J.P. and Amarante, V. (forthcoming). *Desigualdad, Concentración Del Ingreso y Tributación Sobre Las Altas Rentas.*

Jiménez, Juan Pablo, and Isabel Lopez Azcúnaga. 2012. *¿Disminución de La Desigualdad En América Latina? El Rol de La Política Fiscal.* 33. Desigualdades Working Paper Series. Berlin: Desigualdades.net.

Jiménez, J.P. et al. (2012). 'Imposición a la renta personal y equidad en América Latina: Nuevos desafíos,' *CEPAL Working Paper No. LC/L.3477 119.* Santiago de Chile, CEPAL.

Jiménez, J.P. and Tromben, V. (2006). *Política Fiscal En Países Especializados En Productos No Renovables En América Latina.* Santiago de Chile, CEPAL.

Kaldor, N. (1963). 'Will underdeveloped countries learn to tax?' *Foreign Affairs,* vol. 41, no. 2, pp. 410–419.

Lavinas, L. (2013). 'Latin America. Anti-Poverty Schemes Instead of Social Protection,' *desiguALdades Working Paper No. 51.* Berlin, Freie Universität.

López-Calva, L.F. et al. (2010). *Declining Inequality in Latin America: A Decade of Progress?* New York/Washington, DC, United Nations Development Programme.

Lustig, N. et al. (2000). 'Crises and the poor: Socially responsible macroeconomics.' *Economia,* vol. 1, no. 1, pp. 1–30.

Mahon, J.E. (2011). 'Tax reforms and income distribution in Latin America,' in Blofield, M. (ed.) (2011). *The Great Gap: Inequality and the Politics of Redistribution in Latin America.* University Park, Penn State Press.

Mirrlees, J.A. (1976). 'Optimal tax theory : A synthesis.' *Journal of Public Economics,* vol. 6, no. 4, pp. 327–358.

Musgrave, R.A. and Thin, T. (1948). 'Income tax progression, 1929–48.' *Journal of Political Economy,* vol. 56, no. 6, 498–514.

Musgrave, R.A. (1959). *The Theory of Public Finance: A Study in Public Economy.* New York, McGraw-Hill.

Musgrave, R.A. and Musgrave, P.B. (1979). *Public Finance in Theory and Practice.* New York, McGraw-Hill.

Piketty, T. (2014). *Capital in the Twenty-First Century.* Cambridge, MA, Harvard University Press.

Piketty, T. and Saez, E. (2006). 'The evolution of top incomes: A historical and international perspective.' *American Economic Review,* vol. 96, no. 2, pp. 200–205.

Piketty, T. et al. (2011). 'Optimal Taxation of Top Labor Incomes: A Tale of Three Elasticities,' *Working Paper No. 17616.* Washington, DC, National Bureau of Economic Research.

Slemrod, J. (1994). *Tax Progressivity and Income Inequality.* Cambridge, MA, Cambridge University Press.

Sokoloff, K. and Robinson, J. (2004). 'Historical roots of inequality in Latin America,' in de Ferranti, D. et al. (eds.) (2004). *Inequality in Latin America: Breaking with History?* Washington, DC, World Bank.

Stiglitz, J.E. (2012). *The Price of Inequality.* New York/London, W.W. Norton & Company.

Tanzi, V. (2013). *Tax Reform In Latin America: A Long-Term Assessment.* Washington, Woodrow Wilson International Center for Scholars.

Tuomala, M. (1990). *Optimal Income Tax and Redistribution.* Oxford/New York, Clarendon Press/Oxford University Press.

UNCTAD (2012). *Trade and Development Report, 2012.* New York/London, United Nations.

UNDP (2010). *Regional Human Development Report for Latin America and the Caribbean 2010—Acting on the Future: Breaking the Intergenerational Transmission of Inequality.* New York, UNDP.

Valdés, M.F. (2015). The Recent Inequality Reduction in Latin America: The Role of Tax Policy, Ph.D. thesis. Freie Universität Berlin.

Vegh, C.A. and Vuletin, G. (2013). 'The Road to Redemption: Policy Response to Crises in Latin America,' 14th Jacques Polak Annual Research Conference. Washington, DC, November 7–8 2013. International Monetary Fund.

Vegh, C.A. and Vuletin, G. (2014). 'Social Implications of Fiscal Policy Responses During Crises,' *Working Paper No. 19828.* Cambridge, MA, National Bureau of Economic Research.

Woo, J. et al. (2013). 'Distributional Consequences of Fiscal Consolidation and the Role of Fiscal Policy: What Do the Data Say?' *IMF Working Paper No. 13/195.* Washington, DC, International Monetary Fund.

Zee, H. (2004). 'Inequality and optimal redistributive tax and transfer policies.' *Public Finance Review,* vol. 32, no. 4, pp. 359–381.

Annex 10.1: Crisis years

Country/ Year	Argentina	Chile	Colombia	Mexico	Peru*
1990	c,i,s,d,e,b				
1991					
1992					
1993					
1994					
1995	b			c,i,s,b	
1996					
1997					
1998		s	c,s		
1999			c,s		
2000	s			s,b	
2001	s,d,e,b				
2002	c,i,d,e,b				
2003					
2004					
2005					
2006					
2007					
2008		c,s	s	c,s	
2009	d				
2010					

c = currency crisis

i = *inflation* crisis

s = Stock market crash

d = domestic debt crisis

e = external debt crisis

b = *banking* crisis

* There is no data on financial crises for Peru.

Source: Own calculations based on Vegh and Vuletin (2013; 2014). For the analysis, I considered the last 3 years to be crisis years—this in order to calculate correlation coefficients.

Annex 2: Output gap (%) and breaking points

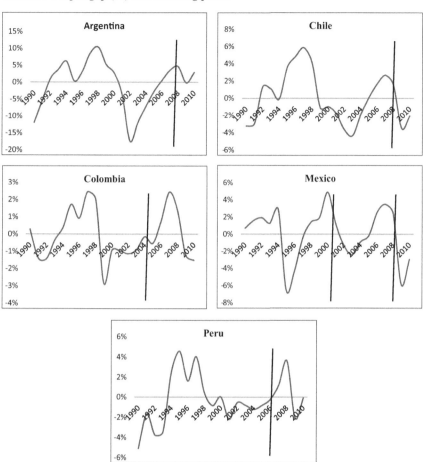

Source: Own calculations based on data from Capalstat. Own calculations based on Valdés (2014).

Chapter 11
Vulnerability of Tax Revenues in Developing Countries

Christian von Haldenwang

Introduction

It has been conventional wisdom for quite some years now that a narrow tax base combined with an excessive reliance on a few commodity exports exposes countries to the risk of increased revenue volatility and, ultimately, lower tax collection. Beyond this general statement, however, there is still a knowledge gap regarding the relationship of exogenous shocks and public revenue in a broad (and increasingly diversified) range of low- and middle-income countries. Facing heterogeneity of cases combined with limited access to data, academic research has found it difficult to even develop consistent measures of tax capacity and tax performance in developing countries[1]—let alone addressing the question of how revenue systems react to unforeseen external events.

But why is it important to analyse the relationship of shocks and taxes in particular? This chapter argues that beyond the general impact of shocks on economic growth there are specific effects on revenue systems that shape the capacity of governments to react to adverse external events and sustain development expenditure. These effects vary not only with the kinds of shock affecting the economies, but also with the characteristics of these economies (welfare levels, dependence on natural resources, etc.), the political and administrative capacity of states to react to changing situations, and the structure of the tax systems. At the same time, it is important to keep in mind that shocks not only affect the level of tax collection, but also (perhaps even more importantly) the stability and predictability of revenue. It can be argued that the latter is critical with regard to the adaptation to exogenous changes as well as the financial ability of states to recover from adverse external events.

This chapter summarizes the results of an empirical study that analyses the impact of several kinds of shocks on revenue systems in a broad set of countries, and in developing countries in particular.[2] Findings indicate that non-democratic and non-resource-rich countries are particularly vulnerable to shocks affecting income taxes and non-tax revenue. In the case of resource-rich countries, no clear patterns emerge: their revenue structure, though more *volatile* than that of non-resource-rich countries due to a higher dependence on non-tax revenue, could be less *vulnerable* to external shocks.

With regard to Latin America, these findings bear particular relevance, as many countries of the region combine a democratic polity with an increased reliance on natural resources and commodity exports. The good performance recently shown by the region in facing the

---

1 See Fenochietto and Pessino (2013) for a recent approach to this issue.
2 See von Haldenwang et al. (2013). The study was co-authored by Oliver Morrissey, Maksym Ivanyna, Ingo Bordon and Armin von Schiller. Funding by the European Commission is gratefully acknowledged.

global economic crisis corroborates one of the study's key messages: if well managed, a resource-based development path does not necessarily lead to increased vulnerability of public revenue.

Exogenous Shocks and Vulnerability

External shocks are the outcome of factors beyond the control of those bearing the consequences. Although they are not necessarily unforeseeable as such, they are often unpredicted in their concrete manifestation. Further, while some shocks are temporary events, with external conditions quickly returning to pre-shock levels, other shocks may indicate a permanent change of conditions. Consequently, the vulnerability and resilience of tax systems depend on their (in)ability to cope with exogenous shocks in two dimensions: (i) a magnitude dimension (shock absorption and avoidance), referring to the sensitivity of tax revenues facing exogenous shocks, and (ii) a time dimension (shock counteraction), referring to the capacity of tax revenues to recover from the impact of exogenous shocks. Such an understanding is in line with other studies on developing countries' economic or fiscal volatility and vulnerability against external shocks.[3]

The IMF defines an exogenous shock "as a sudden event beyond the control of the authorities that has *a significant negative impact* on the economy" (IMF, 2003: p. 4—my emphasis). This definition is in line with common understandings of what constitutes a shock—usually, the term is meant to refer to a major event with a large impact on those suffering the shock. The approach chosen by the IMF is also pragmatic in the sense that it limits the range of events to be taken into account. At the same time, significance levels are always difficult to determine *ex ante*, which may lead to arbitrary decisions regarding what constitutes a shock as opposed to other external events of minor significance.

Against this background, the study summarized here starts by using a general definition of exogenous shocks without references to threshold values, significance levels or directions of impact. However, it is important to note that the impact of exogenous factors on tax revenues *could* in fact be non-linear. For instance, complex revenue systems may be able to cope with minor changes in the terms of trade or commodity prices. Once these changes reach a certain "tipping point," the system could shift from one state to another and experience major disruptions. Among others, Schumacher & Strobl (2008) find such a relationship with regard to the impact of natural disasters on wealth and income in different groups of countries. In order to control for these non-linear effects, the study also looks at the upper 10 percent of year-country observations, in line with the approach taken by the IMF.

The commodity boom of the last decade as well as the recent global financial and economic crisis have both spurred academic debate on the impact of *different kinds* of exogenous shocks in developing countries. Researchers are often particularly interested in commodity or energy price shocks. However, the debate focuses almost exclusively on economic growth and the distribution of rents and income as dependent variables (Anand and Prasad, 2012; Bourguignon, 2012—but see CEPAL, 2013 for explicit references to tax reforms). In contrast, empirical studies covering the impact of shocks on public revenue in developing countries are scarce and mostly related to managing windfall profits from extractive industries.[4]

---

3 For instance, see Fanelli et al. (2011); IMF (2013); Loayza and Raddatz (2007).
4 For instance, Ross (2012); van der Ploeg and Venables (2011); Villafuerte et al. (2010).

Negative external shocks deteriorate the tax basis via several channels. The most commonly employed measure for external shocks is the volatility of terms of trade (Rodrik, 2001). With regard to the business cycle in more open developing economies, world price shocks play an important role (Kose and Riezman, 2001). According to Raddatz (2007), changes in commodity prices are the most important external source of GDP fluctuations in low-income countries. This effect has also been observed with particular reference to Latin America (Jiménez and López Azcúnaga, 2012; Fanelli et al., 2011; see Bertola and Ocampo, 2012 for an historical account of economic volatility in the region). Further, there is evidence that GDP instability is a good proxy for exposure to shocks (Ebeke and Ehrhart, 2011; Lledó and Poplawski-Ribeiro, 2013).

Another type of shock occurs as an outcome of natural disasters that affect entire societies, countries or regions. Natural disasters lead to situations of "concentrated resource scarcity" (Nel and Righarts, 2008). Much of this debate focuses on geophysical events commonly ascribed to global climate change: floods, droughts and fires, etc. In this context, several studies have explored the economic or social impacts of weather changes and rainfall (Deschenes and Greenstone, 2007; Fisher et al., 2012), even though few papers have addressed these issues with regard to low-income countries, due to data challenges. However, natural incidents other than rainfall or even unrelated to climate change, for instance earthquakes, volcano eruptions and accidental oil spills, may also have disastrous impacts on the economies and fiscal revenues of developing countries (Keefer et al., 2011). According to the IMF, "between 1997 and 2001, the average damage per natural disaster was over 5 percent of GDP in low-income countries" (IMF 2003, pp. 4–6).

Hence, the study analyses *three kinds of shocks:* First, the exchange rate (ER) pressure index is taken as a proxy for export demand and foreign capital flows shocks. The ER pressure index has been widely used in international finance literature.[5] It is generally defined as a weighted average of percentage changes of policy variables in response to current account or financial account shocks. The second indicator we use is the terms-of-trade index—scaled as the unit-price of imports divided by unit price of exports. The third indicator refers to the intensity of natural disasters, measured on the basis of people killed and affected by natural disasters in every year and every country.[6] With access only to annual data, we look for contemporaneous effects—assuming that the effect of shocks on revenue will materialise in the same calendar year.[7]

---

5   See Candelon, Dumitrescu, & Hurlin, 2010 for a recent discussion. We use the following definition: $PI_{it} = w_{E,i}\frac{\Delta E_{it}}{E_{i,t-1}} - w_{RES,i}\frac{\Delta RES_{it}}{RES_{i,t-1}}$, where i identifies the country, t is the year, E is the exchange rate in local currency units per USD, RES is the size of reserves, and wE,i and wRES,i are country-specific weights. The logic behind the index is that in response to an adverse balance-of-payment shock a country could employ different strategies: the government could devaluate the currency, but it could also use its international reserves to defend the exchange rate. Both policy variables should be considered in measuring the magnitude of external shocks.

6   As an additional test, the study explores GDP decline as a proxy for a general output shock. In this case, however, all coefficients are statistically insignificant and very close to zero. These results indicate that on average tax systems are neutral, i.e. the elasticity of revenue with respect to output is close to 1—independently of the country income group. For a detailed discussion of measures, indicators and econometric methods used in the study please refer to von Haldenwang et al. (2013).

7   As a robustness check, government revenue in the following year is used as the dependent variable. None of the shocks is found to significantly affect the revenue in the next period, once the current government revenue is controlled for. However, government revenue has a sizeable autoregressive component, i.e. current revenue depends on last year's revenue, so external shocks may have an indirect lasting effect on government finance as they affect current revenue.

Taxes and Country Groups

Countries differ with regard to their tax structure. Most Latin American countries rely heavily on indirect taxes and corporate income taxes, but obtain comparatively little revenue from personal income taxes, property taxes or social security contributions (CEPAL, 2013; Gómez Sabaini and Morán, 2013; OECD/CEPAL/CIAT, 2014). This sets them apart from most OECD member countries, where the latter three tax types tend to play a much bigger role.

In addition, many governments obtain substantial income through non-tax revenues, above all from the extractive industries. Main sources of income in this context are profits from state-owned enterprises and production-sharing contracts in the oil and gas sector. In some countries, royalties (especially those levied as a fixed amount per product unit) are treated as non-tax revenues in fiscal accounts. Other non-tax revenues include proceeds from auctions of exploration or extraction rights and from rents and leases (Collier, 2010; von Haldenwang, 2011).

The study consequently opts for a broad understanding of the term "taxes." The dependent variable used in most regressions is general government total revenue without grants as a share of GDP, including tax revenue, social contributions and other revenue (from property income, interest payments, sales of goods and services, etc.).

Several studies have explored issues of tax performance and volatility with regard to the composition of the tax system. Specific emphasis has been placed on the mix of direct (corporate and private income) vs. indirect (consumption) taxes, the changing relevance of trade taxes, and the weight of revenue from extractive industries. (Ebeke and Ehrhart, 2011) show that tax revenue instability (measured as the standard deviation of the log difference) remains high in Sub-Saharan African countries but has declined from a peak in the late 1980s as the tax composition changed. Corporate and trade taxes tend to be the most unstable, so the gradual decline in overall tax instability is attributed to increased shares of relatively more stable indirect taxes. Tax instability tends to increase with instability of GDP, less consistently with dependence on natural resource rents, and in some specifications is lower in countries with higher trade openness (the trade volume measure) and per capita GDP. Although limited, this is further evidence that instability is associated with exposure to exogenous shocks and related to the composition of public revenue (see (Ehrhart and Guerineau, 2013).

Accounting for data limitations, the study distinguishes *four categories of revenues:* (i) income taxes on personal and corporate incomes; (ii) general taxes on domestic consumption (sales taxes, excises and value-added taxes); (iii) trade taxes; and (iv) non-tax revenue.

Most studies exploring the impact of different variables on tax effort or tax performance assume that there are sub-sets in the sample characterised by specific properties. The literature provides us with some initial clues regarding the identification and tax performance behaviour of specific country groups, but there are only few cases where categorisations are driven by, and provide feedback to, theory:

- *Country income groups* (following the World Bank classification) are frequently used to control for differentiated effects in poorer and richer countries. For instance, Le et al. (2012) observe that the world-wide increase in tax revenue between 1998 and 2009 is particularly pronounced in low-income countries. This could be due to the commodity-based structure of many poorer economies, given that global commodity prices have been on the rise over the last decade. Gupta (2007) also creates income-group-specific indexes for tax effort. The study presented here groups countries in two groups, (i) high- and upper-middle-income countries and (ii) lower-middle- and low-income countries. During the observation period, several Latin American countries moved upwards from the lower- to the higher-income group.

- *Revenue from extractive industries* can be expected to strongly influence tax revenue, even though the impact is not easy to model, as rents from fuels and minerals are sometimes obtained through taxes and sometimes through non-tax sources of income, such as profits from public enterprises (Burgess and Stern, 1993; Collier, 2010). Some studies use dummies for oil producers or exporters, or focus specifically on this group of countries, without, however, producing robust evidence concerning the positive or negative effect of rents from non-renewables on tax collection (for instance, Bornhorst et al., 2008; Herb, 2005; Knack, 2008; McGuirk, 2013). The IMF has identified revenue from extractive industries as a major area of concern for more than 40 developing countries (IMF, 2012). The IMF classification is used to distinguish resource-rich from non-resource-rich countries.

- As mentioned above, *governance levels* affect tax performance (i) by influencing the political debate and the formulation of common-interest-oriented tax policies and (ii) by shaping the capacity of states to enact tax legislation and manage tax systems (von Haldenwang and Ivanyna, 2012). In particular, countries are grouped according to political regime type. The study splits countries according to their political regime characteristics, based on their Polity IV score: On a scale ranging from 10 to -10, a country is considered a democracy if its Polity IV score is higher than 6, and a non-democracy if otherwise (see Marshall et al., 2010).[8]

In addition, regional patterns may affect tax performance in various ways, including competition for investments, shared beliefs or cultural values, colonial histories, contagion from neighbours and patterns of world market integration. Several authors find those patterns, even though the issue is not explored from a conceptual perspective (see von Haldenwang and Ivanyna, 2012; Davoodi and Grigorian, 2007; Profeta et al., 2011; Le et al., 2012). Others look at regional tax performance with more detail, but focus on individual regions (such as for instance Bird et al., 2004; Bird and Zolt, 2013 on Latin America).

With regard to the research design, the study summarised in this chapter proceeds in an incremental fashion which unfolds the complexity of the topic before focusing on the most relevant aspects. The initial stage of the analysis derives measures of fiscal capacity and revenue instability for each country in the sample. We then introduce the three kinds of shocks mentioned above and identify how each of them affects revenue sensitivity. The following stage of the empirical investigation identifies the effects of shocks on tax revenue in various groups of low- and lower-middle-income countries. Finally, to identify possible channels through which external shocks act on government revenue, these shocks are regressed on various types of revenue as dependent variables—non-tax revenue, trade taxes, sales taxes and income taxes.

---

8   Please refer to the Appendix for lists of countries according to income group, regime type and natural resource endowment.

Results of the Analysis

Tax performance and volatility

The range of structural variables which determine fiscal capacity is derived from the literature and includes measures of trade openness, welfare levels and the sectorial composition of the economy.[9] However, unlike most contributions to the debate, the study takes a more detailed look at trade openness: Rather than using a combined measure, the shares of agricultural, mining, manufacturing, and fuel exports to GDP along with imports to GDP are taken as individual control variables. This is justified by the fact that exposure to external shocks is not only driven by trade openness in general but also by the composition of trade and the differentiated response of exports and imports to changes in the external environment.

Looking at the full sample we observe positive effects of mineral and fuels exports on tax revenue, whereas agriculture and manufacturing are negatively associated with tax revenue. Yet, different stories emerge once the sample is divided in two groups: high- and upper-middle-income countries and low- and lower-middle-income countries. The positive relationship between mineral exports and tax performance seems to be driven above all by higher-income countries, whereas the negative impact of manufacturing exports on tax revenue is driven entirely by the lower-income group. The share of agriculture is negatively associated with tax performance in both groups (as expected), but the effect is much bigger in magnitude in the higher-income group. The near-zero effect of imports to GDP in the regression with the full sample is explained by the opposite ways this variable acts on tax performance in countries at different income levels: its effect is negative in higher-income countries, while positive, large, and statistically significant in lower-income countries.

The negative relationship between manufacturing exports and tax revenue in lower-income countries appears counter-intuitive at first glance. From the literature we would expect manufacturing to be positively related to tax performance: Higher shares of manufacturing in the economy are expected to indicate a relatively larger formal sector and, as this is easier to tax than the informal sector, are expected to be associated with higher tax revenue. It is also the case that formal firms, in contrast to informal microenterprises, are more likely to export. One explanation could be that manufacturing in poorer countries achieves global competitiveness primarily through low labour costs and margins. The results are also consistent with the global fragmentation of production: manufacturing exports of poor countries are often based on adding a small amount of value added to imported intermediate inputs. Hence, the sector makes no significant contribution to domestic tax revenue.[10] In Latin America, this finding is especially relevant for several small Central American countries that are integrated in the North American economic zone primarily by providing cheap labour in sweatshop, assembly or "maquiladora" industries.

In a general sense, high volatility of tax revenue can be regarded as an indication for less revenue stability, lower predictability and, ultimately, lower revenue on average. Our

---

9   For instance, see Baskaran and Bigsten (2013); Gupta (2007); Pessino and Fenochietto (2010); Profeta and Scabrosetti (2010); Tanzi (1992); Teera and Hudson (2004); von Haldenwang and Ivanyna (2012).

10   Findings partly coincide with the results presented by Teera and Hudson (2004), who observe a negative impact of manufacturing (as a share of GDP) to taxes in low-income countries in some specifications (but a positive effect on Sub-Saharan African countries in others). Their observation period is 1975–1998.

data analysis confirms this relationship. The relation is more pronounced for high- and upper-middle-income countries, non-resource-rich countries and democratic countries (see Figures 11.1–11.3). With regard to their counterparts (lower-income, resource-rich and non-democratic countries), the former groups appear to be more homogenous and thus exhibit a closer resemblance to the pattern one would assume, i.e. higher total tax volatility being associated with lower total revenues on average.

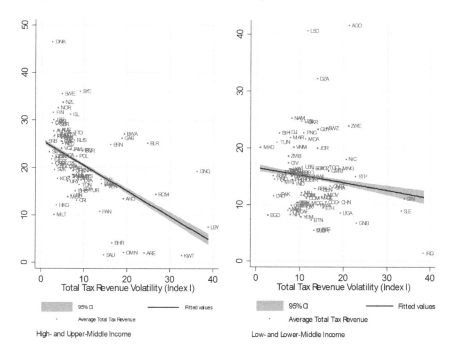

Figure 11.1   Average total tax revenue vs. total tax revenue volatility by country income groups

Shocks and revenue sensitivity

Obviously, different shocks have different effects on revenue, but in general terms it can be said that the effects are more pronounced and statistically stronger in poorer countries compared to the richer group.

- Exchange rate (ER) pressure contributes negatively to tax revenue in all specifications. If all countries are used in the estimation, an increase in the index by 10 percent would reduce tax revenue roughly by 1.3 percentage points. The effect is large and significant for both income groups.
- Adverse shocks to terms of trade also reduce tax revenue, and the result is statistically significant for the whole sample as well as for the group of low- and lower-middle-income countries. In this case, richer countries seem to suffer less from shocks.

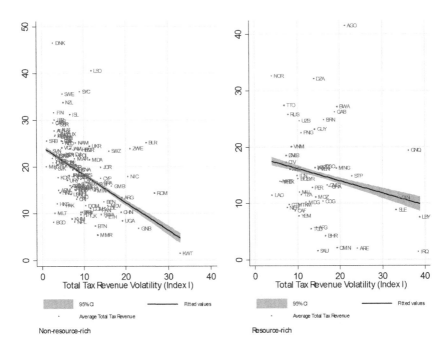

**Figure 11.2   Average total tax revenue vs. total tax revenue volatility by
resource endowments**

- The intensity of natural catastrophes also affects tax revenue negatively. The result is primarily driven by the group of poorer countries, where the effect is statistically significant. This finding would be in line with expectations, as richer countries should be in a better position to respond to natural disasters by relying on tax measures and other public policies.

As mentioned above, most studies on shocks in developing countries start from a definition that contains a magnitude criterion—a shock being a major event with a large impact on the economy. In contrast, the study presented here uses continuous variables along with an approach employed by the IMF to identify large shocks. If large-shock dummies are included in the regressions alone their effect is often significant in the low- and lower-middle-income group, but for most shocks there is little evidence that their effects are non-linear in the sense specified above: Large shock dummies are usually insignificant if included together with the linear specification of the shock. The only exceptions are large ER-shocks in lower-income countries. In this case, the non-linear effect is pronounced and weakly significant, while in high-income countries it is practically non-existent. Hence, we do not find convincing evidence for an approach that focuses exclusively on large shocks when analysing revenue systems. Vulnerability of public revenue to exogenous factors is not only a matter of exposure to major events. It already manifests itself in the context of the insignificant changes experienced day by day.

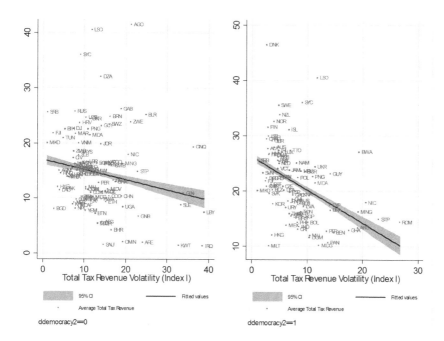

Figure 11.3   Average total tax revenue vs. total tax revenue volatility by regime types

Country groups

The study explores differences between groups of countries with regard to the sensitivity of their tax revenue to external shocks. Countries are grouped according to their respective income levels, endowment with natural resources (resource-rich vs. non-rich) and the character of their political regime (democracies vs. non-democracies), as introduced in the preceding section.

As for *natural resource endowment*, results indicate that ER pressure has a negative effect in both resource-rich (RR) and non-resource-rich (non-RR) countries, but in the former group the effect is much bigger and statistically significant. In contrast, the coefficient of terms-of-trade shocks is negative and statistically significant in both groups of countries, but the effect is more pronounced in non-RR countries. High- and upper-middle-income countries (especially those rich in natural resources) are practically unaffected, which may be the consequence of the fact that their budgets generally rely less on external trade taxes. Finally, the negative effect of natural disasters' intensity seems to be driven entirely by non-RR countries. The reason could be that the extractive industries—the main sources of tax revenue in RR countries—are usually less affected by natural catastrophes than other types of economic activity.

Further, the study shows that the positive effect of fuel exports to GDP on revenue in the poorer countries is driven primarily by resource endowment, as expected. Interestingly, the picture is less clear with regard to mineral exports. This suggests a lack of transparency (or, less probably, a low level of profitability) in the mining sector in many lower-income countries—in contrast to the hydrocarbon industry.

With regard to *political regime type*, the two income groups produce different stories: In general terms, democracies and non-democracies are not dramatically different in their vulnerability to shocks in the higher-income group. Among the low- and lower-middle-income countries, however, democracies fare clearly better than non-democracies in their revenue sensitivity to all three shocks we consider. The coefficients on shocks in democratic countries are smaller in magnitude (even positive in the case of terms-of-trade shocks), yet not significant in statistical terms. For non-democratic countries, the effects of the three kinds of shocks are negative and statistically significant. Imports do not seem to affect government revenue in democratic states, unlike in non-democracies, where the effect is large and significant. The coefficient on fuel exports is much bigger in democracies, and interestingly the coefficient on mineral exports is bigger and negative.

The latter finding is diametrically opposed to the results from the higher-income countries, where the coefficient is much bigger and usually positive. One possible explanation could be that the stability of democratic rule is much lower in the group of lower-income countries compared to the higher-income group. As mining industries often operate with long amortisation and production periods, stability of political context factors may play a key role –independently of the regime characteristics.

Types of taxes

To identify possible channels through which external shocks act on government revenue, four types of government revenue are explored in detail: non-tax revenue, trade taxes, sales taxes, and income taxes. The findings suggest that different shocks act on government revenue through different channels. Even though most coefficients do not reach statistical significance, probably due to the limited number of observations, the results support the following conclusions.

- For the whole sample of lower-income countries, ER pressure has a significant negative effect on trade and income tax. In contrast, its effect is negative yet not significant on indirect taxes (goods and services tax), and practically zero on non-tax revenue. The effect is particularly strong and significant in non-democratic as well as in non-resource-rich countries. Apparently, these groups experience more difficulties in counteracting the impact of ER pressure shocks.
- Terms-of-trade shocks have significant negative effects on non-tax revenue. The reason is perhaps that these shocks are likely to reduce profits of public enterprises that act as commodity exporters. The effect is negative and significant for all sub-groups except democracies, but stronger for non-resource-rich compared to resource-rich countries. Terms-of-trade shocks also affect income tax revenue in non-democratic and non-resource-rich countries.
- Natural disaster intensity affects mostly trade and income taxes, although the coefficient is not significant in any specification. One interesting finding, however, refers to the fact that the point estimates regarding the effect on the sales tax are negative and weakly significant in non-resource-rich countries and positive (yet insignificant) in the other group. This could indicate a higher resilience towards the adverse impacts of natural disasters in resource-rich countries.

Comparing the effects of ER pressure as well as terms-of-trade shocks on income tax in democratic and non-democratic countries reveals slightly different pictures. Both shocks affect income tax negatively in non-democratic countries, with significant results for ER pressure. In contrast, results are insignificant in democratic countries and the coefficient of terms-of-trade shocks is even positive. This could point to a greater capacity of democratic countries to increase revenue collection in the face of exogenous shocks. In general terms it can be said that income tax and non-tax revenue seem to be most sensitive to external shocks, while indirect (sales) taxes appear to be the most stable revenue source.

All in all it can be inferred that non-democratic and non-resource-rich countries are particularly vulnerable to shocks affecting income taxes and non-tax revenue. In the case of resource-rich countries, no clear patterns emerge: their revenue structure, though more *volatile* than that of non-resource-rich countries due to a higher dependence on non-tax revenue, could be less *vulnerable* to external shocks. At least, there is no robust evidence pointing to volatility of revenue from natural resources being directly connected to increased vulnerability vis-à-vis the shocks analysed here. This finding is somewhat unexpected, as conventional wisdom and the literature on rent incomes from (principally) oil would suggest resource-rich economies to be particularly vulnerable to global price and capital shocks. From the present study we get the impression that it is much more the non-resource-rich countries we should be worried about.

Conclusion

Research on developing countries in general and on public finance in particular is often confronted with limited data coverage and questionable data quality. Even though in recent years many countries have made important progress in generating information and providing data, reflecting technological progress as well as international initiatives in this field, challenges still persist. These affect above all those countries that are most relevant from a development perspective, i.e. the poorest and most fragile countries. However, in the context of empirical methods demanding long time series the problems of poor or unavailable data extend to other countries as well. For many countries, data from past decades are not easily available, and even in those cases where they exist their consistency and comparability is sometimes undermined by changing rules for accounting and reporting. Against this background, the results presented above should be read as identifying statistical relationships and not necessarily causal links. Where causal relationships are suggested, they are plausible to expect and theoretically grounded but due to data limitations they cannot be tested properly.

Regarding the *Latin American* region the study does not produce a single pattern of behaviour. With some countries belonging to the lower-income group and others belonging to the higher-income group (and several countries moving from one group to the other), it would make little sense to look for messages that cover the region as a whole. In addition, small sample size makes it difficult to achieve statistical significance when looking at individual regions. One interesting observation, however, refers to the fact that the negative effect of manufacturing exports on tax revenue discussed above applies above all to the *higher-income group* in Latin America, whereas it is primarily a *lower-income* phenomenon in the rest of the world. Or, put the other way round: Manufacturing exports in the upper-middle-income countries in Latin America appear to share some characteristics with manufacturing exports in the low- and lower-middle-income countries in the rest of the world. This might entail a *caveat* for a region that has done comparatively well in dealing with external shocks in the recent past.

Looking at *tax performance*, it becomes evident that splitting the sample into two subsets according to income groups produces two different "stories" on tax performance. This is in line with previous research findings (for instance, see Gupta, 2007; Profeta and Scabrosetti, 2010; Teera and Hudson, 2004). Perhaps less explored so far, however, is the differentiated impact of imports and various kinds of exports. Typically, research on tax effort in developing countries uses one single trade openness measure (lumping exports and imports) combined with several sectorial value-added variables (agriculture, manufacturing, mining/fuels). Findings indicate that at least regarding manufacturing and mineral exports as well as imports, the effects on tax performance are quite dissimilar, sometimes even converse in both groups. It is particularly striking to see that manufacturing exports are associated with less revenue in the lower-income group. This could be due to lower value-added and lower productivity of this sector, leading to lower levels of taxation or higher subsidies granted by governments in order to ensure the international competitiveness of the sector.

The data analysis confirms the initial assumption of *revenue volatility* being negatively associated with levels of revenue (in percent of GDP) and dependence on natural resources. The effect is more pronounced in richer countries compared to poorer countries, in non-resource-rich countries compared to resource-rich countries, and in democracies compared to non-democracies. This association is stronger when looking at taxes alone and weaker when non-tax revenue (without grants) is included (as in the base specification), meaning that non-tax revenue adds to volatility, especially in lower-income and resource-rich countries. Revenue volatility has been historically identified as a major weakness of Latin American public finance systems (CEPAL, 2013; Bértola and Ocampo, 2012), but in line with our findings and accounting for recent prudent macro-economic and financial management in some parts of the region it appears as if several Latin American countries may be prepared to build more resilient revenue systems now.

Regarding the *sensitivity of revenue to exogenous shocks*, low- and lower-middle-income countries are more affected by shocks than richer countries, as could be expected. More importantly, the findings indicate that vulnerability to shocks should not be regarded exclusively as an issue of major adverse events hitting an economy. It may be important for governments, donors and international organisations to prepare for such events and to develop the appropriate financial tools to deal with them. But it is also important to keep in mind that minor events also have significant effects on revenue and that long-term structural reforms (in particular regarding income tax and non-tax revenue) are a necessary ingredient of any strategy targeting vulnerability of revenue in developing countries. In this context, a broad tax portfolio could contribute to making total revenue less susceptible to individual shocks. In Latin America, the need to broaden the tax base, in particular through strengthening direct taxes on private households, has been a consistent observation by researchers and international organisations alike.

Moreover, results suggest that there is a *'democracy rent'* in the sense of lower vulnerability to shocks being associated with democratic rule in lower-income countries. This difference could be connected to a larger capacity of democratic regimes to avoid or compensate revenue losses through public policies and political bargaining, both on the revenue and expenditure side. It should be noted, however, that the effect levels out in the higher-income group (both democratic and non-democratic regimes behave similarly). Also, causality is particularly difficult to establish in this context. Reflecting the focus of this study, findings have been interpreted as *outcomes* of democratic rule (for instance, assuming a higher ability of democratic governments to impose short-term hardships on their citizens). Yet, there is also evidence in the literature pointing from higher and more stable revenue to sustained democratic rule, for instance because governments can spend more on public services. Still, reforms aiming at accountability, transparency and rule of law could have an important positive effect on revenue resilience, as governments may acquire the legitimacy to build broad-based revenue systems, as well as additional short-term manoeuvring space to respond to adverse external events. Several Latin American countries were able to use this manoeuvring space in the course of the global financial and economic crisis (CEPAL, 2013), and Chile raised the corporate income tax by three percentage points in response to a major earthquake suffered in 2010.[11]

Bibliography

Anand, R. and Prasad, E.S. (2012). 'How should emerging market and low-income country central banks respond to commodity price shocks?' in Arezki, R. et al. (eds.) (2012). *Commodity Price Volatility and Inclusive Growth in Low-Income-Countries.* Washington, DC, International Monetary Fund.

Baskaran, T. and Bigsten, A. (2013). 'Fiscal capacity and the quality of government in sub-Saharan Africa.' *World Development,* vol. 45, no. 1, pp. 92–107.

Bértola, L. and Ocampo, J.A. (2012). *The Economic Development of Latin America Since Independence.* Oxford, Oxford University Press.

Bird, R.M. et al. (2004). 'Societal Institutions and Tax Effort in Developing Countries,' *International Studies Program Working Paper Series No. 0406.* Atlanta, GA, Andrew Young School of Policy Studies, Georgia State University.

Bird, R.M. and Zolt, E.M. (2013). 'Taxation and Inequality in the Americas: Changing the Fiscal Contract?' *International Center for Public Policy Working Paper No. 13–15.* Atlanta, GA, Andrew Young School of Policy Studies, Georgia State University.

Bornhorst, F. et al. (2008). 'Natural Resource Endowments, Governance, and the Domestic Revenue Effort: Evidence from a Panel of Countries,' *IMF Working Paper No. 08/170.* Washington, DC, International Monetary Fund.

Bourguignon, F. (2012). 'Commodity price volatility, poverty and growth inclusiveness in Sub-Saharan African countries,' in Arezki, R. et al. (eds.) (2012). *Commodity Price Volatility and Inclusive Growth in Low-Income-Countries.* Washington, DC, International Monetary Fund.

Burgess, R. and Stern, N. (1993). 'Taxation and development.' *Journal of Economic Literature,* vol. 31, no. 2, pp. 762–830.

Candelon, B. et al. (2010). 'Currency Crises Early Warning Systems: Why they should be dynamic,' *Working Paper No. RM/10/047.* Maastricht, Maastricht University.

CEPAL (2013). *Panorama Fiscal de América Latina y el Caribe: Reformas tributarias y renovación del pacto fiscal.* Santiago de Chile, CEPAL.

Collier, P. (2010). 'Principles of resource taxation for low-income countries,' in Daniel, P. et al. (eds.) (2010), *The Taxation of Petroleum and Minerals: Principles, problems and practice.* London, Routledge.

---

11 The increase was introduced as a temporary measure, but was made permanent in 2012. This was justified with expenditure increases on education in response to widespread student protests. See http://www.bloomberg.com/news/2012–04–27/chile-to-raise-corporate-tax-rate-as-student-protests-resume.html (retrieved 07 April 2014).

Davoodi, H.R. and Grigorian, D.A. (2007). 'Tax Potential vs. Tax Effort: A Cross-Country Analysis of Armenia's Stubbornly Low Tax Collection,' *IMF Working Paper No. 07/106.* Washington, DC, International Monetary Fund.

Deschenes, O., and Greenstone, M. (2007). 'The economic impacts of climate change: Evidence from agricultural output and random fluctuations in weather.' *American Economic Review,* vol. 97, no. 1, pp. 354–385.

Ebeke, C. and Ehrhart, H. (2011). 'Tax revenue instability in Sub-Saharan Africa: Consequences and remedies.' *Journal of African Economies,* vol. 21, no. 1, pp. 1–27.

Ehrhart, H. and Guerineau, S. (2013). 'Commodity price volatility and tax revenue: Evidence from developing countries.' *Document de Travail No. 423,* Paris, Banque de France.

Fanelli, J.M. et al. (eds.) (2011). *Volatilidad macroeconómica y respuestas de políticas.* Santiago de Chile, CEPAL.

Fenochietto, R. and Pessino, C. (2013). 'Understanding Countries' Tax Effort,' *IMF Working Paper No. 13/244.* Washington, DC, International Monetary Fund.

Fisher, A.C. et al. (2012). 'The economic impacts of climate change: Evidence from agricultural output and random fluctuations in weather: Comment.' *American Economic Review,* vol. 102, no. 7, pp. 3749–3760.

Gómez Sabaini, J.C. and Morán, D. (2013). 'Política tributaria en América Latina: agenda para una segunda generación de reformas,' *Serie Macroeconomía del Desarrollo No. 133.* Santiago de Chile, CEPAL.

Gupta, A.S. (2007). 'Determinants of Tax Revenue Efforts in Developing Countries,' *IMF Working Paper No. 07/184.* Washington, DC, International Monetary Fund.

Herb, M. (2005). 'No representation without taxation? Rents, development, and democracy.' *Comparative Politics,* vol. 37, no. 3, pp. 297–317.

IMF (2013). *Managing Volatility: A vulnerability exercise for low-income countries.* Washington, DC, International Monetary Fund.

IMF (2012). *Macroeconomic Policy Frameworks for Resource-Rich Developing Countries.* Washington, DC, International Monetary Fund.

IMF (2003). *Fund Assistance for Countries Facing Exogenous Shocks.* Washington, DC, International Monetary Fund (Policy Development and Review Department).

Jiménez, J.P. and López Azcúnaga, I. (2012). 'Disminución de la desigualdad en América Latina? El rol de la política fiscal,' *desiguALdades.net Working Paper No. 33.* Berlin, Freie Universität.

Keefer, P. et al. (2011). 'Earthquake propensity and the politics of mortality prevention.' *World Development,* vol. 39, no. 9, pp. 1530–1541.

Knack, S. (2008). 'Sovereign rents and the quality of tax policy and administration,' *Policy Research Working Paper No. 4773.* Washington, DC, World Bank.

Kose, M.A. and Riezman, R. (2001). 'Trade shocks and macroeconomic fluctuations in Africa.' *Journal of Development Economics,* vol. 65, no. 1, pp. 55–80.

Le, T. M. et al. (2012). 'Tax Capacity and Tax Effort. Extended Cross-Country Analysis from 1994 to 2009,' *Policy Research Working Paper No. 6252.* Washington, DC, World Bank.

Lledó, V.D. and Poplawski-Ribeiro, M. (2013). 'Fiscal policy implementation in sub-Saharan Africa,' *World Development,* vol. 46, no. C, pp. 79–91.

Loayza, N.V. and Raddatz, C. (2007). 'The structural determinants of external vulnerability.' *The World Bank Economic Review,* vol. 21, no. 3, pp. 359–387.

Marshall, M.G. et al. (2010). *Polity IV Project: Political Regime Characteristics and Transitions, 1800–2009, Dataset User's Manual, dataset version 2009.* Vienna, VA, Center for Systemic Peace.

McGuirk, E.F. (2013). 'The illusory leader: Natural resources, taxation and accountability.' *Public Choice,* vol. 154, no. 3–4, pp. 285–313.

Nel, P. and Righarts, M. (2008). 'Natural disasters and the risk of violent civil conflict.' *International Studies Quarterly,* vol. 52, no. 1, pp. 159–185.

OECD/CEPAL/CIAT (2014). *Revenue Statistics in Latin America/Estadísticas tributarias en América Latina, 1990–2012.* Paris, OECD.

Pessino, C. and Fenochietto, R. (2010). 'Determining countries' tax effort.' *Hacienda Pública Española/Revista de Economía Pública,* vol. 195, no. 4, pp. 65–87.

Profeta, P. et al. (2011). *Does Democracy Affect Taxation and Government Spending? Evidence from Developing Countries.* Paper presented at the XXIII Conference of the Societá Italiana di Economia Pubblica, Pavia.

Profeta, P. and Scabrosetti, S. (2010). *The Political Economy of Taxation: Lessons from developing countries.* Cheltenham, Edward Elgar Publishing.

Raddatz, C. (2007). 'Are external shocks responsible for the instability of output in low-income countries?' *Journal of Development Economics,* vol. 84, no. 1, pp. 155–187.

Rodrik, D. (2001). 'Why is there so much economic insecurity in Latin America?' *Cepal Review,* vol. 73, no. 1, pp. 7–29.

Ross, M. L. (2012). 'The political economy of petroleum wealth in low-income countries: Some policy alternatives,' in Arezki, R. et al. (eds.) (2012). *Commodity Price Volatility and Inclusive Growth in Low-Income-Countries.* Washington, DC, International Monetary Fund.

Schumacher, I. and Strobl, E. (2008). 'Economic Development and Losses Due to Natural Disasters: The Role of Risk,' *Cahier No. 2008–32.* Palaiseau: École Polytechnique/ Paris Tech.

Tanzi, V. (1992). 'Structural factors and tax revenue in developing countries: Aa decade of evidence,' in Goldin, I. and Winters, L.A. (eds.) (1992). *Open Economies: Structural Adjustment and Agriculture.* Cambridge, Cambridge University Press.

Teera, J.M. and Hudson, J. (2004). 'Tax performance: A comparative study.' *Journal of International Development,* vol. 16, no. 1, pp. 785–802.

van der Ploeg, F. and Venables, A.J. (2011). 'Natural Resource Wealth: The challenge of managing a windfall,' *OxCarre Research Paper No. 75.* Oxford, University of Oxford, Oxford Centre for the Analysis of Resource Rich Economies.

Villafuerte, M. et al. (2010). 'Riding the Roller Coaster: Fiscal Policies of Nonrenewable Resource Exporters in Latin America and the Caribbean,' *IMF Working Paper No. 10/251.* Washington, DC, International Monetary Fund.

von Haldenwang, C. (2011). 'Taxation of Non-Renewable Natural Resources—What are the Key Issues?' *Briefing Paper No. 05/2011.* Bonn, German Development Institute/ Deutsches Institut für Entwicklungspolitik (DIE).

von Haldenwang, C. and Ivanyna, M. (2012). 'A comparative view on the tax performance of developing countries: Regional patterns, non-tax revenue and governance.' *Economics: The Open-Access, Open-Assessment E-Journal,* vol. 6, no. 32, pp. 1–44.

von Haldenwang, C. et al. (2013). *Study on the Vulnerability and Resilience Factors of Tax Revenues in Developing Countries.* Brussels, AETS.

Appendix

List of countries by income group

High-income group/Upper-middle-income group: Algeria (since 2006), Angola (since 2006), Antigua and Barbuda, Argentina (since 1996), Australia, Austria, Bahamas, Bahrain, Barbados, Belarus (since 2006), Belgium, Belize, Botswana (since 1996), Brazil, Brunei Darussalam, Bulgaria (since 2006), Canada, Chile (since 1996), China (since 2006), Colombia (since 2006), Costa Rica (since 1996), Croatia, Cyprus, Czech Republic, Denmark, Dominica (since 1996), Dominican Republic (since 2006), Ecuador (since 2006), Equatorial Guinea (since 2006), Estonia, Fiji, Finland, France, Gabon, Germany, Greece, Grenada, Hong Kong, Hungary, Iceland, Iran (since 2006), Iraq (until 1995) Ireland, Israel, Italy, Jamaica (since 2006), Japan, Jordan (since 2006), Kazakhstan (since 2006), Kuwait, Latvia (since 2006), Lebanon, Libya (until 2005), Lithuania (since 2006), Luxembourg, Macedonia (since 2006), Malaysia (since 1996), Malta, Mauritius (since 1996), Mexico, Montenegro, Namibia (since 2006), Netherlands, New Zealand, Norway, Oman, Panama (since 1996), Poland (since 1996), Portugal, Rep of Korea, Romania, Russian Federation (since 2006), Saudi Arabia, Serbia, Seychelles, Singapore, Slovak Republic, Slovenia, Solomon Islands, South Africa, Spain, St. Kitts & Nevis (since 1996), St. Lucia, St. Vincent & Grenadines (since 2006), Sweden, Switzerland, Thailand (since 2006), Tonga, Trinidad & Tobago, Tunisia (since 2006), Turkey (since 1996), United Arab Emirates, United Kingdom, United States, Uruguay, Vanuatu, Venezuela.

 Lower-middle-income/Low-income group: Afghanistan, Albania, Algeria (until 2005), Angola (until 2005), Argentina (until 1995), Armenia, Bangladesh, Belize, Benin, Bhutan, Bolivia, Bosnia & Herzegovina (until 2005), Botswana (until 1995), Burkina Faso, Bulgaria (until 2005), Burundi, Cambodia, Cameroon, Cape Verde, Central African Republic, Chad, Chile (until 1995), China (until 2005), Colombia (until 2005), Comoros, Costa Rica (until 1995), Cote d'Ivoire, Djibouti, Dominica (until 1995), Dominican Republic (until 2005), Ecuador (until 2005), Equatorial Guinea (until 2005) Egypt, El Salvador, Eritrea, Ethiopia, Gambia, Georgia, Ghana, Guatemala, Guinea, Guinea-Bissau, Guyana, Haiti, Honduras, India, Indonesia, Iran (until 2005), Iraq (since 1996), Jamaica (until 2005) Jordan (until 2005), Kazakhstan (until 2005), Kenya, Kosovo, Kyrgyz Republic, Lao PDR, Latvia (until 2005), Lesotho, Liberia, Lithuania (until 2005), Macedonia (until 2005), Madagascar, Malaysia (until 2005), Malawi, Maldives, Mali, Mauritania, Moldova, Mongolia, Morocco, Mozambique, Myanmar (until 2005), Namibia (until 2005), Nepal, Nicaragua, Niger, Nigeria, Pakistan, Panama (until 1995), Papua New Guinea, Paraguay, Peru (until 2005), Philippines, Poland (until 1995), Rep of Congo, Russian Federation (until 2005), Rwanda, Samoa, Sao Tome & Principe, St. Lucia (until 1995), St. Vincent & Grenadines (until 2005), Senegal, Sierra Leone, Sri Lanka, Swaziland, Syrian Arab Rep., Tajikistan, Tanzania, Thailand (until 2005), Timor-Leste, Togo, Tunisia (until 2005), Turkey (until 1995), Turkmenistan (until 2005), Uganda, Ukraine, Uzbekistan, Vietnam, Yemen, Zambia, Zimbabwe.

List of countries coded as democracies

Albania (2002–2010), Argentina (1983–2010), Armenia (1991–1994), Australia (1980–2010), Austria (1980–2010), Belarus (1991–1994), Belgium (1980–2010), Benin (2006–2010), Bolivia (1982–2010), Botswana (1987–2010), Brazil (1985–2010), Bulgaria

(1990–2010), Canada (1980–2010), Cape Verde (1991–2010), Chile (1989–2010), Colombia (1980–2010), Comoros (2006–2010), Costa Rica (1980–2010), Croatia (2000–2010), Cyprus (1980–2010), Czech Republic (1993–2010), Denmark (1980–2010), Dominican Republic (1996–2010), Ecuador (1980–1999; 2006), El Salvador (1991–2010), Estonia (1999–2010), Fiji (1980–1986), Finland (1980–2010), France (1980–2010), Gambia (1980–1993), Georgia (2004–2006), Germany (1980–2010), Ghana (2004–2010), Greece (1980–2010), Guatemala (1996–2010), Haiti (1990; 1994–1998), Honduras (1999–2010), Hungary (1990–2010), India (1980–2010), Indonesia (2004–2010), Ireland (1980–2010), Israel (1980–2010), Italy (1980–2010), Jamaica (1980–2010), Japan (1980–2010), Kenya (2002–2010), Rep. of Korea (1998–2010), Kosovo (2008–2010), Latvia (1991–2010), Lebanon (2005–2010), Lesotho (1993–1997; 2002–2010), Lithuania (1991–2010), Luxembourg (1980–2010), Macedonia (2002–2010), Madagascar (1992–2008), Mali (1992- 1996; 2002–2010), Mauritius (1980–2010), Mexico (2000–2010), Moldova (1993–2010), Mongolia (1992–2010), Montenegro (2006–2010), Netherlands (1980–2010), New Zealand (1980–2010), Nicaragua (1995–2010), Niger (1992–1995), Nigeria (1980–1983), Norway (1980–2010), Pakistan (1988 1998), Panama (1989–2010), Paraguay (1992–1997; 1999–2010), Peru (1980–1991; 2001–2010), Philippines (1987–2010), Poland (1991–2010), Portugal (1980–2010), Romania (1996–2010), Senegal-(2000–2010), Serbia (2006–2008), Sierra Leone (2007–2010), Slovak Republic (1993–2010), Slovenia (1991–2010), Solomon Islands (1980–1999; 2004–2010), South Africa (1993–2010), Spain (1980–2010), Sweden (1980–2010), Switzerland (1980–2010), Thailand (1992–2005), Timor-Leste (2006–2010), Trinidad & Tobago (1980–2010), Turkey (1983–2010), Ukraine (1994–1999; 2006–2009), United Kingdom (1980–2010), United States (1980–2010), Uruguay (1985–2010), Venezuela (1980–2000), Zambia (2008–2010).

List of countries coded as resource-rich

Afghanistan, Albania, Algeria, Angola, Bahrain, Bolivia, Botswana, Brunei Darussalam, Cameroon, Central African Republic, Chad, Chile, Congo, Rep., Cote d'Ivoire, Ecuador, Equatorial Guinea, Gabon, Ghana, Guatemala, Guinea, Guyana, Indonesia, Iran, Iraq, Kazakhstan, Kyrgyz Republic, Lao PDR, Libya, Madagascar, Mali, Mauritania, Mexico, Mongolia, Mozambique, Niger, Nigeria, Norway, Oman, Papua New Guinea, Peru, Russian Federation, Sao Tome and Principe, Saudi Arabia, Sierra Leone, Syrian Arab Republic, Tanzania, Timor-Leste, Togo, Trinidad and Tobago, Turkmenistan, United Arab Emirates, Uzbekistan, Venezuela, Vietnam, Yemen, Zambia.

Chapter 12

Social Policy, Inequality, and Development: Notes on Brazil in the First Decade of the 21st Century

Eduardo Fagnani

Introduction

In the first decade of the 21st century, Brazil made important social progress. This chapter supports the hypothesis that the key factors in achieving such progress were economic growth and improved coordination between economic and social objectives, all in a favorable international context. After over two decades, growth reclaimed space on the macroeconomic agenda, consequently driving social spending and the labor market, also potentializing the redistributive effects of Social Security as established in the 1988 Constitution.

The Bolsa Família program played a role in mitigating hunger and other vulnerabilities associated with extreme poverty. But it was, definitively, not the determining factor in the recent improvement on the social scene, despite the common liberal take to the contrary. Strategies for social development cannot do without initiatives focused on those subject to hunger or precariously placed within the job market (more than 70% of the adult beneficiaries of the Bolsa Família program are currently employed). The error here would be to make initiatives such as these into a "one size fits all" or preferential strategy in tackling social issues as a whole.

This view clashes with the hegemonic liberal interpretation of social policy under the administrations of President Luís Inácio "Lula" da Silva (2003–2010), which falsely insists that Brazilian social protection is limited to the Bolsa Família and that improvements in quality of life over the period in question are the direct results of the program.

This mirage, repeated like a mantra by multilateral organizations, works to sing the "virtues" of so-called conditional cash transfer programs (CCT), nuclei of an international strategy in operation for over three decades in developing countries. With the international financial crisis of 2008, this strategy was reinforced. The response from global leaders was to implement the initiative known as the Basic Social Security Floor, with an ample coalition formed around the concept in its defense.

Given this situation, it is argued that the exaggerated praise for the Bolsa Família seems to be a deliberate ideological push designed to elevate the Brazilian program's status to that of a global success story to be followed by other countries, via such a Basic Social Security Floor. This move to sell the illusion of the program's protagonism in the improvement in Brazilians' quality of life, meanwhile, seems to be a valuable marketing weapon in the move to spread this new global initiative. For a start, the article presents critical notes on the liberal interpretation of the Lula administration's social policy (section 1). The following parts seek to deconstruct said interpretation.

This itinerary will begin with an analysis of the evaluations carried out by the Economic Commission for Latin America and the Caribbean (CEPAL) on the social progress attained on the continent over the 2000s, indicating trends contrary to those propagated by principal international agencies: CCTs played a modest role, next to variables related to the growth of the economy and per capita income (section 2).

The next step is to criticize the misguided minimalistic vision of the Brazilian social protection system instituted by the 1988 Constitution and its redistributive role during the Lula administration. The article attempts to demonstrate that it is both broad and diversified, and was the product of the social movement that fought for a redemocratization of the country in the 1970s (section 3).

The next topic paves the way for analyzing social policy under the Lula administration, situating it within a historical perspective marked by two movements with opposite vectors. The first, previously mentioned here, points toward the structuring of the protection system, inspired by key values of the welfare state. The other points in the other direction entirely, to wit, the attempt to impede the consolidation of such conquests. This drive was reinvigorated in the 1990s, when Brazil opted tardily to adhere to a neoliberal doctrine. From 1990 to 2002, social protection was torn between two opposing paradigms (minimal state vs. welfare state) (section 4).

After this brief incursion, the article moves to analyze social policy under the Lula administration, marked by continuing tensions between antagonistic paradigms. This friction remained intense from 2003 to 2005, taking on new intensity from 2006 to 2010. In this last stage, the administration attained improved synchronicity between economic and social objectives, in comparison to the past. And it began moving towards constructing a less perverse model than had been in place previously (section 5).

The following section emphasizes that recent progress, although positive, has not erased the deep marks of chronic Brazilian social inequality that superposes old and new issues yet to be addressed. In the 21st century, the country still displays unacceptable levels of income and wealth inequality; the labor market still has some of the characteristics of peripheral economies; and access to basic goods and services is still unequal across regions and social classes (section 6).

In the conclusion, it is emphasized that, from a progressive perspective, facing down inequalities is one of the principal challenges of the 21st century. The assumption here is that social matters are rooted in the country's political and economic underdevelopment. Strategies for the future will require an agenda for transformation conceived from a developmental perspective.

Critical Notes on the Liberal Interpretation

The liberal interpretation of social policy under the administration of President Luís Inácio "Lula" da Silva (2003–2010) disseminates the false vision that Brazilian social protection is limited to the Bolsa Família program and that the recent improvement in quality of life is the exclusive product of that program. This vision is repeated like a mantra by international organizations. In an article from *Carta Maior*,[1] which references a report from the Organization for Economic Cooperation and Development (OECD), for example, it was

---

1   OCDE: Brasil tem avanço extraordinário e redução da pobreza inédita. André Barrocal, *Carta Maior*, 26 out. 2011.

emphasized that poverty and inequality have never fallen so fast as in Brazil. For OECD, this advance was driven almost wholly by the Bolsa Família program, "an example of social policy copied across the world, even in more developed countries." The organism plays down the role of economic growth, job creation, the valorization of the minimum wage, and income transferences from Social Security.

Studies from the International Labor Organization (ILO) argue in the same vein. Bolsa Família is considered "one of the broadest-reaching social assistance programs in the world," (Cichon et al., 2011: p. 10) as in the year 2008 it addressed the needs of almost 50 million people. IMF Director-General Christine Lagarde sees the impressive improvements in the indicators of poverty, inequality, and development across Latin America as due to the role played by CCTs, with emphasis on the flagship Bolsa Família (Brazil) and Oportunidades (Mexico) programs which, in managing to break the intergenerational transmission of poverty, became models for the rest of the world.

The World Bank is among the principal institutions driving the spread of CCTs worldwide. It's understandable for multilateral institutions to defend CCTs as a global strategy for social development. The surprising part is that popular and progressive sectors and administrations across Latin America have uncritically embraced neoliberal dogma, forging a grand consensus with conservatives over the values of the minimal state. The ideological victory is patent when it also wins over the hearts and minds of those who were elected to implement programs as alternatives to neoliberalism.

These sectors seem unaware that the CCT programs are instruments to exorcise the ideology of the welfare state in favor of that of the minimal state, one being the negation of the other: targeting vs. universality; assistance vs. rights; social insurance vs. social security; commodification vs. public services; flexible contracts vs. workers' and labor rights.

In liberal doctrine, the state is only responsible for taking care of basic education ("equality of opportunity") for the population "below the poverty line." Those who have "left poverty" must go to the private market to seek the provision of the goods and services they need (Lavinas, 2013).

This "one-size-fits-all strategy" opens the door to the privatization and commodification of social services, following the Chilean model adopted in the 1980s. In the next decade, privatization was imposed on essential sectors such as welfare (World Bank, 1994), healthcare (World Bank, 1993), sanitation, and public transit.

The most paradoxical move is attributing an immoderate success rate to Bolsa Família on one hand, and putting forth a different interpretation on the other—attributing a key role to the rise in work income and Social Security transfers in the reduction in social inequality:

> "Over the period 2001/2011 ... work income continues to contribute the most to the fall in inequality. Nearly 60% of the fall in the Gini index stems from the fact that the work market became less unequal. Welfare was the second-most important factor, followed closely by PBF [Bolsa Família], a program that, while representing a tiny fraction of income, caused a drop in inequality of over 10%" (IPEA, 2012: p. 27).

Many in the progressive camp do not realize that the inspiration for CCTs is classically liberal. The security of a minimum income was first proposed by Hayek (1944). Later on, Friedman (1962) popularized the defense of a negative income tax as the most desirable procedure in combating poverty, although he preferred charity.

For a long time, Latin America was a testing ground for neoliberal experiments to deal with the external debt crises of the 1980s. Social protection could not undercut fiscal adjustment. CCTs, being cheap, worked within the macroeconomic adjustment applied in the region during the 1980s and 1990s, pushing towards the liberal reform aims of the state—which, among other points, included the privatization and commodification of the array of social services through the suppression of universal public policies.

After Chile, it was to Mexico and Brazil that these programs were rolled out for the first time on a large scale, during the 1990s. The programs would spread feverishly over the next decade. In 2007 the World Bank informed that practically all the countries in the region had adopted some kind of CCT, as well as more than 30 other countries on other continents (Lavinas, 2013).

International financial crisis and reinforcement of the minimal state

The importance of CCTs was underscored after the international crisis of 2008, when the state was forced to save capitalism from capitalists. Paradoxically, the reaction to the failure of neoliberalism was a doubling down on neoliberalism; and the minimal state was prescribed as a remedy for the ills of the minimal state.

The response from global leadership was to implant the so-called Basic Social Security Floor initiative (OIT, 2011). The implicit concept is to concede financial resources to the poor so that they can buy the goods and social services that they need on the market. According to OIT representatives, provision of universal access to potable water, for example, would be possible through a concession free of cost—"or [via] providing people financial resources so that they can acquire the necessary quantity of water" (Cichon et al., 2011: p. 5).

The initiative revisits a well-known World Bank proposal (Holzmann and Jorgensen, 2000), which consisted of ensuring income for the poor themselves to buy what they need—with freedom of choice in managing their own social risks.[2] In 2009, this initiative was highlighted by the signers of the Global Jobs Pact as a response to the global financial crisis. It was recommended that countries "build adequate social protection for all, drawing on a basic social protection floor" (OIT, 2009: p. 6). Since then, a truly striking avalanche of adhesions have been noted. A broad global coalition has emerged in defense of CCTs, including principal global leadership organizations (the G7 and G-20), the IMF, the World Bank, NGOs, and 19 UN agencies.

In the effort to spread this initiative across the world, international organizations have spoken with basic and unacceptable imprecision. For example, the ILO refers to the basic social security floor as a new paradigm for Social Security, contradicting Convention no. 102, approved by the organization in 1953. OIT, which is coordinating the implementation of the initiative, has thus taken a step back from its founding principles, signed over 60 years ago.

According to the Bachelet Report, "the social protection floor concept focuses particularly on the use of income transfers as a means of ensuring access to basic services" (OIT, 2011a: p. 7). Among the experiments inspiring this initiative are, in particular, Mexico (Oportunidades), Chile (Chile Solidario) and Brazil (Bolsa Família).

But the true star of the new global consensus is the Brazilian program. There seems to have been a deliberate attempt to elevate Bolsa Família to the status of a global success story, the only agent behind social advances in the country. This false vision does not seem to be the product of ignorance. One might venture the hypothesis that it seems to befit a set of clear objectives by virtue of its utility in supporting the apparent virtues of the basic social security floor.

---

2   A critique of this postulation of "social risk management" may be found in Lavinas (2009, p. 5).

The victory of ideology

Neoliberal ideology has amply built up a consensus around the myth that the eradication of poverty and social welfare may be obtained exclusively through targeted programs. This construction has nuances that may evade comprehension through common-sense reasoning.

Ultimately, programs of this kind are weapons that economic power uses to capture public funds meant for society and citizens. Above all, CCTs function for macroeconomic adjustment and residuals for the promotion of more egalitarian societies. Social policy has become a compartment separate from economic policy. The caring souls of the market reserve 0.5% of GDP for so-called progressives to have fun promoting welfare.

For this vein of thinking, this objective may be attained without job creation, work income, the valorization of the minimum wage, universal social policies, or even economic growth, all factors that strongly contributed to curb inequality.

Another subtlety implicit in these dogmas has to do with the definition of poverty. The internationally established criteria that are used across the world by progressives and conservatives alike run extremely low when classifying indigence (an individual who receives up to US$1.25 per day) and poverty (up to US$2.5 per day).

This criterion masks the true dimension of the population living under severe restrictions on monetary subsistence. One does not need to be a specialist to admit that an individual who starts receiving slightly more than US$2.5 per day has in no way left poverty. Based on these monetary parameters, it is not morally acceptable to transform the fiction of poverty reduction into the principal measure of social welfare.

Faced with these facts, one must shine a light on the obvious: programs of this nature alleviate critical situations of vulnerability and hunger. This is precisely why they are necessary and must be a part of a broader strategy for facing social matters. But they cannot eradicate or even reduce poverty in its true dimensions.

Beyond income insufficiency, poverty should also be seen as "capability deprivation" (Sen, 1999) stemming from the absence of public policies to ensure employment and basic services such as healthcare, education, and sanitation, for example. However, the aim of expanding the public offering of these goods and services is not a part of the CCTs and basic social security floor, which do not stray beyond a residual social protection model. They exist precisely in order to act in the opposite direction: the shrinking of public and universal welfare systems. As Lavinas (2013) rightly indicates, the acceptance of these programs' success represents a serious downsizing in social protection in the name of the poor. This model essentially guarantees a marginal income that, in isolation, cannot ensure the incorporation of these most vulnerable groups into the market, and will not create egalitarian societies.

The formulators of the Basic Social Security Floor have also made promises they cannot fulfill. OIT directors see the objective of the initiative as being "to guarantee that people do not go hungry, suffer from avoidable diseases, go without education, have to make use of unsanitary water, or go without housing" (Cichon et al., 2011: p. 5). However, they indicate no concrete measure in terms of attaining these laudable humanitarian aims. The bidimensional conceptual strategy envisioned in the social security staircase invokes promises and hopes of a "vertical" ascension to the "second floor"—which, in theory, would be the ideal level invoked by Convention 102, from 1952 (Fagnani, 2011). But there are no guarantees that monetary transfers alone can ensure "universal access to essential social services in the areas of healthcare, water and sanitation, education, food security, housing, and other areas defined in terms of national priorities," as the Bachelet Report puts it (OIT, 2011a: p. 7).

The initiative's limitations are reinforced by the burden of responsibility placed on the individual in terms of guaranteeing his or her own welfare. Few have perceived the apparent contradiction: "the state imposed on beneficiary families the burden of finding non-existent services in order to prove their 'responsibility' and their worthiness to keep receiving the meagre sums they were being offered," in the words of Lavinas (2013). The author sees the responsibility placed on the individual as a part of the strategy of privatization and commodification of the provision of goods and social services which is implicit in the model. In her vision, this movement has clear links to the current stage of capitalist competition, marked by the domination of financial capital.

It is hardly chance that liberal fundamentalism should associate the eradication of poverty to the emergence of a "new middle class" in Latin America (World Bank, 2013). In many societies, the true middle class tends to buy a part of the social services it needs on the private market. There seems to be no doubt that the implicit aim of this formulation is to increase the centrality of the commodification of public services within the agendas of developing countries.

Growth and Social Inclusion in Latin America

In CEPAL's vision, variables related to the growth of the economy and per capita income were decisive in reducing social inequalities and poverty on the continent over recent years. Contrary to what has been disseminated by many international organizations, the role of programs targeting poverty was fairly modest. Improvement in macroeconomic fundamentals potentialized social spending and its social component. Economic activity contributed to a fall in unemployment rates, job creation, a rise in labor income, and increased job formalization.

The Brazilian case has some similarities with the wider situation in Latin America and the Caribbean. In the 2000s, the global economy grew as a result, among other factors, of the so-called China effect. The exceptional economic growth of the country in question, led by sectors focusing on metal and industrial commodities, expanded demand for these goods as well as the external purchase of food products (Prates and Marçal, 2008).

CEPAL saw international commerce as driving economic growth and the improvement in macroeconomic fundamentals for countries on the continent. Positive figures in the commercial balance had a positive impact on the external debt, and on the reserves of foreign currency that contributed to reducing external vulnerability.

Countries on the continent expanded their economic activity in a rhythm above that of the global average, making for an improvement in macroeconomic fundamentals. The increase in fiscal revenue and debt reduction opened spaces for broadening public spending. In South America from 1991 to 2000, public spending in relation to GDP hit an annual average of 17.1%; this rose to 21.4% for the period 2001–2010. Public social spending followed the same trend, going from 14.5% to 17.9% of GDP from 2001 to 2009. Over the same period, it rose as a relative percentage of public spending from 58.5% to 62.3% (CEPAL, 2012: pp. 171–177). From 1990 to 2009, social spending per capita went from 318 to 819 dollars (Lavinas, 2013).

The job market saw a fall in the unemployment rate (from 11.2% to 6.6%, from 2002 to 2011) and a rise in salaried work as opposed to informal employment. The rise in the real minimum wage was brought about, above all, by the real valorization of the minimum wage (38.2% in Latin America and 49.7% in South America, from 2003 to 2010) (CEPAL, 2012: pp. 222–233).

For the first time in several decades, a considerable subset of countries in the region obtained positive results in terms of distribution, as CEPAL (2012: p. 24) affirms. From 2002 to 2011, the number of people in poverty as a part of the total population fell from 43.9% to 30.4%. The percentage of indigent persons dropped from 19.3% to 12.3%. This performance produced the lowest levels of these indices seen over the past three decades. Despite liberal interpretations, CEPAL sees the role of CCTs as relatively modest when compared with factors related to economic growth and its repercussions on the labor market (CEPAL, 2012b: p. 18).

The real valorization of the minimum wage, evidenced in a number of countries in the region, also had a decisive role in poverty reduction. Countries where the growth of the real minimum wage was most notable (Argentina, Bolivia, Brazil, and Ecuador) are among those with the greatest reductions in poverty. At the other extreme lies Mexico, always referenced as a successful model in terms of targeted income-transfer programs (Lavinas, 2013).

In order to maintain this progress, CEPAL (2012 and 2014) rightly proposes an integrated vision of development that might include economic, social, and environmental aspects.

Far Beyond Bolsa Família: The Brazilian System of Social Protection

Brazil during the 1980s did not present fertile soil for the seeds of neoliberal doctrine. The social movement fighting for the redemocratization of the country sought to settle scores with the military dictatorship, and their path led to the National Constituent Assembly. After marches and counter-marches, the Constitution of the Republic definitively established democracy and forged the basis for a system of social protection inspired in welfare state values such as universality, security, and citizenship (Fagnani, 2005).

For the first time in the country's history, social citizenship was guaranteed by the 1988 Constitution. Social rights were extended to the areas of education, healthcare, work, security, social welfare, protection for maternity and childhood, social assistance, and nutrition.[3]

The Constitution stipulates that the unified national minimum wage, as defined by law, should meet the vital needs of Brazil's workers.[4] Moreover, it tied the minimum wage to the floor established for welfare and assistance benefits. In the case of social welfare benefits, it determines that no benefit which replaces the contribution salary or labor earnings of the insured shall have a monthly amount lower than the minimum monthly wage.[5]

The Constitution extended the welfare benefits of urban workers to the rural sphere. Rural welfare thus became a noncontributory benefit, a typical element of Social Security. Similarly, in the case of Social Assistance, the Constitution establishes "the guarantee of a monthly benefit of one minimum wage to the handicapped and to the elderly who prove their incapability of providing for their own support or having it provided for by their families, as set forth by law."[6] Later on, this program would be dubbed the Continuous Cash Benefit (BPC), tied to the minimum wage.

---

3   Art. 6.
4   Art. 70.
5   Art. 201.
6   Art. 203.

Inspired in the European experience with social democracy during the postwar period, the Unified Health System (SUS), formally introduced in 1988, is based on the principles of citizenship, security, and universality. In the same vein, the constitution guarantees the right to universal, free education at all levels.

In terms of protection for unemployed workers, mechanisms for sustainable financing were created for the Unemployment Insurance Program.[7] This Program had been instituted in 1986, but without a defined financial base. The Constitution allocated 60% of the resources of PIS-PASEP[8] to finance protection for unemployed workers.

Healthcare, welfare, and unemployment insurance were thus incorporated into the nucleus of Social Security.[9] In order to ensure sustainable sources of financing for its development, the Social Security Budget was created.[10] The constituents established a system of tripartite financing, following the classical model inherent to welfare state regimes. The Social Security Budget includes both contributions (from workers and businesses) and general taxes as part of the exclusive financing of these sectors.

Social Security is at once the most important mechanism for social protection in Brazil and a powerful instrument for development and redistribution. In addition to monetary transfers for families, welfare, work, and social assistance, it includes the provision of universal services provided by the Unified Health System (SUS), the Unified System of Social Assistance (SUAS), and the Unified System of Food and Nutritional Security (SUSAN) (both implemented in 2005).

Note that, from 2001 to 2012, total benefits from Social Security (substituting income) went from 24 to 37 million, a bump that occurred across all brackets. In Urban Welfare, benefits grew 48% (11.6 to 17.2 million); Rural Welfare went up 38% (6.3 to 8.7 million); in Social Assistance, only the Continued Cash Benefit (BPC) saw a bump of 83% (2.1 to 4.1 million); and Unemployment Insurance saw a rise in the number of benefits issued (4.1 to 7.5 million) (Fagnani and Tonelli Vaz, 2013a).

This considerable volume of benefits is associated to a considerable distributive effect, which becomes even more evident if we also count indirect beneficiaries. According to the FIBGE (2002), for each direct beneficiary there are 2.5 indirect beneficiary relatives. Social Security thus benefited over 120 million people in 2012, both directly and indirectly.

Recall that nearly 2/3 of the benefits meant to substitute families' income (approximately 34 million) correspond to the minimum wage. And, given the aggressive policy of valorization carried out over the course of the past decade, this sector saw its income elevated more than 90% above inflation since 2003.

Beyond these benefits, there are others that complement work income, such as Bolsa Família (3.6 million families in 2003, 13.8 million in 2013), for example. This set of benefits came to R$407 billion in 2012, the equivalent of 9.3% of GDP. This sum represents 53.9% of the federal government's net tax income (ANFIP, 2013).

Liberal fiction prefers to ignore these facts. The deeper issue is that market forces never accepted the social advances guaranteed by the 1988 Constitution, given that these rights flew in the face of the market strategy for developing countries. This point will be the focus of the next section.

---

7   Art. 239.
8   Contribution taken from the payrolls of public and private workers.
9   Art. 194.
10   Art. 195.

Brazil, 1990–2002: Tensions Between Clashing Projects (Minimal State vs. Welfare State)

Over the past four decades, the trajectory of Brazilian social policy has been marked by two clashing movements (Fagnani, 2005). The first drives toward structuring of the social protection system around certain values of the welfare state. The second movement seeks to impede the consolidation of these very bases—a drive that took on new vigor after 1990, when Brazil tardily opted for neoliberalism.

In this context, in the period 1990–2002, social protection underwent a tug of war between two opposing paradigms (the minimal state vs. the welfare state), at two specific points (Fagnani, 2008). The administration of Fernando Collor de Mello (1990–92), formulated an agenda for liberalizing reforms with an eye to constitutional reform in 1993. This revision never came to pass, however, due to the president's impeachment. While awaiting the revision, the administration sought to disfigure the conquests of 1988 while the complementary constitutional legislation was in the process of being passed. The second point came during the two administrations of Fernando Henrique Cardoso (1995–02), which were marked by the return to liberalizing reforms.

Before analyzing this stage, one must emphasize that the redemocratization of Brazil and its social protection reforms coincided with the fading of the National Developmentalist State, which played a decisive role in the process of industrialization (increasingly intense after 1930). The international crisis of 1982 increased external vulnerability, indebtedness and inflationary pressures. Placed at the epicenter of the crisis, the state lost control of its macroeconomic policy and growth initiative.

This situation was aggravated starting in 1990, when Brazil saw the formation of a "broad consensus favorable to adjustment policies and reforms proposed by the Washington Consensus," in the words of Fiori (1993). In the economic sphere, there was a passive choice for the liberal model. The ruling elites were conquered by the conviction that "there is no other path" (Schwarz, 2013). Thereafter, governments gave up on exercising a more active style of macroeconomic policy.

The Real Plan was successful in stabilizing the currency, but social and economic costs were elevated. This opening of trade exposed industry to unbalanced competition, which led to internationalization and the destruction of the production chains in key sectors. The material and financial bases of the national state were mined by privatizations and growing indebtedness.

The opening of trade and the valorization of the exchange rate destabilized the country's external accounts. The short-term "solution" involved raising the basic interest rate to attract capital and accumulate reserves of foreign currency. During periods of international crisis (Mexico, Asia, and Russia), the basic interest rate went up to over 40% per year.

As a consequence, the public debt doubled in 8 years (30 to 60% of GDP from 1994 to 2002). The increase in spending on interest rate (over 8% of GDP, in many years) led to a rise in the tax burden from 1995 to 2002 (25% to 32% of GDP), under the FHC administration.

The greater pressure exerted by financial expenses on the budget squeezed the limits of financing for social spending. Note that between 1996 and 2003, the ratio of federal social spending as a part of total effective government spending dipped 10 percentage points (from 60 to 50%), while the percentage of financial expenses grew 16 points (from 17 to 33%) (Castro et al., 2008). These choices led to economic stagnation and a crisis in the labor market. Per capita income stalled out, the unemployment rate hit 13% in 2002, and social mobility was interrupted Quadros (2003).

In terms of social citizenship, the state's macroeconomic adjustment and liberal reforms demanded the elimination of the chapter on Social Order in the 1988 Constitution. As they function within a fiscal adjustment, income-conditioned transfer programs came to face down universal policies. It is from this perspective that we can understand the strength of the ideas that seek to impose targeting as the only possible social policy for Brazil. This alternative gained strength within the context of the changes effected as a result of the agreement with the IMF in late 1998.

Economic and Social Policy under the Lula Administration (2003–2010)

Lula's social policy fits within this long series of tensions between paradigms begun in 1990 and comprises two clearly defined stages. The first (2003–05), is marked by a thorny spell during which these tensions remained uncompromising. The second (2006–10) is characterized by the cooling of tensions between the values of the minimal state and the welfare state—although they remained fully active.

Moreover, a favorable international context helped growth reclaim a certain centrality in the macroeconomic agenda, something which hadn't happened for over two decades. The economy began growing again, and the administration attained a more positive synchronicity between economic and social goals. There cam an expansion in social spending, the creation of formal jobs, a drop in unemployment, a real elevation of the minimum wage and work income. This set of factors potentialized the redistributive effects of Social Security as instituted by the 1988 Constitution. Differently from the liberal vision, here it is argued that these events were decisive in the improvement in social indicators (distribution of work income, mobility, familial consumption, reduction in extreme poverty), which grew more intense in the second half of the last decade.

From 1999 to 2002, the Workers' Party (Partido dos Trabalhadores) had already drawn up a social-developmentalist platform with the objective of "rebuilding Brazil after the neoliberal hurricane" (Mercadante and Tavares, 2001). The 2002 election renewed hopes for change. But, in the middle of the campaign, this push was checked. Largely because financial agents began betting against Brazil. "The markets really blackmailed Brazilian voters," affirms Belluzzo (2005).[11]

In this context, between 2003 and 2005, macroeconomic policy essentially continued within the parameters adopted by the previous administration. Reforms demanded by the market were soon implemented, with emphasis on tax and welfare reform. This continuity with economic orthodoxy limited the potential of social policies. As in the past, there remained a basic incongruity between economic strategy and social development. The direction of social policy remained undefined. The nucleus of Lula's social strategy was the Zero Hunger Program; but in 2003, the Bolsa Família Program became the administration's primary social policy—reinforcing targeting as the "one-size-fits-all" strategy in vogue.

Starting in 2006, the social-developmentalist project was partially resurrected. After three decades of marginalization, growth was once again included in the administration's agenda. The government opted for less restrictive fiscal and monetary policies, with

---

11   Belluzzo, L.G. (2005). Interview. Medo da Esperança. *Carta Capital*, 11 de julho.

emphasis on the expansion of public credit and the reduction of goals for the primary surplus and basic income rates.

From 1990 to 2005, GDP grew at an average annual rate close to 2.5%. In the three-year period 2006–2008, this percentage rose to close to 5%; it fell back (-0.2%) in 2009 (global crisis); and then bounced back to 7% in 2010. Rates of investment leaped from around 15% of GDP to 19% of GDP from 2000 to 2012. Per capita income began growing once again, after remaining virtually stagnant during the 1980s and 1990s. Economic growth stimulated fiscal revenue, improving public finances and reducing restrictions on social spending (Barbosa and Souza, 2010).

This growth-positive posture had been reinforced in 2007 with the launch of the Growth Acceleration Program (PAC), which sought to reinforce the state's role—hamstrung by liberalizing reforms—in the coordination of public and private investments oriented towards economic and social infrastructure. In its first four years, the program helped double Brazilian public investments (from 1.62% of GDP in 2006 to 3.27% in 2010, http://www.pac.gov.br/).

With the emergence of the international financial crisis, this posture was redoubled. Countercyclical measures were adopted, and public banks took on an aggressive strategy of broadening credit, practically doubling availability from 2003 to 2010 (from 24% to 49% of GDP). Under these conditions, economic and social objectives began to mesh. Growth had positive effects on public spending, the job market, and Social Security. These factors contributed to elevating familial income, driving the internal mass-consumption market—the foundation of the growth cycle.

From 2003 to 2010, over 18 million formal jobs were created, and the unemployment rate fell from 12.3% to 5.5%. The activation of economic activity also led to the growth of fiscal revenue, improving public finances and opening up space for the expansion of social spending. Federal Social Spending (GSF) per capita saw a real increase of nearly 60% from 2004 to 2010 (from US$946 to US$1,498).[12] In terms of absolute values, it went from US $169 to R$282 billion; and in relation to GDP, it rose from 13.2% to 15.5% (Castro et al., 2012).

The principal item in terms of expanding social spending was income transfers from Social Security (Urban and rural welfare, social assistance, and unemployment insurance). Social spending was also driven by an expansion in the offer of social services. Federal spending on education, for example, doubled from 2000 to 2010 (from US $9.5 to US $20.4 billion), and federal spending on healthcare grew more than 60% in real terms over the same period (from US $18.5 to R$31.0 billion, Castro et al., 2012).

One might also register the growth in spending on affordable housing through the Minha Casa, Minha Vida Program—which hit the mark of 1.3 million houses delivered in August 2013. This improved coordination between social and economic policies contributed to improving indicators of work-income distribution, social mobility, familial consumption, and a drop in extreme poverty.

Per capita household income, after ten years of stagnation, began rising in the middle of the decade. GDP growth per capita was a decisive factor in terms of improvements in income distribution. In 2011 the country hit its lowest level of income inequality as measured by the Gini index, returning to levels last recorded in 1960 (IPEA, 2012).

---

12   1 US$=2.22 BRL (May 2014).

Social inequality among wage earners declined strikingly: real average income for workers rose close to 30%, while the 20% poorest saw growth over 70%. The rise in work income was responsible for around 60% of the drop in social inequality (idem).

Social mobility became reascendent after two sluggish decades. Familial income grew most notably in the lowest brackets, expanding the domestic market of mass consumption.

A less perverse economic model than the historical trend

In short, over the first decade of the 21st century, there were created alternatives to the economic model that had been in the process of implementation since 1990; and these alternatives resulted in an improvement in the standards of living for the Brazilian population. The economy grew and distributed income, something which had not occurred for 50 years.

Recognition of this fact does not necessarily imply rubber-stamping the idea that a new pattern of development has been implanted. In truth, the tendency was towards the construction of a less perverse economic model than historical trend.

The vision of progressive administrations elected in Brazil and other countries in Latin America as "postneoliberal" (Sader, 2014) also appears questionable. It is true that a new stage in the fight against neoliberal doctrine was inaugurated. But, despite this march, the continent is still quite far from "overcoming and turning the page on neoliberalism."

In a more prudent tone, historian Perry Anderson[13] indicates that, at the turn of this century, neoliberalism continues to deepen its hold worldwide. In this context, the progressive administrations of South America cast the continent as the bearer of "a hope that exists in no other place in the world today." In his vision, Brazil is on the front lines of this process of opening up crannies in the search to move "against the tide of the dominant global ideology."

Sectors within the Workers' Party are more critical. Frei Betto, a representative of the progressive segment of the Brazilian catholic church for example, will point out that "Brazil saw great advances in a decade. However, from his perspective, the country was unable to set up an alternative model, besides neoliberalism and the capitalist developmentalist-consumerist model. The author also writes that "in 10 years of governing, the PT has not brought about a single structural reform, not even the most important and widely promised in their founding documents—agricultural land reform."[14]

The profound marks of social inequalities[15]

Although positive, recent social progress has not erased the profound marks of chronic Brazilian social inequality, with historical roots sunk deep into the nation's slaveholding past (Carvalho, 2001), the specific nature of late capitalism, the country's short democratic experience in the 20th century and the accelerated process of urbanization in the absence of agrarian reform and urban and social policies.

From 2001 to 2011, the Gini index fell significantly (from 0.594 to 0.527), and income concentration shrank back to 1960 levels. Nevertheless, it remains among the highest in the

---

13   O Brasil e a América Latina, segundo Perry Anderson. *Carta Maior.* 15/10/2013.

14   "Frei Betto: Lula e Dilma foram 'governo social-popular desenvolvimentista.'" Interviewed by Carlos Miguélez Monroy, released in Hemisferiozero, 13–01–2014.

15   This section is based on the 22 articles examined in Fagnani and Fonseca (eds.) 2013a, 2013b.

world: over the past decade we went from the 3rd to the 15th worst on the global ranking, still far from more egalitarian countries, where the Gini index is under 0.4. Regional inequalities are combined with extreme inequalities of opportunity between social groups.

The problem of agrarian land reform is still very much alive in Brazil—a concern that long since ceased to be an issue for central countries. These nations carried out land reform in the name of the modernization of capitalism. Brazil, on the contrary, oversaw various abortive attempts and the issue remains current here, despite the protests of prevailing liberal thought. The centuries-old concentration of agrarian wealth in Brazil remains untouched: around 1% of landowners control one half of all lands.[16]

The inequalities in Brazilian society are also reflected in the physical appropriation of urban space. Recent advances in social inclusion are insufficient to ensure a more just city, in the words of Maricato (2013). As she sees it, "it is not enough to distribute income"; one must also "distribute the city."

Inequalities are also present in the current tax system, in place since the mid-1960s. Indirect taxes (on consumption), which have the greatest proportional impact on the poorest, represented 49.2% of total tax revenue. Direct taxes on income and net worth came to 19.0% and 3.7% of revenue, respectively. The tax burden amongst OECD member countries comes to 33% of total revenue (Lavinas, 2013b).

The structure of the job market still bears the marks and characteristics of developing or peripheral economies: elevated heterogeneity, a broad presence of underemployment, a structural excess of manual labor, highly concentrated income, low salaries, and high turnover in work posts.

Racial and gender inequalities are woven into society. The total of white students ages 18–24 in higher education is nearly double that of black or mixed-race (brown, or *pardo*) students. On the job market, the proportion of black or mixed-race workers in informal positions far exceeds the white population in similar conditions (36%). The violent death rate amongst young blacks is nearly three times higher than in the white population. Among the 10% poorest Brazilians, more than 2/3 are black or mixed-race, according to the IBGE (2013).

Women not only earn, on average, 25–30% less than men, but they are also subject to a blatant disadvantage in terms of access to decommodified public services such as daycare, full-time schools—and now, in a new phase of demographic transition, eldercare. That is why they cannot manage to invert the markedly unequal division of domestic work in their favor, with an impact on job opportunities.

In spite of being more educated than men, female job opportunities remain highly concentrated on precarious and part-time jobs in order to help conciliating wage activities and domestic duties.

Inequalities are also manifest in terms of access to social services. Universal policies demonstrate regional and class-based lacunas.

The country is still far from an ideal level of equality in terms of educational opportunities: Brazilians' average level of schooling is low in relation to international parameters; illiteracy among youths and adults remains elevated; the universalization of educational services still is still peppered with lacunas in primary, secondary, and higher education; being in school does not guarantee effective learning; and the matter of quality remains troublesome.

---

16 "30 anos do MST." Interview. João Pedro Stédile. *Estado de São Paulo*, January 19, 2014.

Even after 25 years, Social Security still has not been consolidated in accordance with the principles established by the Constitution. Strong opposition and attempts at backpedaling from market forces have been decisive factors in the sidestepping of the constitutional principles of the organization of social security, the Social Security Budget, and social control (the National Council on Social Security) under all administrations since 1989.

Economic growth reversed the decline in welfare coverage for active workers that had begun in 1992. In 2010, levels returned to what they had been 18 years before. This inflection, however, was not enough to alter the general situation of low welfare coverage. Currently, 50% of active workers in the private sector do not contribute to welfare, are not actively protected, and will not be protected once they retire.[17]

The Constitution established the Unified Health System (SUS) as a universal, public right, free of charge and based on federal cooperation between levels of government. But, since the 1990s, Parliament and the three federal bodies of executive power have not prioritized investments towards broadening the public offering of services, especially systems of medium and high complexity. Many sectors of the population lack adequate access to these services. SUS emerged as an antithesis to the privatist policies adopted by the military dictatorship; but Brazilian democracy was not able to keep commodification out of the sector.

The advances within the institution of the Unified System of Social Assistance (SUAS) in 2005 must be consolidated, especially in terms of the articulation with the other sectors that comprise Social Security, as well as the strengthening of the provision of assistance-related services, which calls for effective accountability on the part of the three federal entities responsible for action and in terms of its financing.

The Unemployment Insurance Program presents an anomaly specific to the Brazilian labor market: the demand for unemployment insurance rises when the unemployment rate falls. This paradox is explained in great part by the high employment turnover rate.

One must recall that Brazil has no history of national policies for affordable housing, sanitation, and mobility with adequate financial and institutional resources fit to the problems created by the accelerated process of urbanization underway since the mid-20th century. As a consequence, housing policy was made inaccessible for many years for low-income sectors. As for sanitation services, more than 40% of Brazilians still lack adequate access to water, and over 60% have no adequate sewage-collection system. The chaotic state of metropolitan public transit reveals a chronic insufficiency in the supply of mass transit systems. There remains an urgent need for an integrated policy of mobility between national, state, and municipal governments.

Given these chronic inequalities, and being in opposition to liberal doctrine, the path cannot be exclusively towards conditioned income transfer or the targeting of universal policies. Facing down this challenge calls for the strengthening of the universal public systems conquered in 1988, not dismantling them.

Ensuring the same social rights for all, even the poorest, requires a two-way street. On one side, the specific ministries responsible for administering universal policies must work to broaden the array of services being offered to regions and populations currently not being covered. This is not a matter of targeting universal policies, but rather expanding those policies to cover poorer sectors as well.

---

17 Consult: http://www1.folha.uol.com.br/mercado/2014/01/1405007-emprego-com-carteira-assinada-ja-supera-50-dos-trabalhadores.shtml.

This opportunity to transform poor Brazilians into citizens with rights cannot be missed; Brazil is one of the few developing countries that, amidst neoliberal doctrine and capitalist competition under the dominance of international finance, has managed to preserve the nuclei of its universal public systems—though still subject to tensions and pressures of every kind, as mentioned earlier.

Conclusions and Challenges

Brazil is caught in the dispute between two clashing projects. Liberalism vs. developmentalism. Market vs. State. Minimal state vs. the values of the social welfare state. Exclusive targeting vs. the universalization of citizenship. Both projects fight for space within society, and, contradictorily, within the government itself. This dispute has obvious and contradictory implications for the paths to be followed in terms of future policy.

The liberal interpretation is absolutely hegemonic, and has the support of broad sectors in society. The most heated defense of such a vision comes from the international establishment, which has spent over three decades defending CCTs as an exclusive strategy for developing countries to deal with social issues. The international financial crisis of 2008 reinforced this strategy. The Basic Social Security Floor initiative is setting off a new wave of CCTs in peripheral countries—as well as in central countries hobbled by the financial crisis.

The developmentalist current has seen the recent improvement in quality of life as a consequence of economic growth driven by international trade and internal measures, which resulted in an improved alignment between economic and social aims in relation to the past.

As was the case for the countries of Latin America, even under the global hegemony of neoliberalism and the exacerbation of finance-led capitalist competition, the first decade of the 21st century saw a move toward the construction of a less perverse model than the historical trend.

The importance of debate and comprehending the driving reasons behind recent social progress is fundamental in defining the paths to be taken in the future. Each of the projects in question is pushing for agendas and options with diametrically opposed political implications.

The liberal project reinforced by the Basic Social Security Floor initiative would call for a greater targeting of the poor as a one-size-fits-all strategy, and for the commodification of social services meant to meet the needs of the so-called "new middle class" (those with an income starting at just over US$130 a month). From this perspective, growth, job creation, the valorization of the minimum wage, and universal policies are not necessary in terms of improving "well-being." Why consolidate a national public health system if the "new middle class" recently risen from poverty can buy healthcare on the private market? Wouldn't it be better to subsidize the financial institutions that administer private plans?

In this sense, the formulators of the Basic Social Security Floor, and their national followers, make promises that they cannot fulfill; they offer no concrete measure for obtaining the humanitarian aims that make up their social security staircase. Their objectives actually work against the promises of vertical mobility to the "upper floor. Ultimately, for the reasons laid out here, this residual model of social protection will bring about the shrinkage of public and universal welfare models, in practice and as an ideal model.

Regarding the Brazilian case, the developmentalist angle asserts that the challenge ahead lies in facing Brazil's chronic social inequality, the profound marks of which have not been erased by recent progress. We are still subject to serious levels of concentration of income and wealth, severe poverty, fiscal injustice, structural problems in the job market and piecemeal access to basic goods and services. These are profound marks of underdevelopment that must be overcome if we want a more just and civilized nation.

The universalization of social citizenship will depend on the completion of a series of structural changes. Financing for social policies depends on tax reform oriented towards fiscal justice, with taxes on gains and net worth, not consumption. Another point has to do with the revising of policy on tax exemptions, which currently limit the sources of financing available for social security (ANFIP, 2013). Such a reform would also call for a revision of the federalist pact, a serious approach to facing down the processes of commodification and privatization of services being offered, and the strengthening of state administration, currently undercut by the advance of a number of mechanisms of private administration that wind up producing redundancies, fragmentation, segmentation, and a host of difficulties in terms of efficient functioning.

The complexity inherent in these topics has returned the redistributive conflict between capital and labor to center stage in the national debate. The dispute for public funds is just one facet of the conflict. Overcoming this clash in such a way that society comes out on top depends on its ability to appropriate the resources brought in by economic power through speculative gains on the public debt and through countless mechanisms related to tax transfers.

This will require blazing utterly new paths in the effort to construct a national agenda for development that prioritizes income distribution and social justice. Such a task necessarily calls for a reinforcement of the state's role, economic growth, and the universalization of social citizenship.

In countries under late capitalism, the state must be reinforced in order to take an active role in the transformations demanded by society. This is not a trivial undertaking, as the material and financial foundations of the Brazilian state were sapped during the 1990s.

Economic growth is a necessary condition for development. The question at hand is whether this model of development is sustainable and viable in the long term, considering that the nation's integration into the world economy remains dominated by the exportation of raw materials. Similarly, the theoretical underpinnings behind the so-called macroeconomic tripod must be reexamined; as Biancarelli and Rossi (2013) argue, such principles do not mesh with social-developmentalist goals.

The task is complex both in terms of the structural nature of the phenomenon and the conservatism of the elites at a time in which prevailing forces favor globalized finance. But there can be no other path if the country indeed seeks to face down chronic social inequality, the backdrop for our contemporary malaise.

Bibliography

ANFIP (2013). *Análise da Seguridade Social 2012,* Brasília, Associação Nacional dos Auditores-Fiscáis da Receita Federal do Brasil e Fundação ANFIP de Estudos da Seguridade Social.

Barbosa, N. e Souza, J. (2010). 'A Inflexão do Governo Lula: Política Econômica, Crescimento e Distribuição de Renda,' in Sader, E. e Garcia, M.A. (orgs.) (2010). *Brasil, entre o passado e o future.* São Paulo, Boitempo.

Biancarelli, A. e Rossi, P. (2013). 'A política macroeconômica em uma estratégia social-desenvolvimentista,' in Fagnani, E. e Fonseca, A. (orgs.) (2013a). *Políticas sociais, universalização da cidadania e desenvolvimento: economia, distribuição da renda, e mercado de trabalho.* São Paulo, Fundação Perseu Abramo.

Carvalho, J.M. (2001). *Cidadania no Brasil: o longo caminho.* Rio de Janeiro, Civilização Brasileira.

Castro, J.A. et al. (2008). 'Gasto social e política macroeconômica: trajetórias e tensões no período 1995–2005,' *Texto para Discussão No. 1324.* Brasília, IPEA.

Castro, J.A. et al. (2012). 'Gasto Social Federal: uma análise da prioridade macroeconômica no período 1995–2010,' *Nota técnica 9.* Brasília, IPEA.

CEPAL (2012). *Cambio estructural para la igualdad—Una visión integrada del desarrollo.* Santiago de Chile, CEPAL.

CEPAL (2012b). *Panorama social da América Latina.* Santiago de Chile, CEPAL.

CEPAL (2014). *Pactos para la igualdad—hacia un futuro sostenible. Trigésimo quinto período de sesiones de la CEPAL.* Santiago de Chile, CEPAL.

Cichon, M. et al. (2011). *La iniciativa del Piso de Protecional Social de las Naciones Unidas.* São Paulo, Friedrich-Ebert-Stiftung.

Crespo, A.P. e Gurovitz, E. (2002). *A pobreza como fenômeno multidimensional.* São Paulo, FGV.

Fagnani, E. (2005). *Política social no Brasil (1964–2002): entre a cidadania e a caridade.* Tese de Doutorado, Universidade de Campinas.

Fagnani, E. (2008). 'Tensão entre paradigmas: notas sobre a política social no Brasil (1988–2008).' *Revista Ciência & Saúde Coletiva,* vol. 14, no. 3, pp. 710–712.

Fagnani, E. (2011). *Seguridade social: a experiência brasileira e o debate internacional.* São Paulo, Friedrich-Ebert-Stiftung.

Fagnani, E. e Tonelli Vaz, F. (2013a). 'Seguridade social, direitos constitucionáis e desenvolvimento,' in Fagnani, E. e Fonseca, A. (orgs.) (2013b). *Políticas sociáis, universalização da cidadania e desenvolvimento: educação, seguridade social, infraestrutura urbana, pobreza e transição demográfica.* São Paulo, Fundação Perseu Abramo.

Fagnani, E. e Fonseca, A. (orgs.) (2013a). *Políticas sociáis, universalização da cidadania e desenvolvimento: economia, distribuição da renda, e mercado de trabalho.* São Paulo, Fundação Perseu Abramo.

Fagnani, E. e Fonseca, A. (orgs.) (2013b). *Políticas sociáis, universalização da cidadania e desenvolvimento: educação, seguridade social, infraestrutura urbana, pobreza e transição demográfica.* São Paulo, Fundação Perseu Abramo.

FIBGE (2002). *Perfil dos idosos responsáveis pelos domicílios no Brasil—2000.* Rio de Janeiro, Fundação Instituto Brasileiro de Geografia e Estatística.

Fiori, J.L. (1993). *Ajuste, transición y gobernabilidad: el enigma brasilero.* Washington, BID, mimeo.

Friedman, M. (1962). *Capitalismo e Liberdade.* São Paulo, Nova Cultural.

Hayek, F.A. (1944). *O Caminho da Servidão.* São Paulo, Editora Globo.

Holzmann, R. and Jorgensen, S. (2000). *Social Risk Management: A new conceptual framework for social protection and beyond.* Washington, DC, World Bank.

IBGE (2013). *Síntese dos indicadores sociais,* Rio de Janeiro, IBGE, http://biblioteca.ibge. gov.br/visualizacao/livros/liv66777.pdf/

IPEA (2012). *A Década Inclusiva (2001–2011): Desigualdade, Pobreza e Políticas de Renda.* Brasília, IPEA.

Lavinas, L. (2009). 'Programas focalizados de transferência de renda: ensinamentos do Bolsa-Família no Brasil,' *Sessão Políticas de Transferência de Renda e Combate à Pobreza na América Latina I.* Rio de Janeiro, June 12, 2009, LASA.

Lavinas, L. (2013b). 'Notas sobre os desafios da redistribuição no Brasil,' in Fagnani, E. e Fonseca, A. (orgs.) (2014a). *Políticas sociais, universalização da cidadania e desenvolvimento: economia, distribuição da renda, e mercado de trabalho.* São Paulo, Fundação Perseu Abramo.

Lavinas, L. (2013). '21st century welfare.' *New Left Review,* vol. 84, no. 6, pp. 5–40.

Lavinas, L. (2014). 'Lena Lavinas: Bolsa Família é mudança positiva, mas insuficiente,' *Viomundo,* 3 April, http://www.viomundo.com.br/politica/lena-lavinas-bolsa-familia-e-mudanca-positiva-mas-insuficiente-na-ausencia-de-servicos-publicos-beneficia-sistema-financeiro.html

Maricato, E. (2013). 'Cidades no Brasil: neo desenvolvimentismo ou crescimento periférico predatório?' *Revista Política Social e Desenvolvimento,* vol. 1, no. 1, pp. 16–50, http://revistapoliticasocialedesenvolvimento.com/2014/08/14/desenvolvimento-e-questao-urbana-como-enfrentar-a-crise-das-cidades/

Mercadante, A. e Tavares, M. da C. (2001). 'Eixos de um novo Modelo,' *Debate: Um outro Brasil é possível.* São Paulo, Fundação Perseu Abramo.

Narayan, D. (2000). *Voices of the Poor—Can anyone hear us?* Washington, DC, IBRD.

OIT (2009). *Iniciativa del Piso de Protección Social de las Naciones Unidas. Sexta Iniciativa de la JJE em respuesta a la crisis financiera económica y global y su impacto en el trabajo del sistema de las Naciones Unidas.* Ginebra, OIT.

OIT (2011). *Seguridad social para la justicia social y una globalización equitativa. Discusión recurrente sobre la protección social (seguridad social) en virtud de la Declaración de la OIT relativa a la justicia social para una globalización equitativa, Sexto punto del orden del día.* Ginebra, OIT.

OIT (2011a). *Piso de Proteção Social para uma Globalização Equitativa e Inclusiva Relatório do Grupo Consultivo presidido por Michelle Bachelet, constituído pela OIT com a colaboração da OMS.* Ginebra, OIT.

Prates, D. e Marçal, E. (2008). 'O Papel do Ciclo de Preços das Commodities no Desempenho Recente das Exportações Brasileiras.' *Revista Análise Econômica,* vol. 26, no. 49, pp. 163–191.

Quadros, W. (2003). 'Classes sociais e desemprego no Brasil dos anos 1990.' *Economia e Sociedade,* vol. 12, no. 1, pp. 109–135.

Sader, E. (2014). 'Eles e nós: para a hegemonia pós-neoliberal.' *Carta Maior,* 4 March, [Online] Available at http://www.cartamaior.com.br/?/Blog/Blog-do-Emir/Eles-e-nos-para-a-hegemonia-pos-neoliberal/2/30394 (Accessed 5 August 2014).

Schwarz, R. (2013). 'A situação da cultura diante dos protestos de rua.' *Blog da Boitempo,* 23 de julho [Online]. Available at http://boitempoeditorial.files.wordpress.com/2013/07/roberto-schwarz.jpg (Accessed 5 August 2014).

Sen, A. (1999). *Development as Freedom.* New York, Knopf.

World Bank (1993). *Investing in Health.* Oxford, Oxford University Press.

World Bank (1994). *Envejecimiento sin Crisis: Políticas para la protección de los ancianos y la promoción del crecimiento.* Oxford, Oxford University Press.

World Bank (2001). *O combate à pobreza no Brasil. Relatório sobre a pobreza, com ênfase nas políticas voltadas para a redução da pobreza.* Washington, DC, World Bank.

World Bank (2013). *Economic Mobility and the Rise of Latin American Middle.* Washington, DC, World Bank.

Chapter 13
Protection Without Redistribution? Conceptual Limitations of Policies Meant to Reduce Race and Gender Inequalities in Brazil

Sérgio Costa

Introduction

Studies of social inequalities that involve examining the variables of race/ethnicity and gender have been quite widely spread throughout the various countries of Latin America. Beyond national scholarship, multilateral organizations such as CEPAL, the World Bank, and UNDP, among others, have also analyzed inequalities through this sort of lens. Broadly, persistent inequality is observed across all countries—especially when one uses income as an indicator—favoring men over women and the white population over the black (or of African origin) and/or indigenous population (see, among many others, Thorp and Paredes, 2010; Antón et al., 2009; IPEA, 2011).

In any case, although exceptions can be found for each particular indicator, there does appear a general tendency by which social inequalities between men and women have been less persistent lately than inequalities related to the categories of race and ethnicity.[1] This divergent development of inequalities between men and women and those relating to racial or ethnic ascriptions may be explained at least in part by differences in the corresponding compensatory public policies and programs. These tend to be more efficient and longer-standing in the case of gender inequalities as opposed to inequalities relating to race and ethnicity (Reygadas, 2007).

The aim of this chapter is not to weigh the different measures developed in Brazil in order to evaluate their impact on reducing social inequalities related to gender and race/ethnicity. The proposal here is to discuss the conceptual limits of the programs adopted. To this end, the first part of the text introduces an analytical-theoretical debate concerning the asymmetries between men and women and whites and blacks in Brazil as categorical, durable inequalities, in the terms proposed by Charles Tilly (1999). This first part also examines the mechanisms by which social inequalities are reproduced, which define, as per the relevant literature, the historical persistence of certain patterns of inequality. The

---

1 In keeping with the vocabulary commonly used in studies of inequality indicators in Brazil, in this text, "gender inequalities" refer to inequalities between men and women. "Racial inequalities," meanwhile, refer to inequalities between whites and blacks. That is to say that gender and race are represented, pragmatically, as statistical categories. However, in their sociological application and within the social relations, race and gender, as well as ethnicity, correspond to discursive and conceptual frameworks that are both extremely broad and interconnected, as amply demonstrated by the extensive bibliography on the subject (for a pioneering study, see Stolcke, 1991).

second part presents some general characteristics of inequalities in Brazil and indicators of inequality, income above all, between men and women and whites and blacks. The third section presents a brief discussion of the main initiatives included in the "National Plan for Public Policies for Women" (SPM, 2013) and "National Policy for Promoting Racial Equality" (SEPPIR, 2013), currently in action in Brazil today. Lastly, by way of a conclusion, comes a discussion of the limitations of the conceptual structure of the measures listed in the effort to combat the mechanisms of reproduction of social inequalities.

Persistent Categorical Inequalities

In step with the perspective adopted by the research network *desiguALdades* (see Braig et al. 2013), social inequalities are understood here in a broader sense, being the distance between the *positions that individuals or groups of individuals* occupy in socioeconomic hierarchies (access to the goods and services valued in a given society) and in power relations.

Within this definition, three key aspects come to the fore. The first is the emphasis on inequality of results, reflected in the distances between social positions, over an emphasis on the inequality of opportunities, seen frequently in analyses of race- and gender-based inequalities. The second aspect is a focus on inequalities in a broader sense (Kreckel, 2008), as this refers not only to socioeconomic inequalities but also power inequalities, involving one's ability to effect political action and defend one's own interests. In this sense, power inequalities are made concrete not only in the political-legal structure, but also through a variety of forms of insertion in formal and informal social networks (see Reygadas, 2004a). Lastly, there is the aspect that will be most fully discussed in this text, being an emphasis on not only inequalities between individuals, but also between groups.[2]

Obviously, the decision as to which group-defining categories are analytically relevant in the study of inequalities between groups involves a complex theoretical debate as to what may be considered cause and what effect—to wit, an attempt to determine whether it is the existence of social inequalities that shapes said groups, or whether it is the previous existence of such groups that makes it possible to trace horizontal inequalities (Stewart et al. 2005; Stewart, 2010). The text at hand embraces the perspective proposed by Charles Tilly (1999), which resolves the issue historically, leading from what he calls durable categorical inequalities—found inscribed in the very nature of modern institutions, in the law, and in social relations.

Tilly refers explicitly to inequalities between men and women, whites and blacks, foreigners and citizens, Jews and Muslims, which can be retraced back to the history of colonial domination, slavery, and the formation of modern nation-states. According to the author, such inequalities are largely unaffected by individual attempts at social mobility:

"Large, significant inequalities in advantages among human beings correspond mainly to categorical differences such as black/white, male/female, citizen/foreigner, or Muslim/

---

2   A fourth key aspect for the desiguALdades network, but one which will not be explored in this text, is the scale on which inequalities are observed. While conventional scholarship seeks to study inequalities on a local or national scale, this network is principally interested in understanding the transnational or global entanglements present in the social inequalities observed in Latin America (see Costa, 2013).

Jew rather than to individual differences in attributes, propensities, or performances" (Tilly, 1999: p. 7).[3]

Using the literature available and principally the works of Göran Therborn (2006, 2013) and Charles Tilly (1999; 2007), as well as those of Luis Reygadas (2004b) on Latin America, one may identify the principal mechanisms by which social inequalities in general and "categorical inequalities" in particular are maintained and reproduced over time. They are:

1. Hoarding of resources for the production of value: inequalities in the positions held within social hierarchies by groups can largely be explained by the previous accumulation of goods and assets through which value, in the economic sense, can be generated.[4] In general, the rights of inheritance and correlated property rights guarantee that this inheritance may be transferred over generations. The example most commonly referred to in the literature is that of land holdings, as seen since the works of Karl Marx on primitive accumulation, then in those of Rosa Luxemburg and Karl Polanyi (for a recent take, see Fraser, 2013). That aside, the idea of original accumulation has been expanded in recent debate, presented as a constant dynamic within capitalism. That is, according to such interpretations, the generation of profit always implies a previous process of appropriation and legal guarantees of property over resources that may be used to generate value. This applies to lands, but also to the appropriation, for example, of opportunities in the virtual economy or in the telephony or healthcare markets (Dörre, 2012; 2013). The various possibilities afforded to individuals or groups in terms of appropriating resources for the generation of value largely explain the reproduction and persistence of existing patterns of social inequality.

   The effects of the previous accumulation of resources on the reproduction of inequalities may be mitigated by the restrictive regulation of property rights, impeding the concentration of productive resources, and/or through fiscal measures that tax property and profit, reducing their impact on the distance between the positions of individuals and/or groups in social hierarchies.

2. Distanciation: According to the typology of societal mechanisms of resource distribution suggested by Therborn (2013, pp. 62), distanciation refers to structural mechanisms as well as to individual and group initiatives to maintain or widen

---

3 Today, more than 15 years after the publication of Tilly's important book on durable inequalities, studies in a variety of fields have demonstrated the importance of intermediate categories between in the pairs he presents in determining social inequalities. For example, it has been shown that within the categorical pair citizen/foreigner there is a key series of gradations such immigrants' legal status, their country of origin, etc. that determine their rights and possibilities, varying significantly for different varieties of "foreigners" (see, for example, Gongora-Mera et al., 2014). Moreover, the positions adopted by individuals or groups may vary considerably over time, with groups who defined themselves as peasants later identifying themselves as indigenous or of African origin. That is to say that persistent inequality uses to be expressed in different categories over different historical periods (see Costa, 2012). That aside, the definition for categorical inequalities proposed by Tilly remains analytically useful in the sense that it reinforces the importance of social ascriptions in organizing persistent inequalities.

4 In his description of the mechanisms for the reproduction of inequalities, Therborn (2006; 2013) does not refer to the accumulation of opportunities, but rather to exclusion. Though quite suggestive, the author's terminology only emphasizes current processes of exclusion. The reference to the accumulation of opportunities, as proposed by Tilly, allows for an appreciation of the historical processes that lead to the formation of lasting hierarchies of power or access to socially valued goods.

the distance between social positions.[5] Although in liberal discourses distanciation is treated as the result of conquests derived from individual achievements, the social distances found in modern societies are better explained, again according to Therborn, as ascriptive characteristics not subject to individual action.[6] Normally, references to distanciation are found in studies examining inequalities between individuals. However, when one observes the persistence of inequalities in access to education, for example, and the labor market in Latin America, it becomes clear that ethnic, racial, or general ascriptions considerably shape opportunities for social mobility. This mechanism for the reproduction of inequalities may be counteracted by measures that allow for the social ascension of groups positioned on the lower rungs of the social ladder through the provision of educational services, professional training, etc.

3. Hierarchization: Refers here to formal or informal mechanisms that segment access to material resources and power through the creation of privileged access for certain groups and restricted access for others. The formal instruments of hierarchization, such as, for example, the special cells afforded to authorities and defendants with college degrees (still present in the Brazilian penal code), tend to disappear from contemporary democratic constitutions. However, the informal instruments that operate on the level of institutions and interpersonal relations continue serving as instruments of hierarchization and the reproduction of social inequalities. One example of an effective mechanism for hierarchization in gender relations that has not been formalized, but has been increasingly studied in the Latin American literature, is the division of labor within the family in terms of domestic chores and the care of children, the elderly, etc. Studies show that the distribution of work in this sphere, in burdening women far more than men, hampers women's insertion into the paid labor market (see, e.g., Esquivel et al., 2012).[7] Attempts may be made to combat such informal mechanisms of hierarchization through punitive policies targeting hierarchizational practices or policies encouraging families to overcome established hierarchical forms, such as family policies that seek to strengthen men's role in housework and childcare.

---

5   The notions of distanciation and hierarchization are developed by Therborn (2006; 2013). Charles Tilly prefers to describe the formal and informal processes that generalize and crystallize categorical inequalities generated within the processes of accumulation of opportunities and exploitation through two separate categories: "emulation" and "adaption." "Emulation" comprises "the copying of established, categorically based organizational models and/or the transplanting of existing social relations from one setting to another". "Adaption" covers "the elaboration of daily routines such as mutual aid, political influence, courtship, and information gathering on the basis of categorically unequal structures" (Tilly, 1999, pp. 174).

6   A broad study conducted by Telles and Bailey (2013) corrects the still-persistent interpretation that inequalities related to race and ethnicity are explained by the Latin American population as being the result of varying individual merits. According to the results of the study, carried out in Bolivia, Brazil, Colombia, the Dominican Republic, Ecuador, Guatemala, Mexico, and Peru, "robust majorities of Latin Americans across these eight countries, and both dominant and minority populations, supported structuralist explanations for racial inequality. In addition, numerical majorities in seven of eight countries explicitly recognize the unequal treatment of ethnoracial minorities" (p. 1586).

7   In the case of Brazil, in the population over age 10, women spend an average of 25.1 hours per week on domestic work, while men spent just 10.1 hours on the same activities (cf. Alves and Cavenaghi, 2012, pp. 99).

4. Exclusion: Referring to the various instruments that impede the access of individuals or groups to goods and services, via the establishment of mechanisms of formal or informal membership that block the participation of non-members. This is the case with the operation of the right to national citizenship, for example, which, as a rule, excludes non-nationals from the array of political and social rights afforded to national citizens.[8] They constitute typical mechanisms of exclusion that may affect stigmatization and discrimination both formally and informally. In Brazil, stigmatization and discrimination tend to operate informally, on the level of social relations, as they are generally prohibited by law.

    In the fight against exclusion, anti-discrimination policies and laws are employed alongside measures that seek to expand access to socially valued goods and positions to all the members of a given society, beyond ascriptions of class, gender, or race.

5. Exploitation: the concept of exploitation as used in contemporary research on inequality is quite broad, as may be observed in C. Tilly:

    > "It [exploitation] occurs wherever well-connected people control valuable resources from which they extract returns by deploying the effort of others, whom they exclude from the full value added by that effort. The 'value' in question may of course be monetary, but it may also take the form of power, deference, perquisites, services, goods, or protection" (Tilly, 1998, p. 91).

    This definition reveals that exploitation may occur both on the level of interpersonal relationships—such as when, for example, families exploit domestic servants (generally female maids), through unpaid or poorly paid work—or structurally, for instance, through regressive taxation or the monopolization of the markets of goods and services (Therborn, 2013). Exploitation may be combated through pertinent legislation, supervision, and initiatives to increase awareness on the part of victims.

In observing the operation of these distinct mechanisms in the process of reproducing social inequalities in Latin America, one can confirm that the importance of each changes over the course of history, as Reygadas sums up (2004b: p. 92):

> "In more simplified versions, it is expected that with the elimination of all kinds of discrimination, inequalities will be significantly reduced. But the reproduction of asymmetries in Latin America functions neither exclusively nor principally via class exploitation and direct discrimination. These were quite notorious in the past and remain fundamental, but over the course of history they flowed into an unequal distribution of lands, property, access to resources, educational opportunities, and capacities."

---

8   As they generally take the limits of the nation-state as a reference for the definition of their object of analysis, conventional investigations tend to ignore the ascriptive nature of nationality and its importance in shaping the global structures of inequalities. More recent studies, examining structures of inequalities on a global, rather than a national level, have revealed that "the ascribed characteristics of nationhood and citizenship are considered to be as important for global stratification as class, usually considered to depend on levels of achievement" (Boatcă, 2011: p. 17).

Of course, Reygadas' generalized observation must be confirmed and documented in each particular case and context. Even so, it indicates important tendencies which, in a way, contradict the general perception that discrimination is the main instrument for reproducing inequalities, particularly inequalities related to gender, race and ethnicity. One important proviso, however, must be made, at least in the Brazilian case, to Reygadas' affirmation as to the declining importance of class exploitation in the shaping of social inequalities. In important sectors of the Brazilian labor market, exploitation—often outside the limits of the law or in legal loopholes, continues functioning as an important mechanism for producing and reproducing inequalities of class, gender, and race, as shown by studies on maids (e.g. Brites, 2007) or on the processes of productive restructuring and the correlated expansion of subcontracting and outsourcing in sectors such as the service industry and agro-industry (e.g. Sproll, 2013; Nogueira and Jesus, 2013).

Categorical Inequalities Relative to Race and Gender in Brazil

Following the general tendency over recent years in Latin America, income inequality has fallen in Brazil, although still below the drop recorded in countries such as Bolivia, Argentina, and Uruguay, as may be seen in the graphic (Figure 13.1) below:

The average reduction in Gini as documented in the graphic fits into a larger tendency of falling inequality in Brazil: the index was 0.640 in 1999, falling to 0.559 by 2011. In 2012 the index rises again, up to 0.567 (CEPAL, 2013: p. 90). When comparing the portions of income appropriated by varying income groups, it becomes clear that Brazil remains the only country in Latin America where the richest fifth of the population appropriates

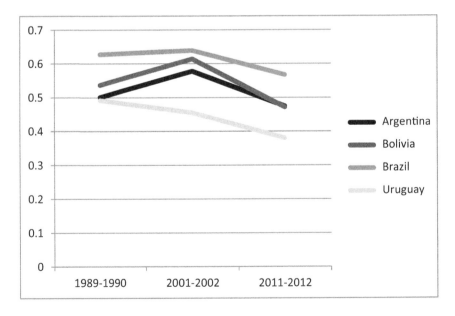

Figure 13.1   Gini coefficient of selected countries
Source: ECLAC, selected years.

the greatest proportion of income, even more so than in countries which, in terms of their Gini coefficients, are even more unequal than Brazil. According to CEPAL (2013: p. 23), the 20% richest in Brazil brought in 55.1% of income in 2012, while the 20% poorest took in just 4.5%. By way of comparison, in Uruguay, the least unequal country in the region, the 20% richest bring in 34.8% of total income, with 10% for the poorest fifth.

An explanation for the apparent contradiction between an important reduction in inequality and the considerable concentration of income in the richest fifth of the population lies in Brazilian tax policy. The tax burden is reasonably heavy,[9] but with a strong emphasis on indirect taxation, making it so that lower-income groups pay proportionally more taxes. Using data from 2008, IPEA (2009) calculated that while workers earning up to two minimum wages spent 53.9% of their income paying taxes, those earning more than 30 minimum wages spent 29% on their taxes.

As for social inequalities between groups, inequalities between men and women and between whites and blacks likely represent the most persistent categorical asymmetries in Brazilian society. These inequalities are rooted in history, in the ways in which blacks and women were integrated into the dynamic of the formation of capitalism alongside colonial expansion and the exploitation of slave labor. Even after independence from Portugal and the abolition of slavery in 1888, there remained formal and informal mechanisms that continued to reproduce accumulated inequalities (Costa, 2011). Specific public policies aimed at reducing categorical inequalities related to race and gender, some of them in place for decades, have had a limited effect on reducing existing inequalities, as shown by persistent differences in income.

The Figure 13.2 lays out the income inequalities between men and women and between whites and blacks. Accompanying evolving data since 1995 reveals a slight reduction in categorical inequalities in both cases. Considering, however, that this is a cycle of almost 20 years marked by deepening democratization, the expansion of social rights and the dissemination of a key array of specific measures meant to combat racial and gender inequalities, the results at hand are very modest. Women and the black population continue to bring in monthly earnings that represent practically half of men's, and of the white population.

Figure 13.3, for the time period 1995–2012, seeks to detect the effect of the combination of the variables of gender and race, and, to an extent, the region of residence, in inequalities as a whole. Here it becomes evident that certain sectors of the population accumulate several disadvantages. The average monthly earnings of black women come to less than a third of the average monthly earnings of white men. When the region of residence is included as a variable, considering the five geographical regions into which Brazil is divided—South, Southeast, Center-West, North, and Northeast—these disparities are exacerbated even further. The most extreme case of inequality may be found in the comparison between black women living in the Northeast (NE) and white men in the Center-West (CW). It appears that black women in the Northeast earn a fifth of the average monthly earnings of white men living in the Center-West.[10]

---

9   In 2009, the Brazilian tax burden represented 32.6% of the country's GDP, comparable to the average percentage across OECD countries, 33.8%, and far above the Latin American average of 19.2%. Indirect taxes came to 44% of Brazilian tax revenues in 2009, while property taxes amounted to just 3% (see Paes, 2013).

10   The data in the graphic come from average figures for the rural and urban populations, taken as a whole, and do not reflect the fact that urban populations across all categories and regions have much higher average monthly earnings than the rural population.

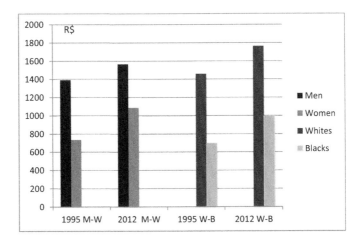

Figure 13.2   Average monthly earnings by sex and race/color* Brazil 1995 and 2012 (in R$ as of September 2012)**

Source: PNAD - IBGE, selected years.

* Data on inequality used here combines the *pardo* (literally: brown, representing 43% of the total population) and *preto* (literally: black, representing 8% of the total) into the "black" column, comparing aggregated indicators with those for the white population (48% of the total). The other census categories for race or color, being indigenous peoples with 0.4% and *amarelo* (Asians), with 1% of the total population, are not considered here—the parenthetical percentages represent rounded figures from the 2010 Census. See: http://www.ibge.gov.br/home/estatistica/populacao/censo2010/ (last accessed: 08/02/2014).

** Average earnings from the main occupation of population over 16 years old. Adjusted for Inflation by INPC.

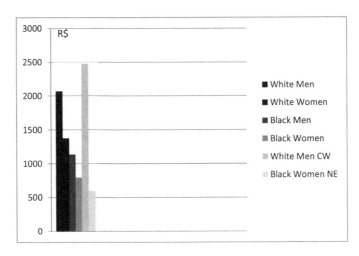

Figure 13.3   Average monthly earnings in R$ intersection of inequality factors: Sex, race, and region Brazil (figures in Brazilian Reais as of September 2012)*

Source: PNAD-IBGE, selected groups.

Legend: CW= Center-West Region, NE= Northeast Region. * Average earnings from the main occupation of population over 16 years old. Adjusted for Inflation by INPC.

As for average education in terms of completed schooling years, women fare better than men. Conversely, in terms of racial educational inequalities, the current situation is of persisting inequalities. As compared to 1995, in 2012, differences in education levels in favor of the white population dropped only slightly—as shown by Figure 13.4

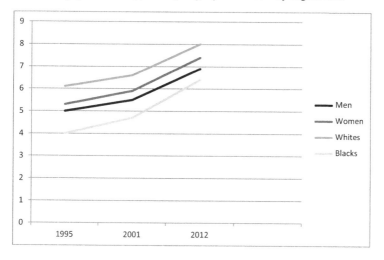

Figure 13.4   Years of education for people 15 years or older by sex and race Brazil, 1995, 2001, 2012
Source: PNAD-IBGE, selected years.

In analyzing income between the white and black populations, one must consider that there has been a significant rise in the percentage of blacks among the highest-income groups; but, at the same time, the percentages of blacks in the lowest-income groups have persisted and even grown, as seen in Table 13.1 (overleaf).

The data in the table suggest that mobility for blacks in the highest-income groups has improved, while mobility among the poorest blacks remains low. However, one must consider the fact that the data are influenced by varying self-declarations of race over the period. To wit, since tendencies to self-declare as *preto* or *pardo* in socio-demographic statistics rose from 1995 to 2012, black participation also raised across all income groups. Thus, the greater growth in black participation in the highest income groups may have been driven by a proportional increase in the number of blacks among the richest segments of the population, or by the fact that general predisposition towards self-declaring as black (*preto* or *pardo*) may have grown amongst blacks in the highest income brackets.

Policies Promoting Gender and Racial Equality

Within the scope of this chapter, it would not be possible to analyze the vast number of policies and measures, dedicated to combating gender and race inequalities, adopted over the last decades in Brazil. For our purposes here, the analysis will thus focus on two recent documents that seek to bring together and harmonize the principal federal policies in existence in the field. These are the PNPM, "National Plan for Public Policies for

Table 13.1   Percentage of the black population by household income bracket Brazil, 1995–2012

Income Deciles and Last Centile	1995	2003	2012
Decile 1	70.1	71.7	74.0
Decile 2	65.7	66.5	71.2
Decile 3	59.3	61.7	65.7
Decile 4	54.3	57.8	62.9
Decile 5	48.0	52.1	57.0
Decile 6	43.2	46.6	52.9
Decile 7	36.4	40.9	47.8
Decile 8	32.1	35.0	42.3
Decile 9	25.5	27.7	36.6
Decile 10	15.2	17.7	25.9
Centile 100	8.3	9.6	15.8

Source: PNAD—IBGE selected years 1995–2003–2012.

Women" (SPM, 2013), and the PNPIR, "National Policy for Promoting Racial Equality" (SEPPIR, 2013).[11]

The PNPM presents the standing plan of action by the Federal Agency for Women's Policies, while the PNPIR encompasses the primary initiatives of the Federal Agency for Policies Promoting Racial Equality. Both agencies enjoy the status afforded to ministries, and were created in 2003, during the first year of President Lula's administration.

The PNPM is a fairly broad and detailed document, encompassing 10 chapters in 140 pages, which describe specific initiatives across the various fields of activity for the period 2013–2015, including:

- the world of work,

---

11   The use of these documents in the chapter at hand, which compile a number of extremely varied documents, may be justified by virtue of this being an analytic-theoretical examination of the conceptual limitations of policies adopted, and not an analysis of the efficacy of specific initiatives. A study interested in measuring the efficacy of such policies would, naturally, have to examine the design and concrete results of specific public policies in different sectors, as did Lima (2010) in a discussion of policies targeting racial inequality, particularly in terms of health and education, Medeiros and Guareschi (2009) in their study of women's health policies, or Sorj (2013) in investigating policies related to care.

- education,
- healthcare,
- combating violence,
- political participation,
- sustainable development,
- access to land,
- culture,
- combating discrimination, and
- attention to youths, senior citizens, and the disabled.

For each of these fields, the report presents detailed current and future initiatives meant to promote, amongst other aims, "effective equality between men and women, across all spheres" (SPM, 2013: p. 9).

The PNPIR's dimensions are more modest: it is just 28 pages long, half of those taken up by photographs, which defend "racial equality" as a principle, emphasizing the state's role in its promotion. The main initiatives proposed by the document are:

- implementing a model for administering racial equality policies,
- supporting the remaining quilombola communities[12],
- affirmative action,
- development and social inclusion, mainly through social policy,
- international cooperation, and
- the production of knowledge in order to promote racial equality.

When one compares both documents, a few important differences stand out. While the PNPIR's main thrust is the incorporation of racial inequality into the government's agenda, the PNPM presents a considerably wider and more varied scope of action, including initiatives and measures in the fight against gender inequality that go beyond state action, such as initiatives meant to favor a less disadvantageous integration for women into the labor market.

Although neither plan goes into an explicit discussion about what either means by "inequality," it is clear that basically all of PNPIR's initiatives are oriented around combating inequalities of opportunity and treatment between whites and blacks. In the case of the PNPM, most of the measures also refer to promoting equality of opportunities. However, the policies concerning gender favor a substantive vision of equality, one which implies a reduction in the distances between the relative positions held by men and women in the social hierarchies prevailing in Brazil.

Just as worthy of emphasis is the difference between the two programs' understandings of the "transversal," i.e. intersectional, character of inequalities. In the PNPIR's view, the transversality of inequalities simply refers to the complementarity of inequalities related to gender and race and the need to incorporate the variable of race into government initiatives as a whole. The PNPM, meanwhile, refers repeatedly to the imperative to understand gender inequalities in the context of their superposition with "racial, generational, and class" inequalities, "among others" (SPM, 2013: p. 10), thus emphasizing the need for a corresponding "transversality" in public policies.

---

12 Quilombolas refer to the population of quilombos that are settlements created by black people who escaped from slavery, only officially abolished in Brazil in 1888.

Reproduction of Categorical Inequalities and Social Policies in Brazil

The first section of this chapter opted for a broadened understanding of inequality, incorporating the distances between the positions occupied by men and women and whites and blacks, in terms of both power asymmetries and socioeconomic differences. The second section made it clear that inequalities in earnings between men and women and whites and blacks remain significant. In terms of access to education, women are better placed than men; inequalities between whites and blacks, however, continue to rise. No indicators were presented in order to study the behavior of power asymmetries between men and women and blacks and whites. Despite this, the growing number of specific public policies and the very creation of two federal agencies with ministerial status dedicated to women's policies and the promotion of racial equality indicate that the political power of women and blacks has grown in Brazil in recent years.

When one considers the five existing mechanisms for reproducing the inequalities that are the previous accumulation of resources, distanciation, hierarchization, exclusion, and exploitation, it becomes clear that the programs meant to fight inequalities of race and gender, catalogued in the two documents at hand, contain certain conceptual limitations that may restrict their effectiveness in reducing power asymmetries and socioeconomic inequalities.

The measures to mitigate the effects of the previous accumulation of resources are limited, in both documents, to an emphasis on the need to favor land access for Quilombola communities and female rural workers, thus addressing only a small portion of the black and female populations as a whole. Neither document includes any reference to tax measures or other forms of redistribution of accumulated resources, which might contribute to reducing race- and gender-related inequalities in urban areas, where 84% of the Brazilian population currently live.

In terms of distanciation, the PNPM refers to specific measures for broadening women's agency, as well as seeking to promote their levels of education and qualification for the labor market. The PNPIR, meanwhile, limits itself to defending affirmative action policies that, in terms of any decisive importance for long-term reduction of power asymmetries between whites and blacks, have a very small impact in promoting socioeconomic mobility for black men and women in Brazil, as it is, by design, oriented towards serving a relatively small portion of the Brazilian black population.

The hierarchization of access to goods and services, between whites and blacks and women and men, occurs via informal mechanisms in Brazil, as formal mechanisms of this kind are, with a few exceptions, forbidden by law. In this sense, the measures in both plans, and which seek to assist and support women and blacks in the awareness and defense of their rights, are initiatives that, in the long term, may favor a reduction in the processes of hierarchization. The PNPM also addresses hierarchization when it turns to inequalities in the distribution of time that men and women, respectively, spend on household chores.

In terms of exclusion, the emphasis on anti-discriminatory policies observed in both documents may lead to a reduction in at least one of the instruments of exclusion, namely, discrimination. That said, restrictions on access to quality healthcare, education, and cultural instruments defined by mechanisms of the market, are not referred to in either plan. The inclusion of measures to revert the exclusion to these goods would mean establishing a more decisive connection between the variables of gender, race, and class than is found in the plans. After all, women and blacks are excluded from access to these goods not necessarily by virtue of their color or sex, but by virtue of their class. In this sense, although "transversality" of social policies is referenced, both plans lack specific measures operating at the intersections of gender, race, and class inequalities.

Finally, exploitation is referenced in the PNPM in terms of the need to protect domestic servants against inadequate working conditions and to protect youths and adolescents against sexual exploitation. The PNPIR, meanwhile, presents no such explicit measures against exploitation.

In conclusion, one may affirm that the principal focus of the two plans lies in combating discrimination, being one particular manifestation of one of the five highlighted mechanisms of reproduction of social inequalities. In terms of the other mechanisms that reproduce inequalities, the PNPIR is largely silent. The PNPM, while limited as well in its ability to act on the various inequality-reproducing mechanisms, is a bit more ambitious than PNPIR in that it incorporates initiatives focused on promoting women's social mobility in an attempt to fight back against their exploitation, both in terms of interpersonal relations as well as in the labor market.

In part, the varying scopes of the two documents reflect the differing political trajectories and levels of institutionalization of the aims of the movements for gender and race equality in Brazil. While the Brazilian state's incorporation of the claims of anti-racist movements is more recent, effective channels of communication between women's movements and the state were established as early as the first years of redemocratization. In tentatively indicating conceptual limitations on the body of measures adopted to combat gender and racial inequalities in Brazil, this chapter does not seek to minimize the importance and legitimacy of such measures and the institutional bodies in which they are inserted. The intention here is rather to indicate possibilities for broadening the scope of the measures in question in order to more effectively combat the full array of mechanisms by which gender and racial inequalities in Brazil continue to reproduce themselves.

Bibliography

Alves, J.E. and Cavenaghi, S. (2012). 'Indicadores de Desigualdade de Gênero no Brasil.' *Mediações,* vol. 17, no. 2, pp. 83–105.

Antón, J. et al. (2009). *Afrodescendientes en América Latina y el Caribe: del reconocimiento estadístico a la realización de derechos.* Santiago de Chile, CEPAL.

Boatcă, M. (2011). 'Global Inequalities Transnational Processes and Transregional Entanglements,' *desiguALdades.net Working Paper No. 11.* Berlin, Freie Universität.

Braig, M. et al. (2013). 'Soziale Ungleichheiten und globale Interdependenzen in Lateinamerika: eine Zwischenbilanz,' *desiguALdades.net Working Paper No. 4.* Berlin, Freie Universität.

Brites, J. (2007). 'Afeto e desigualdade: gênero, geração e classe entre empregadas domésticas e seus empregadores.' *Cadernos Pagu,* vol. 29, no. 2, pp. 91–109.

CEPAL (2013). *Panorama Social de América Latina.* Santiago de Chile, CEPAL

Costa, S. (2013). 'Entangled inequalities in Latin America: Adressing social categorizations and transregional interdependencies,' in Schwarz, T. et al. (eds.) (2013). *Interdependencies of Social Categorizations.* Frankfurt, Vervuert.

Costa, S. (2012). 'Freezing differences: Politics, law, and the invention of cultural diversity in Latin America,' in Araujo, K. and Mascareño, A. (eds.) (2012). *Legitimization in World Society.* Farnham, Ashgate

Costa, S. (2011). 'Perspectivas y políticas sobre racismo y afrodescendencia en América Latina y el Caribe,' in Hopenhayn, M. and Sojo, A. (eds.) (2011). *Sentido de pertenencia en sociedades fragmentadas: América Latina en una perspectiva global.* Santiago de Chile, CEPAL.

Dörre, K. (2013). 'Landnahme. Triebkräfte, Wirkungen und Grenzen kapitalistischer Wachstumsdynamik,' in Backhouse, M. et al. (eds.) (2013). *Die globale Einhegung—Krise, ursprüngliche Akkumulation und Landnahmen im Kapitalismus.* Münster, Westfälisches Dampfboot.

Dörre, K. (2012). 'Landnahme, das Wachstumsdilemma und die "Achsen der Ungleichheit".' *Berliner Journal für Soziologie,* vol. 22, no. 1, pp. 101–128.

Esquivel, V. et al. (eds.) (2012). *Las lógicas del cuidado infantil. Entre las familias, el Estado y el Mercado.* Buenos Aires, IDES.

Fraser, N. (2013). 'A triple movement? Parsing the politics of crisis after Polanyi.' *New Left Review,* vol. 81, no. 1, pp. 119–132.

Góngora-Mera, M. et al. (2014). 'The Frontiers of Universal Citizenship: Transnational Social Spaces and the Legal Status of Migrants in Ecuador,' *Working Paper Series No. 71.* Berlin, desiguALdades.net.

IPEA (2011). *Retrato das Desigualdades de Gênero e Raça.* Brasília, IPEA/SEPPIR/ SNPM/ ONU Mulheres.

IPEA (2009). *Receita pública: Quem paga e como se gasta no Brasil.* Brasília, IPEA.

Kreckel, R. (2008). 'Soziologie der sozialen Ungleichheit im globalen Kontext,' in Bayer, M. et al. (Hgg.) (2008). *Transnationale Ungleichheitsforschung. Eine neue Herausforderung für die Soziologie.* Frankfurt, Campus Verlag.

Lima, M. (2010). 'Desigualdades raciais e políticas públicas: ações afirmativas no governo Lula.' *Novos estudos Cebrap,* vol. 87, no. 2, pp. 77–95.

Medeiros, P.F. and Guareschi, N. (2009). 'Políticas públicas de saúde da mulher: a integralidade em questão.' *Estudos Feministas,* vol. 17, no. 1, pp. 31–48.

Nogueira, C. and Jesus, E. (2013). 'A pequena produção avícola familiar e o Sistema de Integração no oeste catarinense: "uma prisão de portas abertas".' *Cadernos CRH,* vol. 67, no. 3, pp. 123–138.

Paes, N.L. (2013). 'Uma análise comparada do sistema tributário brasileiro em relação à América Latina.' *Acta Scientiarum Human and Social Sciences Maringá,* vol. 35, no. 1, pp. 85–95.

Reygadas, L. (2007). 'La desigualdad después del (multi)culturalismo,' in Giglia, C. and Teres, A. de (comp.) (2007). *¿A dónde va la antropología?* México, DF, Juan Pablos.

Reygadas, L. (2004a). 'Las redes de la desigualdad: un enfoque multidimensional.' *Política y Cultura,* vol. 22, no. 2, pp. 7–25.

Reygadas, L. (2004b). 'Más allá de la clase, la etnia y el género: acciones frente a diversas formas de desigualdad en América Latina.' *Alteridades,* vol. 14, no. 28, pp. 91–106.

SEPPIR (2013). *Política Nacional de Promoção da Igualdade Racial.* Brasília, SEPPIR.

Sorj, B. (2013). 'Arenas of care at the intersections between gender and social class in Brazil.' *Cadernos de Pesquisa,* vol. 43, no. 149, pp. 478–491.

SPM (2013). *Plano Nacional de Políticas para as Mulheres 2013–2015.* Brasília, SPM.

Sproll, M. (2013). 'Precarization, Genderization and Neotaylorist Work. How Global Value Chain Restructuring Affects Banking Sector Workers in Brazil,' *desiguALdades.net Working Paper No. 44.* Berlin, Freie Universität.

Stewart, F. (2010). 'Por qué persisten las desigualdades de grupo? Las trampas de la desigualdad horizontal,' in Jiménez, F. (ed.) (2010). *Teoría económica y desigualdad social. Exclusión, desigualdad y democracia.* Lima, Fondo Editorial de la PUC.

Stewart, F. et al. (2005). 'Why Horizontal Inequalities Matter: Some Implications for Measurement,' *CRISE Working Paper No. 19.* Oxford, University of Oxford.

Stolcke, Verena (1991). 'Sexo está para gênero assim como raça para etnicidade?' *Estudos Afro-Asiáticos,* vol. 20, no. 106, pp. 101–119.

Telles, E. and Bailey, S. (2013). 'Understanding Latin American beliefs about racial inequality.' *American Journal of Sociology,* vol. 118, no. 5, pp. 1559–1595.

Therborn, G. (2006). 'Meaning, mechanisms, pattern, and forces: An introduction,' in Therborn, G. (ed.) (2006). *Inequalities of the World.* London/New York, Verso.

Therborn, G. (2013). *The Killing Fields of Inequality.* Cambridge, Polity Press.

Thorp, R. and Paredes, M. (2010). *Ethnicity and the Persistence of Inequality. The Case of Peru.* Houndmills, Palgrave Macmillan.

Tilly, C. (1999). *Durable Inequality.* Berkeley, University of California Press.

Tilly, C. (2007). *Democracy.* Cambridge, Cambridge University Press.

PART IV
"Final Insights and Future Challenges"

Chapter 14
An Outline for the Future:
Latin America vis-à-vis the World

Hans-Jürgen Puhle

In the various contributions to this volume many interesting points have been made, including some provocative ones, rich evidence has been presented, and we have learned a lot. As many of the more general issues that should be mentioned in a final comment have already been raised by other authors, I can be brief and try to summarize some of my impressions from our debates in seven short and sketchy points focusing a bit on what could, and what should, or what might be done.

1. What can be said about the general direction of a tentative agenda for the future? It appears that there is a broad consensus that reforms should be continued, and that it should be "good" reforms, adequate reforms, reforms conducive to more equity, social justice and fairness, to more incorporation and inclusion, to more equal life chances and opportunities, along the lines, grosso modo, of the principles set out by John Rawls, Amartya Sen and others. Redistributive policies, direct or indirect, can be one important policy cluster among others in the more comprehensive set of reform policies, and, in any specific case, the question will always be how much can be done by redistribution (and what cannot?), how it could be achieved best, and where the spaces for it could be found. In order to implement their concepts, among other things, reformers will have to redesign and reorganize politics and policies, build strong social coalitions (as Göran Therborn has emphasized), fight for a broad consensus on goals, build institutions, and at the same time fight against waste, corruption and populist temptations, and look for the adequate models for reform. "Adequate" here refers to those features that correspond (more than others) to the particular trajectories of development of a given country or society, and can address its specific needs and mobilize its specific strengths and chances. Their identification requires detailed and broad analysis in the *longue durée*, including the analysis of repercussions, entanglements and unintended consequences of political measures. Good politics and policies, first of all, require good analysis of what is the case and how things are interrelated.

We also know that most reforms which later became structures, have been brought about by piecemeal, often trial-and-error reactions to a given crisis, or to an ongoing critical situation. It seems that "blueprint" reforms have not been so common, that Beveridge has been an exception, and that even the various implementations (and "real types") of the Keynesian Welfare State have been mixed bags. Nevertheless, the most convincing approach is undoubtedly a universalistic approach, because it corresponds best to the normative orientation towards more and more equal life chances for everybody along the lines of Rawls and Sen, as a good, and necessary semi-utopian point of orientation. Even if, in political reality, for many reasons, the implementation may again be broken down into consecutive steps of the piecemeal type.

2. There are some preconditions and requirements involved. One important requirement is that we have to see the various sectoral policies that could contribute to reduce inequalities

as related to each other. This not only applies to the usual conglomerate of social and welfare policies, anti-poverty programs, labor market, minimum-wage, health and pension policies, but also to its broader corollaries like tax policy, budget, fiscal, monetary and trade policies, the whole macroeconomic program, not to forget educational, R&D and environmental policies, and all others that might affect people's life chances from early childhood to old age. In the better cases, the various policies should be integrated into a more comprehensive policy concept directed at promoting more equality and inclusion with regard to life chances and opportunities. The sectoral policies' relatedness and interactions, and their embeddedness into their various trajectories, contexts and constellations, nationally and internationally, are central points that should be kept in mind.

3. Many observations in the various papers joined here have centered around problems of "effectiveness", "stability", "reliability", and their prerequisites in the structures of a sufficiently robust and sustained stateness. Whether the problems and the actors involved (at least many of them) be local or transnational, the agency and jurisdiction to address the problems, in Latin America, still predominantly reside in the traditional nation states (no matter at which level). This brings the state back in into our debates, not only as a central sectoral actor or facilitator, but also as a comprehensive process, and as a structure, enabling, promoting, containing, limiting. Just one important, perhaps crucial, at least basic example: for adequate reform programs the state needs money. And it has been demonstrated that in most Latin American countries tax revenue is much too low and unbalanced, and hence should be improved. In order to improve tax collection, however, not only more, and more efficient, tax collectors are required (as it has been emphasized), but also a whole set of rules, institutions and sanctions, and the adequate mechanisms to make them work, which also includes an attitudinal and behavioral dimension: the creation of a somewhat "civilized" habit, the predisposition to pay taxes (eventually even raised taxes!). Here education matters.

It appears to be obvious, and has been emphasized, in one way or another, in many of the contributions to this volume, that the Latin American countries need more of the good old "Steuerstaat" (Schumpeter). It should be built, promoted and empowered. The modern "Steuerstaat" (tax state) has been one of the inventions of European absolutism (the component of "discipline," in the terms of Gerhard Oestreich), but also the Anglo nations have copied it, and all modern democracies have come to terms with it. In the Latin American countries, with their particular trajectories and constellations (cf., e.g., Bértola/Ocampo 2012), it might not always look like in Europe or in the North, but there may be no realistic alternative but to look for functional equivalents. We have learned that tax revenue has lately become higher and more balanced in Brazil, and that some inroads have also been made in Argentina and Bolivia. This raises the question whether (and what) the others could, perhaps, learn from Brazil, and how, in case, that could be done.

4. Christian von Haldenwang, at one point, has stated that "it pays to be democratic". I think this could be generalized, with regard to policies of more equality of life chances and inclusion, and also to the policies of redistribution that have been debated: democracy helps. But the question is: which one? Which elements, sectors, partial regimes, characteristics and features of our more complex and ambitious concept of an "embedded democracy" (Merkel/Puhle et al. 2003; Merkel 2004) can be considered to be particularly helpful with regard to redistribution and social reform policies in Latin American countries? This is not an unimportant question, as most Latin American democracies are what we have called "defective democracies" (ibid.), or what others

prefer to call "incomplete democracies", and hence have their particular strengths and weaknesses in coping with democratic requirements in the various partial regimes of a democratic system. Here the mechanisms of open contestation and participation, of the rule of law and of democratic accountability and control appear to be crucial. It is interesting that it can be shown in many of the relevant indices of the quality of democracy and governance, that, on the whole, the chances for sustainable social reform, better life chances and redistribution are greater in more democratic countries. One good example here are the results of the Transformation Index of the Bertelsmann Foundation (BTI), particularly if we relate the democracy and governance indicators to the indicators, e.g., on social safety nets, equal opportunity, environmental policy, education policy or R&D (cf. www.bti-project.org).

5. We do, however, have to account for variation. The world is full of "varieties", not only varieties of democracy, varieties of capitalism, varieties of welfare regimes, etc., but also varieties of state and nation building, of institution building, and of the different ways and modes of interaction between "agency", i.e. the corporate agreements of political and social actors, and the institutions, which are of particular importance in processes of transformative and reform policies. Here we have to look at both the constellations of actors and the constellations of context and circumstance, and at a third level that might be called the constellations of interdependencies, within Latin America and between Latin America and other parts of the world. Notwithstanding the need to identify the particular constellations and trajectories of every single country and society, a tentative initial typology of the Latin American countries would obviously come up with three types or classes: first, Brazil, which is different, not only with regard to tax collection, and as it has been pointed out, the only Latin American country playing in the league of the BRICSs, bigger, stronger, more powerful, more diversified, in a way more globalized, and at present, as it appears, institutionally and policy-wise more inventive than others, not least due to a more effective use of its federal structures. Second, we have the usual other more developed and better-off countries, and third, the less developed and/or more problematic ones. In any case, the activities of political actors in the various countries are channeled, the spaces for social coalitions delimited and the political processes shaped differently by the countries' particular trajectories and constellations.

6. Agency is important, particularly good, convincing and strong leadership (meaning democratic leadership) and the ability to build sufficiently broad and sustained social and political coalitions. Hence politics matter. Good leadership, however, also implies a sense for the particular chances for social reform policies and for the right moment to negotiate them (cf. Puhle 2012; also Göran Therborn in this volume). The "kairos" is important. This could be a severe economic crisis, or substantial external shocks (as it has been pointed out), provided they leave space for manoeuvre; it could be a ("fashionable") trend, "la force des choses" of various types (or TINA, for the British), international influence, or the result of learning processes which may also depend on the ways and modes of political intermediation (cf. the vast literature on that). In a general mood for reforms (not to speak of a whole climate of "reform mongering") and the underlying "optimism'" it requires it is much easier to launch policies in favor of more equality, inclusion and redistribution. Such a general mood, of course, depends on context, and it usually is much more likely to be found in Brazil than, e.g., in Guatemala.

7. One last observation on the general outlook, or the "outline for the future," as it has been ambitiously phrased in the title for these final remarks: If we take all the messages

together that have been presented and debated, we might, somehow, agree on a number of general points like the following:

- All Latin American countries need policies of reform toward more equal life chances and opportunities, more inclusion and participation (i.e. the normative undercurrent). The various policies of redistribution are important components of this broader project which can serve as a guideline and inspiration (and also as a "benchmark", for economists) for sectoral policies, perhaps the more so the more it is seen as an encompassing universal, semi-utopian project.
- One important challenge for sectoral policies (like those of redistribution) is to see to it that they "fit" into the direction of the broader project, to monitor their embeddedness, to minimize encumberedness, and to maximize conduciveness.
- There are a number of factors that can support and promote policies of reform: It helps to have the structures of a "Steuerstaat", including an efficient and robust administration, it helps to be democratic and to have an effective and determined leadership. And, of course, it helps if the reform policies can be launched in an ambiente and in constellations and moments that are conducive to reforms.
- We should, however, also take into account that there can be no master plan, and that there always will be a broad variety of different projects corresponding to the various trajectories and combinations of factors of the respective societies and regions, at all levels, national, regional and local.

In some of the debates we have had it has remained an open question which policy measures should be launched at which level of the state, and whether, more in particular, policies of social reform and redistribution could be better implemented in a more centralized or in a more decentralized way. This will, of course, have to be determined by more detailed empirical analysis of every single case. I must confess, however, that in general, *ceteris paribus*, and if constellations permit, I have a bias in favor of decentralized and local politics, of autonomies and federations of all kinds, because I think that they can help to provide more participation and control, to make elite coalitions more transparent, and to better cope with the various constellations of (also transnational) interdependency and embeddedness. They also have clear advantages when it comes to design and implement reforms as political measures and in a political way, and not as a technocratic top-down process of "public administration" or "public management". As we are talking politics here, it would be good if it would, as much as possible, be the politics of autonomous citizens.

Bibliography

Bertelsmann Stiftung, ed. (2014). *Transformation Index BTI 2014. Political Management in International Comparison*. Gütersloh: Bertelsmann Stiftung. (Data in: www.bti-project.org)

Bértola, Luis and Ocampo, José Antonio. (2012). *The Economic Development of Latin America since Independence*. Oxford: Oxford University Press.

Merkel, Wolfgang. (2004). 'Embedded and Defective Democracies,' in Croissant, Aurel/ Merkel, Wolfgang, eds., Special Issue of *Democratization: Consolidated or Defective Democracy? Problems of Regime Change,* 11(5), pp. 33–58.

Merkel, Wolfgang and Hans-Jürgen Puhle et al. (2015). *Defekte Demokratie, vol. 1: Theorie.* Opladen: Leske+ Budrich, 2003, 2nd ed. Wiesbaden.

Puhle, Hans-Jürgen. (2012). 'El liderazgo en la política. Una visión desde la historia,' in Mees, Ludger/Núñez Seixas, Xosé, eds., *Nacidos para mandar. Liderazgo, política y poder. Perspectivas comparadas.* Madrid: Tecnos, pp. 23–43.

Index

For Product Safety Concerns and Information please contact our EU representative GPSR@taylorandfrancis.com Taylor & Francis Verlag GmbH, Kaufingerstraße 24, 80331 München, Germany

Printed and bound by CPI Group (UK) Ltd, Croydon, CR0 4YY
01/05/2025
01858355-0010